What readers have said about

I Believe –
I Think....

I Believe –
I Think….

Stories and Struggles in Christian Ministry

CHRISTOPHER
JENKIN

To my family, friends

and patient parishioners

in four dioceses

CONTENTS

1 Introduction   1

2 The roots of my faith   9

3 My Conversion   23

4 What is Conversion?   35

5 Living as a Christian   67

6 What is a Christian?   93

7 Christian Service   103

8 Called to the Ministry   111

9 The Meaning of Ordained Ministry   123

10 The Problem and Privilege of Baptism   161

11 Charismatic Conflicts   185

12 Theological College and Ordination   223

13 The Start of Parish Ministry   241

14 Further Parish Experiences   261

15 Caulkheads and Overners   285

16 Hills of the North   315

17 Gender, Sex and Sexuality   351

18 What Next?   373

19 But is there a "What Next"?   405

Index   419

1

Introduction

Y ou can read the title of this book in two different ways. It *could* mean, if you take the two verbs in parallel, that I believe, and I also think. That is true, I hope. I have a faith, and it is very important to me. It is a faith with many different elements: a series of propositions about "life, the universe and everything"; a personal relationship of trust with Jesus Christ, who died for me; and a way of dealing with everyday decisions and problems, which seeks to involve and rely upon God. But I also have an intellect; not a super-high-powered one, but an ordinary one, which enables me to read, and listen, and discuss, and reflect upon ideas and events in the world around me. So I believe, but my faith is not a faith without intellectual content; it is not like that of the person who said, "I know what I believe – don't confuse me with facts." (I have met plenty of people like that, whether what they "believe" is religious, or anti-religious, or political, or about a variety of other topics.) I believe, and I also think; I seek to use such mental powers as are bestowed upon me to believe intelligently. In the pages that follow I try to explore and explain my own personal experience of the interaction between faith and intellect.

1

But there is a second way of reading the title. The second phrase, "I think", especially with those dots (called an ellipsis) after the words, implies a hesitation, an uncertainty, about what I believe, and even about whether I really do believe after all. Am I kidding myself? Do I believe what I say I do, or am I hiding from all the attacks upon religious faith that seem to be gathering pace and intensity at the start of the twenty-first century, by refusing to look at them? Do I really, in my heart of hearts, have a nagging suspicion that all my apparently confident assertions of faith could easily be blown away by a puff of cold reality? Am I reluctant even to admit to the forefront of my mind the possibility that there is no God?

I want to be honest – dangerous though honesty is. I do indeed, probably like most religious people, have elements of doubt and questioning about my faith. At times – maybe in the wee small hours, when life has been battering me, or perhaps when I am suffering from indigestion – these doubts threaten to overwhelm me, and I wonder whether my whole life, and especially my nearly fifty years of ordained ministry in the Church, has been based on a lie, an illusion, or a pretence.

Many, many Christian ministers before me have had to face this struggle, and it has taken many forms, and has had many different issues. Some have come to feel that they can no longer believe at all, and they have moved away decisively from all creeds and outward forms of religion, even perhaps turning against it and savagely or derisively attacking the faith which was once so precious to them, but which they now feel deceived and enslaved them.

Others no longer feel able to continue in a liturgical and preaching ministry, but continue to respect those who give their lives to traditional church life; for themselves, service in some social sphere appeals more, and they find a rewarding and satisfying ministry in Amnesty International, Christian Aid, Samaritans, or some other such organization – whether overtly Christian or not – and they indeed do valuable work there.

Some turn to other forms of spirituality, which may or may not have any compatibility with orthodox Christian faith; whether in meditation, or healing, or paranormal experiences such as clairvoyance or various so-called "New Age" practices.

Others, sadly, struggle on with their week-to-week ministry, from which the heart has evaporated. They have to lead worship, say the creed, and read prayers, but it is little more than a charade. They perhaps hope that they can conceal from their congregations or their colleagues the vacuum in their faith; but those who have to listen to their contentless sermons soon discern that there is a void at the centre. Perhaps this is what lay behind the remark of one vicar approaching retirement, who was heard to say that what he was looking forward to most of all was not having to go to church any more. I confess that such an attitude leads me to question why on earth such a man was still in the ministry at all. Surely he could have found some other means of gainful employment. While I never can condemn a man who has lost his faith, I find it hard to feel much sympathy for one whose ministry has degenerated to sheer hypocrisy. Any shred of integrity would lead such a person to be honest about his position, and most people would then respect him for coming clean.

Others stay within the official Christian ministry, but develop a form of belief that may be far from the biblical roots of orthodox faith. John Robinson wrote "Honest To God" in the 1960s, a book which was enormously controversial at the time, but also very influential; drawing on the writings of theologians like Rudolph Bultmann he sought to redefine the faith in a way which – for him at least, and probably for many others – was indeed more "honest to God" than the traditional language to which most people were

3

accustomed. Phrases like "The ground of being" to describe God, and "the Man for others" to describe Jesus, became in some circles (they even appear in hymns of the period) a normal way of expressing a faith for which traditional phraseology and dogmas no longer had any resonance. Older ways of speaking about God no longer "rang bells", he wrote.

I recall, some years after I had left my evangelical theological college, going to a lecture given by a man who as a student had been a leading light both of that college and, before that, of the OICCU[1], the strongly conservative evangelical Christian Union at Oxford University. I had known him quite well in those days, and indeed he had been something of a mentor to me at Oxford when I was struggling with some aspects of evangelical and biblical doctrine. But when I heard his lecture it quickly became apparent that he had moved a very long way from his conservative theological and biblical roots. In his dissection of the accounts of the Resurrection in the New Testament, he no longer had any inclination to regard these stories as having historical credibility. Indeed, one story – the encounter two disciples had with Jesus on the road to Emmaus[2] – he dismissed as wholly mythical, with parallels to accounts of "walks with angels" which can be found in various other forms of literature of the same period.

I do not at this point mean to discuss the validity of this view; I simply adduce it as an example of a man with a strongly conservative theological background for whom intellectual honesty compelled him, as he saw it, to move to a much more radical standpoint. Inevitably, for me this raised the question, "Is he lacking in faith, or simply more honest than I am?" Is it sheer cowardice or obscurantism that makes me reluctant to go down

---

[1] Oxford Inter-Collegiate Christian Union
[2] Luke 24. 13-35.

the same road, and persuades me that I can still maintain my belief in the essential truthfulness of the Bible as the Word of God?

Other evangelical ministers, however, while facing the same mental struggles as these men I describe, have come to different conclusions. The famous evangelist, Billy Graham, who came from a background in the Southern Baptist church of the United Church, which some would describe not just as evangelical but as fundamentalist, became aware at an early stage of his preaching ministry that he was not intellectually capable of dealing fully with all the radical approaches to theology which increasingly he was encountering as he moved onto a wider world stage in his great mission "crusades" (as they were called in those days). After an agonising struggle he found a resolution by accepting that there were many things in life which he could not fully understand, but which were true, and which he was happy to use in his day-to-day life – things like television, or even a simple light switch. He could not give much of an account as to how they worked; but they *did* work, and he would continue to use them. In a similar way, he found that the simple (some would say simplistic) declaration of the Gospel of Jesus Christ, which had transformed his own life, was also "working" in transforming the lives of the thousands who responded to the appeals he gave at his mission meetings. He did not pretend to know all the answers to all the theological or philosophical questions that might be thrown at him; but he believed that if he continued to trust God, and the Bible as the Word of God, God would honour that and would bless his ministry. Few could deny that this indeed happened throughout his remarkable ministry.

The Church of England evangelist, preacher and writer, David Watson, wrote movingly in his last book, "Fear No Evil", written during his final illness with the cancer that was to kill him, about his inner struggles in the wakeful hours of the night. He had always made the ministry of healing a central plank of his teaching, and had assured people that God was still active in bringing healing miracles; and he had many stories to tell of instances in his own experience where this had occurred. But, despite the healing ministry he had personally received from his friend, the American charismatic leader, John Wimber, shortly after his cancer was first diagnosed, it was becoming increasingly clear that he had not – yet – been healed. Throughout his ministry he had spoken and written confidently of the eternal life in glory with the Lord to which every believer in Jesus could look forward with total assurance; but now, when an early death was threatening him personally, he faced the question, "When the chips are down, do I really believe it?" And he admitted he lay there in the dark hours, weeping and sweating with fear. But even *in extremis* he emerged victorious from this crisis of faith, and was able to trust in the God of the Bible to whom he had given his life.

An important question is this: does a man *choose* whether to believe or not? Does he face the issues, the big questions, the puzzles, the mysteries, the enigmas which face each one of us at some point, each in our own way, and then make the choice, the personal decision: "Yes, I *will* believe that behind it all there is God! I don't pretend to know all the answers, or even most of them, and I don't suppose I will in this life. But I choose to believe that there is a final answer, a Theory of Everything – and that answer is God." Or he may make the opposite choice: "No, I choose to reject all religion, and all religious answers, dogmas and theories. There is no God, and never has been; God was simply a construct in the minds of frightened, primitive humans as they contemplated the vastness of nature looming over them. But I choose to believe that we know better now. I renounce God!"

Yes, I would maintain: each of us must choose. We are not compelled. We *decide* which route to take; which answers to accept, and which reject; which great thinkers, wise philosophers, brilliant scientists, or men or women of awesome goodness, to seek to identify with.

The Psalmist wrote three millennia ago, *"The fool has said in his heart, 'There is no God!'"*[1] There are three interesting things about this repeated assertion. First, that in those long ago days the writer was familiar with atheists. They were not of course modern, rationalist, scientific atheists, but they were atheists nonetheless. Secondly, he uses the word "fool", which is more than just a term of insult or abuse. It does not mean an unintelligent person, a person with an inadequate intellect. It means a person who makes a choice which is folly, often contrasted with wisdom. Thirdly, note *where* the fool formulates his atheist philosophy: "in his heart". Not his intellect; his "heart" denotes the seat of emotion and of will. It implies that his reasons for coming to this conclusion involve moral issues, matters of pride, and deep-seated, often sub-conscious motivations. Perhaps he finds the idea of God watching over him threatening or even terrifying. Maybe the whole "God thing" is strongly associated in his mind with some profoundly unhappy experience, with memories of harshness, cruelty or abuse. Or he may have encountered some person claiming to be a Christian who has been so deeply unpleasant that his wholly understandable reaction has been, "Well, if that is religion, you can keep it!" So he has *chosen* to reject the concept of God. He will of course then find all sorts of rational justifications to support his decision; but he originally made the choice "in his heart".

I would maintain that this is still so; and also that believing in God – or not believing - is not a one-off choice, but a choice which may need to be repeated a number of times throughout life. I can

---

[1] Psalm 14.1, 53.1

well imagine that in the final days of my life, when like David Watson I am facing eternity, I will have to decide again whether to believe. I will write more on this in my final chapter.

So I venture to write these pages not to compare myself, and my more trivial musings, with the titanic battles of those giants of faith, but to offer to the reader some of the answers, or at least some of the ways of living with the questions, which I have found helpful. If you find any of them helpful too, I will be delighted; if not, then consign this book to the bin, or preferably to recycling. At least it may do some good that way.

2

ᑫᡕᠺᡝᠴᠣ

The Roots of my Faith

Though I am one of those who can point to the day and hour when I was "converted", that day (11ᵗʰ November 1957) was by no means the day when faith in Christ began for me. A phrase widely used by Christians of an evangelical persuasion is "born again". The phrase was used first by Jesus[1], though Christians of different standpoints may well assert that he didn't mean by it what evangelicals have meant by it in the past century. I will discuss later my understanding of the phrase; suffice it to say at this juncture that the imagery of birth perhaps presupposes a period of gestation – a time, by no means in this case of predictable duration, when seeds are being sown, and hidden and subtle changes and developments are going on in preparation for the actual crisis of birth.

Perhaps I was being prayed for before I was born; certainly I was born into a family where "church" was a part of life. I was baptised as an infant when a few weeks old; my godfathers were my father and the clergyman who baptised me, the Revd. Perry Austin, and my godmother was a very old family friend, May

---

[1] John 3. 3.

Nugent. This baptism took place in California where I was born, and where my parents had lived for about eight years; and a week or two later the whole family moved back to England where my father's job had relocated him.

I only ever met my godfather, Perry Austin, once after that: he and his wife visited us in Oxford when I was about 12. By the time I left college and visited the States he was dead, though I did stay with his widow, Camilla, in Santa Barbara for a few days. When I was ordained she sent to me his silver Communion Set for the sick, with an inscription in his memory engraved on the base of the paten. Even though I scarcely knew him this was a precious gift, and it has been much used throughout my parish ministry.

My second godfather, my father, died when I was about two. My godmother, May Nugent, however, did survive until I was in my 30s, and was a part of my growing up. She was a spinster who was a little eccentric in some ways, but was a very caring and affectionate person. She had loads of godchildren, but she tended to keep all her friendships in separate boxes, and the only other of her godchildren I ever met was Ronald Gordon, who was Bishop of Portsmouth when I went to be Vicar of St. John's, Newport, in the Isle of Wight. I do not recall May ever coming to church with us, or giving me any present of religious significance – though she was unfailing in the matter of presents at birthdays and Christmas. I don't think she came to my Confirmation, and I'm not sure she was even there when I was ordained deacon or priest. I have no idea at all whether she had any faith of any kind. But she was chosen as my godmother, and I was very fond of her. (When I was a very small child, she was about to come and stay, and as I also had an Auntie May, who was my father's sister, my mother tried to help me distinguish between Auntie May and Godmother May. I was heard, in my cot, rehearsing: "Not Annie May; Mothercock May..." Mothercock she remained till her death!)

10

So the direct religious influence of any of my godparents upon my faith would seem to have been slight. When I became a committed Christian, I came to feel that the business of being or choosing a godparent was very important, and not to be done lightly, or purely on the basis of friendship or affection. When I have been invited to be a godparent, I have always given it long and prayerful consideration, sometimes to the hurt of the friends who have invited me. Not long enough, perhaps, for at least one of my godchildren I have scarcely seen since she was a small child. Her parents were parishioners in Walthamstow where I was a curate, and within a year of the baptism I moved to a new parish; though I tried to keep in touch, fairly rapidly the contact dwindled to once a year with the exchange of Christmas cards.

Choosing godparents for our own children has also not been an unqualified success; several have also receded to the Christmas-card-only level, though others have remained dear friends of ours and faithful supporters of our children. I still believe it is important to ponder the matter of choice carefully, the primary consideration being whether the potential godparents themselves are people with a living faith. But nearly as important is to weigh the strength of the friendship; if we move apart, is our friendship such that we will want to remain in touch, with visits, correspondence and phone calls (and nowadays, no doubt, emails and texting!), or are we likely to drift apart? But circumstances change, and so do relationships, and the durability of a friendship is not at all easy to predict.

But other influences on my childhood years were undoubtedly formative for my developing religious faith and understanding. Going to church was something we always did on Sundays, and I could not imagine Christmas Day without church. The prep school I attended for nine years, the Dragon School, Oxford, always had its own Sunday service in the school hall. It was a curious kind of anthology of readings from many sources, interspersed with

11

hymns from the school's own hymnbook. Some of the hymns were what one might call "mainstream" hymns – "Praise my soul", "The Lord's my shepherd", and suchlike. But others I have never encountered since, though I remember them well. One was:-

> Courage, brother, do not stumble,
> Though thy path be dark as night;
> There's a light to guide the humble –
> "Trust in God, and do the right!"

This last line came as a repeated refrain throughout the hymn. Another hymn had the refrain, "Be strong, be strong!" But though I could sing its fine tune, I have forgotten the rest of the words.

The readings – taken entirely by the boys, a line of whom sat on chairs upon the platform – were chosen by the elderly, senior headmaster, known as Hum (he was the father of the other headmaster, known as Joc – Jocelyn Lynam - who did most of the business of running the school). Hum (the nickname derived, I think, from his rather mumbling, droning style of speech) also selected the readers, and rehearsed them carefully in his drawing room before the service. (We were not allowed either to mumble or to drone!) There were readings from Scripture, of course; but others came from poems, or from biographies or other stories. There were prayers, and there was a sermon, usually from a visiting preacher. The greatest advantage of the service was that it only lasted three quarters of an hour.

Certainly in term time, that was where we always "went to church", not only when I was a boarder but also when I was a dayboy, as I was till I was 11. In the holidays, when we had to go to our parish church for a standard Book of Common Prayer service of Morning Prayer, we boys tended to find this more of a trial. Those Dragon School services, slightly odd though they were, were influential upon me. I recall some of the sermons affecting me deeply; and perhaps the stories of heroes of faith like David Livingstone also sowed seeds.

At home, from my earliest years, saying prayers were part of bedtime. They started, "God bless Mummy and Daddy" – even though Daddy had died of throat cancer when I was 2. But it was taken for granted that prayer for him continued.

In later years, I came to believe that prayers for the departed are inappropriate; we can remember them before God with thanksgiving, but making requests for them implies that their circumstances can change. Unless you believe in something like purgatory, which I do not, there is nothing to change. Either the dead person died in faith, in which case he is with Christ in glory, and nothing more can be sought for him; or he did not, in which case he is lost eternally, and my prayers cannot alter that. We do not have to make our own judgement as to which was the case with any particular individual, though we may be utterly convinced of the salvation of certain loved ones; their eternal salvation and judgment is God's business, not ours.

But such considerations had no place in the childish prayers of a little boy at his bedside. Daddy was part of the family, even though he had died, and so of course he must have a mention in the prayers.

The absence of my father from my family life from the age of 2 had, no doubt, many effects upon my developing character. But although I was too young when he died to have any but the haziest recollections of him, my mother spoke of him frequently, so that the image of fatherhood growing in my mind was a wholly positive one. She told me many stories about him, especially of the eight years when they lived in California. She even told me stories about his relationship with me as a baby and a toddler; that he called me "Toffee", as a pet abbreviation of Christopher (whether always or only occasionally, I would not know); or the story of how, aged 2, when they were loading the car for an outing, I ran back indoors and slammed the front door, so that they were locked out, and I was alone in the house. (Apparently he talked to me through the letterbox, and instructed me how to get a chair so that I could reach the latch and let them in.)

I have met people who grew up, as I did, in a one-parent family, for whom the whole idea of fatherhood is a vacuum. Not only can this hinder them in being adequate fathers themselves, but it may also make the concept of God as a heavenly Father totally alien and incomprehensible. For me this was never the case, and I am sure the main reason for this was my mother's care to ensure that I still in some sense knew, respected and loved my earthly father.

My earliest recollection of a direct sense that God was concerned with me and my life was when I was about 7. I had been given my first fountain pen – before that we wrote with pencils (it was before the days of ballpoints). So this new pen was a much-prized possession, and a token of becoming a big boy now; and when it was lost it was a disaster. I prayed very earnestly that God would help me find it again, and I assured him that if He did, I would be very, very good. I don't remember how or where, but I did indeed find it again, and I was deeply impressed with this prompt answer to my prayers. How long the "being good" lasted I am not sure!

When I won a small exhibition to Shrewsbury School and went there at the age of 13, I started the experience of a regular, daily service in Chapel (except Saturdays), and twice on Sundays. I also joined the Chapel Choir; and this was where I learned to sing the traditional Anglican repertoire of hymns, psalms and canticles, as well as a variety of anthems and musical settings of the canticles. These five years of classical Church music were the root of much of my experience and appreciation of liturgical worship which has lasted all my life. Even though in later years I came to value the newer forms of music associated with the charismatic renewal, and also became aware how difficult and alien is the chanting of psalms to people without any church background, for me personally it was never a problem. Likewise the singing of plainsong, like the Merbecke setting of the Holy Communion service, is still something I can slip into with ease, even though it has not been a regular part of the worship of any church I have ministered in for more than thirty years.

Another memory of those school Chapel services concerns the sermons. We had a variety of visiting preachers, as well as sermons from the two chaplains and the Headmaster. Inevitably some were better than others; but I sometimes found myself thinking, "I bet I could do better than him!" I had no particular idea of what I would say – but I was sure I could say it better than some of these chapel preachers! Was this the first inkling of a call to the ministry, even though it was years before I had found a personal, committed faith? I have met other clergy who discerned a similar sense of vocation, even before their conversion.

I was confirmed at the beginning of my second year in the school, when I was 15. This was not, of course, compulsory, but it was regarded as the norm that at that stage you joined the confirmation class, and most of us did; those who declined were seen slightly as rebels. One boy in my confirmation class was two years older than the rest of us; it was his third time of going through the preparation course, as he had felt on each of the two previous occasions that he was not yet ready to be confirmed. He was in fact confirmed on this occasion. I was very struck by his intensity and earnestness.

I remember very little of what we were taught in the classes, though I am sure the assistant Chaplain, the Reverend Michael Tupper, was faithful and conscientious in trying to explain Christian commitment to us. It was not his fault that I very nearly withdrew from the actual Confirmation at the last minute, because of a crisis of conscience.

This concerned rules about playing games – what nowadays might be called "doing sport". I was never any good at games, but a school rule prescribed that you had to play games of some sort, involving changing into games kit and having a shower afterwards, every weekday, and there was a chart on the House notice board in which to fill in what you had done. It could be swimming, fives, football, running, or, in summer, rowing or cricket. It was called "Doing a Change", and to cut it was an offence punishable by caning. On two occasions in the weeks leading up to the day of the Confirmation Service I tried to get away with not "doing a change", writing some false claim on the chart on the board. On the second occasion, I actually got as far as changing into games clothes, but as the day was damp and chilly, instead of going out to the football field I went and hid in the latrines for half an hour, and read a book.

Somehow I was found out, and was summoned to Headroom, the House Monitors' room, to face cross-examination by the Head of House. "Jenkin, did you do a change today?"

Confident of the impenetrability of my alibi, I answered boldly, "Yes, I did a football practice."

"Who did you do it with?" he asked.

My heart fell; but I had seen two or three other boys going out in football boots, so I named them. But then my heart fell further, for one of the other monitors was dispatched to interrogate those I had named. The inevitable discovery was made that they had seen no sign of me during their game; and so I was punished with six strokes of the cane by the Head of House, not only for cutting games, but also for telling lies about it.

And the next day I was to be confirmed! The sense of shame hurt far more than the cane. How could I stand up before the

Bishop and make these solemn vows, when I was such a despicable liar? There was only one thing which stopped my withdrawal from the ceremony, and that was the fact that my mother had come up from Oxford and was already staying in the area; I felt I could not let her down.

But my sense of guilt and unworthiness ensured that I approached the service in a very real spirit of penitence, and I hung on every word of the service and of the Bishop's sermon. His text was "More than conquerors"[1], and one of the hymns was that old favourite for confirmations, "O Jesus, I have promised", sung to the tune Wolvercote. (It is sung to various tunes, but to me, this one will always be the best. "Day of Rest", known to some as "the old tune", I have always regarded as weak and insipid; the one from Geoffrey Beaumont's "Twentieth Century" collection, though often used in schools, is trivial, reminiscent of "Lullaby of Broadway". But "Wolvercote" is strong and robust, and fits the words admirably.)

Although my confirmation was such a memorable occasion, some six years later when I had the experience of conversion I came to feel that, despite all my earnestness, I had not at the time of my confirmation yet come to understand what becoming a Christian was about; I was not converted; I had not been born again. At that stage I saw "being a Christian" very much in terms of trying hard to be good, going faithfully to church, and saying my prayers. Nevertheless though this is a very inadequate understanding (which vast numbers of faithful churchgoers no doubt still hold, and perhaps they will be puzzled by my assertions of its inadequacy), I believe now that God in his grace was at work in my life, and accepted my adolescent repentances and misunderstandings; and indeed the very experience of such earnest but ignorant religion helped me in later years to be able to

---

[1] Romans 8. 37

identify with the many church members I was to meet who were still at that point in their faith and understanding.

A year after my confirmation, I had another crisis of faith. Again it involved strong feelings of inadequacy and guilt, probably largely concerned with the normal problems of adolescence. I felt that all those heartfelt vows taken a year earlier had come to nothing, and I prayed passionately for some kind of forgiveness and help. I came to a sensation of absolution and peace; and I sat down to write a poem about my feelings. This poem – acutely embarrassing in retrospect – was actually published in the school magazine, *The Salopian,* and no doubt still exists in some archive of past issues. My only wish now is that it might be burnt, or, failing that, irretrievably lost, at least until after my death.

The years passed; my attendance at chapel continued (it had to, being compulsory), and in the choir I rose to the dizzy heights of Choregus – the leader of the choir who carried the cross in procession. Perhaps the only other event worthy of note in connection with my religion at school is that I took 'O' level Religious Knowledge, and failed it!

Two years of National Service in the army followed. I was called up into the Dorset Regiment – quite logical, I suppose, as I had requested the Queens Own Cameron Highlanders with which I had strong family connections. I lived in Gloucestershire, so perhaps there might have been some logic in drafting me into the Gloucesters; I had never, so far as I know, visited the county of Dorset – so, in the Army's typical way, to the Dorset Regiment I went!

As a Public School boy (I remember being surprised how very few of us there were with that background – about three or four in an intake of perhaps sixty; it is an indication of how sheltered my upbringing had been!) I was "creamed off" from the rest after only

four weeks, designated a "P.O." or Potential Officer, and sent to
Brigade HQ in Exeter where all the P.O.s did their basic training.
After being selected by WOSB (pronounced "Wosby", but
standing for the War Office Selection Board) to be an Officer
Cadet, I had sixteen weeks at Eaton Hall, Chester. There I held the
record for the number of "Extra Parades" as punishment for
scruffiness and inefficiency! Then I received a National Service
Commission as an officer – a Second Lieutenant in the Cameron
Highlanders (at last!). This led to the remainder of my two years
being served in Inverness, Singapore, Malaya, Aden, and Bahrain,
broken by two weeks' leave in Kenya.

Religion was still part of my life there, though not a very large
part. I met various Padres, and was not very impressed by any of
them. In Exeter there had been no Army padre, and so the Padre's
Hour was taken by a visiting vicar, a well-meaning elderly man
who totally failed to communicate with a large group of
unchurched young men. When I was stationed in Aden, our
Companies took it in turns to do a two-months' stint up on the
Yemen border in the mountains, where armed dissidents were a
fact of life; but we enjoyed those months, not only because of the
change of scene and more pleasant climate than that of the arid
coastal town of Aden, but because we were a satisfactorily long
way away from the Battalion HQ, and life was more relaxed. I was
asked by my Company Commander to be responsible for a
Sunday service, on the basis that I was a churchgoer; this was an
open-air affair, lasting about 15 minutes – a couple of hymns, a
reading and some prayers. There I was again, before my
conversion, leading worship! (I did *not* attempt a sermon.)

There were two other significant events concerning religion
during my time in Aden. One was my very first encounter with
"choruses", the short children's songs published in the songbooks
of the Children's Special Service Mission – the CSSM, later
subsumed into the Scripture Union. The Anglican church on

Steamer Point had a regular Family Service, which I sometimes attended; and it was there that I found myself, with the congregation which included a number of young families, singing "Wide, wide as the ocean", and "Do you want a pilot?" I was unfamiliar with such songs, but was charmed by them.

The other incident arose from my wanting to play the piano. I have never been a very competent pianist, but I have always enjoyed playing, and having access to an instrument was important to me. I found a piano in the back room of a little undenominational chapel in Steamer Point in Aden; I never asked anyone's permission, but I often used to sneak in by the back door, which always seemed to be left unlocked, and spend perhaps half an hour playing the piano there. On one occasion I found a hymn book open on the piano – not very surprising, perhaps; it was a book with which I was unfamiliar, from an evangelical, free-church tradition, and it was open at a hymn, totally unknown to me, which had the refrain, "When the roll is called up yonder, I'll be there!"

I was astounded and deeply offended by this sentiment. All my background had inculcated in me the necessity of not boasting; in the ethos of a public school, showing "side" (i.e. conceit) was totally unacceptable. In religious matters, any kind of "holier than thou" attitude was abhorrent, and this of course included any suggestion that a person could possibly claim to *know* they were going to heaven. Humility surely dictated that one might say "I *hope* I'll be accounted good enough to go to heaven, but we will never know until the day comes – will we?" This so-called humility I took for granted to be the proper religious attitude; so the bold declaration of assurance in this hymn-writer's personal eternal salvation I found profoundly offensive. How could anyone be so conceited as to say, "I know I'm so good that I am bound to go to heaven?"

20

Years later I came to enjoy singing that hymn, though it was never part of the regular repertoire of any church where I served (it is No. 759 in Mission Praise). A year or two after this episode I did come to understand the true basis of Christian assurance. My sense of outrage at the sentiments of the hymn was due to my complete ignorance of the grounds of Christian salvation. But how I discovered that is a later story.

I Believe – I Think...

3

Conversion

I chose to do my National Service before I went up to Oxford, despite the efforts of the Principal of Brasenose to dissuade me; "Scholarship is a tender plant," he asserted, "and the Services are not kindly soil." Had I acceded to his recommendation, my life might have taken a very different direction; I would have read "Mods and Greats" – Classics and Philosophy – and it is anyone's guess what sort of career this might have led me to. However that is not what happened. My brother Michael, who had also served in the Camerons for two years before going up to Brasenose, persuaded me that I would get far more out of Oxford if I had the experience and added maturity that National Service would give; he spoke of the very marked difference he had seen in his time at Oxford between boys fresh from school, and young men with forces life behind them.

Perhaps the Principal's worst fears were realised. I had had no particular reason to choose Mods and Greats as a degree course; I had done Classics at school, and got my place at Oxford by doing Latin, Greek and Ancient History, simply by default – I had found myself on "the Classical Side" at school, and had never seen any particular reason to change. (One considerable disadvantage of that was that in all the five years I spent at Shrewsbury, I never learned a word of any scientific subject; the only rudimentary science I knew was what I had learned in one lesson a week at the Dragon School. This became a serious problem to me later.) I had no idea what career I wanted; suggestions of the Diplomatic Service, among others, had been vaguely mentioned, but I hoped that in some way my path would become clear by the time I had to make some kind of decision.

During my time in the army I had enjoyed two weeks' leave in Kenya and Tanganyika (as Tanzania was called in those days), and this had included two nights staying with the warden of the Ngorongoro Crater Game Preserve. I found his way of life totally fascinating, surrounded as he was by all the wild creatures of the African bush: the elephants sometimes trampling down his garden fence; the waterbuck coming out of the trees at dusk to graze on the hillside outside his living room windows; having to take care about letting the dogs out for a run in case there was a leopard about. What sort of job could I aim for which would lead to such a life? What University course might prepare me for a career in such a setting? I cannot remember who it was who suggested Forestry, but by the time I came home to be demobbed, that was where my mind was firmly set. Oxford was one of the four Universities in Britain that offered a Forestry degree course (the others being Aberdeen, Edinburgh and Bangor); and after making enquiries, I blithely wrote to my College a fortnight before the beginning of my first term, and informed them that I was not going to do Classics, I was going to do Forestry.

It is perhaps noteworthy that in these two major decisions – to do National Service first, and to make the change from Classics to Forestry – it never occurred to me to pray about whether they were the right decisions. Consulting God simply never entered my mind. It was just not something I did. Yes, I was still a regular churchgoer, and a believer in God; but the way I made life-changing decisions would seem to indicate that my faith barely impinged on aspects of life outside of the overtly religious.

It is perhaps surprising that the college authorities accepted this change of direction without demur; but on arrival at Brasenose I found my name on lists of those taking scientific courses. But study courses were not what was pressing for my attention first of all. Rather it was the bewildering array of University clubs and societies which deluged me with invitations, programme cards and recruiting leaflets. Sporting clubs, dramatic, political and religious societies, social and philosophical groups, and so on and so on – they all clamoured for my support, and assured me that I was the person they really needed as a member.

One of them was the OICCU, the college group of which invited me very soon after the start of term to what was called a "Freshers' Squash". This seemed to be a meeting at which a speaker would describe the purpose of the Christian Union, and there would be an opportunity to meet the existing members. With a feeling that it would be good to meet some men who were, like me, churchgoers, I went along. (The term "squash" for such gatherings denoted that we would all be crammed into a smallish room; perhaps it was meant to suggest that it would be an enormously popular occasion, so I shouldn't miss it. One unfortunate freshman in another college, unfamiliar with the jargon, turned up in white shorts and carrying a squash racquet...)

I found the meeting slightly embarrassing. Everyone was exceedingly friendly, but the speaker was a bit over-familiar, to my mind, in the way he spoke about God; I was not quite comfortable with this kind of earnestness. However, when we were invited to put our names on a list if we wanted to be kept in touch with future events, I added my name, perhaps feeling it was a bit rude not to do so – it would almost have implied that I was not interested in God. This small action was to have profound consequences; the immediate result was that one existing member of the college group took it upon himself to "follow me up". It rather felt as if he was pursuing me. Whenever we met around the college he greeted me warmly. He often sat beside me in Hall for meals. He kept inviting me to various meetings, especially the Sunday evening evangelistic services in the City Church. But I politely declined all his solicitations.

He even, upon hearing that I was joining the University Walking Club, said that he thought he would do so too. This Walking Club was not a Rambling Club, but a sporting body that went in for competitive race walking, and what lay behind my joining was an experience in the Army in Aden. As I mentioned before, I have never been particularly athletic or sporting, though at school I was involved in cross-country running (I was "Senior Whip" or vice-captain) and in rowing. But in Aden an Inter-Company Athletics Tournament was being organised for the Camerons, one event of which was to be the Two Mile Walk – eight laps around a ¼ mile circuit. Major Alan McCall, my Company Commander, said breezily: "Come on, Jenkin, you've got long legs; you can represent us in the Two Mile Walk."

To everyone's surprise, not least my own, I won, and the result of that was that two months later, when an Inter-Unit sports day (involving the RAF and other forces bodies) was arranged, I was to represent the Camerons. I don't remember how much training I did; but on the great day, striding out with hips waggling and arms pumping, I forged into the lead at the start of the final lap and, to a thunder of applause from all the Camerons in the stands, breasted the tape. I even was awarded a medal for it, though I was given to understand that this was not to be worn when in uniform.

So when the leaflet of the Oxford University Walking Club landed in my pigeon hole, it seemed a good idea to join; and poor Bruce, my Christian Union minder, went along too. The first event was a 6-mile walk against some club like the Tooting Harriers – gnarled and muscular men twice our age; and off we went, waddling through the centre of Oxford for maximum publicity. Very quickly Bruce got left miles behind; as I was half way back on the return lap, I met him only half way along on the outward lap. When he finally reached the finish, he seemed unabashed that he was several miles behind the leaders, and assured me that he had enjoyed it!

It honestly never occurred to me that his sole reason for joining and putting himself through such torture was to keep in touch with me; he saw me as a quarry to whom God had directed him, and he was going to use all means to seek to win me. In the fifth week of Term he had his chance.

The OICCU was organising a student Mission that week, with the Reverend John Stott as the main speaker. John Stott, Rector of All Souls Church, Langham Place (next door to Broadcasting House, the home of the BBC), was already gaining a reputation as a formidably effective evangelist, particularly among student audiences, though at that stage I had never heard of him. My OICCU pursuer, Bruce, was determined to get me to one of the Mission meetings in St. Aldate's Church. Could I go on Sunday night? No; on Sunday evenings I went to College Chapel. What about Monday? On Monday I went to rehearse with the Oxford Bach Choir. Tuesday, then? No, 'fraid not; Tuesday evenings were for Scottish Country Dancing. How about Wednesday? At this point I ran out of credible excuses. "Oh, all right!"

So on Wednesday evening I joined the great crowd of students (being Oxford in the 1950s, overwhelmingly of men) queuing to get into St. Aldate's. After a short time of worship – a hymn, a Bible reading; a prayer or two, and a second hymn – John Stott started his address. At this stage in the week – though each address stood on its own, he was following a course of topics – he was dealing with the theme of the cost of following Christ. Up to this point I was of course regarding myself as a Christian, a believer – not a doubter or enquirer. I found him easy to listen to,

27

with a certain compelling rhetoric, and a sprinkling of amusing anecdotes. There was nothing which made me want to disagree with him. But then he came to a particular illustration of his theme: a student he had known at an Art College, who had won her place there by submitting another artist's work as her own. When she responded to the challenge of Christ's invitation to follow him, she had realised that this would just not do any more, and she confessed her dishonesty to the college authorities, which resulted in her being summarily expelled.

This story pierced me to the heart. I suddenly remembered that two and a half years earlier I, too, had cheated. In those days, a year after 'A' level, there was a further exam called 'S' or Scholarship Level; I think the papers were the same as those taken by 'A' level students, but with a much higher pass-mark. If the candidate achieved this mark, he or she had won a State Scholarship, which awarded a grant towards University fees. I had won such a State Scholarship, but in the Ancient History paper I had taken into the exam room a slip of paper with a list of crucial dates, always something I found hard to remember. I slipped it under my blotter, and consulted it surreptitiously once or twice when answering questions. I do not know whether this was critical in making the difference between a pass and a fail; I think I got 63% in that paper, and 63% was the mark required for a State Scholarship. But then I gave it no further thought, and it entirely slipped from my mind – until, as John Stott spoke that Wednesday evening, it slammed into my view once again with a jolt which shattered all my comfortable complacency.

John always ended his mission addresses the same way. He closed his main talk, but said that all those who would like to learn how, in practice, to respond to the message and commit their lives to Jesus Christ should stay behind for a brief after-meeting. Bruce asked me if I wanted to stay, and I said I did. The after-meeting talk lasted perhaps five minutes; it spelled out very simply the A-

B-C-D of becoming a Christian. (This pattern became something of a cliché in subsequent years, but I still regard it as a useful pattern for explaining the Christian response, just because it is so simple.)

'A' stands for Admit – that I am a sinner, and need to be forgiven by God. I need a saviour. 'B' is for Believe – that Jesus came to be the Saviour I need, by dying on the cross for my forgiveness, and rising again. 'C' stands for something to Consider – that there is a cost to following Christ, as he requires his followers to turn away from all that is wrong in their lives, and to be prepared to be mocked for his sake. 'D' is something to Do; it's not enough just to understand and believe; action is required, to make one's personal, decisive response to Jesus.

The verse of Scripture that John Stott introduced me to that evening was Revelation 3.20:

Behold, I stand at the door and knock; if any one hears my voice and opens the door, I will come in to him and eat with him, and he with me.

This, he explained, was the risen Lord Jesus Christ speaking, and he was knocking on the door of our hearts and lives. He has the authority to demand entry; he has the power to force his way in. But he does not; he knocks, and waits for us to hear, and to respond. He waits until we ask him in. John told the story of the famous picture, "The Light of the World", by the Victorian artist, Holman Hunt, illustrating this verse. (Hunt painted this picture three times; one copy is in St. Paul's Cathedral in London, a second in Keble College Chapel in Oxford, and the third in Manchester.) It portrays Jesus, dressed in a long white robe, with a crown of thorns on his head, and carrying a lantern in his nail-pierced hand. He is knocking on a door; the door has obviously not been opened for a long time, as it is half-covered with weeds and creepers.

When the picture was first exhibited, it created a considerable stir and large crowds went to see it. One man, however (John Stott told us), felt he had to speak to the artist. "It's a wonderful picture, Mr. Hunt," he enthused, "but – I hope you don't mind me saying this – you have made just one mistake." "Oh?" responded the artist; "what is that?" "There's no handle on the door!" pointed out the man.

"No, that is not a mistake," replied Hunt quietly. "The handle is on the inside!"

So John explained to us that Jesus was knocking on our door; but the handle was on the inside. It was up to us to decide whether or not to open the door and let him in, or to keep him out. He told us of his own experience. As a youth he had kept Jesus outside for years. He had said his prayers through the keyhole; he had pushed pennies under the door. But for a long time he had not wanted Christ inside – that would be too demanding.

As I sat there listening I identified totally with that description. For the first time in my life, I felt, someone had explained Jesus' call to me, in a way I could understand. But it was also horribly clear to me that it was not, for me, a simple matter of opening the door – not now; there was the matter of that cheating to be dealt with. If I confessed it to the College authorities, what would happen? Would I lose my place? Would I be "sent down" in disgrace? What would my family think – my mother, my two brothers who had university degrees, my grandparents, and my uncles and aunts who had helped to pay for my expensive education? The horror of this vista opening up before me I found almost overwhelming.

At the end, John Stott invited all those who wanted to respond, to join him, not out loud but secretly in their hearts, as he said a prayer of commitment, "opening the door" to Jesus. But then he challenged those who had done so to confess it, publicly, by coming forward to him as others left. "I ask you to do this for three reasons," he said. "First, because whenever Jesus called people he called them publicly. Secondly, because I would like to meet you, shake your hand, and write your name down in my book so that I can pray for you. But thirdly, because it is difficult! If you come forward while others head for the doors, you will be going against the stream. But if you have given your life to Jesus, you will be going against the stream for the rest of your life, so you may as well start now!"

But because of the turmoil and battle raging in my heart I was unable to make this response, and I joined Bruce and the rest of the congregation leaving the church. As we walked through the dark streets towards Brasenose, Bruce was, I think, aware that I was deeply moved but also disturbed, and tentatively asked me how I felt about the evening. I was very close to tears; but I needed to speak to someone, and I hesitantly stumbled through an explanation of how I was feeling. "I see," he said thoughtfully and sympathetically. To my relief he expressed no shock or disapproval at what I had done, but tried to help me think through what I needed to do. The advice he came up with was that I should discuss the matter with John Stott himself. There was a telephone number printed in the Mission publicity, for those who wanted to see him personally; so before I went to bed that night I had called the number, and made an appointment for a meeting in his hotel room next morning.

John was very friendly and welcoming. It turned out that he was acquainted with my old school chaplain, Michael Tupper. I was able to pour out to him my problems. The first one was about the whole issue of commitment.

"I think I understand what you were inviting us to do last night," I said; "but there were several times in my schooldays when I tried to serve Jesus – when I was confirmed, and a year or two later; but it never lasted. I am afraid of yet another failure – I just don't think I can keep it up."

"You are afraid that if you start to follow Jesus, you won't be able to keep it up?" repeated John. "But I am not asking you to promise to follow Jesus. If you tried to do that, you're quite right – you couldn't keep it up! But no, I'm suggesting that you should ask Jesus into your life – and then *he* will keep *you* up!"

This was a different slant on it, and I pondered it. But then there was the matter of the cheating. I explained what had happened. What was I to do?

"You will recall," said John, "that I told the congregation last night that I didn't feel that it was necessary or helpful to go raking through your entire past to uncover sins of long ago. I don't want to stifle your conscience if you are really troubled by this sin; but my judgement would be that you are obviously deeply penitent for what you did; you have no intention of ever cheating again. Is that right?"

"Yes, of course," I assured him.

"Then I suggest you leave it at that. Ask God for his forgiveness; turn resolutely away from such behaviour; and then put it behind you. I don't feel any further action would be necessary."

I was enormously relieved by this advice. After a few more minutes of chat, he gave me a little booklet, called "Becoming A Christian", written by himself, and bade me farewell. "I'll see you this evening, perhaps!" he ended.

There were two sequels to his advice about the cheating issue; but they are for a later chapter.

When I left him, I returned to my college room, and sat down straight away to read his little booklet. My first reaction to the title, "Becoming a Christian", was a negative one; that did not apply to me, of course – surely I had always been a Christian. But I ignored that, and read through the booklet – it took perhaps a quarter of an hour. I found it simple and straightforward in its explanation of what Jesus had done for me by his death and resurrection, and its invitation to respond. It was very similar to what he had said in his after-meeting the previous evening. It concluded by saying something like, "If you feel you are ready to 'open the door' to Jesus, you might find it helpful to use this prayer…" On the final page was a prayer using the A-B-C-D pattern.

I read carefully through the prayer. I remember thinking, "Well, this is what I want. I'm still not sure I will be able to 'keep it up', but if John Stott was right in his promise that Jesus would 'keep me up', then – here goes!" And I read through the prayer again, this time consciously making each phrase my own. At the end I sat quietly, reflecting on what I had done, and wondering what the result would be. There were no blinding lights, no angelic choirs, no sensation of ecstasy or divine inspiration. There was just a quiet assurance that I had done something very important. I had turned a corner, and set off in a new direction.

I Believe – I Think...

4

⚜

What is Conversion?

The concept of conversion is one of the defining characteristics of evangelical Christianity. Christians of other traditions do not commonly speak of it except in connection with turning to Christianity from a non-Christian faith position, involving baptism. They do not usually use the phrase "being converted" of the experience of someone who, being already within the Christian tradition and perhaps even a baptized, confirmed, communicant worshipper, then finds that their faith becomes more real and more personal.

Especially they would be very reluctant to say to anyone that they *need* to be "converted". But this is exactly what an evangelical would say, or at least believe – however gently and tactfully they might try to put it into words to the person concerned. And I am afraid that some of us evangelicals are far from gentle or tactful! As one who would now be happy to admit to being an evangelical Christian, let me explain how I see the matter.

As always, I turn to the Bible for my authority. There are various different phrases and concepts which describe or refer to this experience, and I want to consider these in turn.

Being born again

The first one I want to look at is one I have already mentioned: Jesus used the phrase "born again". He said, *"No one can see the kingdom of God unless he is born again."*[1] He said, *"You should not be surprised at my saying, 'You must be born again.'"*[2]

Peter in his first Epistle takes up this idea, when he writes: *"In his great mercy he has given us new birth into a living hope through the resurrection of Jesus Christ from the dead."*[3] So Jesus said to Nicodemus – a deeply religious Pharisee – "You must be born again." Peter wrote to his readers, most of whom were probably Jews who had turned to Jesus Christ, "We have been born again."

Why did Jesus use this particular image? Birth is something familiar. It is the start of life on earth. Yes, of course we know that the beginning of human life, biologically speaking, is at conception, when the sperm cell merges with the egg cell in the womb, forming a linked cell or zygote containing chromosomes from both the parent cells. This becomes the embryo, and later the foetus. But that's not the way in ordinary human terms that we think of our life. We celebrate our birthday, not our conception day. We welcome babies into the world at birth. So birth represents a major, fundamental beginning.

Jesus links this with the idea of breath. *"Flesh gives birth to flesh, and the Spirit gives birth to spirit."*[4] In other words, ordinary, human, physical birth gives rise to ordinary, human, physical life; but spiritual birth leads to a different kind of life – spiritual life. The Greek word for 'spirit' is 'πνευμα', 'pneuma', which can also be translated 'wind' or 'breath'. At the moment of physical birth, the first sign of life is the breath of the baby, usually emerging as a yell or a squawk. Jesus is linking this familiar experience –

---

[1] John 3.3.
[2] John 3.7
[3] I Peter 1.3
[4] John 3.6

36

associated with all sorts of emotions of joy, wonder and hope – with a new kind of beginning. Most English translations of John's Gospel start the first Spirit in the verse with a capital letter, making it a reference to the Holy Spirit.

There is in the same passage a comparison with a different kind of 'pneuma'. *"The wind blows wherever it pleases; you hear its sound, but you cannot tell where it comes from or where it is going. So it is with everyone born of the Spirit."*[1] There are other passages in Scripture where the Holy Spirit is compared with the wind; we think of the wind moving over the waters at creation[2], and Ezekiel's vision of the valley of dry bones[3]. The wind is something invisible, mysterious and yet very powerful. We cannot control it, but we can see its unmistakeable results and effects. The work of the Holy Spirit is like this – especially this particular work of bringing a new kind or dimension of life.

There is another passage in John's Gospel, which should be studied alongside this teaching of Jesus in Chapter 3. That is in the Prologue in Chapter 1, where John writes concerning "the Word", which is his title for Jesus:

"He was in the world, and though the world was made through him, the world did not recognise him. He came to that which was his own, but his own did not receive him. Yet to all who received him, to those who believed in his name, he gave the right to become children of God – children born not of natural descent, nor of human decision or a husband's will, but born of God."[4]

Here the birth image is used again; and John says that it is those who "receive" or "believe in" Jesus who are thus "born of God". They are the ones who can be called children of God. They

---

[1] John 3.8
[2] Genesis 1.2
[3] Ezekiel 37
[4] John 1. 10-13

are children of God *not* by natural descent – not by being of Jewish birth, not even just by being of the human race, which is the way many people use the phrase "children of God" – but in one way only: they have received Jesus Christ; they have put their trust in him.

We begin to see in these passages a very black-and-white, a very yes-or-no understanding of spiritual life. Unlike the way many of us prefer to think of these things, in innumerable shades of grey, John is saying: "Either you are a child of God, or you are not. Either you have been born again, or you have not. Either you have received spiritual life, or you have not." He spells this out even more starkly in his first Epistle:

> *"God has given us eternal life, and this life is in his Son. He who has the Son has life; he who does not have the Son of God does not have life."*[1]

He couldn't make it much clearer than that, could he? And here John uses another word to describe this new, spiritual life, which starts with the new birth: he calls it "eternal life".

So we start to grasp the enormous significance of what happens when a person "receives" or "believes in" Jesus Christ as the Word or Son of God.

1. He (or she, of course – but for simplicity's sake I will stick to "he") accepts Jesus – unlike those who rejected him or did not recognise him for who he was.
2. He believes in Jesus – and this is not just a matter of accepting statements or doctrines about him, but starting to trust him personally, to rest or rely on him.
3. The Holy Spirit is at work in him, bringing about a fundamental change.
4. He receives a new dimension of life, spiritual life.

---

[1] I John 5. 11,12.

5.   This is also eternal life – which does not just mean something that starts when he is dead; it starts when he receives Jesus, but it never stops, even when he dies physically.

6.   Entering into this new, eternal, spiritual life is new birth, spiritual birth, and it makes a person a child of God.

7.   Such a person – and only such a person - then has the right to call God "Father".

I believe this is what happened to me, that morning in November 1957 as I sat in my room in Brasenose College, Oxford, with a little blue booklet in my hands, and deliberately "opened the door" to Jesus. I was born again; I received Jesus – after all, this is what happens when you open the door to someone! I received spiritual life. I received eternal life. I became a child of God.

Although evangelical Christians have used the language of "new birth" for centuries, it really only hit the popular, secular awareness when Jimmy Carter became President of the United States. He frequently spoke of himself as "born again", and the world's press started to ask what on earth he was talking about. As so often when non-Christian journalists start writing about Christian matters, they got it wrong and misunderstood it; and the popular understanding of the phrase from then on was that it was something to do with a dramatic experience of conversion. Even in Christian circles, people began talking about "born-again Christians", as opposed to other kinds of Christians.

But if you think carefully about those verses of Scripture mentioned above, you will see two things that contradict these ways of thinking:

1. Though the *spiritual results* of being born again could indeed be said to be dramatic, there is nothing there that carries the necessary implication that the actual *experience* has to be a sudden or dramatic one. I myself can tell you the day and almost

the hour when it happened to me (it was Thursday November 11th 1957, at about 10.45 a.m.!), but it doesn't have to be this way. For many people it has been a much more gradual process, over a matter of weeks, months or even years; images like a flower opening up to the sun have been used – and though we have all seen the speeded-up photography of flowers which makes this appear a sudden "whoosh", we know it isn't really like that. Some people can point to a moment when all the thinking and pondering began to move towards an answer, all the elements gradually fell into place, or as their understanding clarified – when this culminated in a particular moment when they said a mental "Yes!" to Jesus. C. S. Lewis wrote of how it happened to him on the top of a bus going up Headington Hill in Oxford. It was a decisive moment, but not a startling or dramatic revelation, not a "Hallelujah!" event.

I think of another man I knew who had no Christian background at all; he seldom thought of religion, and if he did he was inclined to regard people who took that sort of thing seriously as stupid and foolish. But he didn't mind that his two little girls went to Sunday school; his wife had done so as a child, and the kids seemed to enjoy it. Then one day his six-year-old said,

"Daddy, you must come to church on Sunday – my class is singing a song in the service!"

"Oh – must I?" he asked reluctantly. But he loved his little daughter, and couldn't refuse her; and somewhat nervously he turned up at the church door on Sunday.

Two things surprised him. One was that he saw several people there that he knew – but he had had no idea that they went to church. And they seemed fairly normal people! The second surprising thing was that he actually enjoyed the service, and said to his wife afterwards, "I wouldn't mind going again sometimes!"

So about once a month he went with his wife; and gradually his ideas of what "religion" was about began to change. At

Christmas he went to the Carol Service, and found it profoundly moving. About that time he bought himself a "Good News" Bible, and began to read it. Then one frosty winter day as he walked to work, he was mulling over in his mind all the ideas and experiences he had been having; and he found himself thinking, "I used to think that Christian believers were fools; but all the time it was me who was the fool! I was the stupid one!" And as this thought went through his mind it was as if a warm glow pulsed through him, and all the rest of the way to work, that frosty morning, he felt like the old Readybrek advertisement ("This is the way we glow to school!"), with an inner warmth radiating from him.

It was some weeks later that an evangelistic appeal was given in church, and those who wanted to commit their lives to Jesus were invited to raise their hands. Both he and his wife did so. That was the first time I – their vicar – became aware that anything of spiritual significance was happening in their lives; when I went to call on them a day or two later, he told me his story.

I couldn't define, and nor could he, exactly when the moment of his "new birth" occurred; was it the "Readybrek moment", or was it when he responded to the appeal, or some time in the weeks or months before these events? Who knows? Who cares? It had been a process. There was no doubt, though, that it had happened, and I rejoiced with that young couple at what they had found.

For others, there have been no "moments" of conversion at all, even as vague as that man's; just a gradual dawning of light, a number of "pennies dropping", a dealing with negative attitudes, a journey of seeking and questioning – and not necessarily a steady journey all in one direction, either: the dawning light may have flickered and dimmed, there may have been times of drifting away again; but in the end a conviction has been reached, and they are able finally to say, "I believe! Jesus is Lord!"

2. The other fallacy in the secular idea of being born again is that there are "born-again" Christians and other kinds of Christians. Look again at those conclusions I have drawn from the various verses I quoted on this subject: if my conclusions are right, *all* Christians are born again! A person who has not been born again cannot be described as a Christian, a disciple of Christ, at all.

I hope that the first point I made, that a sudden or dramatic conversion is not a necessary feature of being born again, does something to remove the offence from this assertion. I am not, of course, saying that if you cannot pinpoint the precise day of your conversion, I refuse you the title of Christian. (For a discussion about the true definition of the word "Christian", see below on page 93.) What I am saying is that any man, woman or child who is a committed believer in Jesus Christ, irrespective of the way or process through which they reached that faith, *is* a "born-again Christian." If you hadn't realised what had happened to you – whenever or however it happened – I want you to grasp it, and wonder at it, and praise God for it.

But if it *hasn't* yet happened, and you are still – as I was, for years – relying on good behaviour, a habit of churchgoing, and an assent to certain statements in the Creed, to give you your identity as a Christian, then I want you to realise – these things, though important and valuable, are quite inadequate as a way to find eternal life, and there is something wholly different you need to discover! You too can come to know Jesus in a personal way as your Lord and your Saviour, and God as your Father! So before you hurl this book across the room in fury and frustration, please read on, and ask the Holy Spirit to use these pages to speak to you in a new way.

Life, Death and Resurrection

Another set of images that the New Testament uses to illustrate the difference between a person who has come to faith in Christ and one who hasn't – yet! – is the contrast between life and death. A key passage is in Paul's letter to the Christians at Ephesus.

"As for you, you were dead in your transgressions and sins, in which you used to live when you followed the ways of this world and of the ruler of the kingdom of the air, the spirit who is now at work in those who are disobedient. All of us also lived among them at one time, gratifying the cravings of our sinful nature and following its desires and thoughts. Like the rest, we were by nature objects of wrath. But because of his great love for us, God, who is rich in mercy, made us alive with Christ even when we were dead in transgressions – it is by grace you have been saved. And God raised us up with Christ..."[1]

Paul is piling on the images here! Ideas like death and life, sin, wrath, grace, resurrection: all are intertwined, and quite hard for the newcomer to disentangle. Let me try to unwrap it all for you.

1. Paul is saying that both he himself and his readers were all sinners. They could all look back on a period in their lives when their behaviour was governed by three factors:

   a. *"The ways of this world"* – the cultural standards, values and assumptions of their age. They just did and thought what everyone else did and thought.

   b. *"The cravings of our sinful nature"* – our own natural tendency to selfishness, greed, lust, and all the rest.

   c. *"The spirit who is now at work in those who are disobedient"* – a hard idea for some to accept, but Paul is talking about the Devil, a spiritual

---

[1] Ephesians 2. 1-6

43

force of evil. (Do these three phrases ring bells with those who are at all familiar with the Church of England Baptism Service? That service refers to "The world, the flesh and the devil". This Bible passage is one of the places from which that phrase is derived.)

2.   Paul asserts that one result of this life of sin is that we fall under the wrath of God – "we were by nature objects of wrath". This too is a concept modern people are uneasy with, with overtones of Victorian preachers thundering about fire and brimstone, hellfire and damnation. (I heard about such a preacher who published a book of his sermons, and he used the phrase "The Wrath of God" so frequently that the printer ran out of capital W's!) Any doctrine can be exaggerated or distorted – or mocked and derided. The "wrath of God" is not the bad temper of some vengeful deity; it is rather the implacable hostility against sin, of a God who is utterly holy. Sin *cannot* be tolerated; it is an offence against God's very nature – and that nature is what holds the entire cosmos together! But this understanding must be held in conjunction with that of grace – see below.

3.   The second result of our sin is death. *"You were dead in your transgressions…"* This reminds us of the story of Adam and Eve who were warned that if they disobeyed God and ate from the Tree of the Knowledge of Good and Evil they would die. I will examine this story in more detail later in this chapter; let me just say now that one concept frequently found in the Bible is that death is the result of sin – not just physical death, but spiritual

death. In this passage in Ephesians, Paul is maintaining that all of us, until we turn to Christ, are dead already – spiritually dead, because of our sin.

4.   That is our helpless situation – until a loving God steps in to rescue us. This is what Paul means when he writes, *"it is by grace you have been saved."* "Grace" is a major Bible concept, worthy of a whole chapter on its own, but at this point I will just say that a good definition is "God's boundless love to us, who are totally undeserving of it." It was this love for dead, helpless, undeserving sinners that prompted God (who is *"rich in mercy"*) to step in to rescue us.   And what dead people need is resurrection!

5.   This then is what God has given us, *"because of his great love for us"*: new life, when we were dead. *"God raised us up with Christ!"* Paul asserts. As surely, and as miraculously, as he raised Jesus on the first Easter Day, conquering death, so he raised us – potentially, at the same moment as Christ's resurrection; but actually and in our experience, when we decisively respond to the invitation of Christ to receive him.

So there are two different images – new birth, and resurrection – both of which indicate a massive change in a person's situation, a totally new life. The Bible is saying not just that coming to faith in Christ is *like* these things, or that it may feel like that; it is saying – in these passages I have quoted, and in numerous others – that this is something which in the spiritual realm has actually happened. A person has either been born again of the Spirit, or he hasn't, and is still solely living on the earthly, human plane. He has either been raised from spiritual death, and given eternal life, or he hasn't, and is still spiritually dead – and when he comes to the end of his earthly life, the difference between these two states becomes irretrievable and eternal. It is the difference between Heaven and Hell.

Sin and Salvation

This is another area about which we need to get our ideas straight, and which is a fundamental aspect of the experience of conversion. In the "Death and Life" section above, I mentioned Paul's reference to sin which causes death. So let's consider sin.

We must get one thing straight from the very beginning. Every human being – except Jesus himself – is a sinner. This of course includes born-again Christians; they may sometimes regrettably give the impression that they think every one else is a sinner, but not them – but this of course is utter nonsense. Paul not only says "we" (including himself) in that passage about being dead in sin before we were raised by God's grace; but in other passages in his letters he makes it abundantly clear that he is all too aware that he is still a sinner. The difference is – now he is a forgiven sinner.

The very word "sin" has almost dropped out of normal secular English usage by the start of the 21st Century. A generation ago this was not so; one context in which it used to be found quite frequently was in the more salacious Sunday papers, especially the *News of the World*, which used to specialise in stories with headings like *"She opened the door in her nightdress"*. They used the word "sin" quite frequently, and almost invariably it had a sexual connotation. (I read a recent copy of the paper to see if they still wrote like that; and though I felt it my duty to peruse with great care every story with such a theme – there were still a good many of them – I found no mention of "sin"!)

It is correct not to use the word "sin" in a secular context, for it only has any real meaning in relation to God. Those who have no room for God in their thinking will also have no place for the concept of sin; for what sin is in its essence is an offence against a holy God. *"Sin is lawlessness,"*[1] wrote John; and the "law" referred to is not any civil or secular legislation, but the eternal law of God. Remove the concept of the Law of God, and the concept of sin evaporates.

I am not of course claiming that without religion there is no morality. Morality can be derived from all sorts of philosophical positions, and rest upon various bases such as the common good, conscience, cultural consensus, civil laws etc. But breaking of a cultural consensus, however morally wrong it is regarded to be, is not "sin".

From the early chapters of the Book of Genesis onwards, the Bible maintains that God is the origin of all goodness, and therefore to resist or disobey what God has commanded is sin. (James adds a condition to this basic overall concept, and that is that the offender must be aware of the law or command: *"Whoever knows what is right to do and fails to do it, for him it is sin."*[2]) Moreover Bible writers insist that the consequences of sin are dire: *"The wages of sin is death."*[3]

The story of Adam and Eve and the Tree of the Knowledge of Good and Evil vividly expresses this truth[4]. When God put the human pair in the Garden of Eden, he assured them that everything was freely available to them. Everything they could possibly need or desire was there for the taking. There was one prohibition, and one only – and it was made clear that the prohibition was for their benefit: they were not

---

[1] I John 3.4
[2] James 4.17
[3] Romans 6.23
[4] Genesis, chapters 2 and 3

allowed to eat the fruit of one specific tree "in the middle of the garden". They were told categorically that if they disobeyed this one command, they would die.

There is no suggestion in the story that the tree was evil. (Nor was it the "Tree of Knowledge", as I have heard suggested, as if knowledge itself was forbidden them – implying that all scientific study is in defiance of God.) It was "the tree of the knowledge of good and evil"[1]. The very fact that it was there, and that they had to make a moral decision about it, was in itself a gift of God: whether they obeyed God or disobeyed him, the fruit of that tree would be a focus of moral decision. They could learn what good and evil meant, only if such a decision was available to them.

They might have looked at that fruit, and considered carefully, and said to themselves or to each other, "This fruit cannot be evil or harmful in itself, because God is good, and he would not put something in the garden which is evil or poisonous. But he has commanded us, in his love, not to eat it; although it looks tasty and nutritious, let us trust that it is out of love that he has forbidden it, because he knows what is best for us. We will not eat it." If that had been their free choice and decision, they would have learned a very important lesson, one essential to being a human being and a child of God: that they could choose to obey or disobey God, to do either what is good or what is evil. To have made the alternative decision would have been evil, and they had rejected it. Thus the tree would still, in my fantasy re-writing of the tale, have been for them "the tree of the knowledge of good and evil".

Tragically they made the opposite decision; they chose evil, and they instantly began to experience it in their minds,

---

[1] Genesis 2.17

their wills, their emotions, and all aspects of their lives, in ways that God had not wanted for them; for mere humans are not able to experience evil without being corrupted and destroyed by it. They had been warned that disobedience would lead to death, and it did. Physical death was not instantaneous (the human race would have stopped right there if it had been); but, as Paul wrote, *"Death came into the world through sin"*[1]

This simple and ancient tale brilliantly portrays the nature and the results of sin.

1.   Their relationship with each other was spoiled. The awareness of nakedness[2] is *not* (as so often asserted) the discovery of sexuality; they had already been told to have children[3], and there is only one way of doing that! It had also been said that the man would *"be united to his wife, and they will become one flesh"*[4] – a term that denotes sexual intercourse. No; their instinct to conceal their nakedness from each other is a pictorial way of expressing their hiding of their most personal and intimate natures from each other. It was the estrangement of human being from human being, as well as of man from woman. From this beginning stems all mistrust, misunderstanding, deceit, hatred, anger, killing and war.

2.   Their relationship with God was spoiled. That lovely intimacy suggested a few verses further on, by God's expectation that they would walk with

---

[1] Romans 5.12
[2] Genesis 3.7
[3] Genesis 1.28
[4] Genesis 2.24

him in the garden in the cool of the day[1], had been lost: and they hid from him. Humanity has been hiding from God ever since – but has also been aware of the depth of that loss, resulting in the desperate attempts to find, invent or create a deity or some substitute that will show us who we are and how we fit into the universe.

3.   The man's attempt to find excuses for his sin – *"The woman you put here with me – she gave me some fruit from the tree, and I ate it"*[2] - is an early manifestation of three things:

   a.   He is trying to evade responsibility for his actions – an early "Not me, Guv!"

   b.   He is blaming someone else, namely his wife.

   c.   He is even blaming God: *"The woman you gave me..."*

4.   Their relationship with nature was spoiled. *"Cursed is the ground because of you..."*[3]

5.   Their enjoyment of work was spoiled. They had been told earlier that they were to till and keep the garden, and this had been designed as a joyful sharing of the work of God's creation, fulfilling and satisfying[4]. But now, *"In toil shall you eat of it... in the sweat of your face..."*[5]

6.   Their personal and family life was spoiled. Childbearing would be an agony; the relationship between husband and wife would no longer be the

[1] Genesis 3.8
[2] Genesis 3.12
[3] Genesis 3.17
[4] Genesis 1.28, 2.15
[5] Genesis 3.17,19

easy and delighted intimacy of *"bone of my bones and flesh of my flesh!"*[1], but a matter of dominance: *"He shall rule over you."*[2]

7.   Physical death became inevitable, and they would *"return to the dust"*.

8.   Most dreadful of all, they were excluded from the eternal life that God intended for them: the way to the *"Tree of Life"*[3] was barred to them.

And yet...

And yet, despite these tragic and disastrous repercussions of what might have seemed a minor and trivial sin, but which was actually a rebellion of huge significance, despite the inevitable consequences, and the severe judgement of God upon their disobedience, God was still showing love and mercy!

1.   Even before a word of judgement was spoken to the human pair, God indicated an ultimate salvation. When speaking to the serpent – no longer just a reptile but the embodiment of the Tempter – God promised:

"I will put enmity between you and the woman,
and between your offspring and hers;
he will crush your head,
and you will strike his heel."[4]

This has always been seen as the first prophecy of the Messiah, and Christians apply it to Jesus; he is the one who, through enormous suffering, would ultimately crush the power of the Devil.

---

[1] Genesis 2.23
[2] Genesis 3.16
[3] Genesis 3.24
[4] Genesis 3.15

2. Even before God had expelled them from the Garden, he clothed their nakedness with garments of skins[1]. This is not only an amazing act of graciousness in covering a result of their sin, but it should be noticed what the clothes were made of: skins. Such a covering was not only a good deal more adequate than the pathetic, self-help attempts by the couple themselves, using fig leaves, but it was much more significant than this: animals had to die for human sin to be covered. This was the first sacrifice for sin, once again foreshadowing the sacrifice of Jesus, the Lamb of God.

3. Finally, even what seems at first the severest judgement of all, the exclusion from the Garden and from the Tree of Life, in fact is an act of mercy: God was ensuring that sin would be finite. *Sinful man could not be allowed to live forever*[2]; only when sin had been eternally dealt with could the way to the Tree of Life be opened once more.[3]

I have discussed in some detail the Genesis story of the Fall of Man, as it is commonly called, because so much of the nature of sin and its results is seen there. But before discussing the moral and theological implications of the story, I must address the question that will inevitably be in the mind of the reader: "Are you really trying to tell us that you believe that this story is historically, literally true?" It would not be honest to dodge this legitimate question.

Many evangelical Christians would, no doubt, say in categorical terms, "Yes, of course it is true! It's the written word of God."

---

[1] Genesis 3.21
[2] Genesis 3.22
[3] Revelation 22. 1-5

Other people who would stoutly affirm their right to the name of Christian would take an opposite view, and answer, "No, of course it is not *literally* true. It is simply an ancient legend, a myth dreamed up by simple and primitive people to explain life as they saw it. It is no more *literally* true than the story that God physically shaped man with his hands from the dust of the earth."

At one period in my Christian exploration, I might have agreed whole-heartedly with the first answer. But perhaps the answer I now feel bound to give will not be accepted as a "straight" answer at all, but a typical and infuriating fudge!

First, I believe that the story expresses concepts about God, about human beings, and about good and evil which are indeed profoundly true. We would be quite wrong to dismiss such ideas as merely quaint and primitive; on the contrary, they offer us essential insights into the whole area of human moral choices, and their relationship with God and his holy will.

Secondly, I am perfectly ready to accept that the way that this story of human moral choice is presented – the stealing of forbidden fruit – may not be literally true. There was, indeed, a crucial choice with cosmic and eternal consequences; whether it actually, literally, involved fruit from a tree is unimportant. C. S. Lewis, in his sci-fi novel, *Voyage to Venus* (earlier entitled *Perelandra*), portrays a world (he places it on the planet Venus) in a Garden-of-Eden state, but where the focus of moral decision for the man and woman was different: his was a world of huge oceans, and the human couple lived on floating islands of vegetation, but there was solid, dry land too, which they often explored. The one thing they were forbidden to do was to sleep on the dry land; they had to return to the floating islands for the night. The lengthy account in the book of the satanic temptation revolved around that choice. The "fruit of the tree" story could well have been a simple, pictorial, metaphorical way of portraying what was a real moral choice which actually involved some other, perhaps less tangible, decision.

[It is impossible to separate the question of the truth of the Fall story, in Genesis 3, from the question of the Creation of Man stories, in Genesis 1 and 2. This is a huge issue (however summarily and contemptuously it is dismissed by most modern British writers), which I will only mention briefly at this point. It is possible, indeed, that the theory of evolution of mankind is actually what happened. It is just a theory, and I accept totally that "evolution" as a process, such as Darwin posited from his examinations of the Galapagos finches, is satisfactorily proven and has often happened: one species of finch has evolved into another, one species of gastropod or trilobite has evolved into another. It is unproven that evolution on a much vaster scale has occurred – not just between species, but between genera, families and even orders. That human beings evolved from earlier prehistoric creatures, and ultimately from unicellular forms of life, is unproven, and I am not totally convinced that it offers a sufficient explanation for the existence of mankind. But supposing it *is* true, it simply means that this was the mechanism God chose to create mankind. And I can accept that the picture in Genesis 2 of God forming or moulding the man from the dust of the earth, could be a vivid, poetic way of describing the process that started with slime at the bottom of a shallow sea, and ended up with *Homo sapiens*.

But, yes, I believe there was a "Fall". At some point in the development of the *Homo* genus, there came the point where God saw that he was ready for the next stage – the capacity for spirituality, for a personal relationship with God himself. Maybe that is what is meant by the sentence, God *"breathed into his nostrils the breath of life, and the man became a living being"* (AV: "soul")[1].]

---

[1] Genesis 2.7

Let us return to the story of the Fall in Genesis 3. From that point on, sin is regarded in the Bible as something of enormous significance. Again and again the holiness of God is contrasted with the sinfulness of humanity. Again and again, it is demonstrated how a sinful person dare not, *cannot* approach a holy God, unless some provision is made for his sinfulness; and almost invariably the prescribed provision involves some form of sacrifice.

In the Law of Moses, the sacrifices required are spelled out in great detail, and in enormous variety according to the specific occasion. Sometimes offerings of oil or grain were commanded; but whenever sin was the issue, the slaughter of an animal or bird, the shedding of blood, was required. As the Epistle to the Hebrews, that New Testament book which sets out to interpret Jewish law in the light of Christ, sums up a millennium and a half later: *"Without shedding of blood there is no remission of sins."*[1]

Sin is described in different ways, and a number of words are used; these are not identical in meaning, but point to different aspects of sin. Three in particular are significant, and all are used in the first two verses of Psalm 51, that Psalm in which David, deeply convicted of his own sinfulness, pleads with God for forgiveness.

"Have mercy on me, O God, according to your unfailing love;
according to your great compassion blot out my transgressions.
Wash away all my iniquity
and cleanse me from my sin."[2]

The three words are
(a) "Transgressions": "Transgression" means, literally, a stepping over; stepping over a line, disobeying a sign that says "No Admittance". It is a word which points to a

---

[1] Hebrews 9.22
[2] Psalm 51.1,2

55

deliberate, flagrant rebellion against a known command. It reflects the defiant attitude which says, "I don't care what God says: I am going to do what I want!"

(b) "Iniquity": a word which points to the inner predisposition to go wrong, a deep flaw in human nature. In verse 5 David writes, *"Surely I was sinful at birth, sinful from the time my mother conceived me."* This is *not* (as sometimes wrongly interpreted) a suggestion that there is something intrinsically wicked about sexual intercourse, the act through which he was conceived – this is something that the Bible never says or implies, even though at certain points in church history such an idea has gained credence. Rather it is the recognition that as soon as human life existed, that life which was to become "me", it was sinful life – *even before this had manifested itself in any specific wrong action.* He was sinful because his parents, and theirs, had been sinful. As surely as dogs have puppies and cats have kittens, sinners have sinners.

(c) "Sin": this is the general word to refer to any particular sinful act. In David's case, what had brought him to this lament of penitence involved adultery, lies and murder, namely his affair with Bathsheba[1].

What sin does, always and inevitably, is that it separates: it separates us from one another, but more importantly and fundamentally it separates us from God. It did both these things in the Garden of Eden, and it still does. The separation from God is clearly affirmed in the first two verses of Isaiah, chapter 59. He was answering the complaints of his contemporaries, "Why doesn't God listen to our prayers? Why doesn't he reach out his arm and help us?" Isaiah answered:

"Surely the arm of the Lord is not too short to save,

---

[1] II Samuel 11

nor his ear too dull to hear.
But your iniquities have separated you from your God,
your sins have hidden his face from you, so that he will not hear."

And he goes on to spell out in vivid and poetic language the wrongdoing of the people of his day.

I am not saying (and neither, I think, was he) that every time a prayer of a believer is not apparently answered, it must mean that it is the fault of his own sins. The question of unanswered prayer is more complex than that! Isaiah was simply setting out a principle: this is what sin does. It cuts us off from God. And until sin is dealt with, we remain cut off from him.

This is a fundamental truth that lies at the heart of Biblical faith. Sin separates us from God. Ultimately, if this is not dealt with, it will separate us from him for all eternity; and this is Hell.

What can be done about it? *"What must I do to be saved?"* is the desperate cry of the Philippian gaoler to Paul[1], and it is the cry through the ages of everyone whose eyes have been opened to the appalling consequences of sin.

Paul's answer was, *"Believe in the Lord Jesus, and you shall be saved!"*

In a way he was saying, "Friend, there is *nothing* that you can do! Nothing that you could ever do will make the slightest difference! No amount of effort to be good; no acts of charity, no religious observances. None of these things can put away human sin! We have sinned; we cannot deny it; we must plead guilty before the Judge of all the earth. And his eternal law says, 'The wages of sin is death.' "

"So must I be eternally damned?" comes the appalled cry.

"Yes, if you hope that something *you* can do might save you. But in fact God has already done something! While we were still sinners, he sent his Son, Jesus, to die for us. When he died on the

---

[1] Acts 16.30

cross, he took upon himself all the results of human sin: the guilt, the darkness, the separation from God. He suffered Hell for us. And after death, he rose again! The wages of sin is indeed death; but the free gift of God is eternal life, through Jesus Christ our Lord!

"So all you can do is trust – trust Jesus, trust what he has done for you. Reach out your hand to receive that free gift – a gift that you could never, ever earn or deserve, or purchase by your own efforts. Believe in the Lord Jesus, and you shall be saved!"

This is what is meant in the New Testament by that somewhat mysterious word, "Salvation", and the associated words, "saved" and "Saviour". There are many things we may need to be saved from: physical dangers like a burning house, illness, poverty, injustice, hopelessness, despair. All of these can ruin a person's life, and it is not God's will that humanity should be subject to them. Much Christian service is dedicated to bringing "salvation" to people suffering from one or another of these woes, and this is surely right. But what people need most of all is salvation from *eternal* suffering, *eternal* hopelessness, *eternal* death. This, above all, is what Jesus came to bring us.

The name he was given, revealed both to Mary his mother and to Joseph before he was born, "Jesus", means "Saviour", or "God saves." From his very conception he was God's answer to humanity's need of salvation – salvation from sin and its consequences; and ultimately fulfilling the purpose for which he was born took him to the cross. When a Christian calls him "Saviour", it is above all his death on the cross that is in our thoughts.

"Are you saved?" is the question sometimes asked by earnest street evangelists, often to the confused embarrassment (or profound irritation) of their hearers, who usually have no idea what the question means. What does it mean? If I am "saved" it means that because I have put my trust in Jesus and his death for me, I can be sure that my sin is dealt with. I am forgiven. I am loved. I am accepted by God. I have been welcomed into his family, and have been born again. I have become a child of God. I have been given the free gift of eternal life. I have been promised a place in heaven.

Are *you* saved?

Some other "conversion" words and phrases

Evangelicals sometimes use words and phrases to refer to conversion which, though much loved, are not in fact biblical. One is "inviting Jesus into your heart". (No one but an evangelical would say that!) There are variations – maybe "heart and life" is used. But you will not actually find the phrase in Scripture.

You will find similar forms of words, or related concepts. Paul says that he prays for his Christian friends at Ephesus, *"that Christ may dwell in your hearts through faith"*[1]; he is not referring to conversion, but a steady, continual indwelling. It is similar to the teaching of Jesus, when he tells his disciples, *"Remain in me and I will remain in you"*[2]; it speaks of a close and intimate relationship, and in Jesus' teaching it is in the context of an illustration of a vine and its branches. You could argue that the start of such a relationship could be described as "inviting Jesus into your heart"; but over-emphasis on this can make the believer lose sight of the need to nurture this relationship, which is what Paul is talking about.

The verse which John Stott used to help me to respond to the Gospel, about "opening the door"[3], is a similar idea; the door is metaphorical, of course, and it can only be a metaphor for our "heart and life". That verse is very precious to me, not only because of my own conversion experience, but also because I have

---

[1] Ephesians 3.17
[2] John 15.4
[3] Revelation 3.20

used it many times to help other people make a decisive step of Christian commitment. But it is often argued that to use the verse in that way is a dishonest use of Scripture, as it totally ignores the context of the passage. So let me pause to examine it a little more carefully.

The overall context in chapters 2 and 3 of the Book of Revelation is a series of seven messages from the risen Christ to the seven churches of Asia. Because seven is such a symbolic number, we are surely justified in extending the messages beyond the seven 1st Century Christian communities in western Turkey – valuable though it is to study each message in relation to what is known about these cities at the time – to all Christian communities everywhere in all ages. The seventh message is to the church of Laodicea.[1]

This assembly of believers was deeply complacent. The Lord describes them as *"lukewarm – neither hot nor cold"*, and he virtually says they make him sick! Though they were so self-satisfied, he saw them as *"wretched, pitiful, poor, blind and naked"*, and he summons them to *"be earnest, and repent"*.

Then he speaks to each individual within this church which was hardly more than nominally Christian:

"Here I am! I stand at the door and knock. If anyone hears my voice and opens the door, I will come in and eat with him, and he with me."

Every man, woman or child, though members of a Christian community which had so sadly lost its way and its very purpose for existing, is being personally addressed by the Lord in words of challenge and of invitation. Each one individually has to decide how to respond; each one can hear the voice of the Lord and his knock on the door. To each one the Lord Jesus promises a life of future warmth and intimate fellowship with him. All he or she

---

[1] Revelation 3. 14-22

needs to do is listen, respond to the knocking, and make the decision to open the door.

This vivid image wonderfully encapsulates the essence of the evangelistic message. Yes, in context it is addressed to members of a moribund church (and how many Christian congregations today are all too similar in spirit to the Laodicean church); but I can see no reason why it is inappropriate to apply the same message even to people who are not and never have been members of any church. Surely the Lord makes the same promise, that *"I will come in and eat with him"*, to each one, whatever his personal history!

Another phrase that has become common to refer to conversion is "make a commitment". Perhaps this is used where the speaker feels reluctant to say "become a Christian", "get saved", or any of the other terms that are sometimes used. In contexts where the hearer is clear what you are talking about, it is a harmless phrase, but of course it is not only non-Biblical, it is totally unspecific. A commitment to what or whom? If it is made clear that it is commitment to Jesus Christ – not to "religion", or "the church", or even "Christianity" – then it may be acceptable; it is linked with the term "a committed Christian", to distinguish such a person from purely nominal Christians. But even then the phrase, "make a commitment", has one drawback, in that it places the emphasis on what the person concerned is doing, on his decision or determination to follow Christ. Such determination is wholly admirable, of course – but our eternal life, our spiritual life, depends not upon our determination but upon the Lord and the power of his Spirit within us. This was something I personally had to grasp when considering my response to the message; I felt it all depended on me, and I was so aware of past failures that I feared I could never "keep it up". I had to be assured that it was not a matter of what *I* would decide to do; it was an invitation for another power, the power and person of Jesus himself, to come into my life and change its direction from the inside. I think I really prefer "ask Jesus into your heart and life"!

The first recorded words of Jesus' ministry according to Matthew – or perhaps just Matthew's summary of his message – were *"Repent, for the Kingdom of heaven is near."*[1] Mark puts it a bit more fully: *"The time has come. The kingdom of God is near. Repent and believe the good news!"*[2] The word "repent" needs a bit of unpacking, because so often people understand it solely in terms of being sorry for what you have done wrong. But though that is included in the meaning it is a far richer word than that.

The Greek word for it (I'm sorry we keep going back to the Greek, but as the New Testament was written in Greek, it is a vital means of understanding the full meaning of words!) is "Metanoia" (μετανοια). The prefix "meta" usually has the connotation of "change" – as in metamorphosis, change of form or shape. The "noia" bit is derived from the word "nous" which means "mind". So "metanoia" means a change of mind.

This might seem a fairly trivial thing; "no, I won't have the soup; I've changed my mind and will have the avocado." A more significant change of mind might be if a man is on the road heading for his mistress's house; and then he feels really bad about this, and does a U-turn, and heads home to his wife. This certainly illustrates an aspect of "metanoia": it is a change of mind, which leads to a change of direction. But repentance in the New Testament sense is right at the far end of this scale: it involves a recognition that my entire life has been going in the wrong direction, and I must turn right around. Not just my behaviour and my actions – we all have things to repent of there; but my priorities, my values, my attitudes, my hopes and ambitions, my relationships, all must change. Most fundamentally of all, my attitude towards God and towards Jesus must change.

When a person has been living an obviously wicked life, of crime or gross immorality and depravity, it's obvious that a great deal has to change. But most of us are not like that, and may feel that we are really pretty decent, good-living people. Talk of "repentance" to us may seem a bit exaggerated and over the top. The odd minor correction, working a bit harder over our bad habits, cutting down on the drink or the bad language, perhaps – is anything more than that required? Yes, indeed. The basic question to ask is this: where has Jesus been in my life?

For many people the honest answer is, "Well, nowhere; he has hardly ever figured in my thoughts at all. I have totally ignored him. I don't know whether I believe he is God's son or not, but honestly I don't care much either. The Cross, the Resurrection stories – what are they to me?" *That* is what calls for a deep and radical repentance! If Jesus is the One of whom God himself said at his transfiguration, *"This is my Son, whom I love; listen to him!"*[1]; if Jesus is right in claiming to be the Resurrection and the Life, and the One who one day will judge the world – and that judgement will be on the basis of every person's relationship with, and attitude to, him: then to ignore him, and shut him out of our lives, and live as if he had never been born, and never called upon our allegiance, and never died on the cross, and never risen again, and never promised to return in glory one day, is to make one big mistake – a mistake which, if uncorrected, will have dire and eternal consequences. So if that has indeed been my attitude towards Jesus, *how* I need to repent of it! A total change of mind towards him is called for; a total change of the whole direction of my life is required. This may indeed also result in incidental changes like cutting down on the drink or the bad language, or

---

[1] Matthew 17.5

63

giving up robbing banks – but those are essentially minor consequences of the major reorientation of my whole life. It is above all towards Jesus that I must repent.

This is even so for those who are, as I was, quite religious and even regular churchgoers. Jesus *did* have a place in my life; but he was on the margins, the periphery. He was not at the centre where the major decisions of life were made. But that is where he wants to be – at the core, the heart, the central focus of every person's life, so that our attitude towards him and our relationship with him colours and directs every single other relationship and value we have. Repentance means recognising how wrongly centred our life has been, acknowledging it to ourselves and to God, and seeking his help in reorientating it.

There are other words and phrases which occur in the New Testament, to denote the act of responding to Jesus. *"Turn to the Lord"*[1] is one, which is very similar in thrust to "be converted" or "turned". Others found are *"became obedient to the faith"*[2], *"accepted the message"*[3], *"were added to their number"*[4], *"accepted the word of God"*[5], *"believed in the Lord"*[6], *"were brought to the Lord"*[7], or just *"believed"*[8], or in the challenge of Jesus, *"believe the Good News"*[9].

Most of these phrases are self-explanatory, and require no comment. Two of them, however, merit some further exploration.

"Were added to their number" is significant, with its clear implication that being converted, or turning to the Lord, or whichever other phrase is used to describe a personal response to

[1] Acts 9.35, 11.21
[2] Acts 6.7
[3] Acts 2.41
[4] Acts 2.41,47
[5] Acts 8.14
[6] Acts 9.42
[7] Acts 11.24
[8] Acts 13.12, 14.1, etc.
[9] Mark 1.15

Jesus, is not solely a private and individual matter – something of which our Western, individualised culture needs constantly to be reminded. When I am called by Jesus to respond to him, or to "open the door" to him, I am in fact being called to become a member of his community of followers – not to become a secret disciple on my own. It is expected that any new believer will join the fellowship of believers if this is possible.

If you read the early chapters of Acts, and examine what newly converted people actually did, in almost every case they joined the "church". I put the word "church" in quotes, because although the Greek word, "ecclesia" (εκκλησια), just means "assembly" (I will look at the implications and connotations of this word more fully later), to us "church" is packed with a heavy weight of less helpful connotations – ancient buildings, formal rituals, centuries of tradition, ecclesiastical hierarchy, and so on – none of which was conveyed to the 1st Century reader. What we find in Acts, in contrast to all that, is a close, loving fellowship, deeply committed to one another, meeting wherever they could find a place – whether in the courts of the temple in Jerusalem, in a lecture hall in Corinth, in the open air or in someone's home. They met for worship, prayer, and teaching by their leaders. A passage which makes this clear is Acts 2. 41-47 – the immediate aftermath of Peter's great Day of Pentecost sermon:-

"Those who accepted his message were baptised, and about three thousand were added to their number that day. They devoted themselves to the apostles' teaching and fellowship, the breaking of bread and prayer... All the believers were together and had everything in common... Every day they continued to meet together in the temple courts. They broke bread in their homes and at together with glad and sincere hearts, praising God and enjoying the favour of all the people. And the Lord added to their number daily those who were being saved."

This degree of sharing of possessions (sometimes misleadingly referred to as "communism", but unlike 20th century communism it was entirely spontaneous and voluntary) was an early explosion of enthusiasm in the brand new church, and did not last as the church spread and became more settled in later decades; but the principle that "Turn to Jesus" includes "join the disciples" was laid down then, and remained a basic assumption. The claim, which all modern clergy have met with wearisome regularity, that "you don't have to go to church to be a Christian", has no support in the New Testament. (Obviously there are exceptions where circumstances do not permit joining a fellowship; the Ethiopian who was baptised by Philip on his way home to Ethiopia[1] was going to a place where, at first at any rate, he would be the only Christian. We can however assume that as he shared his newfound faith, he would soon be joined by others.)

The other word that perhaps needs enlarging upon is "believe". This might be open to misunderstanding, and should be understood by looking at the phrase used by John and already mentioned: *"To all who received him, to those who believed in his name, he gave the right to become children of God."*[2] This is a key passage for explaining what "believed" means. "Believed in his name" is used in conjunction with "received him". It is so much more than believing in your head that something is true or finding an argument convincing, though these may be part of the process and are important. But what "believing" means in its full sense is having a personal encounter with Jesus, starting a relationship with Jesus, putting your trust in him. In particular it should be seen in connection with the crucifixion; "I believe" means "I believe that Jesus died for me." I will enlarge upon that idea in a later chapter.

---

[1] Acts 8. 26-39
[2] John 1.12.

5

❧

Living as a Christian

In the days following my conversion there were a number of changes in my lifestyle. I had always been a churchgoer, so that didn't change. But my newfound faith did start to bring about other changes.

First I joined the OICCU. I was slightly hesitant to do so at first, because I had read (I forget where) a description of the OICCU (pronounced "Oi-kew") as a "fundamentalist organization"; and I understood the word "fundamentalist" to mean someone who believed that every word in the Bible was literally true. That meant believing that the world was made in six literal days, and so on; and however grateful I felt to the OICCU for sponsoring the Mission which had brought John Stott to Oxford, I didn't feel I could identify with "fundamentalism" in that sense. But when I asked Bruce, the undergraduate who was now becoming something of a mentor to me, about this, he explained that though OICCU members did take the Bible extremely seriously, and regarded it as the inspired word of God, they fully recognised that it contained different kinds of literature – poetry, for example – not all of which was designed to be taken literally. I was still left with some questions, but put them aside for the moment, and signed up as a member.

The OICCU had college groups, and also university-wide meetings. Our college group consisted of about twenty members who met one evening a week for Bible study, and also had a regular prayer meeting. The Bible study was what I started attending first, and from the beginning I found it enjoyable, stimulating and thought provoking. Normally different students (in Oxford called undergraduates, not students) took it in turns to prepare and lead the meeting, but we all took part in discussing the passage under consideration. This was not just an intellectual argument, but very definitely a matter of trying to work out what the Bible was saying to us about God and what he wanted us to be and to do.

When I had been confirmed at school at the age of 15, Michael Tupper, the assistant chaplain who had led the classes, had tried to encourage us to start reading the Bible regularly; but my efforts in that direction didn't last longer than a few weeks. I only possessed an Authorised Version (an ancient copy which had belonged to my father), and I found it heavy going; and I do not recall that we were given any help in the way of study notes. So fairly rapidly personal Bible study had faded out of my life. But now after my conversion I felt I must take serious steps to revive the habit, and in this I was strongly encouraged by Bruce and my other new friends in OICCU.

Under their guidance three practical steps were taken. First I bought a new Bible in a modern translation, the Revised Standard Version or RSV, which was the one favoured by most OICCU members. Secondly I was taken to the little evangelical bookshop the other side of Magdalen Bridge (I think it was called the Gospel Book Depot) where I was encouraged to buy a booklet called *The Quiet Time*. I had found that a daily time of personal prayer and bible study was known, in the circles in which I was beginning to move, as a Quiet Time, sometimes shortened to QT (I am afraid that I started to learn and adopt quite a lot of rather esoteric jargon of this sort!). I bought this booklet and studied it, and found it a helpful introduction to the disciplines of personal prayer and bible study. And thirdly I was introduced to a set of study books, written specifically for Christian students, called *Search The Scriptures*. Each book provided a year's worth of prescribed readings, and the whole set of three took you through the entire Bible. They did not contain the actual Bible text (we were expected to use our own Bibles), but the chapter and verses to be read each day, with some brief notes, and several questions which the reader was meant to answer by studying the Bible text. In order to do this more seriously, I bought a notebook in which to write my answers –followed over the coming weeks and months by numerous further notebooks.

I was encouraged to decide upon the best time in the day for my Quiet Time, but it was generally recommended that first thing in the morning was the most satisfactory. After all, it was said, a musician doesn't tune up his instrument when the concert is over! So it's a good idea to start the day with God, before all the other concerns of the day come flooding in to distract you. I have kept up this custom to the present day, more than fifty years later (though I confess that there were a few years when my children were little that I allowed it to lapse); I still find that if I don't have my Quiet Time first thing in the morning, it is highly probable that I don't have it at all. I know that other people find other arrangements suit them better – a mum may have hers once the children have gone to school; an office worker in the City may slip into a church in his lunch hour. But for me, early morning is best.

Search The Scriptures, like any other system, has its faults – perhaps it tends a little too much towards an academic rather than a devotional study – but its use for all those first three years of my Christian life gave me an all-round familiarity with the Bible for which I am profoundly grateful. Having been a churchgoer all my life, as well as doing "Scripture", "Divinity" or "R.E." throughout my schooldays, I thought I knew the Bible fairly well; but I soon found that I was only familiar with a few isolated stories in the Old Testament or the Gospels, and one or two "purple passages" in the Epistles, like the Armour of God passage in Ephesians. The majority of this Book I discovered to be totally unfamiliar, and much of it I found, with the help and guidance of *Search The Scriptures*, absolutely fascinating. I sat down with my Bible, notebook and pen for about three quarters of an hour every morning, and religiously wrote down my answers to the questions posed by the book. Though I have never regularly used a pen and notebook since those years, I still believe that such a discipline is a very valuable way to focus one's mind to think seriously about what the passage is saying, and to seek ways to apply it to one's own life.

As well as my private Bible study and the college group studies, I was introduced to another new way to encounter the Bible. Very soon after my conversion Bruce suggested that he and I should get together a couple of times a week and study the Bible together. I was a little taken aback by this, but in my new attitude of being hungry to learn anything I could about God in any way that was suggested, I agreed, and thus we started our regular meetings in which we worked our way through St. Paul's Letter to the Philippians. This too I found to be a helpful and enlightening experience; though at first much of the input was from Bruce, he encouraged me to come up with my own ideas and interpretations of the text – even though occasionally he gently suggested that perhaps an alternative understanding might be preferable to my slightly eccentric contributions.

Another aspect of these one-to-one times was prayer. For the first two or three times we met, Bruce said a prayer at the beginning and the end. This was perhaps my first introduction to the unfamiliar custom of praying out loud in one's own words, rather than reading or reciting a set prayer from a book; but I quickly accepted it and got over any initial embarrassment. But then one day Bruce said:

"Why don't you say a prayer to start us off, Chris?"

I was appalled. "Me? I don't think I'd be any good at that!" I stammered.

"It's quite OK; just say anything you want," he responded; and bowing his head and closing his eyes, he waited for me to pray. I had no choice; we were either going to sit in total silence, or I had to say something! So I opened my mouth and stumbled through some kind of prayer, and Bruce said "Amen" fervently at the end. He made no comment, in criticism or praise, about my effort, but just started off our study for the day.

Thus I took my very first hesitant steps in extemporary prayer. In later years I have often had to remind myself of what an ordeal I found it that first time, when I have been trying to encourage some of my parishioners to pray aloud, and they have insisted that such a thing is totally beyond them. But there have been many times over the years when I have sat and listened to someone praying his or her first-ever prayer; and I have invariably found it a deeply moving experience. They may have been hesitant and inarticulate; they may not even have been quite "correct" theologically (I recall hearing a nine-year-old boy at a Beach Mission, after we had been reading part of the crucifixion story, saying a prayer for Pontius Pilate!) but it is still exciting to hear a new child of God, whether literally a child or an adult or even an elderly person, speaking to their Lord in their own, unrehearsed words. I have not infrequently been moved to tears.

It was soon after that that I started attending the College group's prayer meeting. For the first few times I sat in silence, apart from an "Amen" at the end of the prayers of the others; but one day, after several deep breaths, I dared to join in more vocally.

The central meetings of the OICCU, in the North Gate Hall, also consisted of Bible studies and prayer meetings. These Bible studies were not discussions but expositions by a series of visiting speakers, many of them well known and of high calibre. Usually as well as leading the Bible exposition on the Saturday night, these men (they were always men in those days) were preaching in at least one of the city's churches on the Sunday. If they were Anglicans, they would probably preach in St. Ebbe's, the church attended by most of the C. of E. OICCU members; but they may have been from any of a variety of other denominations, as the OICCU was an inter-denominational body. But whatever their allegiance, on the Sunday evening at 8 o'clock they would invariably be the speaker at the OICCU's own evangelistic service at the City Church in The High.

Perhaps I should just explain what these words, "evangelical" and "evangelistic" mean. They are not interchangeable, though I have often heard people use one when they mean the other! "Evangelical" is a description of a specific kind of Christian, or a particular theological approach to Christian faith. An evangelical is marked by two main characteristics: first a conviction that the Bible is the authoritative and inspired word of God which the individual Christian should study and seek to understand (though different evangelicals may take differing views on particular matters of interpretation)[1], and secondly an expectation that every person needs to be converted, to make a personal act of commitment to give his life to Jesus Christ. From these two foundational standpoints may come a variety of minor manifestations – a particular phraseology, a style of prayer or of worship, an approach to certain moral or social issues. But it is the

---

[1] While the wisdom or experience of clergy, theologians or other experienced readers can be valuable and should be taken seriously, it is still the responsibility of each Christian to study the Word of God for him- or herself, unmediated by priest or ecclesiastical tradition.

twin issues of reverence for the Bible and a personal experience of turning to Christ that define the evangelical.

"Evangelistic" describes the approach to uncommitted people to urge or encourage (or sometimes, I am afraid, bully!) them to turn to Christ in faith. This does not mean that no one would be moved to respond to God in some other kind of service, even if it was not specifically evangelistic; any faithful preaching of the word of God, on any topic, can become a specific word of challenge or invitation from God to a listener, and people may be converted by some quite unexpected event. One man at my theological college said he was converted at a performance of Handel's Messiah! But these Sunday night services in Oxford were all specifically evangelistic events, planned for that one purpose. The preachers, I am sure, were told firmly that that was their brief; they were not there to give teaching on prayer or meditation, or to expound an approach to moral or social issues, or to tell us about world mission. All those things were important, but Sunday night was to be evangelistic. OICCU members were all urged to invite their non-Christian friends to the service, and to pray that they might be converted. Almost invariably the service ended with some sort of appeal; not usually (perhaps not ever) an invitation to "come up to the front" before the whole congregation (that would have been too embarrassing, and word would soon have got about among undergraduates that these were occasions to be avoided at all costs), but usually a more gentle invitation to join secretly in a prayer of commitment led by the speaker, and then, if you have done so, to make yourself known to the preacher afterwards.

The OICCU lunchtime prayer meetings were primarily geared towards these services, as members prayed aloud for their friends whom they were trying to evangelise.

"Lord, we pray for a man from Trinity that I was speaking to yesterday, and who seemed interested; please let him come on Sunday night!"

"Lord, I ask you to touch a St. Hugh's girl who's got a lot of problems; she said she might come on Sunday – please let nothing stop her, and let her become a Christian!"

Week after week there was a steady stream of such prayers; and sometimes there would be thanks offered when prayers had been gloriously answered, and someone "had stayed behind" – which was almost another way of saying, "had become a Christian".

With my own experience of conversion, I needed no urging to seek to evangelise my friends. When I heard John Stott preaching at the Mission services, and then explaining at the after-meetings how to make a personal decision for Christ, I felt that I had never in my life had this explained to me before. Why had no one told me how to become a committed Christian? Later I realised that of course they had; I had just never taken it in. Indeed I came to understand that it is God, and only God, who opens a person's mind to understand the Gospel, and moves his heart to respond. I am sure that Michael Tupper had done his best to make the message clear; indeed when I met him again some years later and told him about my faith, he assured me that he had used verses like the one about "opening the door" during the confirmation classes. But at that point in my life I was not ready; putting it another way, it was not God's chosen time for me to hear and respond. Even on my first Sunday at Oxford I heard an evangelistic sermon at St. Aldate's from Dr. Cuthbert Bardsley, the Bishop of Coventry, and I learned later that another Forestry student whom I got to know well, and who later sought ordination, owed his faith to that sermon. But at the time it passed me by; I remember saying to someone afterwards that I felt that the Bishop was an eloquent speaker, but had said nothing of substance. Again – that wasn't God's moment for me.

But in my early days as a Christian, I naïvely assumed that if I could only explain the Gospel as it had now been explained to me, my hearers would instantly respond and turn to Christ, and I was quite taken aback and disappointed when it didn't work out that way. I fear I was a bit of a nuisance to some friends at the time, seizing every moment to buttonhole them and earnestly explain some aspect of the Gospel. An old friend from Shrewsbury came to visit me in Oxford for a weekend, and so I took him to church not once but twice. He was polite about it, but obviously felt no compulsion to give his life to Jesus. Perhaps it didn't help that his visit happened to coincide with some major building project that was being launched at St. Ebbe's, and poor Joe had to sit through *two* lengthy appeals to give generously.

Another aspect of my new faith was the growing conviction that God had a plan for my life, though I had as yet no idea what it might be. As I mentioned earlier, I had earlier had no conception of such a thing, and despite thinking of myself as a Christian and a believer in God, it had simply never occurred to me to consult God before making even major decisions that were likely to affect the whole direction of my life. It was John Stott, once again, who helped me to reorientate my thinking; his words of wisdom occurred during that conversation in his hotel room on the day of my conversion.

"What are you reading?" he asked me.

"Forestry," I replied.

"Well, God may well have a plan for you in that sphere, and may want you to serve him as a Christian forest officer somewhere in the world; but he might want you to be a missionary in South America! You never know what is going to happen once you put your life in God's hands. One thing you can be sure of, and that is that he *has* a plan for you, and the most important thing you can do is to seek his will for your life."

This thought had a profound influence upon me. I had been doing classics up until my 'A' and 'S' levels and my Oxford entrance exams, but I had never had any idea what sort of career I wanted. My decision to change to Forestry as a degree course had been influenced by nothing more significant than my enjoyment of the scenery and wildlife of Tanganyika. But now I started to ask another question: not, "What do I want to do with my life?" But, "What does God want me to do with my life?" – or indeed, "God, what do you want to do with my life?"

Because of John's words, I even began to consider being a missionary in South America! He had only mentioned that, I'm sure, as a "for instance", not because he felt that it was a word of guidance from God about my future; but it was the only guidance I had at that point, and so I took a small step in that direction. The OICCU had a number of overseas missionary interests, and regularly arranged visits of missionaries from various parts of the world. These usually addressed "Missionary Breakfast" meetings – which always caused mild amusement because they sounded like the sort of event that cannibal tribes might enjoy! But though we didn't consume the visiting missionaries, they spoke at the breakfast meetings about their sphere of service. The actual breakfast was usually arranged by the Missionary Prayer and Support group that covered that part of the world.

It must have been about that time that the visiting speaker at a Missionary Breakfast was from South America, representing a very small Missionary Society called the West Amazon Mission; so I joined the prayer group for that Mission and helped to plan and arrange the breakfast. (I seem to recall that, for a touch of local colour, we wrote the menu in Spanish – or was it Portuguese? - and called the fruit juice "Ipecacuanha".) For a year or two I attended the group that prayed for that Mission, and read their newsletter. But I never felt particularly moved or directed towards being a missionary in that or any other overseas society. However I still prayed on a regular basis that God would guide me to the right career or sphere of service. But it was another three years before his plan for me started to emerge.

I began to hear from other OICCU members about a variety of Christian activities in which they took part during vacations. As we were approaching the Easter vac, someone told me about VPS Camps. VPS stood for Varsity and Public School; the so-called camps were not in fact under canvas, but house parties that took place in boarding schools. They were for boys from Public Schools (I do not remember if there were any for girls, but if there were they did not concern me), and the "Varsity" bit referred to the fact that undergraduates from Oxford and Cambridge, men who were themselves from Public Schools, took part as "Senior Campers", who had no specific leadership role, but helped to run the games and activities and do various chores. The particular one to which I was invited was at a school called Clayesmore at Iwerne Minster in Dorset. It was generally just known as "Iwerne" (pronounced "Yew-ern").

It was when I was planning to go there as a Senior Camper that my mother first began to be aware that something odd and religious had happened to me, as I had to explain why I was going to be away from home during part of the Easter Vacation. "I want to go to this Christian camp," I started to say.

"Camping in April is likely to be a bit cold, isn't it?" objected my mother.

I explained about the accommodation. But it was when I tried to explain the "Christian" bit that I saw a guarded look come over her face. I could read her mind: "Oh, help – what's he got into now? Has he got caught up in the Oxford Group[1] or some other strange movement?" she was obviously thinking.

The very word "Christian" was a problem that caused misunderstanding and even resentment then and in a number of subsequent conversations with my mother.

---

[1] Founded in 1921 by Frank Buchman; later called Moral Re-Armament or MRA

"When you speak about 'Christians' in the way you do, of your friends at Oxford, you seem to be calling into question *my* faith. Don't you regard me as a Christian?"

That was a difficult one; I loved and respected my mother, and she had always brought me up to say my prayers and go to church. She was herself a regular worshipper, and "church" was part of her life. But so it had been of mine up to the time of my conversion; and that experience, and the wholly new way in which I was now working out my relationship with Jesus Christ, made me feel that before my conversion I had *not* been a Christian (despite my initial doubts about the title of John Stott's booklet, *Becoming a Christian)* – not in the true sense. But I did not at all want to hurt or insult my mother by saying bluntly, "No, you are not a Christian." Because I have found the word "Christian" causes so much misunderstanding, I have devoted a later chapter to it.

The OICCU and other Christians

The OICCU, in common with similar student Christian Unions affiliated to the Inter-Varsity Fellowship (or IVF) in other universities, tended to be very dismissive of student religious societies of different Christian traditions. In those days the main options, for students who did not feel at ease with the strongly conservative evangelical ethos of the OICCU but who wanted to join some Christian fellowship, were the Student Christian Movement (SCM), the denominational societies, and the college chaplains' groups. The emphasis of the SCM tended much more towards the social implications of religious faith, less towards nurturing personal faith, and scarcely at all towards evangelism. As a result these two bodies tended to regard each other with deep suspicion. I remember one, and only one, joint meeting during my time at Oxford, and that was a debate on the issue of Fundamentalism. The speaker in the OICCU corner was Dr. James Packer, who had written the newly-published paperback,

Fundamentalism and the Word of God; I am afraid I cannot remember the name of the SCM's speaker, which perhaps indicates that I was not very interested in him or his arguments, but only in whether "our" man would win. It was an interesting debate, but as an exercise in reconciliation or fellowship across the traditions it was a non-starter.

It illustrates the narrow and intolerant attitude of that particular manifestation of evangelicalism at the time. There was a strong feeling in OICCU that we were the only sound and faithful Christians; the rest were either woolly-minded compromisers or probably not Christians at all. And as for Roman Catholics, they were virtually regarded as the enemy, and there were books on the OICCU bookstall pointing out the many serious errors of Roman Catholic theology. During my time at Oxford a Mission was arranged (by the chaplains, I think) at which the speaker was Michael Ramsay, the Archbishop of Canterbury. In common with most OICCU members, I did not go to any of the meetings because of our suspicion that he was not "sound" on the Gospel. One member of our college group did attend, and came back full of admiration for the Archbishop's intellect and godliness; but I fear that only made us start to regard the OICCU member with loving concern that he was going off the rails.

Another negative aspect of OICCU's ethos in those days was its strictness regarding such things as alcohol, dancing, films and the theatre. These were all regarded as "worldly" and thus a threat to the morals of a godly Christian. There was a much-recommended book on the OICCU bookstall called *The Problem of Worldliness*, which I recall as having about a dozen chapters, each dealing with some aspect of social life which was "worldly" and therefore to be avoided. In this attitude the OICCU was conforming to the ethos which was standard in all strongly evangelical churches in Britain.

Curiously evangelicals in other countries had different standards of what was or was not acceptable. When the famous American evangelist, Billy Graham, started coming to lead evangelistic missions in Britain, a frisson of horror ran through many evangelical churches when it was noticed that his wife wore make-up. This was regarded as an unmistakeable sign of worldliness, and even perhaps of loose morals; yet the faithfulness of Billy Graham and his team, and God's blessing on their preaching of the Gospel, were undeniable. I also heard of a conference held jointly between British and Dutch evangelical students; the British were horrified that most of the Dutch people smoked heavily, while the Dutch strongly disapproved of the British habit of playing, even at a religious conference, frivolous ball games like "crocker"[1]!

For a few years I largely went along with avoiding activities that were frowned on by OICCU; though I never became a teetotaller, I generally avoided alcohol during my student years, and I have never smoked. What I now regret more than that was my missing out on the wealth of cultural activities at Oxford like films and plays. In the years since those days evangelical attitudes have relaxed enormously, and few churches still proscribe all those activities previously dubbed "worldly". Smoking is perhaps the only one where disapproval is as strong as ever, and a clergyman seen smoking will almost certainly be of a "catholic" tradition.

But though I am now, and have been for many years, a modest consumer of alcohol (mostly wine, rather than beer or spirits, purely for reasons of personal preference), I still dislike drunkenness, and deplore the growing habit particularly among young people of drinking heavily at all social occasions,

---

[1] A variety of rounders, but played with a football; it was popular at many Christian holiday events for young people.

apparently convinced that you cannot have a good time unless you get totally smashed. I have always found drunken behaviour unattractive and very seldom amusing; that strand of humour which portrays inebriation as inherently comic simply does not usually make me laugh. This, you may say, is my problem; and I would not deny it. It is also the case that getting drunk has never been a temptation to me – as soon as I begin to feel the slightest bit unsteady, I just don't want to have any more. I know some people feel that because I have never in my life been seriously drunk, or anything more than slightly tiddly, that I have somehow missed out on an essential experience. But I shun the idea of being out of control of myself, and I believe that so many terrible social evils are attributable to an excess of alcoholic consumption, from minor irritations like noisy disturbances to much more serious tragedies like fatal road accidents, not to mention a great deal of crime and domestic violence, that I am convinced that the current trend towards casual, heavy over-indulgence is one to be reversed as soon as possible.

However despite the narrowness of OICCU's brand of Christianity, both in social matters and in its intolerance of other Christians, I will always be grateful for the solid foundation of sound, Biblical teaching I received in those years.

But it was a year or two later that I came under the influence of another strand of Christianity which was eventually to become a central feature of my faith. A fresher arrived one September and joined the college OICCU group. He was friendly and out-going, and soon became a regular contributor to various aspects of OICCU life. I realised he was not an Anglican, but people's denominational labels were of little relevance to us in College, and it was a few weeks before it emerged that he was a member of the Assemblies of God, a Pentecostal denomination.

I was aware that there was an Elim Pentecostal church in Oxford; we had passed it on the bus, on the Hinksey road beyond

Oxford Station. I remember asking a friend at the time when we saw the sign outside:

"What *is* a Pentecostal Church?"

He responded, "Oh, I think they do things like speaking in tongues."

As far as I was concerned he might as well have said they were a sect of snake-handlers; although I was of course aware of the story in the Book of Acts[1] of the Holy Spirit coming upon the disciples on the Day of Pentecost, which led them to "speak in tongues", doing such things in modern times seemed weird and alien, and I thought no more about it. But when this new undergraduate, David, said that *he* was a Pentecostal – though the Assemblies of God were a different branch of the movement from the Elim Church – I was intrigued.

"Is it true," I enquired, "that at the Pentecostal Church people speak in tongues?"

"Yes, that's right," he answered casually.

"Have you ever actually heard it?" I asked with great interest.

"Yes, of course," he replied; "I speak in tongues myself!"

That was quite a conversation-stopper; my jaw dropped, and I didn't know what to say. But David was not in the least abashed or embarrassed, and he went on to tell us not only about speaking in tongues, but, more importantly, about the Pentecostal doctrine of the Baptism in the Holy Spirit.

They believed, he explained, that not only must we be converted; we need also to be baptised in, or by, the Holy Spirit. Without this, we are halfway Christians, believing in Jesus, saved, born again – but without the power of the Holy Spirit to help us to live for him, or to exercise spiritual gifts. But when a believer seeks to receive the Baptism of the Spirit, very often by someone such as a church pastor praying for him and laying hands on him, the

---

[1] Acts 2

Holy Spirit comes down upon him in a powerful and overwhelming spiritual experience, and the initial evidence that this has happened is that he starts to "speak in tongues" – to pray out loud and praise God in an unintelligible language which neither the hearers nor the speaker can understand. It is a praise-language given by God.

Furthermore, when once he has entered into this new dimension of the spiritual life, David went on, all sorts of other spiritual gifts may start to be manifested – gifts like prophecy (spontaneous utterances in one's own language, which are heard as direct messages from God), or healing. Paul gives a list of such spiritual gifts in his first letter to the Corinthians.[1]

I was very intrigued with this conversation, as it seemed to indicate an area of spiritual life of which I had never heard. In addition, I was going through a time in my own faith of feeling dissatisfied and "dry"; the joy and excitement that I had known in the early days after I had been converted seemed to have faded away. Was this the answer? Was it that I needed to be baptised in the Spirit? Was I trying to live the Christian life entirely in my own strength, and not experiencing the power that Jesus had promised and that God wanted to pour into me?

"Look," said David, "Why don't you come along to the Pentecostal Church with me? If you don't want to come on Sunday, come to the Prayer Meeting on Tuesday night?"

This was agreed, and the following Tuesday, in a spirit of some apprehension but also of hesitant anticipation, I turned up at the Elim Church prayer meeting with David.

The little church hall was nearly full, and it immediately struck me that the worshippers were mostly of a different social class from those I usually met in the Church of England, being obviously less well educated. This, to me, was a positive indication

---

[1] I Corinthians 12.7-11

83

of Christian validity – it had always troubled me that the Church as I knew it was almost wholly middle-class and people of a more working class background would simply not feel at ease there. This seemed to be in contrast to Jesus himself, of whom it was said, *"The common people heard him gladly."*[1] These "common people" in the Pentecostal group greeted me with great warmth and friendliness. But it was when the prayer meeting began that I was shaken. I was used to the OICCU prayer meetings; one person would pray aloud, and everyone would listen, and say "Amen" at the end. Often there were long pauses between the prayers. But this was very different!

First, whoever was praying aloud was doing so with enormous fervour, often rising to a loud shout. Meanwhile everyone else was "praying along" with them, with a murmur of, "Yes, Lord!" "Alleluia!" "Ay-men!" "Oh, Lord! Oh, Lord!" " Jesus! *Jeee*sus!" And this murmur also often would rise to such a climax of cries, especially if the person praying mentioned Jesus dying on the cross, that the pray-er could hardly be heard over the hubbub.

And then from the back of the hall came a voice, talking incomprehensibly. This voice was not, like the prayers, noisy and excitable, but quiet, almost prosaic. As soon as this started, everyone became quiet, and the murmur subsided to a hushed silence, broken occasionally by soft mutters of "Oh, thank you, Jesus!"

The speaker in the unknown language came to a stop, and there were a few moments of quiet. It was as if everyone was waiting for something. Then another person spoke out, this time in English; she spoke as if it was God himself speaking to us, and addressing us, his children, in words of love and encouragement. "Behold, my children, I have heard your prayers, and they bring joy to my heart; trust me, my children, I have a great and mighty

---

[1] Mark 12.37, AV

plan and purpose for you! You will witness me pouring out my Spirit upon this place in power...." I am not sure that these were the words spoken, but I am attempting to give something of the flavour of them.

Afterwards David explained to me that this was the "Gift of Interpretation", one of the nine Gifts of the Spirit listed by Paul[1]. A person with this spiritual gift is needed, so that the message spoken by someone else "in tongues" can be understood by the congregation and be a blessing to them.

I left the meeting that night somewhat bemused and shaken. I remember saying to David, "Well, I think I want the Baptism in the Holy Spirit – but I don't think I want Pentecostal prayer meetings!" But that was not in fact the last time I went. I found after that that the OICCU prayer meetings seemed very dull in comparison. Earnest, sincere, yes; but lacking in life and energy! So I took to going to the meeting every Tuesday night, even though I was still worshipping at St. Ebbe's on Sunday mornings. I became accustomed to the exuberant Pentecostal style; and I even occasionally joined in and said a prayer myself (David told me that on those occasions I prayed quite differently from the way I did in OICCU meetings!).

I was still confused about the basic doctrine of "the Baptism of the Spirit", because it was something that had never been mentioned in any Christian circles with which I had associated before meeting David and his Pentecostal friends. Was it possible that something which was – according to the Pentecostals – so vital, had been totally ignored or even denied by all other Bible-believing Christians?

I made an appointment to go and see the Rector of St. Ebbe's, Basil Gough. Basil was a somewhat austere man, but his church was recognised as wholly "sound" and conservative evangelical,

---

[1] I Corinthians 12.10

so I felt that I could trust him to give me wise advice. I started by saying to him, "I have started to wonder about Pentecostalism and its doctrines, because I find their arguments very convincing." Basil listened gravely, and then reached behind him into his bookcase, and drew out a book called HERESIES ANCIENT AND MODERN.

He did not actually find Pentecostalism listed there; but it is significant that that was his initial and immediate reaction – in the light of the growth of the Charismatic renewal that spread through all denominations a few years later, perhaps an astonishing one. But he was not alone among traditional evangelicals in having such a negative attitude towards Pentecostal teaching; I was to meet it many times in the years to come. He spoke to me earnestly about the danger of any version of the Gospel which sought to add to Jesus, and to imply that Jesus alone was not enough. "Beware of 'Christianity plus'!" he warned seriously.

I was a little disconcerted but by no means discouraged. When I discussed Basil's words with David, he was quite cross. "It's not 'Christianity plus'", he insisted. "Of course Jesus is wholly sufficient for salvation – but it was Jesus who promised the Baptism of the Spirit! To ignore or neglect that is 'Christianity minus'!"

So from then on I started very definitely to "seek the Baptism". When I first announced this to the Pentecostal prayer meeting (they always had a time when people were invited to ask for prayer or share any blessings they felt they had received), the pastor and all the people almost cheered. I was invited to come to the front then and there, and the pastor laid his hands on my head and prayed fervently for me; but nothing happened. Once or twice in the following weeks David prayed for me in private; I had confessed to him that I felt that perhaps the blockage was my fear of making a fool of myself, and babbling gibberish as I attempted to speak in tongues, and he felt that ministry in private, with no onlookers to mock or criticise, might help. But again there was no discernible result.

In later years when my thoughts on the matter had matured and modified I often prayed for other people to be filled with the Spirit, and I would be far more ready to accept that the Spirit can move in many different ways; Bible writers use images like dew, as well as wind and fire, to describe the work of the Spirit, which indicates that quiet, almost indiscernible results as well as dramatic ones may follow. But at the time of which I speak I accepted the Pentecostal doctrine that *the* sign of the Baptism is speaking in tongues; if that hasn't happened, you haven't been baptised in the Spirit. Another facet of their teaching was that a time of "tarrying" is often required. This was based on the command of Jesus to the disciples in Luke 24.49 (in the Authorised Version), after promising them that the Spirit would descend upon them in a few days: *"Tarry ye in the city of Jerusalem until ye be endued with power from on high."*

So I tarried, and went on praying for some weeks, awaiting the moment when the Spirit would descend upon me.

One evening I was alone in my digs, reading the biography of the great pioneer missionary to China, Hudson Taylor. It quoted a letter that Taylor had written home when facing a particular problem of danger or opposition: "I need courage, as well as faith!" he wrote.

"Yes, Lord!" I exclaimed aloud, in the quiet of my room. "That's what I need too!" And then an astonishing thing happened: as I spoke aloud to God, suddenly I found that my words of prayer were no longer in English, but in some incomprehensible language. They came pouring out from somewhere deep within me. (Later, when describing the experience to David, I said it was rather like being sick – except it was joyful rather than unpleasant! He roared with laughter, and

87

reminded me of what Jesus had said, *"out of his belly shall flow rivers of living water"*[1].)

I was not in any way in a trance or out of control; I could stop, and think about it, and then open my mouth and continue. I had no idea what I was saying; but it felt like a joyful and enthusiastic prayer of praise. Later I read what St. Paul had written about this: *"If I pray in a tongue, my spirit prays, but my mind is unfruitful,"*[2] which very much matched my experience.

Furthermore I felt that what I had received was not just an enjoyable gift of speaking rubbish – so often people were to say in the days ahead, "But what's the point of it?" and I can sympathise with the question. But I sensed that I had "moved up a notch" in my general spiritual life. The feelings of joy and excitement which I had known in the early days after my conversion, but which had latterly faded, had returned – in spades, to use a perhaps unspiritual phrase! Reading the Bible, praying, worshipping, all seemed to be better, more real, and more alive. Jesus was somehow closer to me than before; some form of barrier within me which had seemed to keep him at a distance had melted away.

But curiously, in the days ahead, very soon after I had "received the Baptism", I started to withdraw from the Pentecostal church, and from the small group of Pentecostal students who met for mutual encouragement. The reason for this withdrawal was theological; although I had no doubt whatever that what had happened to me was from God, I became more and more uneasy about the theological explanation for it that the Pentecostals gave. In particular I was unhappy about the whole "two-phase conversion" idea; first you are converted, and then, later, you receive the Holy Spirit.

---

[1] John 7.38 AV
[2] I Corinthians 14.14

I simply could not see in Scripture any support for the idea that you could be a Christian without the Holy Spirit. Yes, of course for Jesus' disciples this had been their experience; they became followers of Jesus, and then on the Day of Pentecost they were filled with the Spirit. But I did not, and do not, believe that this was to be the universal pattern after Pentecost. I found nothing in the writings of Paul that even hinted at such a thing. Indeed, Paul wrote, *"If anyone does not have the Spirit of Christ, he does not belong to Christ."*[1]

Conversion itself is the work of the Spirit; when you "receive Jesus", you receive the Spirit. Yes, of course there may be subsequent, further experiences of the Spirit, further and greater "fillings" with the Spirit; when Paul wrote to the Ephesian Church, *"Be filled with the Spirit"*[2] he was obviously aware that a Christian community might be not particularly Spirit-filled, and he was saying (the present tense and plural voice in the Greek indicate this), "Go on being, increasingly, a Spirit-filled community." But that is a very different thing from saying, as the Pentecostals did in those days, that there were two different kinds of Christians – those with and those without the Holy Spirit. This, perhaps, was what especially lay behind the hostility of people like Basil Gough – as well as the very British suspicion of any excessive religious enthusiasm and emotion!

So at that time, and for some years afterwards, I was left in a kind of limbo, with no one to go to for support in this particular area of my Christian faith and experience; I could seek the help neither of the Pentecostals (as I was rejecting an important facet of their doctrine) nor of the non-Pentecostal evangelicals like Basil Gough (as I feared they would have been suspicious of my spirit-baptism experience). I still, in my private prayers, spoke in

---

[1] Romans 8.9
[2] Ephesians 5.18

tongues quite often; I still felt that this practice brought life and immediacy to my prayers. But I had no theology to explain what had happened to me, nor did I know where to find one. It was not until the Charismatic movement started to become apparent in the mainline churches, some seven or eight years later, that I started to resolve these uncertainties, as I describe in a later chapter.

One feature of the OICCU, and therefore of my growing Christian discipleship, was the bookstall. Every Saturday night when some three hundred people gathered in the Northgate Hall for the weekly Bible exposition by the speaker of the week, we usually started by going downstairs to the lower hall where there was a substantial bookstall, with a large selection of Christian books. Oxford did (and still does, I think) have a branch of the Christian bookshop, Mowbrays; but Mowbrays caters for the whole spectrum of Christian traditions, with a particular slant towards the Anglo-Catholic. So it was not much patronised by OICCU members. Instead we found all our literary needs catered for by OICCU's own bookstall, and we could be sure that any book displayed there would be "sound".

OICCU, together with sister bodies like CICCU (at Cambridge) and LIFCU (the Liverpool Inter-Faculty Christian Union), was affiliated to the IVF – the Inter-Varsity Fellowship. An offshoot of this was the IVP, the Inter-Varsity Press, which started to produce a whole series of paperback books to give sound Christian teaching to students. John Stott's first book, *Basic Christianity*, was published by IVP, and was regarded by OICCU members as second only to the Bible in giving a solid, carefully-worked-out introduction to the Christian faith; it was, I think, a distillation of the sermons from a series of University missions, such as the one at which I was converted. Another IVP paperback was *Fundamentalism and the Word of God* by J. I. Packer; it had been written as a response to a book by G. Hebert, *Fundamentalism and the Church of God*, which was an attack on the growing phenomenon of evangelicalism. So Packer's book was a splendid armoury for evangelical students, in their polemical arguments with more liberal Christians who did not properly reverence the inspiration of the Bible. (I guess that few of those who read Packer's book ever read Hebert's, to examine arguments on the other side! I hasten to say that I did.)

In my early days as a Christian, I was hungry for teaching wherever I could find it, and I started to build up a collection of such books, buying a new one nearly every week. Some of these were still on my shelves over forty years later, and were only disposed of when, upon retirement, I had to sell or give away hundreds of books for reasons of space when moving into a smaller house. As well as the anti-liberal ("liberal" was a very bad thing to be, for evangelicals!) books like Packer's *Fundamentalism*, I bought books to arm me against Roman Catholics, one of which was Salmon's *The Infallibility of the Church* – described as "massive in learning, devastating in logic".

But I also started a growing collection of second-hand books; one of the first was given to me by David Fletcher, a theological student at Wycliffe Hall who was a Iwerne man, and who took me under his wing to encourage my growth in faith. The book he gave me was *Quiet Talks on Power*, by S. D. Gordon, a somewhat syrupy devotional book by an American author, which nevertheless I found helpful; later I acquired some of Gordon's other *Quiet Talks* books – on prayer, on the Tempter, and others.

As well as books for my own use, another use of Christian books was to lend to non-Christians to evangelise them; I expect a lot of undergraduates had worthy books earnestly pressed upon them by keen men, and then shoved them on to a shelf to be forgotten. But this was no escape, because next time we saw the victim, we would ask him how he was enjoying that book. However, though I gently mock our evangelistic zeal in those days, because it was too often somewhat brash and lacking in sensitivity, nevertheless a steady trickle of undergraduates were converted, whether through personal chats late into the night, or books, or missions, or the regular weekly evangelistic services. I wish that more Christians in our churches today had half the zeal to share the Gospel that we had in those days!

6

What is a Christian?

T he word "Christian" is used in common parlance in a wide variety of senses. Nowadays in the 21st Century, when the great majority of people in Britain make no claims to practising Christian faith, it has become quite common in secular circles to refer to "Christians" as an identifiable minority group. But in the '50s, it was charitably assumed that virtually everyone was a Christian, unless they were very specifically members of some other religious or anti-religious group. I heard of one earnest evangelical who wrote to her MP who was a member of the Cabinet, and asked, "Can you please tell me how many members of the Cabinet are Christians?" She received a somewhat dusty reply: "As far as I know we're all Christians!"

To say of someone "he is not a Christian", would have been regarded as an insult, calling into question his morals and integrity. I well remember my aunt's indignation on one occasion, when she served on the Parochial Church Council of her parish church. Another P.C.C. member, a lady who was perhaps of an evangelical persuasion, had said during a discussion, "My husband is not a Christian."

My aunt was outraged.

"What an appalling thing for a woman to say about her husband, and in public!" she fulminated when recounting the incident later. I suggested mildly that perhaps the husband made no claim to be a Christian. But that was no excuse, in Auntie May's eyes. To say that someone was not a Christian was a shocking accusation, a serious criticism, not merely a factual description of a lack of faith in Christ.

An extension of this understanding of the word was its use as a term of praise, usually about someone's kindness and helpfulness. "You're a real Christian!" "That's what I call a Christian act." This use of the word, usually by people who are not religious or what one might call "practising Christians", has nothing to do with faith in God or in Jesus. The question of whether the person thus described has any faith or connection with the church probably does not enter the speaker's mind.

Similar is the oft-repeated assertion, "You don't have to go to church to be a Christian." Belief in God might be a part of "being a Christian" in this sense, but what really matters is whether you live a good life. (What "a good life" consists of, to those who speak in this way, may again have little to do with the commands of Jesus as seen in the Gospels, or with what Paul writes about how a believer should live; if pressed, the speaker would probably mention avoiding the more serious crimes, and being nice to people.)

Another way of using the word is in contrast to other world faiths. During all the conflict in Lebanon the news media were constantly referring to "Christians" or "Christian villages", as opposed to Muslims. I have no doubt that some of the people thus designated who were caught up in the violence and mayhem of that period were men and women with a genuine faith in Christ; but it was not their living faith that the journalists were referring to, but the traditions of the communities to which they belonged. Many of them would probably be no more "Christian" than the average Briton who, even if he has been baptized, may not have entered a church or said a prayer since, but who is still likely to write "C of E" in answer to a question on a form which asks for "religion".

Because of this multiplicity of understandings of the term, I generally try to avoid the word altogether, unless I know I am speaking to people who will understand it in the same way as me. Otherwise it is a recipe for confusion and misunderstanding.

As always, I prefer to take my definitions from the Bible. The word "Christianity" is not found in the Bible. Again I usually avoid the word. I have heard preachers and others use the phrase "turning to Christianity" to mean conversion. I am not at all happy about that form of words. "Christianity" is a package word, denoting not only personal faith in Christ, but the whole traditional, cultural, political, artistic, architectural, musical, liturgical and ecclesiastical baggage associated with or derived from such faith. Some of this baggage is powerfully redolent of and suffused with Christian faith; other aspects of it have, for the uninstructed observer at least, only the slightest relevance to a personal faith in Jesus. So to "turn to Christianity" might imply little more than starting to take an interest in church history, or the oratorios of Bach, or the beauties of mediaeval church architecture.

The word "Christian" *is* found in the New Testament, but only three times. There are other words far more commonly used there to describe the people whom we might call Christians, such as believers, brethren, saints, disciples, or followers of the Way. The first use of the word "Christian" is in the description of the growth of a community of believers, Gentiles as well as Jews, in the city of Antioch in Syria. *"The disciples were first called Christians in Antioch."*[1]

---

[1] Acts 11.26

The implication was that this newly coined word was applied to the believers by outsiders, even by hostile outsiders. It was a term of abuse or mockery; to get the flavour of it you should think of modern phrases of ridicule like "Jesus freaks" or "God squad". These people were called Christ-ites – in the much same way in which the followers of the twentieth-century Korean self-proclaimed messianic leader, Sun Myung Moon, have been commonly called Moonies.

It is instructive to study the passage in which the word first occurs, to see who it was that the term was applied to, and why. Consider first why that particular word was coined: it can only be because the name "Christ" was so constantly on their lips. I wonder whether, if the word had not been invented then, it would be thought up today to describe modern churchgoers? How often is the name of Christ upon *our* lips – apart from when we are taking part in a service in church, when the unbelievers are unlikely to hear us? In the contexts in which today's believers in Jesus mostly encounter the secular world – at work or in our social life – it is hardly true that the name of Christ is so constant a topic of conversation that those who resent what we stand for would start to abuse us as "Christ-people"! But those followers of Jesus in Antioch around the year 50 AD were so thrilled with their Lord that they could not stop talking about him, and thus acquired a mocking nickname which they were proud to bear.

To see who they were and what they were like, look at the passage that describes them:

"Now those who had been scattered by the persecution in connection with Stephen travelled as far as Phoenicia, Cyprus and Antioch, telling the message only to Jews. Some of them however, men from Cyprus and Cyrene, went to Antioch and began to speak to Greeks also, telling them the good news about the Lord Jesus. The Lord's hand was with them, and a great number of people believed and turned to the Lord.

News of this reached the ears of the church at Jerusalem, and they sent Barnabas to Antioch. When he arrived and saw the evidence of the grace of God, he was glad and encouraged them all to remain true to the Lord with all their hearts. He was a good man, full of the Holy Spirit and faith, and a great number of people were brought to the Lord.

*Then Barnabas went to Tarsus to look for Paul, and when he found him he brought him to Antioch. So for a whole year Barnabas and Saul met with the church and taught great numbers of people. **The disciples were called Christians first at Antioch.**"[1]*

Let's unwrap it, and see who it was that were given this name!

1.　　They were *"disciples"*: the word means pupils, or learners. It was the common term not only for pupils in a school, but also for followers of a particular rabbi or religious leader: those who sat at his feet, hung on his words, and sought to follow his teachings. (It is also linked with the word "discipline" – implying that being a disciple is something you have to work hard at!)

2.　　They *"believed and turned to the Lord"*. They had been converted (a word which means "turned"), and had come to a personal faith. And this faith was focussed on *"the Lord"* – a term which in the New Testament almost invariably means Jesus.

3.　　Their new faith and lifestyle showed *"evidence of the grace of God"*. It was not just a matter of enthusiastic words. Words are cheap. But in these people's lives there were visible signs of change of character – *"evidence"* that God was at work in them. (It is also likely that the evidence Luke mentions included a miraculous element such as healing and other spiritual gifts.)

---

[1] Acts 11. 19-26

4.　　This church was experiencing spectacular growth: "*A great number of people were brought to the Lord*". This indicates that the believers were exuberantly sharing their faith and witnessing to Christ in their local community so effectively that huge numbers were converted.

5.　　The leaders "*met with the church and taught great numbers of people*". The word "church" ("Ecclesia", εκκλησια) simply means "assembly" or "gathering" – it has none of the overtones of ecclesiastical formality, robed clergy, or ancient buildings. (For those 1ˢᵗ Century believers, the first readers of Luke's account, who were familiar with the Greek version of the Old Testament, known as the Septuagint, the word "ecclesia" was used to describe the people of Israel on their wanderings through the desert on their way from Egypt to the promised land, the "congregation" or "assembly" of the people of Israel; so it had overtones of "the people of God on the move", unlike the word "church" which now has to our ears associations of solid, ancient and immoveable stone buildings, old-fashioned traditions, and an established hierarchy of clergy.) So individual believers did not "go to church"; they *were* the church, who met together regularly and expected to be taught.

6.　　There is one more significant use of the word "Christian", and that is in the first Letter of Peter, where he is writing about the common experience of persecution that many believers had:

"If you are insulted because of the name of Christ, you are blessed, for the Spirit of glory and of God rests on you. If you suffer, it should not be as a murderer or thief or any other kind of criminal, or even as a meddler. However if you

98

suffer as a Christian, do not be ashamed, but praise God that you bear that name."[1]

So we can add to the definition: a Christian was someone who had to be prepared to suffer for being one!

How relevant is this multi-faceted definition of "Christian" according to the New Testament, to our use of the word today? Linguistically there is no doubt that many words change their meaning over the years and centuries, and he would be a foolish man who insisted that everyone should use a word like "nice", for instance, only with the meaning that it had in the 19th or 17th centuries. Some words come to mean precisely the opposite of the older meaning – think of "wicked"!

So I cannot stop people using "Christian" to refer to a culture, or to virtuous behaviour. But I can and do maintain that those who apply the Biblical meaning to themselves, have a right to do so – denoting a person who has turned to the Lord Jesus Christ in faith, is seeking to be a disciple and to live out his faith in his personal values and behaviour, is regularly meeting with an assembly of fellow-Christians to worship and learn, and recognises that he may be called upon to suffer for his faith, whether merely ridicule or physical violence. He has a right to value that title with all those implications, especially because the word Christian is based upon the name of the Lord whom we love and reverence. Inevitably this will sometimes lead to hurt feelings, as it did between my mother and me, and I regret this; I never told her that I didn't think she was a Christian, but my very assertion that I had "become a Christian" was perceived to carry that implication.

I have known occasions when this issue has resulted in someone facing the question of whether in fact he or she is a Christian at all, as they have always assumed. When they have encountered a person for whom the word points to a reality of

---

[1] I Peter 4. 14-16

experience and a depth of commitment which is quite unfamiliar, they start to ask themselves, "Why, if I am a Christian, is my experience so different? Am I missing something? If so, how can I find it?"

Discussions about terms like "being born again" can also have this salutary effect, as well as sometimes merely causing irritation and resentment. There is of course the danger that so-called "born again" Christians can indeed assume that those who experience or express their faith in ways different from theirs have no real faith at all, and can deny the name of Christian to all traditions but their own. I have encountered this attitude on a number of occasions (and have even been guilty of it myself), and I deplore it. I have often been taken by surprise by evidence of a very real trust in Jesus and commitment to him, in people whom I might have been tempted to write off as merely "churchgoers" or nominal Christians, and I have felt rebuked for my surprise. So I have learned to be cautious about despising other expressions of discipleship.

Nevertheless I am convinced that in most, if not all, church congregations there are many people who are still in the spiritual state in which I was to be found before the Gospel as proclaimed by John Stott that evening in 1957 reached out and grabbed me. I have heard it suggested that we should always charitably assume that everyone in church is a Christian; but I am convinced, as a preacher and teacher, that it is no kindness to them to hold back from proclaiming and explaining, as boldly, clearly and lovingly as lies within us, what is meant by the invitation of Jesus to "Follow me!" or to "Repent and believe the Gospel!"

I sometimes encounter clergy whose life and ministry raise serious questions in my mind about whether they know Jesus for themselves at all or whether the whole concept of a personal relationship with him is a closed book to them. I rather suspect that in their understanding, Christian faith consists simply in ecclesiastical and liturgical traditions of church worship and the obligation to lead a good life and help to make a caring local community. I do not feel I must repent of such an uncharitable attitude. I recall that John Wesley had been an ordained minister, and even a missionary in America, for some years, before he had the experience of feeling his heart "strangely warmed" as he heard an exposition of the Epistle to the Romans; he was then converted, and he is far from being the only Christian minister who has had a similar experience. I will not go around saying "Oh, that vicar is not a Christian at all;" even less will I accuse him to his face, "You are not a Christian." No; I will pray for him that God will reveal to him more of the reality of Jesus than he has yet found; and if I can personally help him towards this in some way I would regard this as a great privilege.

But all too often I discern a hole at the centre of the ministry of some clergy. They are caring people; they work tremendously hard; they may be learned in theology. But somehow they do not ever seem to speak, whether in personal conversations or in their sermons, of knowing God personally, or of turning to him through trusting in Jesus. Their congregations are not taught how to pray and let all their requests be known to God. No teaching about seeking and finding forgiveness or the assurance of salvation is given. I recall one such priest referring to the illustration of "a vertical relationship with God, and a horizontal relationship with fellow-believers" – and confessing that he had never understood what that meant. "No," I thought at the time, "That was rather what I had suspected!"

But if the minister of the church has never discovered what it means to know the Lord, how can he lead other people to such an experience? And if a church has had a succession of such clergy, whole generations of worshippers may live and die, never knowing the eternal life which Jesus came to purchase for them by his death and resurrection. How tragic is that!

Afterword: What about Baptism?

Some readers might be astonished that I have written about the meaning of conversion and of being a Christian, without mentioning baptism almost at all. I heard a bishop in whose diocese I served say that we must of course regard every baptized person as a Christian. "Some of them we may feel are not very satisfactory Christians; but of which of us is that not true?"

It is arguable that the New Testament writers would regard "Christians" and "those who are baptized" as interchangeable terms; a baptized person *is* a believer and a member of the church. But one cannot transfer the language used of a first generation church composed of baptized converts, into the totally different situation of twenty centuries later in a post-Christian society, in which infant baptism is for millions just a superstition or a social ceremony divorced from any living faith in Christ or commitment to the worshipping people of God. The argument used in my chapter on Baptism on pages 167-169 applies to this situation. For the bishop to equate "unsatisfactory Christians" in the sense that all believers are still sinners, though forgiven sinners, with those who are utterly ignorant of the meaning of genuine Christian faith and have no interest in it at all, is an illegitimate comparison.

My experience has mostly been with people who have been baptized as infants, so when they are converted the matter of baptism does not arise. If they have not been baptized, then of course they should be. Bishop Colin Buchanan when taking parish missions used to invite those who responded to the Gospel appeal, but who had not been baptized, to undergo baptism then and there, with no delay for lengthy instruction classes; this apparently was the New Testament pattern, for example in the case of the Ethiopian eunuch[1] and the Philippian gaoler and his family[2].

---

[1] Acts 8. 36,38
[2] Acts 16. 33

7

❧

Christian Service

As well as being expected to attend Bible studies, prayer meetings and church services, in order to build up our faith and understanding, OICCU members were also encouraged to undertake some form of Christian service. I do not remember whether there were many forms of service brought to our notice; but I found myself taking part in services in hospital wards.

After attending one or two such services in a "back-up" capacity, without having any particular responsibility (perhaps I read a Bible passage), there came the great day when I was to be the one to give "the talk". As we were to be in a maternity ward, I felt it would be appropriate to take "being born again" as my theme! I worked hard to prepare my talk, and ran it past one of the other members of the group for his suggestions. I was desperately nervous, even though my talk probably lasted no more than five minutes; but it was my first one, and I did want to get it right. In the event the captive audience of young mums listened politely, and there were not too many interruptions from the younger patients in the ward.

Later I became one of a team who led services in a children's ward, and this was my first experience of teaching children about Jesus. Probably in those days most of the children were Sunday School members when not in hospital, and it was great fun encouraging their participation in the service. I remember one little boy, aged about 6, who was there for many weeks, as he had been very badly scalded; at first he just lay moaning in pain, but as the weeks went by and his injuries started to heal, he became a more and more lively participant in our little services. As we sang, "Yes, Jesus loves me!" he joined in with enormous enthusiasm, if little tunefulness.

On one occasion I ventured to suggest to one of the team members that when announcing the next hymn or chorus, it might be nice if he did a little more than merely give the number in the book; perhaps he could introduce it by commenting on the theme of the song. To my dismay, next time he announced the song, he went through it line by line first, laboriously explaining what each word meant, while I writhed with embarrassment. But it is only by having a go that you learn; I am sure that my own efforts were sometimes equally ham-fisted.

It is surely a thoroughly healthy principle that people who have come to a new faith in Christ should be urged to serve their Lord in some way; and the fact that they may be nervous or reluctant, or that their early attempts are clumsy and gauche, is no reason to abandon the principle. People can only discover and develop their gifts by trying them out; sometimes this will lead them to change tack and seek different avenues of service, but I cannot be the only person whose future ministry was nurtured by such early experiences.

It is a shame that in most churches this practice is conspicuous by its absence, and the most that lay members are ever expected to do is arrange the flowers or hand round the collection plate. There is so often a conspiracy on the part of both clergy and congregation, to ensure that only the clergyman (or in more recent years, clergywoman) does anything "spiritual" or evangelistic. If a layperson is invited to lead worship, in many more traditional churches it would be resented, both with a feeling of "Who does she think she is?" and also, "This is what the minister is paid to do!" Thankfully this culture is at last changing, and some bishops of the Church of England are vigorously encouraging their clergy to let lay people have a go, to discover what gifts of ministry they may have, even before they have been officially "licensed" to take part in leading some aspect of worship.

As I mentioned before, I also began to explore avenues of Christian service in the university vacations, and my first experiences were with the VPS house parties. I never progressed beyond being a "senior camper", with the more menial tasks to do; but I still sat under the regular teaching of the team of more senior leaders, most of whom were schoolmasters, clergy or theological students. These "camps" had been going for a good many years, though I had never encountered them in my own school years; they were the inspiration of one remarkable man, the Revd. E. J. H. Nash, always known as Bash. He had had the vision for such house parties, specifically to reach public school boys with the gospel. Not only were these young men likely to be the leaders of society and nation in the future, but also they were unlikely ever to go to the sort of Sunday School where a personal response to the call of Christ was expected. All most of them would ever encounter of the Christian faith would be very traditional public school chapel services, and perhaps equally traditional parish churches in the holidays.

So Bash gathered teams of like-minded men (and later, women for girls' camps) to be leaders, and recruited undergraduates from Oxford and Cambridge as senior campers, not only to be general dogsbodies but also to be role models of hearty young Christian men for the boys to observe. Boys were generally invited to the

105

camps by evangelical schoolmasters or chaplains in the public schools, and my impression is that this was done in a somewhat secretive way, to avoid mockery in the schools at large. I learnt later that Michael Tupper had invited a number of boys from my House in Shrewsbury while I was there, but I heard nothing about it; presumably he felt that I was unsuitable, or would not be interested. So there were no brochures or posters for the notice boards inviting interested boys to ask for a booking form; no, a teacher would quietly approach some boy whom he felt might respond, and ask him if he would like to take part in a holiday activity which included games of all sorts, outings and expeditions, and daily meetings when the Christian faith would be explained.

Probably hundreds of young people from the public schools came to faith in that way over the years, and many of them went on to be ordained, some being well-known church leaders such as John Stott himself, David Watson and Bishop David Sheppard; others no doubt took leading roles in many other walks of life. I heard one opinion expressed that Bash – that quiet, retiring, austere man, almost totally unknown outside the sphere of VPS Camps – was perhaps the most effective Christian influence in Britain in the mid 20th Century.

Many of the leaders had been boys at the Camps themselves, and then after leaving school had had a spell as Senior Campers; they had thus had steady, consistent Christian teaching over a number of years, as well as learning to exercise gifts of ministry themselves. The ethos of these houseparties was very "public school", and though the games and sketches were light-hearted, the actual meetings were formal, earnest and serious. I recall one younger leader giving a talk on Christian behaviour, and with all the illustrations of how things can go wrong in this sphere it was hilarious, and provoked gales of laughter. At the following camp the same leader gave a talk on the same subject, and I was anticipating a repeat performance; but instead he gave a very subdued and serious address. I strongly suspect that after his previous effort, he was quietly taken aside and told firmly that such levity in a Christian meeting was simply not the thing.

Bash took seriously his pastoral role in bringing on young leaders, and regularly visited the universities. He had heard that I had started to take an interest in the Pentecostal approach to faith and spirituality, and was obviously quite troubled by this; I was invited to a quiet talk with him on one of his visits to Oxford, and he tried to persuade me of the error of my ways. I never had another invitation to Iwerne Minster, but was encouraged to find alternative spheres of holiday service among young people. This led to my attending my first CSSM beach mission.

The CSSM – standing for Children's Special Service Mission, but usually pronounced "Sizzm" – was a branch of the Scripture Union, and had been running evangelistic missions for children since the late 19th Century at many seaside resorts (and occasionally at inland sites too). A team of young people was gathered and stayed in some suitable, inexpensive accommodation. The main focus of the Beach Mission was the daily Beach Service, centred on the Sand Pulpit. The team went along the beach and invited any children they met, who were on holiday with their parents, to come along to the service. There would be singing of choruses accompanied by a portable harmonium (known as the Pandemonium) and led by one of the team holding up large cards with the words. There was a talk (of course!), which tended to be much livelier than what I had encountered at Iwerne, with sketches, visual aids of all kinds, and a lot of audience participation. Over the sand pulpit (renewed every morning by a hard-working team) was the "C.S.S.M." banner.

There were all sorts of other activities in the course of the mission, including games of beach hockey, early morning Bible

Study groups (known by names such as "gold-diggers"), evening Sausage Sizzles, and a Parents' Tea Party. Nowadays with all the sensitivities and anxieties about child abuse and paedophiles, there would be no way young men could wander along a beach and talk to children, without arousing deep suspicion and hostility; but in those innocent days parents were usually very pleased to have fun activities arranged for their children, without charge, and didn't mind the religious bit. In many resorts the same families came every year, and the Beach Mission was a central part of their holidays.

It was at a CSSM mission at Sheringham in Norfolk that I had an unexpected shove into further public speaking. On the Sunday the inter-denominational team of young people was sent off in pairs to attend all the different churches in the town; and two of us were deputed to go to the Plymouth Brethren assembly. (This was the "Open Brethren", not the "Exclusive Brethren" where we would *not* have been welcome.) It was an interesting service, rather different from anything I had encountered before. We had Communion – called "the Breaking of Bread" – in which the bread and wine were passed from person to person around the congregation. After the service as we chatted to members of the congregation, and explained why we were there, an elderly man told us that on Sunday evenings he went and did some open-air preaching along the coast at Wells-by-the-Sea; would we like to join him there? We agreed, and arranged a time and place to meet him.

When we arrived, we were rather taken aback to find him wearing a large sandwich-board, with a text on the front and the back, and another text board as an extension over his head; it did not say, as in the familiar cartoons, "Prepare to meet thy doom!", but probably texts like "The wages of sin is death, but the gift of God is eternal life." This was not quite the style I was accustomed to, and I felt ill at ease; but worse was to come. After we had chatted for a few minutes, our friend looked at his watch, and said:

"Well, I think it's time we started. Would you like to go first, or shall I?" I was horrified; I had been expecting to be a spectator, or a non-participating supporter. It had not occurred to me that I would have to give a talk, and that without any form of preparation whatever. There was no regular audience either; just a line of people sitting on the sea wall beside the car park, with their backs to us, and various passers-by. However I felt unable just to refuse to take part.

"You go first!" I said hastily, and all through his talk I was alternating between praying hard and scratching around in my mind to think of something to say. When the elderly preacher drew to a close, and turned to me with an encouraging smile, I gulped, took a deep breath and started.

My address was a kind of rehash of a talk that had been given to the children by the team leader at the previous day's beach service, based on the story of Zacchaeus. I remember the words with which I started: "Do you think it is possible to change human nature?" I bellowed at all the backs on the wall. I went on to show how encountering Jesus had changed the nature of the greedy, dishonest tax-collector, of whom Jesus then said, "Today salvation has come to this house." I was amazed that I was able to give my talk, without too much hesitation or stumbling, and draw it to a reasonable conclusion; I was hoarse and trembling by the end, but rejoicing that God seemed to have answered my frantic prayers for help. Whether it did any of the hearers any good I do not know, but it was certainly a valuable experience for me.

One of the families who were regulars at Sheringham was the Wood family; the Revd. Maurice Wood was Vicar of St. Mary's, Islington, and later became Bishop of Norwich. I heard a story about him and a nervous young Christian at an open-air meeting. "Will you give the talk today?" asked Maurice. "Oh, no, Mr.

Wood, I don't think I'm ready for that yet!" demurred the young man. "All right, then; you can do it tomorrow!" insisted Maurice, smiling. Sometimes we need to be pushed into new activities for God; protestations of inadequacy or reluctance are not generally accepted by the Lord as valid excuses! There are several examples of this in the Bible, one of the best being Moses who went on making excuses for several chapters, finally ending up pleading "O Lord, please send someone else!"[1]

Over the next few years I was involved with a variety of camps, house-parties and missions, mostly with children and young people. As well as going to Sheringham two or three times, I joined a CSSM beach mission in Elie in Fife, and an Inland Children's Mission in Nottingham, centred round two adjoining parishes. While I was there one of my tasks was to dress up as a Town Crier, and lead a long trail of children and leaders around the housing estate, ringing my bell, and roaring out an invitation to come to the Mission activities. The local paper was invited to come to this, and my photograph appeared in its pages next day. It so happened that someone who had been in my House at school three or four years earlier lived in Nottingham, saw the photograph and accompanying article, and phoned up for a chat. Unfortunately at school I had disliked him heartily, and I am afraid that instead of greeting him with Christian warmth and forgiveness, I was fairly short with him!

---

[1] Exodus 4.13

8

Called to the Ministry

Ever since my conversion, and the conversation I had had with John Stott in his hotel room, my future life and career had been a matter of prayer for me. From the very start I had taken extremely seriously the proposition that God had a plan for my life. I never understood this in any deterministic way, as if my life were on rails, or in some "It is written!" sense. Rather I believed that God had given me certain gifts, even though I had not yet fully recognised them; he had a purpose for me, in which those gifts would be most fully utilised and expressed in his service. It was sheer logic to conclude that I would be happiest if I was in the centre of God's plan, and therefore the most important thing for me to do was to find out what that plan was.

It was not necessarily to be in some religious sphere; as John had said, God might want me to be a Christian forest officer, as Forestry was the subject I was reading – even though I had chosen it without any reference to God's plan. But I had no doubts that God could have been involved in that decision anyway, and it could well be a part of the whole picture. Moreover I was certain that God would guide me if I sought his guidance; the danger was that I should go off in my own direction, as if I knew better than him what was good for me.

The first crisis involving such an understanding of God's hand upon my life came as I approached the set of exams which came half way through the four-year Forestry course, "Honour Moderations in Natural Science", known generally as Science Mods. Unlike Prelims, the first set of exams for most courses, which were simply a matter of Pass or Fail, Mods were given classes like the degree at the end – you could get a First, Second or Third. For the first two years I was studying Botany, Geology and Chemistry, subjects which were all totally new to me, as those on the Classical Side at school simply did no science of any kind at all. Most of my fellow Forestry students had done two years of Botany and at least five years of Chemistry, even though most of them were as new to Geology as I was.

It was the chemistry – Organic and Inorganic - that I really struggled with. As the exams drew closer, I revised hard, but my panic levels grew steadily higher. I felt as if I was forgetting each page I had revised, by the time I had moved on to the page after the next; and it began to look horribly possible that I was simply going to fail these exams altogether. If that happened, I would probably – as far as I understood it – have to leave university. At the very least it would presumably mean leaving the Forestry course. The prospect of such failure and disgrace filled my heart with lead. What would my mother think? What would my two brothers who had achieved good degrees before me – one of them at Brasenose – think? What would happen to me?

I do not now remember how it was that I discovered a particular verse of Scripture that proved to be a lifeline to me as I was drowning in these feelings of despair. *"We know that all things work together for good to them that love God, to them who are called according to his purpose."*[1] If that was true – and all my recent teaching had inclined me to take such words as a firm promise

---

[1] Romans 8.28 (AV)

from God himself – it meant that I really had no need to worry. I was the person referred to in the second half: I loved God, and was called. So this meant that all things – that included the exams, and their results, whatever they were – would "work together for good" for me. It did not mean that I was therefore bound to pass! It meant that, pass or fail, it was all in God's hands. If I were to fail – even if I had to leave Oxford – then that was all right; God was saying to me, "Trust me! I have your future under my control." If I was not going to be able to get a degree, then that was the best thing that could happen. It would all work together for good.

So could I then put my feet up for the remaining few weeks in some fatalistic way? Not a bit of it. I still had to do my bit, and my bit was to work as hard as I reasonably could at my revision. But I didn't believe that meant I had to study for sixteen hours a day, poring over my books into the small hours. I decided that I would work eight hours a day – including lectures, lab work and essays, as well as revision – and six days a week; on Sunday I would put the books aside and rest. I believed the Sabbath provision was also for my good, and that I would achieve more, not less, if I rested one day in seven.

By hanging on to that promise, and reminding myself of it several times a day, I kept panic at bay. I also discovered some more "trust" verses with which I reassured myself. *"Thou wilt keep him in perfect peace whose mind is stayed on thee."*[1] *"Cast all your cares on God, for he cares for you."*[2] *"Seek first God's kingdom and his righteousness, and all these things shall be added to you."*[3] There was simply no room for worry with a God like this!

Well, that was the theory. It didn't always work quite like that in practice. I would sometimes wake up in the small hours, and lie

---

[1] Isaiah 26.3
[2] I Peter 5.7
[3] Matthew 6.33

there, tossing and turning, consumed with anxiety – until I took myself in hand. "All things…" I reminded myself sternly.

The exams were going to start on a Wednesday; so I decided to go home the previous Saturday and have a long weekend of complete relaxation. I felt I deserved it, and would be the better for it. So I went home to the Cotswolds, and enjoyed three restful summer days. There was only one drawback: my grandmother, whom I loved dearly, lived with us, and several times a day she would say sympathetically, "I know you must be terribly worried about your exams, dear!" Every time she said this my anxiety level was cranked up a further notch, and by the time I returned to Oxford a couple of days before the exams I was in a state of tension as bad as I had ever suffered. However I had two more days, away from well-meaning words of comfort, and once again I concentrated on the promises of God. Even as I sat in the examination room, waiting for the papers to be given out, I used the blotter to write out some of the "promise" verses of scripture, to keep myself calm; and it really did work. While others around me trembled and bit their nails, I sat quietly, thanking God for his promises.

I went home before the results were published; but one of my friends was staying on in Oxford, and saw them as soon as they were posted up on the board. He phoned me at home. I was playing a game of croquet with my mother and my aunt, and was playing a shot when the phone went, so Auntie May went indoors to answer it. A moment later she came running down the steps, exclaiming, "You've got a Second!" I went to the phone, and heard for myself; I had done better than I would have believed possible. When I returned to the lawn and took up my mallet again, my euphoria was such that I could do no wrong; I took absurdly long shots, and the ball sailed through the hoops from the opposite end of the lawn. I have never played with such skill before or since!

So these results seemed to indicate not only that I could stay at Oxford, but also that I should continue with the Forestry degree course. In the year and a half since I started wondering what God wanted me to do with my life, the options seemed to have crystallised to just two. My initial wonderings about being a missionary in South America had receded, as had the possibility of some other kind of overseas missionary work – a calling which was frequently laid before OICCU members for serious consideration. But by this time I was clear that the choice for me lay between a job in Forestry and ordained ministry in the Church of England. In this connection the exam results gave me no indication, one way or the other; so all I could do was continue on my present course until God clearly pushed me in a different direction.

You might ask, what sort of guidance was I looking for? How, precisely, did I expect Almighty God to make his will known to me? I had heard many talks on "Guidance", and all sorts of ways for God's will to be conveyed to the believer had been suggested: a verse of Scripture "leaping from the page" and seeming to speak personally to the seeker; a sermon or talk which strikes home powerfully; advice about one's own gifts and abilities, strengths and weaknesses from godly friends or ministers; and, of course, doors opening and shutting. This image (used more than once in the Bible, especially by Paul) indicated the coming together of circumstances, such as opportunities suddenly opening up, or alternatively closing. Coupled with all or any of these might be a firm, inner conviction. The way of seeking guidance favoured by some earnest souls, the Bible and pin method (opening the Bible at random and jabbing a pin down, and taking the verse indicated as infallible guidance) was definitely not recommended. Nor did I expect some supernatural visitation or voice from heaven.

The "opening the Bible at random" method of hearing God's voice is not, in my experience, as totally ludicrous and superstitious as it might seem, although I would still not commend it to anyone as a substitute for hard and careful thought, prayer and seeking advice. But there have been occasions in my life when something like this has been of significance to me.

One such occasion was in the months before taking my Mods. I was at home for the vacation, and one evening I was feeling very low as I contemplated the science revision which was causing me so much trouble. When my mother asked me what I was moping about, I poured it all out to her, but she was very unsympathetic. "Oh, for heaven's sake, pull yourself together and stop feeling so sorry for yourself! Just buckle down to some work, and get on with it!"

I went into my bedroom, fell on my knees beside the bed, and grabbed my Bible. "O Lord, please speak to me, as I'm feeling so wretched!" I pleaded as I opened it, virtually at random. It fell open, more or less in the middle, at the 40th chapter of Isaiah, and my eye fell on the words at the beginning of the chapter: "*Comfort, comfort my people, says your God.*"

Those words, written some twenty-six centuries earlier, for a totally different situation, nevertheless spoke so powerfully to my heart at that moment that I wept. God was bringing me a word of love and comfort, just when I needed it. There have been other occasions over the years when I have felt that God has spoken to me similarly through random words of Scripture.

After the successful results of my Science Mods I moved on to the second two years of the Forestry course, which were more directly concerned with Forestry proper, rather than just the academic, scientific subjects of the first two years. Silviculture, Ecology, Forest Pathology, Soil Science, Utilization, and such things as Forest Engineering (building roads and bridges) and Colonial Forest Administration. Because we were all starting at the same point, I found these subjects easier, and often very interesting. My feelings about whether this was to be the sphere for my career swithered one way and the other; sometimes I was quite convinced that I was headed for a life in some overseas forest – and then I pictured myself as a Vicar....

St. Ebbe's Church had occasional meetings specifically for those who were wondering about a vocation to the ordained, pastoral ministry (I did not like the phrase commonly used in non-evangelical circles, "Going into the Church", as if lay Christians were not "in the Church" at all). I attended these and found them helpful. In one vacation a week's "parish experience" was arranged, centred on a group of parishes in Islington. This gave a taste of life "at the coal face" of an inner city parish, particularly valuable for those such as myself that had had a sheltered and somewhat privileged upbringing.

As the fourth and final year of the Forestry course started, several of the other students were writing off for job application forms from the Forestry Commission, the Colonial Forest Service, or timber companies; and I felt that I must get a move on and take action, one way or the other. I could not go on waiting for divine guidance forever. One of the other Forestry students – one of the twelve of us in my year – was definitely hoping to be ordained, so I discussed the matter with him. He advised me to apply to attend one of the Selection Conferences for the Ministry organised by the Church of England. "These people are there to help you to discern God's vocation for you," he explained. "They could give valuable advice."

I decided to take this advice, found the address of CACTM (the Central Advisory Council for The Ministry – a title which changed several times over later years), and wrote a letter, applying for a place at a conference. As soon as I had posted my letter, I began to have a feeling, "This is right!" In fact this was completely the wrong way to go about such things; normally a potential ordinand, or candidate for ordination, would have had to go through the Diocesan process, with a recommendation from his

117

vicar, an interview with the Diocesan Director of Ordinands, and so on. I am sure that nowadays such a letter would have received a reply firmly pointing me in the direction of the correct process. However for some reason I had a reply inviting me to a Selection Conference during the Christmas vac. This seemed further to confirm that I was at long last moving in the right direction.

I found the CACTM conference interesting and enjoyable. There were twenty-four men (no women of course in those days), and five members of the interviewing panel, consisting of one archdeacon, three other clergy and a layman. The candidates were a very varied lot, some being still at school, and one man being a retired colonel. There were only three of us who were evangelicals. At the first meeting, each of us in turn around the room was asked to say something about ourselves, and why we were there. This gave a great opportunity for the evangelicals to "give our testimonies", which was something we were well accustomed to from evangelistic work. We were then divided for most meetings into three "cadres" of eight, in alphabetical order; and as the names of the evangelicals began with B, J and W, there was one of us in each cadre.

It was my first real experience of middle-of-the-road Anglicanism since my conversion (apart from attending my village church in the vacations); and I was astonished, and somewhat derisive, at some of the attitudes I encountered. When our cadres were involved in discussions, when I contributed I naturally quoted from Scripture, and found that this was met with astonishment: "Good heavens! Here's someone who knows the Bible!" I was also puzzled by the anxiety expressed, especially by some of the more immature candidates, that they "wouldn't pass". I simply did not see it like that, as a matter of "passing" or "failing", but of trying to find God's purpose for me. But the others seemed to find that an incomprehensible approach.

After several days of discussions, addresses, times of worship, and interviews with each of the five leaders, we were told that we would hear the verdict from our own Bishops in a few days. But by the time I left for my journey home, I felt 90% certain that ordained ministry was what God intended for me. When I received the letter from the office of the Bishop of Gloucester, informing me that I had been "recommended for ordination training", this confirmed it.

The next question that had to be pondered concerned the ordination training itself. Where was I to do it? And was I to go straight to a Theological College after Oxford, or broaden my experience with some secular job first, perhaps by working for a year on a factory floor?

I approached two colleges, Clifton in Bristol, and Ridley College, Cambridge; and each of them invited me for a visit and interview with the Principal. Clifton was known to be a college firmly within the conservative evangelical mould; Ridley was more mixed, with a variety of church traditions being represented in both the students and the staff.

But before I visited either, I was summoned to meet the Bishop of Gloucester (my home parish being in that diocese), and his Diocesan Director of Ordinands. The Bishop was an impressive and somewhat daunting figure. I had been warned that he had little sympathy for evangelicalism, so I was apprehensive and on my guard during the interview. At one point he asked me if I had any theological colleges in mind.

"Yes," I said nervously; "I have written to Ridley, and – er – Clifton."

There was a pause, and the temperature of the room seemed to drop several degrees.

"I would be very happy for you to go to Ridley!" the Bishop said at last. Clifton was not even worthy of a comment. At the end of the interview he said he would give me his blessing, and I was told to kneel before him.

Then I was sent across the Close to see the DDO. He too, I had been told, heartily despised the evangelical tradition. He was much more open about his contempt of Clifton, which, he felt, had no place at all in the Church of England. (I was told by another OICCU man two or three years older than me, who was also from Gloucester Diocese, that this DDO warned him strongly against going to Clifton, because it would totally scupper his chances of ever being a bishop. This was Pat Harris, who later was to become a bishop in South America, before returning to the UK to be Bishop of Southwell.)

However despite the disapproval of the Bishop and the DDO I persisted with my intention to visit both colleges. Tom Anscombe, the Principal of Clifton where I went first, was the first person in the whole Anglican process who actually invited me to pray with him; none of the five CACTM interviewers, nor Bishop nor DDO, had suggested such a thing, and I found it refreshing and encouraging to share with Tom Anscombe a few minutes of prayer together. The same thing happened at Ridley; Cyril Bowles, the Principal, was completely sympathetic to my uncertainty about which college to go to, and in his prayer asked God to guide me clearly. My heart warmed to him too.

While I was at Ridley, I spent a few minutes with a student there whom I had known through Iwerne Minster. He was enjoying the stimulation of the variety of teaching he was receiving at Ridley, but he had been under evangelical teaching and leadership all his life. He felt that for a man who had not had that privilege, a firmly evangelical college might be more helpful.

In later years I met a vicar who would perhaps have benefited from such advice. He had been converted as a teenager through an undenominational youth movement called Crusaders. He had received all his basic Christian teaching in that context, and had been involved in both leadership and evangelism under their auspices. But Crusaders had virtually no links with any particular church, and so when this young man began to sense a vocation to be ordained, he had no help or guidance from his evangelical leaders. The diocesan authorities pointed him in a direction of a college of a theologically liberal position; and sadly his years there virtually destroyed his faith. He lost all his evangelical convictions, and all his spiritual fire and fervour; when I knew him, he was just a well-meaning, middle-of-the-road vicar with no message, no Gospel at all.

I have met more than one man who has claimed that his theological college left him believing in nothing. One friend, however, was saved by the vicar under whom he served his "title", or first curacy. This priest was a man of deep and powerful faith, with a strong grasp of the Gospel, and a belief in a God who both saved and healed; and when his curate left that parish to move on to the next, he too had imbibed the same firm and enthusiastic faith, convinced not so much by theological arguments, but by the ways in which he had seen God at work in people's lives.

I was still not sure what was right for me; and in particular whether a year in industry might be of benefit. At Brasenose I had been allocated a "moral tutor", a science don who was meant to be in a pastoral role for me, although I scarcely ever saw him. However it seemed appropriate for me to discuss this matter with him, especially as he was a Christian – by no means an evangelical, but a regular worshipper at one of the Anglo-Catholic churches in town. He was wholly in sympathy with my sense of vocation, and advised strongly that a year in industry would be a waste of time. "You will learn far more in your first year as a curate than you ever would working in a factory," he insisted.

But, if I were not to have a "year out", would either theological college be able to offer me a place in the coming September? I wrote to each one to ask.

Ridley wrote back to say that they were fully booked for the coming academic year, but they would probably be able to offer me a place in the following year. Clifton wrote back to say that they had been fully booked; but they had just heard that one student had decided to abandon his course in order to pursue a teaching career. So they had just one place, which they would be happy to offer to me. This seemed like a direct answer to prayer; I was reminded of a verse in Scripture, "Your ears shall hear a voice behind you saying, 'This is the way; walk in it.'"[1]

So I wrote and accepted the place at Clifton for a two-year ordination course. When I learned at the end of my time in Oxford that I had got a First, and moreover had been awarded the Oxford University Forestry Prize, it was gratifying, but ultimately irrelevant to the calling I was to pursue.

---

[1] Isaiah 30.21

9

❧❦❧

The Meaning of Ordained Ministry

Within the Christian church there are many different forms of leadership, and many different understandings of it. Even within the Church of England (it has been suggested that "C. of E." stands for "Comedy of Errors"!) there are widely different views; and the terminology used reflects this variety.

There are some for whom the key words are "priest" and "priesthood". This is seen as an indelible anointing of God by the hands of the ordaining bishop and the company of priests who assist at a "priesting" or ordination to the priesthood. (It does not guarantee godliness, or even salvation. One man of this tradition said to me, "A priest may go to Hell – but he will still be a priest!") Only a priest may preside at Holy Communion; only a priest may pronounce benediction. Any service of bread and wine without the presiding of a priest, ordained by the laying on of hands by a Bishop in the apostolic succession, is not a true, valid Communion at all, but just a pale imitation of it.

This has never been an understanding of Christian ministry with which I have had any sympathy, because I can find no support for it in the New Testament; it was a development which occurred in subsequent centuries when the simple,

123

straightforward faith of the Apostles had become corrupted and distorted.

Part of the problem is the variety of meanings which can be given to the word "priest" – a word that is used in the services and formularies of the Church of England, in the *Book of Common Prayer* and the more modern service books such as *Common Worship*. The actual English word "priest" is a compression of the word "presbyter", a Greek word meaning "elder". But the same English word is also used to translate other words from the Hebrew Old Testament and Greek New Testament, as well as Latin words used in later translations of the Bible.

When the word "priest" is found in the English translations of the Old Testament it represents the Hebrew word "COHEN" – found among Jews today as a surname, where it is generally believed to indicate that the family is descended from a priestly family. Such priests, who had to be of the tribe of Levi and the family of Aaron, were the only people authorised by the Law of Moses to offer sacrifices in the Tabernacle and subsequently the Temple in Jerusalem.

We still find such Jewish priests mentioned in the New Testament, particularly in the Gospels and the book of Acts, as the Jewish priesthood was still in operation at the time of Jesus. (The Jewish priesthood is not found now; it should not be confused with the office of a Rabbi.) The Greek word for "Cohen" was "Hiereus" ('ιερευς). The Latin word which was later used, when the Bible was translated into Latin, was "Sacerdos", literally meaning "sacrifice-offerer". So whenever we find the word "priest" in English versions of the Bible, in Old or New Testament, these are the words it is translating.

The Greek word "Hiereus" is used of three classes of people in the New Testament. First, of the Jewish priesthood in the temple; secondly, of Jesus himself, who has a unique priesthood; the sacrifice he offered was the sacrifice of himself on the Cross.

Thirdly, the word is used of all Christians, who are described as *"a royal priesthood"*[1] or *"a kingdom and priests to serve his God and Father"*[2] "Hiereus" is *never* used in the New Testament to denote leaders within the Christian church, as if the leaders were in some way distinct from other Christians. Various words or titles are used of them: "Presbyter" or elder, "Diaconos" or servant (from which the word "deacon" is derived), "Episcopos" or overseer, "Pastor" or shepherd. But never "Hiereus" or sacrificing priest.

Coupled with the erroneous (however common or venerable) view that a leader or minister of a Christian congregation is a "priest", in the sense of a "Hiereus", "Sacerdos" or sacrificial priest, is the doctrine of the Apostolic Succession. This is taken to mean an unbroken chain of bishops, from the time of St. Peter right through to the present day, each one laying hands in sacramental bestowing of authority upon the next; and moreover, it is held, only "priests" ordained through the laying on of hands by a bishop in this unbroken chain are genuine, authentic priests. Furthermore only such a priest is able to preside at Holy Communion, and consecrate the Bread and Wine.

There is not a shred of Biblical support for this theory, even though it is commonly held to be the official doctrine of the Church of England[3] (and of course the Roman Catholic Church), and is probably stoutly defended by the majority of current bishops and clergy. First, as mentioned above, "bishops" in this sense are unknown in the New Testament; the words "bishop" (episcopos, επισκοπος) and "elder" (presbuteros, πρεσβυτερος) are interchangeable.

Secondly there is no evidence whatever that St. Peter was seen as the leader of the worldwide church, from whom all episcopal or

---

[1] I Peter 2.9

[2] Revelation 1.6

[3] There is no mention of the doctrine of the Apostolic Succession in the *Thirty-nine Articles of Religion*, the official statement of the Church of England's faith.

ministerial authority was derived. (The Roman Catholic Church holds that he was the first Bishop of Rome; but in the earliest documents which list bishops, Clement was named as the first bishop of Rome.) Indeed Paul describes how on one occasion, on a vital matter of principle, he had publicly to oppose and rebuke Peter who was behaving hypocritically[1]. It was not that Paul felt he was "over" Peter or "under" him in any hierarchical sense. That was not remotely the issue. What mattered was the truth of the Gospel.

So the "unbroken chain" theory is an irrelevance. Not only is it historically improvable; but what matters is not whose hands have been laid on your head, but whether you are holding to the true Gospel. I have been ordained at the hands of a bishop (the Bishop of Chelmsford) who would doubtless be held to be soundly in this Apostolic Succession. But supposing some historical research were to indicate that at some point in, say, the thirteenth century, the chain had been broken, what then? Would this mean that all bishops since the "break", and all clergy ordained at their hands, were not real bishops or priests at all? So my own ministry for forty years would have been completely invalid? My answer to such an (admittedly improbable) hypothesis is, "*So what?*" What my ministry has been based on is the truth of the Gospel. Sometimes I have got things right, and no doubt sometimes I have got things wrong, both theologically and morally, in matters of judgement and in my relationships with people; those are the factors on which my ministry must be assessed, not whose hands were laid on me or whose on him!

The only "apostolic succession" that we see in the New Testament is a succession of faithful preaching and teaching of the true Gospel. This is well expressed in what Paul wrote to Timothy, "*The things you have heard me say in the presence of many witnesses*

---

[1] Galatians 2. 11-14

entrust to reliable men who will also be qualified to teach others." [1] Look at this succession:

1. Paul taught Timothy.
2. Timothy was to teach the same things to faithful men
3. The faithful men were to teach them to others.

The passing on of teaching which is faithful to the truth of the message of Christ and his apostles is what mattered to Paul and the other New Testament writers. This is particularly significant when you consider the Jewish background from which they came, in which the proper authorization of the priesthood, and the ensuring that all priests were from the right genealogical line, had been considered vital for fourteen centuries. But no such consideration was of any relevance within the church of Jesus Christ, simple because now *all* believers in Jesus are priests, under one High Priest, Jesus himself.

In saying these things I am in no way seeking to devalue Christian leadership and ministry. The call to be a leader in the church is seen in the New Testament as an extremely important one, with a heavy responsibility – to teach the word of God faithfully, to set an example of godliness to the people, to lead them, care for them, guide them, even if necessary rebuke them. But the suggestion that only a "presbyter" could be allowed to preside at the Breaking of Bread, let alone the idea that unless he said particular words or performed particular actions the worship was in some way invalid – such things are never even hinted at. Paul wrote strongly about the misuse of the Lord's Supper, but the issues that troubled him concerned personal relationships within the fellowship, the absence of love, a self-centred attitude; he apparently was totally unconcerned about who presided, or said particular words.

---

[1] II Timothy 2.2

In saying this do I imply that I would be quite willing to allow laypeople to preside at Holy Communion, even in the absence of a priest? In terms of theological conviction, yes, indeed; I can see in Scripture nothing whatever to imply that such a thing is wrong or would in some way invalidate the sacrament. However I am a man under authority, and I believe that my bishop is "over me in the Lord"[1], and is therefore a man who is entitled to my respect. When a priest is instituted into a parish, he or she has to promise publicly to obey his bishop "in all things lawful and honest". Though I am now retired from stipendiary ministry, I believe the principle still holds, and that it would be wrong for me to break the rules and disregard the disciplines of my Church in such a matter, except in the most extreme circumstances. I am sure that some at least of the current bench of Bishops would have a good deal of sympathy with the theological standpoint I have outlined on this matter; but there are other factors at stake, one of which is the unity of the church. When an Australian diocese in the Anglican Communion passed a motion that "lay presidency" was to be permitted, this raised in stark terms the possibility of splitting the Anglican Communion down the middle, since, like it or not, to a substantial proportion of bishops and clergy – and, no doubt, lay Christians – the idea of lay presidency at the Eucharist is totally unacceptable, and a matter on which there can be no compromise. So, for the sake of the conscience and convictions of our brothers and sisters in Christ, we must sacrifice our own freedom to follow our conscience in this matter, and submit to the current rules.

Nevertheless I have always felt some of the practical outworkings of this dogma to be absurd. Suppose there is a parish whose the priest is taken ill or is away: in order for the worshippers to be able to receive Holy Communion an ordained

---

[1] I Thessalonians 5.12

priest from elsewhere, who may be a total stranger to them all, has to be wheeled in to preside. I see no valid reason why some well-loved, respected, godly, lay man or woman should not be in such circumstances permitted to preside at the Lord's Table, so long as the Bishop gives his permission. In some parts of the world the present rules mean that months can go by in which faithful congregations are not able to partake of the Lord's Supper because the nearest priest is hundreds of miles away, with dozens of congregations to care for, and perhaps travel in that region, and at that season, would necessitate an arduous journey of several days. This seems to me outrageous, and a totally wrong sense of priorities. Nevertheless that is the rule, and at present it must be obeyed if the church concerned is not to be expelled in disgrace from the Anglican Communion.

I have sometimes met situations where the rules have been "bent"! When I was a Vicar in the Isle of Wight it was possible to arrange holiday cover by offering the use of our home in exchange for Sunday duty, and this allowed some urban vicar and his family to have a very inexpensive holiday. On one occasion our holiday guest was an incumbent from Gateshead, and we overlapped by one night before our family headed for Scotland for our holiday. As we chatted I asked how he arranged his own holiday cover; and he said that he had a lady Reader in the parish who was willing to take all his services. When I asked, "But what about Communion?" he replied casually that he had consecrated enough wafers and wine for two weeks, and put them in the safe for her to use as required. (When I mentioned this, with a laugh, to a bishop I met at a conference – without of course naming names – he was utterly horrified!)

When I was Curate-in-Charge of Emmanuel Church, Tolworth, in Surrey, one autumn we had a series of house meetings in six homes for a Bible Study course, led by lay people. One leader, a man whose background was in a Free Church though he had been a member, and indeed a churchwarden, in that Anglican church for some years, asked me towards the end of the course if he could borrow the Church Communion silver, as his house group had decided it would be nice if their course could conclude with a Communion service in the home. He was intending to preside at this, and hence his innocent request! I had every sympathy with the desire of the group to express their faith and fellowship in this way, but had to explain gently that it was just not possible. In the end I was able to arrange to preside myself; but I suspect the members would have preferred their little service to be led by the man who had been the leader for the first five weeks of their group.

We have become familiar over the centuries with the concept of the church being divided into "clergy" and "laity"; "clergy" who are priests, or vicars or rectors or parsons (or in the Free Churches pastors or ministers) and therefore in some way "special" in church – to the extent that many people speak about "going into the Church" as a synonym for "being ordained"; and "laity" who are the rest, the ordinary church members, not ordained, not special, not allowed to do the really holy things. And yet the words "laity" and "layman" are derived from the Greek word "Laos" (λαος), which means "people" – and in this context, "the people of God" – *all* the People of God. The word "clergy" comes from another Greek word, "Cleros" (κληρος) which means a "lot" or share; it has various connotations in the New Testament, which apply to all believers, such as sharing the inheritance of heaven – not, it is to be hoped, to be applied only to the "clergy"! Only in later, post-Biblical times, did it come to mean those appointed to a specific office of leadership – which we think of as "clergy". The whole idea of separating the people of God into two classes or categories, "ordained" and "lay" is totally alien to the New Testament writers.

The three "orders" in the Anglican ministry, Bishops, Priests and Deacons, are therefore not to be found in the New Testament, even though all three words are found there. "Deacons" or "diaconoi" (διακονοι) were administrators, people set aside to see that the practical arrangements went smoothly – a very important role in any family or organisation! "Presbyters" (πρεσβυτεροι) and "Episcopoi" (επισκοποι), overseers or bishops, were equivalent terms – two different words to describe the same people, who led the local churches, usually in teams rather than as solitary leaders.

It seems to have been fairly soon after the New Testament period that the latter two words started to refer to separate categories: "presbyters" as those presiding over a local Christian assembly, and "overseers" as leaders who had the oversight of a group of assemblies. Thus the word "episcopos" started fairly soon to take on a meaning similar to the role of Bishops today. I do not believe that this was wrong; leadership is important, not only of the local assembly of worshipping believers, but also of the more extended Christian community. In some denominations today such extended leadership is exercised by a council or committee, but I feel there are advantages to having it in the hands of a single person – committees are not always very caring or pastoral bodies!

The idea of a "deacon" as a probationary presbyter is harmless, even though that is not what the word originally denoted; in recent years the idea of an order of permanent deacons has been revived, particularly in the Roman Catholic Church, which is perhaps a little more like the New Testament idea of a deacon. But it makes sense to have a probationary period for leaders while they learn the practicalities of the job, and if you want to call people at that stage "deacons" I do not object. So although "Bishops, Priest and Deacons" in the Anglican sense cannot be found in Scripture, I do not see these arrangements as *contrary* to Scripture, but as a legitimate development of it – so long as they are not held to be the only valid and true form of Christian ministry.

There are several other weaknesses of the traditional Anglican pattern. One is the idea that each church has one leader – though in rural districts especially this has changed to each vicar having several churches! But the invariable pattern that we see in the New Testament church is of shared leadership; it seems that a team of leaders was appointed in each place. Presumably this team would have had a variety of gifts, strengths and weaknesses; not only would this have been an effective way of sharing out the tasks according to people's individual abilities, but it would also be a valuable safeguard against lopsided or unbalanced ministry. Team members would be able not only to support and encourage each other, but also to correct each other.

Another very serious weakness of the traditional pattern is that it implies that only "the vicar" has gifts of ministry – and that he or she has them all! In fact gifts of ministry (which means "service") are described by Peter as "multi-coloured" or variegated – this is what is implied when he wrote, *"Each one should use whatever gift he has received, faithfully administering God's grace in its various forms."*[1] That is, that the many different gifts and abilities are shared out among all the members of a church, of all ages and both sexes; not only gifts which might be formalised in a particular "office" like being the chief musician or the treasurer, but more casual and spontaneous gifts, such as being able to bring joy and laughter, or comfort and reassurance. We do not want someone to be appointed as the Official Parish Joker (an appalling thought!) – but a joke at the appropriate moment is a lovely thing, and to be able to make people smile is a God-given ability to be valued by all.

---

[1] I Peter 4.10

But personal gifts that might develop into a recognised, and perhaps formalised, ministry must also have a place. How can a person discover if he or she would be able to give a helpful talk, or lead worship in an uplifting way, unless they can try it out? Rules that are too rigid, which dictate that no one may do such things until they have been through a three year course of training and been formally commissioned in the Cathedral, are likely to stifle the development of all the rich variety of gifts which God the Holy Spirit has already given to each church. The gifted person will feel frustrated; and the church as a whole is impoverished.

Thankfully this concept, of the ministry of the whole church, has been increasingly accepted in recent years, though in some churches you might not have noticed it! One blockage to such "body ministry" as it is sometimes called (ministry by all members of the body, to all members of the body) can be the insecurities of the Minister himself. Some clergy need to feel that they are in charge of everything, and feel very threatened by any suggestion that other people may also have gifts to use in church – and may even be able to do some things better than the Vicar! He may even feel, "then what am I here for?"

I am convinced that what the team leader, the Vicar, Priest or Minister, is there for is to be like the conductor of an orchestra, or the manager of a football team. The Minister must learn to see his church members as players – not as audience or spectators; as members of the crew of the ship, not passengers. Because the orchestra concerned includes beginners, and members of all ages, the resultant sound may sometimes seem a little discordant! But the answer to this is not for the conductor to try to rush round the room, playing each instrument in turn; still less is he to be a one-man band at the front, to whom everyone else is expected to listen admiringly. He is to seek to encourage each player, not only to develop their own individual gifts, but to play them in time and in tune with all the other players, as directed and led by the conductor. This way the orchestra will learn to make beautiful, harmonious and uplifting music, bringing satisfaction and fulfilment to the players, and pleasure and inspiration to hearers – who may be encouraged to join in themselves.

This is in fact a much more demanding, but also rewarding, job than just trying to do everything yourself. I have been the Minister of a church whose members take for granted the traditional pattern, that I was expected to do everything, even including organising the Sunday School outing or producing the Christmas pantomime! When I protested, and suggested that surely there was someone else who could undertake some task, this was met with puzzlement or even indignation: "But it's *your* church!" I should of course have answered (as so often, one thinks of the right answer later), "But isn't it yours too?"

A key New Testament passage in which Paul spells out the pattern of leadership which I have outlined above is this:

> *"It was he who gave some to be apostles, some to be prophets, some to be evangelists, and some to be pastors and teachers, to prepare God's people for works of service, so that the body of Christ may be built up, until we all reach unity in the faith and in the knowledge of the Son of God and become mature, attaining to the whole measure of the fullness of Christ."*[1]

In this passage Paul is asserting that the risen, ascended Lord Jesus Christ made provision for his church be giving a variety of leadership gifts. He mentions five – apostles, prophets, evangelists, pastors and teachers. It would perhaps be a mistake to interpret this as prescribing five "orders" of ministry, to replace the three tradition "orders" found in the Church of England, bishops, priests and deacons. First, when taken in conjunction with other lists of spiritual gifts, the passage would seem to

---

[1] Ephesians 4. 11-13

indicate examples of leadership gifts, a "for instance", rather than a definitive list. Further, it is questionable whether "apostles" are a permanent feature of church life; although the word is used in slightly different senses, normally it is taken to mean those foundational apostles, men who had personally known or been commissioned by Jesus.

But I want at this point to focus on the *purpose* of these ministries according to this passage: *"to prepare God's people for works of service, so that the body of Christ may be built up."*

(It is interesting to compare those words from the New International Version of the Bible, with those of the Authorized or King James Version: *"for the perfecting of the saints, for the work of the ministry, for the edifying of the body of Christ."* There it looks as if the three phrases are all in parallel, three different things that the pastors and teachers are meant to do: that it is they, the pastors and teachers, who are to (a) perfect the saints, (b) do the work of ministry, and (c) to edify the body of Christ. But that is wholly misleading – the comma after "saints" is particularly regrettable. What Paul is actually saying is that – in AV words – the saints are to be "perfected" *in order for them to be able to do* "the work of the ministry". The Greek prepositions make this clear, and this meaning is well expressed in the NIV translation.)

So this indicates a progression of purpose:

1. Jesus equips certain people with different leadership gifts.

2. This was in order for them to be able to lead, teach, prepare or train, God's people – the ordinary church members.

3. This training was to equip these church members to minister, or serve (as Peter wrote) in a wide, multi-coloured, variety of ways.

4. It is when everyone is ministering like this that the body of Christ, the church community, is built up – spiritually, morally, and numerically.

This is precisely how I have always seen the aim and purpose of my parish ministry – however imperfectly I have carried it out. There are many aspects of ministry: pastoral, evangelistic, administrative, teaching, leading of worship, strategic planning, vision, spiritual nurture, and many others. (These are not written in any order of priority.)

I do not pretend to have gifts in all these spheres myself, and I would guess that the clergy who do have such a wide portfolio of gifts are few indeed. But I do not believe it was ever my role, in the purpose of God, to try to do all these things myself. Some parish priests behave as if they do see this as their vocation; and the result is inevitable: half the things they take on they do rather badly, because they are simply not gifted in those spheres; they do not have time or energy left to develop and practise the things they *are* good at, and they work themselves into the ground, ending up on the verge of a breakdown. Moreover their church is not "edified" or built up, partly because nothing is being done properly, and partly because those in the congregation who are aware of the gifts they themselves have feel frustrated and under-used, because they do not have the opportunity to exercise them; and those many who have never discovered their gifts are left feeling that they have no contribution to make, no value except as "pew fodder". How sad! How totally contrary to what the Lord intends for his people!

So what will a church led according to the New Testament pattern look like? First, there will be a leadership team, with a mixture of ordained and "lay" people, men and women. How these leaders are to be selected, trained, and recognised is a matter for careful working out, and safeguards need to be built into any system. It is not ideal for each church to work out its own system, but preferable for there to be some recognised approach so that all "best practice" can be adopted. I would envisage a diocesan pattern being recommended, so long as this is not too rigid or tied up with red tape. Existing authority structures like the Parochial Church Council must be involved in the process and not by-passed; but existing leadership roles like churchwardens are not necessarily identical with the gifts needed for a leadership team.

Such a leadership team will meet regularly to discuss and to pray. Probably each member will have some particular area of responsibility, such as youth, music, and pastoral care. A particular church may develop specialised areas of ministry – such as services in old people's care homes, street evangelism among unchurched youth, ministry to the homeless or to local industry or to schools, or to those of other religions or cultures, etc., etc. – both according to the needs that are discerned locally, and according to the gifts of church members to develop and lead such ministry. When a new area of ministry begins to take off, perhaps it should be represented on the leadership team.

But there must also be arrangements for people to leave the team. Probably lay members' terms of office should be time-limited – too often in church life when someone takes on a job like leading Sunday School or the Mothers' Union it turns into a life sentence! But a further consideration is that if someone is found to be unsuitable in a particular role, there must be some means of terminating their membership, which may often be painful.

A second feature of a church seeking to follow New Testament principles of leadership is that it will be taken for granted that every single member of the church has a contribution to make, a spiritual gift which can be used by God to build up his church. Learning to discern and recognise such gifts is itself a valuable gift; very often a person may be totally unaware of their own gift, until someone else points it out to them. Part of the problem is that for generations people have been inculcated with a kind of bogus humility – "I'm nothing special, I'm just a miserable sinner, I'm not well educated, I'm no good at that sort of thing…" – whatever particular sort of thing is under consideration. Congregations need to be taught, regularly and constantly, that God has given them gifts, and values them.

Another aspect of the problem is that we tend to think in terms of filling vacancies rather than using gifts and abilities. We need someone to lead the children's work, or to edit the parish magazine; who on earth can we persuade to take it on? What is needed is a change of mind-set, so that our starting point is at the other end: here is someone with a particular gift – how can it be used to the glory of God? If God has given our church no one with the necessary gifts to lead Sunday School or to edit the parish magazine, then maybe this indicates that, sad though it may seem, that job is not God's priority for our church at this stage!

However one important principle which I believe we should set against this is a favourite saying of a great-uncle of mine: "if a thing is worth doing, it's worth doing badly!"[1] In other words, just because someone is not an expert, it doesn't mean they can't have a go. So often it is only by attempting a task, and making lots of mistakes, that a person starts to develop a very real gift that she has. But the gift of encouragement from other people is also needed, to carry her through those times of feeling a total failure when things don't go right.

The ordained man or woman (assuming there is only one in the team, which would not be so in larger churches) would have the primary responsibility of coordinating and leading the leadership team, and encouraging and developing the gifts of the entire church. He would probably be the person to develop the vision for the future direction of the church and to share it

---

[1] The phrase is generally attributed to G. K. Chesterton, in his book, "What's Wrong With The World?" published in 1910.

constantly with the whole church family. He is likely to be the primary leader of worship, but there would be others in this ministry. Some leaders have musical gifts, but others do not; but they would still value music of all sorts in the worship – traditional and contemporary, instrumental and choral, solo and congregational – and seek members to lead and develop this. Some leaders are good preachers, but others are not; and those clergy who recognise their own limitations in this vital work would encourage laymen and women who show signs of this gift, some of whom may go on to take Readership training and even move towards ordination.

Pastoral care, both of the congregation and of those beyond the active church membership, is vital; but this too is not solely the responsibility of the ordained priest, even though he or she is indeed responsible for ensuring that it is done. But "body ministry" involves virtually every church member caring for one another – learning to listen, to give time, and to pray sensitively for and with one another. This is of course a seven-day activity, but one way it will manifest itself will be on Sunday mornings in church. A congregation which is learning to do this will not just be chatting cheerfully about the weather before or after services; one would expect to see people sitting in pairs or threes around the church, as troubled people, grieving people, harassed people feel able to bring their burdens before their brothers and sisters, and perhaps pray together about them. In some cases it may indeed be right for the trained and ordained person to be involved, but not all.

Evangelism may happen in many ways, and should be happening in some. It will be found that a proportion of the congregation have this gift – not, probably, of preaching an evangelistic sermon, but of chatting to friends and neighbours about their faith, and perhaps bringing them to church activities – especially those which are particularly geared to explaining the faith to the seeker. In recent years Alpha courses have proved particularly valuable in this respect, and lay people are often as effective as clergy in organising and leading these; but of course these are by no means the only approach.

One vital aspect of using and developing gifts is training, and the ordained minister will ensure that there are frequent opportunities to receive it – though he may well delegate this to one of the leadership team who is designated Training Organiser. Such training may take many different forms, from one-off events in someone's home, to several-week courses in the church hall, to residential weekends away, or even nationally-certificated courses based on a university. Some will be laid on from the parish's own resources, others by the deanery, the diocese, or national organizations like Scripture Union or CPAS. But if someone is asked to take on some responsibility within the church, training opportunities should be offered and arrangements made, from baby-sitting to finance, to enable them to make use of it.

Such a church – whether in an affluent suburb, a run-down inner city estate, a country village or a "yuppie" area of a big city – will be welcoming, open to the community, rewarding and satisfying to those who are using their gifts and discovering their potential in it, and therefore it is likely it will also be growing. The ordained priest(s) will not be feeling run into the ground, but neither would they feel in any way surplus to requirements, any more than the manager of a football team would. There would of course be frustrations, disappointments, and even occasionally rows and disagreements; dealing with human beings is like that! But there would also be a sense of excitement and purpose, and of being part of God's mission in the world.

No church in which I have ministered has been quite like this! I have tried to move churches in this direction, and some have got further than others. I of course tend to blame the church members if I am getting frustrated because of what I perceive as their reluctance to move from their familiar patterns; but it was probably at least as much my own failure to share the vision vividly, and to put the necessary mechanisms in place to bring such changes about. Even more fundamental, perhaps, as a cause of failure is the failure of love. If people do not feel that their minister loves them, they are likely to see all his attempts to change the patterns of church life as merely arrogant and disruptive, and all his dissatisfaction with the existing, time-honoured forms of church life as criticisms of them, the church members, personally. You cannot bully or chivvy people into new ways of thinking; you can only lead them gently, one step at a time, into new experiences of God's love, dealing patiently with their fears and their misunderstandings.

The chemistry of the relationship between priest and people, between pastor and flock, is a complex one. A minister who has seen great blessing and what the world calls "success" in one parish, may experience nothing but failure, disappointment and frustration when he moves to another. In some cases this may indeed be because the members of the second church or community are resisting the Holy Spirit and refusing to believe or obey God's message. Several of the experiences and teachings of Jesus certainly indicate that this is a very real possibility. The parable of the sower, with the different kinds of soil representing differing degrees of responsiveness to the word of God, shows this, as does the experience of Jesus in his own home town where he was amazed at their unbelief.[1]

But the question the disciples asked Jesus when he said that one of them would betray him – "Lord, is it I?" – is one that every frustrated minister must ask when things do not go according to plan. Is it my failure to understand these people, their background, their history, and their culture that underlies my

---

[1] Mark 6. 1-6

inability to lead the church forward? Am I assuming that because a particular approach "worked" in one parish that it must therefore be equally effective in another place where certain conditions are very different – and is it mere insensitivity on my part to blame the people for their unbelief and unresponsiveness, when a greater understanding on my part might achieve more?

There is, however, another element to be considered, and that is the purpose of God. I am convinced that God has a plan, and particular timing, not only for each individual but also for each church. I wrote in an earlier chapter about my personal experience of faith: that I had heard the Christian message several times, but my time to respond was still in the future. The same thing is true of churches and parishes. The enthusiastic priest may be impatient for results, but God is not in a hurry. Perhaps my part in his plan is to sow rather than to reap; to lay foundations, rather than to see a fine, new building rising up. This thought was brought before me just at a moment when I needed it, when I was feeling particularly despondent over my failure in a parish where I had worked myself to exhaustion with apparently negligible results. I read a story in a magazine – I cannot remember what magazine, or even whether the story was a true one or apocryphal.

It concerned a missionary who worked for many years in a group of Pacific islands, but who never saw a single conversion. Despite all his faithful labours, travelling from island to island, the people seemed utterly impervious to his message. At length he fell ill, and in his final days he wrote in his diary, "All my work for the Lord in these islands has been a complete waste of time." Shortly after that he died, and the islanders buried him.

It was some years before the missionary society which had supported him was able to find a replacement for that area, but eventually a new missionary was sent. As he landed, he told the people who met him, "I have come to tell you about Jesus."

"Oh, yes," they responded, "We knew him; he used to live here!"

The new missionary was very puzzled, but the islanders led him through the village to the little hut where his predecessor had lived and died. It was untouched, and everything still lay just as it had been when the old man had died, even to the diary lying on the bedside table, still open at his last, despairing entry. The young missionary looked around, and then turned to his guides.

"No," he said, "this was not Jesus, who lived here; but I think it was a friend of his."

Some months later he wrote in his report to his society and his home supporters, "I have never known such responsiveness! Wherever I go, people seem hungry for the Gospel, and are turning to Jesus in faith in large numbers."

Sometimes God calls us to do a work of preparation, so that someone else can take things on to the next stage. This can seem a hard and unrewarding role, and such a minister may need a lot of support and encouragement from his superiors (which too often in the Church of England is not forthcoming). But the role is a vital one for God's plan, and must be faithfully fulfilled, even if it is hard to see any results.

For many clergy, the whole concept of "results" may be an alien one, even an irrelevance. They see their role as twofold: to maintain the pattern of services and sacraments, and to offer a pastoral, caring ministry to the people. So long as people are being baptised and brought to Holy Communion, and loved and cared for in all aspects of their daily life, that is all that matters. "Results" are God's business, not ours. Apart from anything else, in most cases we can't see the really important results, namely someone's growth in personal holiness, and very seldom is it our business to judge what our own contribution has been to any such growth that can be discerned.

In no way do I deride such a standpoint. If you see your role primarily in liturgical and pastoral terms, in conducting worship and ministering to individuals, to be uninterested in assessing results is perfectly logical and legitimate. My problem, perhaps, is that this is not how I have ever seen my ministry. Of course it must include these elements, but I am aware that pastoral gifts are not my strong suit. So often when I have found myself having to try to counsel someone at a time of crisis in their life, I have felt totally inadequate, and unable to give them the support they need, or to offer any words of wisdom to guide them. I can only hope that being there to listen, even if I have nothing helpful to say, has been of some use. (Indeed, probably more use than anything – too often we stop listening and start talking far too soon!)

But I also see my calling as including the following elements:

1. Evangelism. This means – by all and any legitimate means – to seek to lead people to find a personal faith in Jesus Christ, and to make their own response to his love. Inevitably I have to ask myself, "Is it working? Is anyone being converted? Is there a steady flow, or even just a trickle, of men and women, boys and girls, into the Kingdom of God?" If no such results can be discerned, of course I will have to consider why not: is it me, or my methods? Should we try a different approach? What is wrong?

2. Teaching. I am not referring to work in schools, though this can be included, but a steady programme of helping adults as well as children to understand the Christian faith. This should be a large element in sermons, from which I hope, over a period, that my hearers will become familiar with the Bible and what it tells us about God and about Christian living. Paul tells the elders of the church of Ephesus, "*I have not*

hesitated to proclaim to you the whole will of God."[1] I have found that most Anglican Christians are painfully ignorant about their faith; I want to help them not just to know the teaching of Scripture, but to be able to "think Christianly", to apply their faith and spiritual understanding to every aspect of life. Again, I must ask the question, is it working? Are people growing in understanding? Is there evidence of this?

3.   Christian nurture. This follows on from the previous element, and means building people up in their faith and in their relationship with God. That is what the teaching is for; it is not just for theological literacy. It includes learning to live out one's faith, both in personal morality and in relationships; in seeking and finding God's will for one's life; in learning to share one's faith with other people and tell one's own story of faith; in playing one's part in the fellowship of the Christian community, and discovering one's own gifts which can be used to help other people and serve God. I must ask: is this happening to people through their life as members of the church I lead?

4.   Worship. I am not up at the front of the church on Sunday mornings just to go through the words in the service book decently and reverently. I am there to lead worship, which means to bring people to a sense of the presence and the majesty of God, so that they are moved to respond to that majesty in adoration and praise. Every element of worship, including the words in the book, the music, the actions such as the sacraments, and the silences, are all directed to this end. So I must ask myself, are people just coming to

church and going through the service, or are they worshipping? Is there a sense of reverence, of joy, of exultation? Do people leave feeling that they have been brought closer to God – or just that it was a nice service?

5.   Prayer. Joining in the prayer offered in church services is perhaps the start – but it is a pity if it is also the finish! Yes, I must seek to ensure that prayer is led in church, whether by the ordained clergy or by lay people, thoughtfully and helpfully, covering (over a period, not all in one service!) all aspects of the life of the individual, the community, the church and the world, and bringing them before the Lord. But the believer should be discovering his own personal life of prayer, and there is a vast wealth of wisdom and experience in the Christian church to help people in this. The disciples said to Jesus, "Lord, teach us to pray!" They are still saying it, though perhaps they have given up saying it to their clergy, because too often they find no helpful answers. Are they being helped to pray through my ministry?

6.   The building up of the Church. All the above elements could be understood purely on an individual and personal level, and that level is indeed important. But it is the development of the Church as the Body of Christ, expressing his love, showing his reality and telling his message to the world, that is the focus here. The church is "we", not just an aggregation of isolated "I's". The local church has a corporate identity, and every individual believer is a part of it – as Paul expressed it, a limb of the body.[1] We need each other,

[1] I Corinthians 12. 12-27

we support each other, we encourage each other. We pray together, we worship together, we weep together, we laugh together. Together we seek to bring Christ's Gospel to our local community. We welcome seekers or new members into our fellowship. We are responsible for each other. We are our brothers' and sisters' keepers. Is this the direction in which my church is moving?

In all these ways, I cannot avoid looking for results. I cannot avoid the conviction that I am called to work towards all these ends: that this is my vocation as a priest, an elder in the church, a minister of the Gospel. While I am well aware that many of these things can be thought of in organic terms, as growing plants (Jesus often used such similes), and it doesn't help a plant to grow if you keep pulling it up to examine its roots, nevertheless a healthy plant *will* grow. That is the result that the gardener is looking for; and if growth cannot be seen, he will be concerned to find out the reason, and try to work out what can be done to help growth to resume.

It might be much more restful to stop asking these awkward questions, like "am I achieving anything? Is it working? Are people being converted, or growing in their faith? Is the church growing – spiritually as well as numerically?" It would be much easier just to plod along, getting on with my daily tasks, and saying, "I leave the results to God." But I feel that is not so much faith as complacency, and will lead not to progress but stagnation. Yes, of course the results in spiritual terms are indeed God's business: Paul wrote, "*I planted, Apollos watered, but God gave the growth.*"[1] But what farmer, after labouring to plant, or to water, does not look for growth?

---

[1] I Corinthians 3.6

If no growth is visible, what is the farmer – or to leave the metaphor, the minister – to do? Personally, I cannot just shrug, and ignore it! As I have mentioned above, there can be many reasons for such apparent fruitlessness, and they must all be considered. Moreover it is vital to consider the matter not only in a spirit of prayerfulness, bringing the problem before God – "Lord, is it I?" – but to share it with other Christians, both fellow-clergy and lay members of the church fellowship.

A possible reason for lack of results can be, and very often is, that we are failing to understand some aspect of the situation, so that the methods we are using are inappropriate. Where this is the case, deep and careful thinking, study and analysis are required. We have to consider the culture and assumptions of the people to whom we are ministering, because these things determine how they hear and understand what we say and do. Frequently clergy come from a cultural background quite different from that of the majority of their parishioners. This does not necessarily mean that they will never be able to communicate with or relate to them, and some people are extremely good at crossing enormous cultural divides. A priest from an upper-middle-class background, privately educated in Public School and Oxbridge, may find that he or she has no difficulty in relating to industrial or agricultural workers, urban unemployed youth, or the members of the wide variety of ethnic minorities found in modern Britain; but rather more often this facility does not come naturally, and he will have to work at it.

But as well as educational or social barriers, there can also be assumptions built into people brought up in a particular locality which are simply not recognised or understood by the clerical incomer. For example, the enormously influential Alpha Course has, as part of its recommended method, the custom of sharing a meal together. Alpha started life in West London, in a cultural milieu when giving and going to dinner parties is a familiar part of people's lives. But I discovered when I moved to the North West of England that that is alien to most people's experience there, and in the thirteen years in which I worked in that parish, my wife and I were invited to dinner in someone's home just four times – and two of our host couples were not local people but incomers like us. People in that area were far more likely, if they wanted to share a meal with friends, to go out to a hotel or a restaurant, or probably a pub. So to suggest that the way to make guests at an Alpha Course feel at home is to start by inviting them to dinner in a home is not necessarily going to work! The principle is sound – eating together engenders fellowship; but for a different culture it may need some modification and adaptation.

In this kind of issue, as in many others, the use of the gifts and insights of the team is vital. The ordained minister must learn to listen carefully to local people in the team. These may perhaps initially feel intimidated by his obviously greater education and academic intelligence, and so be reluctant to offer their opinions in case they appear stupid or ignorant; but if the minister is to benefit from their native wit and wisdom he must encourage them to believe that their contribution is of enormous value. His own attitude therefore is vital. If he is in any way condescending, or likely to take offence if criticised, a person who could share valuable suggestions or insights is likely to dry up. But if he is ready humbly to learn and to acknowledge his own limitations, the key to a new effectiveness in outreach is likely to emerge.

However the problem may not be cultural, but spiritual. What Jesus said about the towns in Galilee which rejected his message – *"Woe to you, Korazin! Woe to you, Bethsaida!"*[1] – can be equally true of modern communities, whatever their social or cultural level. I believe that this element is seldom recognised, and indeed it is not "politically correct" to suggest that if people are unresponsive to

---

[1] Luke 10.13

the Gospel, this may indeed be because they have deliberately turned their back upon God. Yet it was Jesus who warned, *"Do not give dogs what is sacred; do not throw your pearls to pigs."*[1] He can only have meant that there are some people who can be compared to dogs or pigs, unworthy to receive the Gospel message. A harsh judgement indeed! And certainly not one to be lightly adopted, just because someone, or some community, does not seem to be responding to my ministry. Every other possibility must be explored first, especially all those that seek the problem in the minister, rather than in those being ministered to. But equally it is foolish to dismiss such a possibility out of hand. If Jesus said those strong words – and, in the rather less stark terms of the Parable of the Sower, described hearers of the word of God as stony or weed-choked soil – we must accept that this diagnosis is a feasible one.

Spiritual barriers must also be considered. Here too I am walking on thin ice, liable to evoke ridicule or even outrage. But I believe that there is such a thing as spiritual resistance to the Gospel. This can take many forms. I heard of a church which had had a history of bitter divisions which had manifested themselves over different issues for several generations. More than one vicar had suffered a breakdown while ministering there, and the wife of another had suffered similarly. Finally a new vicar became convinced that the church was infected with some spiritual "virus" which needed radical treatment, and he called upon someone with experience in such matters. I know no details of what was done to diagnose the roots of the problem or to treat it, except that I gathered that some sort of spiritual deliverance ministry – what some would call exorcism – was used. Whatever steps were taken, that church at last turned a corner and seemed to have found healing for its poisonous divisiveness.

---

[1] Matthew 7.6

My own experience is less dramatic, but equally controversial. This concerns Freemasonry. This is a large topic which I cannot go into in depth at this point. Suffice it to say that I do not see the Craft, as its adherents call it, as merely a well-intentioned secret society with worthy objectives even if with some bizarre rituals. Traditionally there have been fairly strong links between Freemasonry and the Church of England, though the Roman Catholic Church and some of the Free Churches have been deeply suspicious of it. But in 1987 the General Synod of the Church of England did at last come out firmly in favour of the view that Anglicans should not be freemasons and that the Craft and the Church were not compatible. Most Masons I have met have been decent men, and these have even included at least one retired bishop for whom I had considerable respect; nevertheless I have become convinced that a strong strand of freemasonry within a local church is hostile to spiritual growth.

In one church where I ministered there was a group of half a dozen men who were freemasons, most of whom regularly attended the evening service. In my years in that parish we experienced a very considerable degree of growth and development. The congregation grew in numbers; the youth and children's work flourished; the musical life of the church went from strength to strength; more and more young families became involved with our fellowship and grew steadily in their faith. But all these developments concerned the morning service; on Sunday evenings church life seemed totally untouched and had no more life and freedom at the end of my years there than it had at the beginning. One of the older men who was a mason once said in my hearing, "My father always told me, 'Go to church regularly, but beware of getting too involved with religion'"! He was expressing his hostility to real spirituality, especially things like earnest prayer, the healing ministry, Bible study groups, and charismatic worship. All my attempts to bring some new life to

151

the evening service failed; there seemed to be a wall of resistance to everything I said and did. All they seemed to want was a regular routine of traditional services. Beyond that, the motto seemed to be, "Do not disturb". My own conviction was and is that this was linked with that group of freemasons and their wives who were the core of the evening congregation.

Experiencing failure, week after week, year after year, is exceedingly disheartening for the Christian minister, as it is in any other sphere. I heard of one Methodist minister who turned up on the doorstep of his Anglican parish priest one Monday morning, utterly distraught. "I had *one person* in the congregation last night! The Spirit of the Lord has left me!" Another minister in that inner-city area committed suicide. I myself, after some years labouring with seemingly little fruit in one parish, was put on anti-depressants by my doctor.

One aspect of this issue which I have experienced is the enormous difference it makes to get some "come-back" from the church members. In Chapter 16 I describe the difficulties I experienced in one parish where I served because of the total lack of response to anything I did in a service. I found this profoundly dispiriting.

Having said all this, it remains undoubtedly true that "results" of parish ministry are in God's hands, and that we can only discern a small proportion of them. It is gratifying to see congregational numbers rise; it is exciting to witness people being converted, or to recognise spiritual growth in individuals. It is encouraging when people say words of appreciation. Nevertheless, I am certain that this is all on the surface, and that it will not be until we are in glory with the Lord that we will discover the real fruits of our ministry and of our lives. I am certain there will be a lot of surprises on that day!

Clergy and buildings

In the previous chapter I mentioned the meetings held by the Revd. Basil Gough of St. Ebbe's in Oxford for those who were wondering about ordained ministry. I recall once Basil telling us that sometimes, when a parish minister is finding building the church of God too demanding and discouraging, he can start to divert his attention to bricks and mortar buildings instead. "If you find a vicar whose main preoccupation seems to be building projects," he said, "beware! He is a man who has lost his vision!"

After forty years of parish ministry I might suggest that that judgement is perhaps a little harsh; but it is an insight not to be wholly dismissed. I have had times when a great deal of my attention and time has seemed to be focussed on material matters, whether church buildings themselves, or the furnishings of them; a new organ, or a proposed reordering scheme, or an extension. In one instance I specifically rejected a possible call to a particular parish largely because I was told that the previous vicar had done marvellous work in seeing through a massive building renewal project, including finding grants and other sources of funding to cover the huge costs, but – I was warned – there was still a great deal to be done before the building would be fully restored. No, I said to myself; God did not call me into the ministry to oversee work with stone, mortar and stained glass, but with living stones to make a temple to the Lord.[1] I knew another vicar whose church building was found to need astronomical sums spent on it to make the roof and huge spire safe. It was a Victorian building – quite a local landmark – which could seat some six hundred people, but which had a congregation of about thirty. Even after the proposed vast sums had been spent – supposing they could be found – the building would not have been altered, developed or improved in any way to make it more fitted for the mission of the

---

[1] I Peter 2.5

church; it was simply a matter of making it safe and weathertight. The vicar was convinced that it would be a totally wrong use of time and money, and that the congregation should move into the fine hall across the road, and convert that into a suitable worship centre – much as we had done in St. Stephen's, Walthamstow, thirty years earlier. The PCC had several stormy debates on the matter, and in the end the majority voted against the vicar – they insisted that their beloved old building must be preserved. So the Vicar said, "OK; if that is your choice, count me out. I am not prepared to preside over such a project for years to come. I will tell the Bishop I want to move."

I have mentioned before that though the word "church" has come to be almost wholly associated in the popular mind – even the mind of worshipping Christians – with buildings, and in most cases old, solid, historic buildings, the Greek word ecclesia (εκκλησια) has no such connotations, but means assembly or congregation; the use of the word in the Greek version of the Old Testament tended to refer to the pilgrim people of God on the move to the promised land. (It is a great pity that the first translators of the scriptures into English chose the word "church" to translate ecclesia.)

The New Testament church of course had no buildings. They were people who gathered where they could, in a hired hall, or someone's home ("the church in your house"[1]) or even in the open air, such as by the riverside. It was not really until the time of Constantine in the 4th Century, when Christianity became the authorised religion of the Empire and therefore safe, that they started to feel they should have their own buildings.

In the 20th and 21st Centuries certain church movements like the Vineyard churches have reverted to the early pattern, and they are often known as "house churches" for that reason. Even if

---

[1] Philemon 2

a residence is not big enough to hold all those who want to come to a meeting for worship, they will hire a hall of some kind. This of course saves enormous costs in maintenance, heating, insurance and so on, so that the giving and focus of the members, once the rent is paid, can be directed to more positive mission projects.

So often the historic churches, however, find themselves in the position where their building is a ball and chain around the ankle of the Body of Christ, stopping them doing anything except maintaining it. Some congregations, who have picked up a vision for mission, and for worship which really involves the whole body rather than a spectator sport led entirely from the front, chafe at this, and sometimes are able to take radical action to be set free from this huge historic impediment. But all too often they love it as it is (like the church mentioned above) and simply cannot see what the problem is. Such a church, instead of being the Body of Christ, obeying the Lord who said *"Go and make disciples"*[1], has degenerated into a Society for the Preservation of Ancient Monuments.

There is an interesting Old Testament parallel to this. The Book of Numbers tells of an episode in the wanderings of the people of Israel when as a judgement of God they were attacked by a plague of poisonous snakes, but Moses was instructed to make a bronze snake and set it up on a pole; if anyone bitten by a snake looked to the bronze snake, he would be saved.[2] (Jesus applied the story to himself, and his crucifixion.[3]) The second Book of Kings tells us what became of that famous bronze sculpture: it was deeply valued as a sacred relic, to the extent that it was worshipped as an idol. King Hezekiah – one of the few kings who *"did what was right in the eyes of the Lord"*, was

---

[1] Matthew 28.19
[2] Numbers 21.5-9
[3] John 3.14,15

uncompromising about this idolatry, and smashed this six-hundred-year-old sacred relic[1]. One can imagine the shrieks of horror and outrage, the "Protect Our Snake" marches and demonstrations! This snake, remember, had been made in obedience to God's direct command; it had been a sacred vehicle of God's healing and salvation. It was even a foreshadowing of the Messiah! But it had become an idol, a substitute for God. It must be destroyed! Of how many ancient sacred buildings could this be true?

The question has to be faced: what is a church building? Some would say it is merely a shelter to keep us warm and dry while we worship. Others would maintain that it is very much more than that: it is a kind of sacrament, "an outward and visible sign of an inward and spiritual reality". They would point to the many people, who have no apparent membership of or allegiance to the worshipping people of God, but who like to visit a church, who want to be married in a church and hope for their funeral to be in a church. That building speaks to them of realities beyond the worldly and trivial; the old purpose of a church spire, to be a finger pointing people to God, has a validity not to be despised. I would accept these assertions.

As so often, it is a matter of balance. One must recognise the very real danger of the building being an idol, or a ball and chain to hold us back in our obedience to Christ and his mission. But in so far as the building we use is a real vehicle of the message, a visual aid to help people to find God, then we must find the time and the funds to maintain it. If it has no positive spiritual value, but is a hindrance to the work of the Mission of Christ, then, if the local community or the nation – or English Heritage or the Historic Churches Preservation Trust – feel it must be maintained, then they must find the funds for this. The worshipping

---

[1] II Kings 18.4

community must resist pressure to turn from their God-given mission.

What of clergy spending a large proportion of their time and imagination on building projects? I suggest that there are two major factors which indicate whether this is right or wrong.

1. Is the proposed project something which, when complete, will positively help the mission and fellowship of the church? Will it be an aid to preaching the Gospel? A new hall or suite of meeting rooms in which the people can meet, learn, have fellowship, and offer services to their community, might well fulfil this criterion. Alterations to the church interior and its furnishings, to allow for greater flexibility, visibility of worship, a sense of family fellowship, facilities for refreshments, are all features which could be absolutely valid. I would regard major projects for organs or stained glass windows as more questionable.

2. Is the vicar the right person to be leading the project? Is that his God-given ministry? Even if he is the one who has the vision and imagination so see what is needed, is there not some other person or team who can do the hugely time-consuming work of researching grants, conducting planning meetings, interviewing architects and so on? A vicar who finds himself spending many hours on such issues must ask himself honestly whether it is an escape from the pastoral and spiritual tasks to which God called him.

However I have known clergy with the opposite attitude: they say "the church building is the responsibility of the churchwardens, not me! I will have nothing to do with any decisions about it." Legally there is some validity to this view – the incumbent is only responsible for the chancel. However such an approach totally ignores the fact that the building is the church's "shop window". As soon as a person enters the door, the building speaks to them. The medium is the message. It can convey a message of loving care, or of neglect. It can say that God is deeply important, or that he does not matter very much. Dirty windows, or heaps of clutter; old magazines or service sheets from events weeks ago, moth-eaten kneelers.... All these things say, loud and clear, that no one cares very much. It speaks of decline and decay. This church once, perhaps, was important, but not any more. Christianity represents the ancient past; it has nothing to do with the living present.

The spiritual leader of that church simply cannot say, "Not my business!" No, it is not his business to spend his time cleaning the windows or repairing the hassocks, but he must care strongly that such things should be done, if his message of a Living God and a contemporary Gospel is not to be fatally undermined by the surroundings in which he is hoping to proclaim them. In exactly the same way, if the children whom the minister is seeking to introduce into church life encounter aged, musty books or pictures, or Victorian imagery and second- or third-rate equipment, which compares horribly unfavourably with what they meet at their bright, modern school, what message do they imbibe about the value of Jesus Christ?

There can be enormous impediments to rendering an old building serviceable for the modern age. I heard of a parish church (was it in Stratford upon Avon?) which, after lengthy and complex discussions and negotiations, had at last decided to strip out all the pews and replace them with comfortable chairs, flexible enough to allow the building to be used not only for Sunday worship but for music and drama and all sorts of other community events, and the membership was excited about their church's future ministry to the community in these ways. At the last minute it was discovered that two of the pews were, for ancient, historical reasons, the legal possession of two families in the town – families from which no member had ever in living memory attended worship. But these families adamantly refused to allow "their" pew to be moved! The entire scheme came to a grinding halt.

However I heard of another ancient church with uncomfortable and very inconvenient, but incredibly old and precious pews, which on no account – the new Vicar was told - could be moved. A couple of years later, a friend from college came to visit that vicar, and was shown round the church, which now was warmly carpeted and furnished with modern chairs. "How on earth did you manage that?" gasped the visitor. "Prayer!" answered his friend. "We prayed hard – and dry rot swept through the whole building, and all the pews had to be removed and burnt!"

Perhaps there is really a role for that fictional official, the Diocesan Arsonist!

10

❧❧❧❧

The Problem and Privilege of Baptism

Some might object that I mention "problem" before "privilege" in this title; I only plead that that was the order in which I first encountered the issue! Even after my initial confusion about baptism while I was at Oxford, controversies and disagreements continued to surround the subject at Theological College and throughout my parish ministry. So even though I came to value my own Christian baptism as a privilege, and I still count it as a privilege to have been able to minister to candidates for baptism and their families in all the parishes in which I have served, the problematical areas have never been far away.

Not long after my conversion, the issue arose that was to bother me for quite some time. As I have mentioned, the OICCU was an inter-denominational body, and quite a number of the members were Baptists, members of the Brethren or Pentecostalists, all of which fellowships do not believe in the baptism of infants; they were and are convinced that Scripture teaches that baptism in water must follow conversion. It is a sign and a witness to the personal faith of the person being baptized; to "christen" a baby, therefore, who can have no faith, is mere superstition and is not baptism at all. Furthermore true baptism,

161

they insist, must involve total immersion in water, not a mere sprinkling.

I cannot remember how I first encountered this point of view, but it began to trouble me. I had been baptized as a baby, as are most Church of England members (and Roman Catholics, Orthodox, Methodists, Presbyterians, Lutherans, and indeed members of most Christian denominations). I had then been confirmed in my teens, in the traditional Anglican way. But now I had been converted; if my Baptist friends were right, my pre-conversion ceremonies of baptism and confirmation were meaningless, and I must be prepared to undergo the total immersion of Believer's Baptism. I was very reluctant to do this, not at this stage for any reasons of theological conviction, but because it seemed to be such a total repudiation of the faith and practice of the church in which I had grown up, and which (at St. Ebbe's) I was still attending, in common with large numbers of faithful OICCU members, who surely were sound evangelical believers. Besides this, a powerful disincentive for such action was another consideration: what would my family think? And yet, if Scripture really did teach what the Baptists said it did, obedience dictated that I must submit.

There were many long discussions about the issue, and various books and leaflets were pored over. David Fletcher, the theological student who had so often helped and encouraged me, tried to allay my misgivings about the legitimacy of infant baptism.

What were the arguments? First, on the Baptist side, it was pointed out that on the Day of Pentecost, Peter said to the crowds who heard his Spirit-empowered sermon, "Repent and be baptized." This was the invariable pattern throughout the Book of Acts; people heard the Gospel, responded to it, and then were baptized. As for total immersion, they point out that the very word "Baptize" is the English form of the Greek word "Baptizo", (βαπτιζω), which actually means immerse or submerge; and when

Paul writes about baptism he compares it with death, burial and resurrection:

"We were therefore buried with him [Christ] through baptism into death, in order that, just as Christ was raised from the dead through the glory of the Father, we too may live a new life."[1]

This is vividly expressed by someone going down into the water, having it closing over his head, and then bursting up out of the water again as if rising from the dead to new life.

Furthermore, they challenge, is there a single instance in the New Testament of a baby being baptized? No, of course not; all the people whose baptism is mentioned were adult believers. Moreover the Anglican Church seems to teach that so long as you have been baptized – even in a ceremony involving totally unbelieving parents, who just want it for their child for traditional or superstitious reasons – you are all right; you are then a Christian, and will go to heaven. What true Bible-believer could go along with that?

This all seemed to me at first to present a virtually irrefutable argument. But then I began to learn that it wasn't quite as cut-and-dried as it seemed.

1.   The Greek word "baptizo" actually has the connotation of being immersed, and not emerging again but *staying* immersed; the word which would be used for dipping into the water and coming up again, like a ship plunging through waves, is a different though related word, "bapto" (βαπτω). So the thrust of "Baptizo" is not about how much water is used, but about being immersed into Christ.

2.   There were many evangelical Anglicans who did *not* remotely believe that if you were baptized, you were

automatically a Christian and would go to heaven; and probably very few Anglicans, even of a non-evangelical tradition, did actually believe that in quite that way. It was a distortion of Anglican faith.

3. Regarding instances of baptism of babies in the Bible:

    a.   There are instances of baptism of whole families; the Philippian gaoler was one (*"Immediately he and all his family were baptized"*[1]), and Lydia was another (*"She and the members of her household were baptized"*[2]). It does not specifically say that these families included children, but they easily might have done. Moreover it does not specify that each member of the family or household, without exception, had actually made a personal response of faith; the way it is worded seems to imply that they were baptized as a communal, family act.

    b.   If Anglicans cannot point to an unmistakeable instance of an infant baptism, neither can the Baptist point to an example of someone born into a Christian family, brought up in that family as a member of the church, but not baptized until he was an adult believer. By the nature of it, the New Testament is describing a first generation church; you cannot expect to find practices that would emerge in the next generation of believers.

    c.   Certainly the practice of baptizing the infants of believers was the norm by very early in the

---

[1] Acts 16.33
[2] Acts 16.15

2nd Century, a generation or two after New Testament times.

4.   All the very earliest Christians were Jews, who were accustomed to the practice of circumcision of 8-day-old baby boys; this was understood as an initiation into the community of the People of God. So when on the Day of Pentecost Peter – a Jew – immediately after saying *"Repent and be baptized"*, said to the Jewish audience, *"The promise is for you and your children"*, it was quite certain that his hearers would have understood this to mean that they and their children – *as children*, not later when they were grown up and old enough to believe for themselves – were being offered baptism, and promised the forgiveness of their sins and the gift of the Holy Spirit.

5.   Paul actually makes the comparison between circumcision and baptism, which would seem to support this: *"In him [Christ] you were also circumcised, in the putting off of the sinful nature, not with the circumcision done by the hands of men but with the circumcision done by Christ, having been buried with him in baptism..."*[1] He is not of course emphasising the age at which it happens, but mentioning baptism and circumcision in the same breath would convey to the hearer – especially the Jewish hearer - that they were comparable rites.

6.   Jesus gave the command to baptize: *"Go and make disciples of all nations, baptizing them in* (literally, *into) the name of the Father and of the Son and of the Holy Spirit, and teaching them to obey everything I have commanded you."*[2] He too was a Jew, and was talking to a group of Jewish

---

[1] Colossians 2.11,12
[2] Matthew 28.19,20

disciples: he was telling them how to initiate new believers into the new People of God, with a new relationship with, and revelation of, God in all his fullness – Father, Son and Holy Spirit. It would have been quite inconceivable, shocking and bewildering to them if he had meant that this *excluded* little children; indeed if he had meant that, he would have had to say so, as they would naturally have taken for granted that the privileges of children under the New Covenant could not possibly be less than they were under the Old.

Such were the arguments that gradually persuaded me that it was not illegitimate or unbiblical to baptize the children of believers. "Believe and be baptized:" yes, indeed; *I* believed, and *I* had been baptized, even if not in that order. God is perfectly capable of varying the order of events in people's lives. After all, though the order of events for those converted through Peter's sermon was (a) believe, (b) be baptized, and (c) be filled with the Spirit, a few chapters later on we find a different order in the case of the Roman centurion Cornelius and his household: for them it was (a) believe, (b) be filled with the Spirit, and (c) be baptized.[1]

Paul wrote, "*When we were still powerless, Christ died for the ungodly… While we were still sinners, Christ died for us.*"[2] It seems to me eminently appropriate that when I was a helpless infant, long before I was capable of understanding or appreciating it, the symbol of the salvation won for me by Jesus was applied to my head. Twenty-one years later, I entered into that salvation whose sign I had much earlier received.

Convinced by these arguments, I decided I did not need to undergo a new baptism. Nevertheless I (in company with many

---

[1] Acts 10.44-48
[2] Romans 5.6,8

young Anglicans both at Oxford and later at Theological College) was still sometimes uncomfortable with the language used in the Prayer Book, which almost seemed to imply a doctrine that it was the sacrament of baptism itself which brings salvation, forgiveness and new birth. For example, in a prayer before the actual baptism we ask "that he, coming to thy holy baptism, may receive remission of his sins by spiritual regeneration..." After the infant has been baptized, the Priest says, "Seeing now, dearly beloved brethren, that this child is regenerate, and grafted into the body of Christ's Church..." As a good evangelical, believing firmly that we receive salvation not through an outward ceremony, however sacred, but through personally receiving Christ by faith, I winced when I heard (or, after ordination, had to speak) such statements!

Eventually I found a way of resolving this. First of all I read in the New Testament about Paul's attitude towards the sacrament of initiation into the Old Testament people of God, namely circumcision. He wrote this:

> *"Circumcision has value if you observe the law, but if you break the law you have become as though you had not been circumcised. If those who are not circumcised keep the law's requirements, will they not be regarded as though they were circumcised? The one who is not circumcised physically and yet obeys the law will condemn you who, even though you have the written code and circumcision, are a law-breaker.*
>
> *A man is not a Jew if he is only one outwardly, nor is circumcision merely outward and physical. No, a man is a Jew if he is one inwardly; and circumcision is circumcision of the heart, by the Spirit, not by the written code. "*[1]

Paul is writing about Jews and Gentiles, in a context where Jews were apt to dismiss the "uncircumcised", i.e. the non-Jews,

---

[1] Romans 2.25-29

the Gentiles, as totally rejected by God. Not so, insists Paul; the sacrament of circumcision, without true obedience of the heart, is empty. Note the actual points he makes:

1. The sacrament, without obedience, is nullified.
2. Obedience, without the sacrament, is accepted by God.
3. The sacrament is only valid if accompanied by obedience.

Let's re-write Paul's words, translating the concepts into the issue of Baptism and Christian faith:

Baptism has value if you have faith in Jesus; but if you have no faith, you have become as though you had not been baptized. If those who are not baptized have faith in Jesus, will they not be regarded as though they were baptized? The one who is not baptized physically and yet trusts in Jesus will condemn the person who, even though he has been baptized, has no faith in Jesus.

A man is not a Christian if he is only one outwardly, nor is baptism merely outward and physical or ceremonial. No, a man is a Christian if he is one inwardly; and baptism is baptism of the heart, by the Spirit, not by mere ceremony.

No, that was not what Paul wrote; but surely it is wholly consistent with what he did write. In a setting where most Jews would have regarded such words about circumcision almost as blasphemous, he dared to say that it is the heart, and the attitude towards God, not the undergoing of a sacred ceremony, which counts with God.

When writing about baptism, Paul uses language just as strong and categorical as the language of the Prayer Book: "*We were buried with him through baptism*"[1] "*All of you who were baptized into Christ have put on Christ.*"[2] I might have wanted to hedge it around with

---

[1] Romans 6.3
[2] Galatians 3.27

ifs and buts: "*IF* the person being baptized is truly a believer in Jesus..." But the language Paul uses assumes that that is the case; and making this assumption, he dares to link the blessing obtained strongly to the sacrament that expresses it or conveys it.

In later years I often liked to use a particular illustration when preaching about baptism, namely that of a cheque. If I give you a cheque for £500, I could truthfully say I have actually given you £500; but from one point of view it is only a piece of paper that I have given you. You can't eat it; you can't wrap it around you to keep you warm and dry, or even decent; you could burn it, but the fire engendered would not afford you much warmth! Nevertheless £500 could buy a lot of food, several garments, or a fair amount of heating energy to warm your house. But in order for it to bring you those benefits you have to take action: you must go to the bank, present the cheque, and thus claim the money, which will then come from my account.

Two other aspects of the cheque illustration convey helpful truths. My cheque will have your name on it, because it is to you personally that I want to give the money. Similarly in baptism the candidate is addressed, personally, by name. God is wanting to give that particular person, whether child or adult, all the blessings associated with baptism, namely forgiveness of all sin, past, present and future, because of the death of Jesus on the cross; acceptance as a child of God, and thus a welcome into the family of God; a personal relationship with Jesus; the fullness of the Holy Spirit; and eternal life, both here and now, and in Heaven. So these amazing gifts are given to him as he is addressed by his name.

(Let me correct a widespread but false impression. I have often heard people say, "I was christened John", or "she was baptized Alice Henrietta." I have baptized many people, both infants and older people, and I have never said to anyone, "I baptize you John!" or "I baptize you Alice!" What I do say is: "John, I baptize you in the name of the Father and of the Son and Holy Spirit." In the Prayer Book service, the minister says to the godparents, "Name this child." So the godparents name the child. In the modern service it is assumed that the vicar has probably met the family, and knows what the child's name is – even if he may need to be reminded, especially if there are several infants awaiting his ministrations, and he is at risk of getting them confused! Either way, when he has been told the name which has been given by the family, the minister then addresses the child by name, and says, "John, I baptize you..." So let's stop using that phrase, "he was baptized John", as if what baptism is really about is giving the child its name. It's not! Mind you, I recall attending a service of baptism in a neighbouring parish, because I was waiting till I could prepare some visual aids there for a St. George's Day Parade Service later in the day. I was dismayed to hear the vicar assuring the congregation of parents and godparents that what this ceremony was all about was giving their child a Christian name... So if even some clergy are so ignorant, no wonder many lay people get it wrong!)

There is another name on the cheque, and that is the signature of the person giving the money. The value of the cheque depends wholly on that name. If I wrote you a cheque for one million pounds, it would be worthless – in the cliché, not worth the paper it was written on, because I do not have a million pounds, and so I cannot give it to you. Putting it another way, I am not worth a million pounds. But if Richard Branson or Bill Gates wrote you a cheque for one million pounds, and signed it, you would have a right to feel quite excited – because they have such funds available. The promises contained in baptism depend not on the worth of the minister, or of the church that he represents; they depend on God himself, for it is Almighty God who is signing this cheque!

So God really does want this particular person to have eternal life; and in baptism he is saying so in a vivid ceremony. While a child is too young to understand, to accept and believe in the gift and the Giver, or to reject and disbelieve, we can be completely confident that God's love and good will and purpose for him are an assurance that those gifts truly belong to our child. If, tragically, the baby dies before reaching an age where he is capable of faith, we can still be totally sure that he is saved and with Jesus.

This is true *whether the child has been baptized or not!* The mediaeval church had developed a dreadful doctrine that babies who died unbaptized could not go to heaven; they had never sinned, so would not go to hell either. Another notional state was therefore invented for them, called Limbo. There is, of course, not the slightest hint of such a doctrine in the Bible. Indeed Jesus said precisely the opposite: he took children in his arms, and said, "*The kingdom of heaven belongs to such as these!*" These babies he was talking about and cuddling were Jewish babies; they had not been baptized, and he didn't baptize them. He just declared that the kingdom of heaven belonged to them! If that was his attitude and his declaration, that's good enough for me, and should be good enough for any believer in Jesus.

Over the years I have met parents who have apparently been infected with something like this terrible, unchristian "limbo" doctrine, and so have a horrible, nagging suspicion that if their beloved child is not baptized, something terrible will happen to her; and that if the worst happens and she dies, she will not – or perhaps just *may not* – go to heaven. So of course she must be baptized – just in case! Often I have found that none of my assurances to the contrary make any impact on this deep-seated fear.

But if, as the words of Jesus tell us, the child is saved whether it is baptized or not – simply because it is loved by God and by Jesus – then, you may ask, why bother to have it baptized at all? That is a perfectly fair and legitimate question. My answer is twofold: First, because I am convinced that God *does* love my child, and *wants* him to have all the blessings of eternal life, it seems to me to be very appropriate to say so, not just in words but in a vivid ceremony. I love my child; and I may say so. But I will also show it, by kissing and cuddling him! I see baptism as God giving my child a kiss – a tangible sign and token of his love.

Secondly, baptism is not just a sign of the candidate's individual and personal salvation, it is also a sign of his being welcomed into the community of the people of Jesus, the Church. I want my child to grow up always knowing that he belongs; he is a member of the Christian family. Maybe one day he will reject this, and move out of the family; I will be sad at this, but he must ultimately decide for himself. But until he decides not to belong, he *does* belong – and baptism conveys this belonging.

The trouble with the Baptist position, of deferring the baptism of the child of a Christian couple until he has professed the faith for himself, is that it seems to be saying to that child, "We hope very much that you will one day decided to follow Jesus; but until you do, you are not really part of this church family. You are welcome to attend our gatherings, of course, but I'm afraid you don't really belong!" Of course no Baptist would say such a thing to a child in so many words – but they can only avoid that implication by removing from their understanding of baptism anything to do with church membership. Sometimes when I have witnessed a baptism in a Baptist church, or a believer's baptism elsewhere like a river or the sea, I am left feeling that there was never any hint that the person was being baptized *into* anything! It is reduced to nothing but an act of witness to a personal faith. It is that, of course; but Scripture has a far richer doctrine of baptism than merely as an act of witness.

"Please will you christen our baby?"

This is another problem area! There are three main pastoral situations where a vicar encounters the non-churchgoer: these are baptisms, marriages and funerals, the technical term for which is "occasional offices". All three give great opportunities for meeting people with Christian love at important moments of their lives; but I have found that it is baptism, above all, which affords the opening for talking to people directly about God, and helping them to engage with the Gospel.

The statistics of infant baptism in the Church of England go down year by year, but it remains the case that large numbers of people express their residual religious faith by asking for their children to be baptized. Different clergy respond to this in very different ways.

Some have the "hosepipe" position – spray the water around as widely as possible, as a sign of the totally unconditional love of God. There is some validity in this position of course, but it tends to remove any element of challenge. Moreover it implies that the words spoken by the parents and godparents in the Anglican service are almost denuded of meaning or truth.

The president then says to the parents and godparents

Parents and godparents, the Church receives *these children* with joy. Today we are trusting God for *their* growth in faith Will you pray for *them*, draw *them* by your example into the community of faith and walk with *them* in the way of Christ?
Parents and Godparents **With the help of God, we will.**

In baptism *these children* begin *their* journey in faith. You speak for *them* today. Will you care for *them*, and help *them* to take *their* place within the life and worship of Christ's Church?
Parents and Godparents **With the help of God, we will.**

A little later comes this bit of dialogue:

Do you turn to Christ as Saviour?
Parents and Godparents **I turn to Christ.**

Do you submit to Christ as Lord?

> *Parents and Godparents*   **I submit to Christ.**
>
> Do you come to Christ, the way, the truth and the life?
> *Parents and Godparents*   **I come to Christ.**

The vicar who accepts all comers indiscriminately, without challenging the parents to ask themselves if they truly mean these words they are saying, implies that the words can be spoken casually, simply because they are the script before them on the service card, without any serious intention of even considering whether they are understood or spoken with sincerity. To be consistent, such a vicar should simply omit these words of promise, faith and commitment, and go straight on to the business with the water.

It is true that God loves these people, and their baby, irrespective of their faith and response. But it is not true that he doesn't care whether they respond or not. Nor does the indiscriminate position do the slightest justice to what the New Testament actually says about the meaning and significance of baptism, with all its connotations of commitment, discipleship, faith and membership of the community of believers.

The opposite position is that of the rigorist, who refuses to baptize any baby until at least one of the parents has been attending church regularly for a specified period; some go further and insist that at least one of the parents, and perhaps all the godparents, must be confirmed church members and regular communicants. There is a consistency in this; the promises about "turning to Christ" are identical to those spoken at a Confirmation, and it is logical to maintain that if a parent or godparent can truthfully say them at a child's baptism, they can also say them when they themselves are being confirmed. This point of view puts the emphasis on baptism as a sacrament of membership; if there is no evident intention to bring up the child as a participating member, then baptism should be deferred until such intention can be detected.

I have a good deal of sympathy with the theology of this position. The problem is that it is pastorally disastrous. People who are totally unfamiliar with church and the language of liturgy, and who have no idea at all what Christian faith and commitment mean, simply hear this response as a rejection. However gently, clearly and lovingly the rigorist vicar tries to explain, the bottom line is, "So you won't baptize my baby?" Frequently such parents have a long history of feeling rejected by those in positions of power and authority. They are so often made to feel inferior, ignorant and inadequate. Now it's happened again. The Church says we're not good enough, and has turned our baby away.

Somehow, despite the logical consistency of the rigorist position, it doesn't feel very like the attitude of Jesus to the outsiders, or to little children. Its result in a community is to leave a lot of hurt, bitterness and anger; often it is other neighbouring clergy who have to try to pick up the pieces. A rigorist vicar can sometimes point to people for whom the policy has "worked", because they have been made to face the challenge of the Gospel, and as a result have been brought to a living and committed faith. But often the other side of the "result", the legacy of hurt and rejection, they do not see, because those people won't come back.

I have always been so aware that in my parish ministry I have been spending most of my time like a salesman of some deeply unpopular product; people generally are not interested in the Gospel, or the Church, or God. But then when they have a baby they actually turn up on my doorstep wanting my ministrations; am I to turn them away?

So I have taken an intermediate position between the indiscriminate and the rigorist ones. I have always taken a good deal of trouble to explain to parents what baptism actually means and so I would arrange to spend an evening with them. We have together looked through the words they will have to say in the service, and tried to unpack what they imply. I have done my best to make it absolutely clear how much Jesus loves their baby, whether he's baptized or not. I have usually offered them an alternative, a service of thanksgiving and blessing, if they perhaps feel that it would not be honest for them to speak these strong promises of faith and commitment to Christ and to church membership. And then I have left it to them to decide and to choose. I cannot read their heart; I am well aware that people's faith, and their ability to articulate their faith, are two very different things. So it is not up to me to judge whether they can sincerely make the promises. That is between them and God.

The trouble is that, so often, they are sure that they already know what baptism means, and so all my earnest words fall on deaf ears. I would say these things, wouldn't I? I'm trying to get them to go to church – that's my job. But as far as they are concerned, baptism is nothing to do with going to church. Going to church is fine for those who like that sort of thing, but "we're not the type". But to suggest that we might decide *not* to have Susie christened, and to have some kind of second-rate alternative? There's nothing second-rate about our Susie, so thank you, but no, thank you! Proper christening is what we want.

So a date is fixed, and I will do my very best to make sure that the baptism service is a wholly positive experience. It will always be a service when the regular congregation is present, preferably including the children, not a hole-in-the-corner affair in the middle of the afternoon; for I do not see how we can welcome someone into the Lord's family if the Lord's family are not there! I often ask them to choose a hymn, so that they will know at least one hymn in the service – but I will also try to choose other hymns that are suitable and familiar. I will chat to the family and greet the baby when they arrive. I will try to ensure that they are near the front so that they can see what is happening, but not at the very front – it is important that there are regular worshippers sitting in front of them, to show them when to stand up or sit down. It is very embarrassing for them if they are occupying the front pews, and suddenly realise that everyone is standing up except them! I will explain what is happening, and give out page numbers. I will try to get the right balance between light-hearted friendliness and humour, and a due solemnity appropriate for such a great moment in their baby's life. I will ensure that the card they are given to commemorate the event is a quality production, and not one with a sentimental style of "Jesus among the bunny-rabbits" reminiscent of a Victorian Sunday School.

And then I have to leave the results with God, both for the infant and for the rest of the family and friends. Sometimes I am privileged to learn that the whole experience has touched someone's heart and drawn them closer to God; much more often I just never know. The old illustration of "sowing seeds" applies; it is up to God to make them grow.

I have had some comic experiences of baptism in my time. In St. Mary's, Walthamstow, where I was merely a junior curate and so had no control over baptism policy, we still had a mid-afternoon service with no one there but the baptism families, and often five or six babies to be baptized. On one occasion there was a large crowd, and the usual hubbub. I managed to baptize all six babies, and after everyone had gone I went in to the Vestry to sign the Register. There were only five names in the book; I have no idea who the sixth baby was. Obviously one family had said to a friend, "Why don't you bring along your Jason to be done too?"

In St. Stephen's, Walthamstow, where I was curate-in-charge, we had a wooden font with a lid; the water was in the Tupperware bowl inside. We always warmed the water before the service, to avoid startling the baby with an icy douche; but on one occasion when I removed the wooden lid, steam belched forth – the water was still quite hot. I called to dear Sister Neate, our Church Army Sister, to bring some cold water to cool it down, and she appeared a few moments later with a tiny cream jug of water. After adding that, I tested the temperature, but judged it still too hot for infant skin, so more cold water was requested. By this time the congregation was helpless with laughter – one person said she expected me at any moment to dip my elbow in to test the temperature! (Why *do* people traditionally dip their elbow into a baby's bath water?)

In Walthamstow I think all the families tended to patronise the same shop for christening clothes, and this establishment seemed to specialise in white, quilted nylon coats. These garments looked quite cute, but had one disadvantage; you picked the child up, and the coat was so slippery that the infant was liable to slither straight out, leaving the startled vicar with an empty garment. It never actually happened – I soon learned to grip the infant thigh firmly with my left hand.

Yelling babies could be a problem, especially when I was wearing a radio mike; the roaring mouth was right against the microphone, and the amplified disapproval of the proceedings thus totally drowned whatever I was saying. My own eldest son bellowed throughout his baptism; it was our fault, as we deliberately kept him awake beforehand in the hope that he would then fall asleep in church. But he didn't oblige; he got more and more tired, and crosser and crosser as the service went on! It was probably quite a good thing – if the minister's son does it, it must be OK! The noisiest one I recall was a little girl of about eighteen months – the older ones were often the worst. She had been showing considerable displeasure throughout the earlier parts of the service, but when I took her in my arms this was obviously the ultimate outrage. Her mouth opened like a trap, and for a few moments her fury was such that nothing came out at all. We too all held our breath, waiting for the explosion – which came with the inevitable roar, and arms and legs flailing in all directions.

But the most upsetting incident of a noisy baby did not involve the one being baptized, but her older sister, a toddler of nearly two. On this particular occasion we had a visiting preacher, who was a man with an internationally famous preaching and writing ministry. It was quite a coup to get him to speak in our little church, and many of us were looking forward to hearing him. But right from the start of his address, the toddler was crying loudly and persistently. The mother knew well that we had a crèche – she was an occasional attender, and her children belonged to our Sunday School. After a few minutes of this hubbub, a churchwarden came forward and quietly suggested that the distressed little girl should be taken out; but the mother refused to move. After a few more minutes, the preacher himself stopped, and very gently suggested that she could be taken for a little walk:" Don't worry about it!" he said; "we've all been there! Why not carry her up and down at the back?" But once again the mother flatly refused to budge; and so the preacher battled on to the bitter end against this persistent competition. I am afraid that not only were his words lost on even the most attentive listeners, but the preacher himself was very tight-lipped when he came back to my house for lunch. I felt he blamed me for the débacle.

But certainly there is no way that I would adopt the practice of a neighbouring vicar, who had been known to stop the service, and say curtly, "When that child is removed we will continue the service!" Word soon got around that children were not welcome in St. Mary's.

Such are the perils of dealing with babies in church! But I have also been privileged to be involved in the baptism of adult believers. On these occasions I fully accept the appropriateness of total immersion, not as something essential to validate the baptism, but as a vivid and striking picture of the death, burial and resurrection of which Paul writes in connection with baptism.

I learned once that in the church of the early centuries, there is evidence that the baptism of believers took place out of the sight of the congregation, with the baptistry being behind curtains. The reason for this was that the candidate entered the water totally naked; if it was a man the officiant was a male priest, but a woman was baptized by a deaconess. The candidate arrived for the service dressed in dirty, dark clothes; when he went through the curtains the dirty garments were stripped off him and cast out, to symbolise the putting off of the old, pre-Christian life. The congregation heard what was going on, but saw nothing. Then the candidate was led down into the water as the words of baptism in the name of the Trinity were spoken; and as he came out of the water, on the opposite side from where he went in (how could he come out at the same place as he went in?), he was clothed in clean, white robes, and emerged before the congregation – clean, shining white, and rejoicing in his new life in Christ!

I confess I have never baptized anyone naked – not even a baby. But there are several baptisms of believers that remain vivid memories. The first one I ever performed was for a lady who had been brought up in the Salvation Army, which does not use the sacrament of baptism at all. She had been worshipping with us for a while, but the turning point in her faith was an Easter Day television service broadcast from St. Michael Le Belfry in York, the church of the well-known preacher and writer, David Watson. When she told me of her new faith – and her husband enthused that he seemed to have a new wife! – I started suggesting that she should think about being baptized. As we studied the New Testament passages about it, she was amazed – despite all her years of churchgoing she had had no idea there was so much in the Bible about baptism; and soon she said she wanted to be baptized.

"What about being baptized by total immersion?" I suggested. At first she was horrified at the idea, as she was scared of water; but after more consideration, she decided it was what she would like. Like the vast majority of Anglican churches, we had no facilities in church for such a ceremony, but just across the road there was a school which had an outdoor swimming pool. I obtained permission to use this. I also approached a local Baptist minister, both to borrow a baptismal gown (a white robe with weights around the lower hem to prevent it floating up as the lady entered the water), and also to get some hints about the practicalities of doing the deed.

When the great day came, there was beautiful, warm, July sunshine. We started the service in church, and it included a personal testimony from the young woman herself. Then the whole congregation moved out of church, across the road, and down the drive to the swimming pool, where we gathered on all sides, and sang a song or two to guitar accompaniment. After that I entered the pool – I was not robed at this stage, but in clerical shirt with collar, and lightweight slacks; I was not of course wearing shoes, but kept my socks on as the Baptist minister had said I was less likely to slip! As I stepped into the water, still thus dressed, all the children gasped. Then the candidate stepped in, wearing her white robe, and I performed the actual baptism, pressing her right under the water, before she sprang up again, dripping but beaming all over her face. As she stepped out, her husband was ready with a huge bath towel in which he enveloped her. The whole event was immensely striking and memorable for all concerned – the regular Anglican congregation, the Salvationists who had come along to support their old friend, and of course the lady herself as well as me.

Another baptism by immersion I recall with great clarity was very different. It took place at a summer Pathfinder Camp (for boys and girls aged 11 to 15) in South Devon. There was a boy whose father was a Hindu but whose mother was British and had become a Christian. He had witnessed an adult baptism by immersion a couple of years earlier, and had felt that if and when he was ever baptized, that was how he wanted it to happen. Now the time had come, and he was to be baptized in the sea one sunny Sunday afternoon.

The beach we used was a delightful sandy bay enclosed on either side by rugged rocks. On Sundays it was open to the public, and there were hundreds of people there. The Pathfinders and their leaders – a total of perhaps a hundred people – gathered on a knoll at the top of the beach, and started with some singing in their usual exuberant style, with several guitars and tambourines. Then the entire party moved down the beach – watched with curiosity and astonishment by the many families on the beach – and formed a large circle in the sea, with the water up to our thighs. (A number of the holidaymakers joined the circle to observe.) The camp Commandant and I were both clergy, robed only in swimming trunks, but carrying guitars! We used the central part of the baptismal liturgy, and as the lad was immersed in the salt water, and then emerged, spluttering, the whole camp cheered lustily. We all returned up the beach, singing as we went, and returned to our knoll. (A little boy from one of the families of holidaymakers came across, saying, "Mum wants to know, what religion are you?" So we assured him we were Christians, and members of the C. of E.!)

It is a shame that so few Anglican churches have an immersion baptistry. On a number of occasions I have the borrowed the facilities of a nearby Baptist or Brethren church, which has always been willingly loaned; but I have felt it is sad that we cannot have the ceremony at the heart of our usual place of worship. Some churches have hired portable birthing pools for such occasions – but this tends to be expensive, and a tremendous palaver; it also requires ample space, and some means of filling, warming and later emptying the pool, and I have never done so. In one church where we were planning a radical reordering of the interior, an immersion baptistry was part of the plan – but for various reasons such as more urgent building maintenance needs the whole project was deferred indefinitely.

I Believe – I Think…

11

❧❦❧

Charismatic Conflicts

As described above, in my later years at Oxford I withdrew from the Pentecostal Church and the group of Pentecostal students in the OICCU. I was not comfortable with their theology and their assumptions; and yet I could not go to the opposite extreme and reject Pentecostalism as a heresy, as was the tendency with most conservative evangelicals at the time. I had no doubt that the experience of Baptism with the Holy Spirit and the gift of speaking in tongues that I had received were from God; I just had no satisfactory theology to define or explain them.

The Pentecostal style of prayer, too, was one about which I was ambivalent. When the Pentecostal students met for prayer on one occasion in a room in Brasenose when the window was open, one of them in particular prayed with such enthusiasm that his urgent petitions echoed across the quad, and I shared the embarrassment of other OICCU members about this (indeed, the emotion of one member could better be described as agonised horror!); and yet I now tended to find the very subdued and dignified prayers in OICCU meetings rather moribund and frankly boring.

When I started my theological training at Clifton the matter slipped into the background of my mind, until one evening when, in a conversation over the dinner table, I mentioned light-heartedly that I had been gently excluded from VPS holidays because I was felt to be unsound on the Pentecostal issue. I noticed another student looking at me hard as I said this, and after dinner he buttonholed me and suggested we should go for a walk and have a chat. As we wandered through the dark gardens, he said that he, too, had had a Pentecostal experience, but generally felt it unwise to talk about it. Moreover he warned me that a certain student at Clifton a few years earlier had been asked to leave because he so assiduously tried to spread Pentecostal notions in the student body. This man had left the Church of England and was now a Pentecostal pastor. All this was in hushed tones, almost as if the theology police might be lurking behind a bush and eavesdropping on our discussion.

When I was a Curate in Walthamstow a few years later, stories began to appear in the church newspapers about strange goings-on in certain parts of the Anglican Communion, particularly in the United States; some priests there had apparently adopted the Pentecostal habit of speaking in tongues. When such rumours started spreading to include well-known British clergy too, eyebrows were seriously raised. I remember my vicar at St. Mary's, Canon K. H. Druitt, shaking his head sadly over reports that a hitherto deeply respected evangelical vicar in Gillingham, Canon J. T. C. B. Collins, had joined the "tongues-speakers". "He's gone right off the rails – right off the rails!" lamented Canon Druitt. As far as I remember, I made no comment; but I was secretly most intrigued and indeed excited.

But it was not until I had moved on to my next parish, Emmanuel Church, Tolworth, and had been there several years, that I began to find a resolution of the conflict between my theology and my experience. In those intervening years the Charismatic Movement (as it was now being called) had gained ground both in Britain and worldwide. The Archbishop of

Canterbury, Donald Coggan, in a major address spoke of the three great strands of Western Christianity – the Catholic, the Protestant and the Pentecostal; and it was in Latin America that adherents to the Pentecostal movement seemed to be multiplying exponentially. Books were being written from many traditions describing and explaining this new movement, and some of these became popular textbooks on the theme, such as the very readable *Nine O'Clock In The Morning*, by an American Episcopalian priest, Dennis Bennett.

One which I found most helpful was by Simon Tugwell, a Roman Catholic priest, who in his book *Did You Receive The Spirit?* used the phrase "the release of the Spirit" to describe the Pentecostal experience. This terminology accepted, and indeed insisted, that every true Christian has *received* the Holy Spirit, but recognised that in so many the life of the Spirit seems to be submerged or suppressed. But when He is "released" the believer enters into a new experience of Christ, and is set free to enjoy and share many spiritual gifts. That description matched my experience well.

During this period, the late 1960s and early '70s, an organisation was set up within the Church of England to unite and focus all the disparate groups and individual Christians who were seeking to explore this new, exciting, but potentially dangerous and divisive dimension of spiritual experience. This was the Fountain Trust, of which a moving spirit and founder member was Michael Harper, a curate at that evangelical Mecca, All Souls', Langham Place – the church beside the BBC of which John Stott was rector. The fact that a minister on the staff of such a famous church was involved in the new movement helped to give it a measure of respectability.

Conferences and worship celebrations were organised, often led by American groups such as the Fisherfolk, from the Church of the Redeemer in Houston, Texas, who opened up new ways of worshipping with joy and exuberance; while some found this distasteful and uncomfortable, others found it liberating and uplifting. There was an explosion of new songs with a totally different style from that of traditional hymns – some noisy and enthusiastic, often with actions and movements, but others quiet, worshipful and meditative. The phrase "Happy-clappy" was coined as a derogatory term for such worship songs, or for the people who enjoyed them; but while some of the new songs and choruses were undoubtedly shallow and lacking in either poetic or musical quality, and soon dropped out of use, the term was unjust towards many of the new songs which in subsequent years have become part of the staple diet of worship of many churches.

But the movement remained seriously controversial, and a source of division both within and between churches. One reason for this was undoubtedly the attitude of many enthusiastic new adherents of the movement, which all too often was lacking in both love and humility. In their newfound exhilaration they would tell anyone who would listen, and many who would rather not, of how God had blessed them; and frequently this gave their hearers the firm impression that they, the hearers, were hardly Christian at all because they, poor benighted souls, had not yet experienced the fullness of the Spirit. This was hurtful and insulting to many deeply devout, committed and godly people. Many churches started to find that among the membership was a group of highly enthusiastic charismatics, who after attending some conference or celebration had returned to their parishes glowing with spiritual fervour, and at once started pressurising others in the church to sing the new choruses, to go to conferences, and especially to accept the exercise of gifts like prophecy and speaking in tongues in their Sunday services. Above all, they were making more traditional Christians feel inadequate and second-class, simply because the latter were not able to express their faith and worship in such extrovert ways. There were, of course, many who had experienced a "baptism in the Spirit" who were much more restrained and diffident; but it was the more extrovert and demonstrative ones who inevitably had a higher profile.

Of all the "gifts of the Spirit", it was the gift of speaking in tongues which aroused the most excitement and the most hostility. The excitement, for those who received the gift, was not only because it is an uplifting sensation (Paul wrote that *"he who speaks in a tongue edifies himself"*[1]), but because it seemed to offer a very clear experience of the supernatural, which was a marked contrast to the wholly rational, academic and prosy worship that they had been used to. This, surely, was God at work; this was the Holy Spirit inspiring the speakers, just as He had in Bible days! Moreover their experience was often that this gift was the one which unlocked their own spirits to worship and serve God in all sorts of new ways; it was a gateway gift, to a whole new way of knowing and serving Jesus.

But for those who had not received it, and were perhaps deeply suspicious of it, it represented all that was unwelcome in the new movement. It was irrational – which could be denigrated as "mindless". It seemed to be pointless; what was the value in speaking gibberish? It had regrettable associations with over-emotionalism (always highly suspect in the Church of England). And it was exercised by people who generally had not had any particular status or position in the church, but who now seemed to think that they were the bees' knees, and spiritually superior to all the rest of us. It is not surprising that people who were made to feel sub-standard and inferior were likely to resent and despise those who aroused such emotions.

There were, of course, those who felt like this because they did indeed have no living faith, and saw their church solely as an exclusive, deeply respectable, dignified club; such people are

---

[1] I Corinthians 14.4

always likely to resent people who have a more personal relationship with God than they do. But too often the newly "Spirit-filled" people tended to dismiss as unspiritual all who were slow to accept the new movement, and this judgement was frequently unjust and lacking in charity.

There was a very real alarm in the higher echelons of the evangelical wing of the church that a serious schism threatened; and the Church of England Evangelical Council called a meeting of many leaders from both sides of the divide to seek to face up honestly and openly to their differences, and to search for a way to unity. This Conference produced an irenic report, "Word and Spirit", which, while not settling all differences (which would have been an unrealistic expectation) set an agenda for mutual respect and loving sensitivity. Probably most church members at the time, whether involved in the charismatic movement and its attendant controversies or not, never heard of the CEEC or this report; but nevertheless it was a valuable turning point which started to bring healing between warring factions, a healing which gradually percolated down into the churches which were in danger of being torn apart over the issue.

In my own church the turning point into a more overtly charismatic direction was a Parish Weekend in 1972. The two churches – Christ Church, Surbiton, the parish church, and Emmanuel Church, Tolworth, the daughter church of which I was curate-in-charge - arranged a joint residential weekend house party at Pilgrim Hall, near Uckfield, to which some sixty members of the two congregations went. There had been a number of such houseparties over the years, and they were usually enjoyable occasions, not only offering opportunities to deepen fellowship with other church members more than years of Sunday-only churchgoing could do, but to explore biblical and spiritual issues in a more concentrated way, with plenty of chances for discussion. The shared informal worship, too, was a new experience for many, and one which almost all found refreshing. This particular weekend was to be led by Reg Sanger, the vicar of St. Mildred's, Lee, in southeast London.

Reg was not a high-powered celebrity preacher or conference leader, but an ordinary parish priest; his down-to-earth and relaxed approach allayed many of the fears of those of our houseparty who initially tended to be deeply suspicious of the whole charismatic issue. (I heard of some parishes where such suspicions had become so intense that the Vicar had been told firmly by the PCC that they did not want the Holy Spirit mentioned at all!) Reg opened up the subject to us, with a mix of homely anecdotes about life and experience in his very ordinary parish, and a clear exposition of the Bible. By the end of the weekend many people had themselves entered into a new experience of the Holy Spirit, and brought a new excitement back into parish life.

But this did not mean that all problems had been solved, for the individuals concerned or for the church. We faced our own conflicts, which I as the minister had to try to resolve. By this time I had made clear my own experience and my sympathies with the charismatic approach; but I was also sympathetic to the hurts of those who felt that the church that they had belonged to and served so long was changing into something in which they no longer felt at home.

At one stage, there were certain church members who felt moved to speak in tongues in almost every service. Usually the moment when one of them did this, and the voice rang out from the congregation, was in the moment of reverent silence after the Blessing at the end of the service. These ladies (they were all women) who did so felt deeply that they were being inspired or even commanded to speak out this message in an unknown tongue; to have held back, they felt, would have been sheer disobedience. But for many people, the interruption of their devotions, especially at this point after the much loved words, "The peace of God, which passes all understanding, keep your hearts and minds…." was deeply unwelcome, disturbing and even offensive.

I didn't know how to deal with the issue. St. Paul wrote, very clearly, *"Do not forbid speaking in tongues"*[1]. He laid down in that chapter some rules to regulate the practice, one of which was that a "tongue" should always be interpreted[2]; this presupposed that someone with the gift of interpretation should be present. At first when this started happening in our church, we had been joined by a man from a nearby Pentecostal church who could always be relied upon to come out with what purported to be an interpretation of the "tongue" (I am not denying that it was; his words were always innocuous, but my mind remained not entirely convinced that they were always inspired by the Spirit).

Though I had spoken in tongues in my private devotions for some ten years or more, I had never received other gifts such as interpretation or prophecy. I was always on edge when the message in tongues was spoken, until the interpretation followed, because I had no glimmering of an interpretation myself. But one evening I was with a group of people at a home meeting, at which our most regular tongues-speaker came out with yet another utterance. Perhaps because this was not public worship with a mixed audience, but an intimate gathering of like-minded people, I was more relaxed about the situation; and as she spoke, I felt that I understood what she was saying. It was not that I could translate the words, as if she had been speaking in a language I knew slightly; rather it was that the general sense or drift of what she was saying seemed to be in my mind as she spoke. So after a short pause, while I waited for someone else to interpret, I spoke out the

---

[1] I Corinthians 14.39
[2] I Corinthians 14. 27,28

thoughts that had been moving through my mind during the "tongue" – as far as I remember, it was a general message of love and encouragement from the Lord.

It seemed to be something of a breakthrough for me, and we were all quite excited that I had apparently now received the gift of interpretation of tongues. Unfortunately, for some reason, I have never again since that day received an interpretation of a message in tongues. But our regular "tongues-speakers" now felt that so long as I was present, they had the go-ahead to speak out their utterances in Sunday services, on the grounds that I was there to interpret. But it just didn't happen; perhaps because I was tense and anxious as soon as someone spoke in tongues, because as the minister leading the worship, I was responsible for what went on, I was totally unable to hear or discern what God might be saying to the congregation through the "tongue" – and our Pentecostal visitor was no longer with us. So it always led to a very awkward and uncomfortable silence.

It was reported to me that one or two long-standing members of the church were speaking of leaving because they found this regular interruption of their worship with alien practices ever harder to tolerate. Action had to be taken; the problem was deciding what that action should be.

With hindsight I can see that I did not handle the issue well. It was made more difficult by the traditional one-person leadership of the church that is the norm in an Anglican church; in a team of leaders, ordained and lay, which seems to have been the pattern in the New Testament church, we could have shared the problem and used a variety of insights to find a solution. But as it was, everyone looked to me to sort things out; and I made my decision.

I announced, both orally and in writing in the weekly news-sheet, that from now on there was to be no speaking in tongues in a Sunday service, but that the gift should be limited to informal meetings in homes. Some members were deeply saddened by this edict, and even shocked that I should have done something which was so clearly forbidden in Scripture (*"do not forbid speaking in tongues"*); many others were enormously relieved, and the danger of haemorrhaging church members was lifted.

I still feel that it was not the best way to have handled the situation. At a later conference of Eclectics, an organisation for younger evangelical clergy, such matters were discussed, and the speaker (the well-known Baptist preacher, David Pawson) dealt with the subject of the feeling of compulsion which some who exercise spiritual gifts like tongues and prophecy claim to feel. He emphasised that this is an illusion – *"The spirits of prophets are subject to the control of prophets."*[1] In other words, no one is *forced* by the Holy Spirit to speak a prophecy or in tongues; they are able to control themselves. "The only compulsion," urged David Pawson, "is the compulsion of love!" That is why the two long chapters about such spiritual gifts, I Corinthians 12 and 14, are separated by the much more familiar chapter 13 about love. This chapter is far too often taken totally out of context, simply as if it were a beautiful poem about love in general; but that is not why Paul wrote it. The theme of that chapter is to draw the distinction between exercising spiritual gifts with love and exercising them without love.

So it might have been far better if, rather than forbidding the exercise of the gift of tongues in Sunday services, I had discussed with the people who were doing so what was the most loving thing to do, in view of the very considerable hurt and distress that their present practice was causing. I do not of course know whether this would have solved the conflict; but I am sure it would have been a better, and more biblical, way of proceeding.

---

[1] I Corinthians 14.32

Spiritual Warfare

Another area of difficulty arising from this realm of biblical teaching and experience that we were exploring concerned what later came to be known as "spiritual warfare". This phrase was used to denote what is known in some circles, especially of a more "catholic" and less evangelical tradition, as Exorcism. This is a term which tended to be associated particularly with certain rituals, an approach with which evangelicals were not comfortable; they tended to prefer the phrase "deliverance ministry". Whatever the words used, what it was about was the belief that demons, or evil spirits (often known in the New Testament as "unclean spirits") were and are a reality, and not just a primitive or medieval explanation for mental illness or conditions such as epilepsy, which had been the comfortable assumption for a century or more.

There had always been, even in the 20th century, Christian teachers who took the possibility of demonic attack very seriously. I first encountered this in the OICCU in the reports of missionaries from Africa, who had no doubt at all that what they had often witnessed was exactly what the New Testament had described in the ministry of Jesus. It seemed that in countries where crudest paganism had ruled for many generations, the arrival of the Christian gospel provoked what a later charismatic teacher, the Californian John Wimber, was to describe in his books as a "power encounter"; when people who were under the power of demonic spirits met the power of Jesus, violent screams and struggles often ensued, and the Christian missionary had no weapons but faith in the power of the name and the cross of Jesus. Many times, we learned, people whose lives had been tortured by physical and spiritual forces of evil were wonderfully set free when unclean spirits were authoritatively commanded to depart in the name of Jesus. We young Christians listened, moved and enthralled; but we still tended to assume that such phenomena were to be met only in what we would now call the Third World.

But when the charismatic renewal began to spread through the churches, with its readiness to believe that the teachings of the New Testament about the spiritual dimension, both good and evil, were to be taken seriously and even literally, this area too was re-examined. As in all matters, some teaching, and some teachers, were wiser and more balanced than others. There was a tendency among some to get over-excited by this obviously supernatural dimension, which had been so readily dismissed for generations as nothing but superstition. Demonic activity was perceived in more and more places and situations, and over-enthusiastic Christians with only a superficial understanding of the issues were tempted to charge in and invoke the name of Jesus to solve all manner of apparent problems.

Sometimes the result of these well-meaning ministrations was no more serious than some embarrassment; but occasionally something much more damaging occurred. One of the worst incidents hit all the headlines, and the tabloids revelled in the story, though a tragedy had ensued. A group of Christians in a northern city had tried to minister to a deeply disturbed man. Whether his problems had indeed a spiritual root I cannot say; but after lengthy prayer and attempts at deliverance ministry, the man went away and committed a horrible and violent murder. The subsequent court trial gave the lawyers a platform for denouncing these ignorant and superstitious meddlers who had made the sick man's problems far, far worse, with terrible results.

Naturally this incident brought all deliverance ministry into very serious disrepute. The Bishops took action, and sought to appoint a specific priest in every diocese who was to be responsible for this area of pastoral and spiritual ministry. They were not denying the genuine need for such ministry (though no doubt the Bishops themselves differed widely in their theological and psychological understanding of the matter); but they laid down firm guidelines to govern how and in what circumstances it should be offered. In particular, they insisted that such ministry should never be offered without consulting the diocesan official Minister for Exorcism.

This regulation was well-intentioned, but not wholly realistic. Certainly it was essential to rein in the well-meaning but untrained lay people who, completely ignorant of the complexities of spiritual and psychological ill-health, and with often only the crudest and most simplistic understanding of biblical teaching on the matter, could do enormous harm by their enthusiastic readiness to rush in and "cast out demons" from troubled people. Clergy, too, despite years of theological training and pastoral experience, often felt very inadequate and at a loss when faced with phenomena with which they were ill-equipped to deal, and to have an "expert" upon whom they could call for help and advice was very valuable. But in real life, things could not always be arranged so tidily, and demonic oppression could suddenly manifest itself in a situation where action had to be taken then and there; it is not always possible to say, "Come back next Tuesday when I have phoned the Diocesan Exorcism Officer"!

I had such an encounter myself. A teenage girl who was a member of our YCF (Young Christians' Fellowship) was doing a part-time job in a shop, and there she met a very disturbed young woman, who told the younger girl that she was sure she – the older woman – was demon-possessed. Apparently she had for some years been involved in various occult practices, including Satanism and witchcraft, and she was now convinced that she was hopelessly under the power of evil spirits, and bound irretrievably for Hell. The young Christian girl was of course very troubled by this, and urged her to turn to Jesus for help, but without success; and so she came to consult me. It was arranged that she should bring the troubled young woman to see me.

This was a year or two before the bishops' appointment of official exorcism officers, and I felt I had no option but to cope on my own. My wife Mary, of course, knew of the appointment, but we agreed that she would stay in the background and support me with prayer. We had two very young children, and a dog; I had once been told that animals should be kept out of the way of any deliverance ministry (was this perhaps with the story of the Gadarene swine in mind?), and so Shuna, the Labrador, was kept in the other room; and we prayed over our two sleeping children before our guest arrived, asking for the protection of their angels.

When the bell rang, and I met the young woman for the first time, I was struck by how her facial appearance seemed utterly dead and devoid of expression. The young Christian girl introduced us, and they came in and sat down. We spoke for a while, and I was told something of the strange and troubled history of the young woman. I asked her the key question: did she *want* genuinely to be set free from all her satanic and demonic past? Did she *want* the help of Jesus? Did she truly repent of, and renounce, all her occult practices? She assured me that she did.

I was starting to say that we would pray, but just as I was about to begin I noticed that she was wearing on a finger a chunky ring in the form of intertwined snakes. I asked her whether this had any significance. "Oh, yes," she answered at once; "that's Satan's ring!" I said that if she was asking to be delivered from Satan's clutches, she had to get rid of anything to do with him, and she instantly took off the ring and flung it into the empty fireplace.

So we then all bowed our heads and I started to pray. One of the problems she had told me about was the struggles she had with lust; I knew no details and had not asked for any, but in my prayer I started with that theme, asking that the pure love of Jesus should replace all corrupt lust. I had only spoken a few words when she started screaming. She screamed and screamed, and it was impossible to continue the prayer; I changed tack, and started to command in the name of Jesus that this evil spirit should leave her.

I learnt later that evening, when our guests had left, that just before this screaming started my wife Mary, who was in the kitchen doing the ironing, had felt a powerful urge to pray. She put the iron down and started praying, not in the least knowing what to ask for; and she found herself praying in an unknown tongue. This was virtually the only time in her life that she has spoken in tongues, but at that moment of crisis, when she did not know what to pray, she was apparently given the words to pray by the Holy Spirit. As she started, she heard the screaming break out in the other room. She prayed in her Spirit-language for a minute or two; and then felt, quite definitely, that she had done what was required; so she stopped and continued the ironing!

In the front room, there was I, for my first ever time, confronting what seemed to be a demonic manifestation; and all I could do was to say, firmly, "In the name of Jesus Christ, I command you to leave her! By the cross and resurrection of Jesus, leave her!" And all the time she was screaming, screaming, and writhing about in her chair. Gradually – I suppose the whole episode took no more than two minutes – she quietened down; the screams faded to moans, and finally she sagged, slumped in her chair, quiet at last, her eyes closed. I caught the eye of the young Christian girl, sitting there ashen faced, but bravely continuing to pray throughout.

After a few moments of stillness, the young woman stirred, sat up, and opened her eyes. She looked at me, and smiled. It was the first truly human expression I had seen on her face since she came in. We prayed again, thanking the Lord for this deliverance and for his victory over the forces of darkness, and praying for him to fill the newly-cleansed vessel with his Holy Spirit.

What, in fact, had been happening? At the time, I was sure that there had been a spiritual battle going on, and that this was a genuine example of what the New Testament describes so vividly: that the young woman was truly afflicted or infected with unclean spirits, which were then forced to go by the authority of the name of Jesus. Even then, I was sure that there was more to come – that her problems were not over; and I urged her to come to church, especially on a Sunday a week or two later when we had a visiting preacher who had considerable experience of such matters.

This preacher was a man named John Linden-Cooke who was what was then called a Lay Reader (a Reader in later years) from a church in Brixton. I had met him when I had preached at his church; and he had told me after that service of some of his dramatic experiences when ministering to apparently demonised people, some of whom reacted to the name of Jesus by crawling on the ground and barking like dogs or exhibiting other similarly startling phenomena. Perhaps rashly, I booked him to preach at Emmanuel Church one Sunday morning; and this happened to be shortly after my first encounter with the demonised young woman.

When John preached that morning, his sermon fulfilled all my expectations of exciting and blood-curdling stories, with accounts of the wonderful, victorious power of Jesus. The young woman was sitting in the front row, just below the pulpit, vibrating like a guitar string. After the final hymn ("To the name of our salvation") and the blessing, John and I went to the vestibule to greet the departing congregation. But after only a few people had left, and the church was still full of worshippers, suddenly we became aware of a nerve-shattering outburst of screaming from the young woman at the front.

This, following on from John's terrifying stories, was too much for some people, who rushed out of the church with their hands over their ears; others who had already left, ran back in again to see what was going on. John and I abandoned our handshaking exercise and hurried back into the church, to find that John's wife had already moved to sit beside the tormented woman. John took over, and started to deal with the situation in his accustomed way, while I urged the clumps of awe-struck church members who were standing around to pray earnestly.

John's method of dealing with evil spirits was to command them, one by one, to declare their names. The Biblical warrant for this was of course the incident when Jesus asked the demon-possessed man in the region of the Gadarenes (or perhaps Gerasenes) his name; and he said, *"My name is Legion", for there were many demons*[1]. But the practice of people like John – I often came across this approach – was to ask each demon "What is your name?", and then to address the demon by that name, and command it to go. This is what John did that Sunday morning; several times a name was forthcoming, the command to go followed, and after a fresh paroxysm of screaming the spirit apparently departed, leaving the sufferer quiet, until the next spirit was tackled. The only "name" I recall was a spirit that called itself "Fear of Old Age".

At last, after perhaps five or six spirits had thus been expelled, it seemed that it was over, and John's wife started quietly singing "Praise, my soul, the King of Heaven", in which the congregation gradually joined.

There were various sequels to this episode. A middle-aged, single lady who had only been coming to church for a few months was one of those who had rushed out in terror when the screaming started. She was a timid soul, and it had been too much for her; she flatly refused ever to come to church again. Another woman who was a very committed worshipper, and whose husband had started occasionally coming to church but was, so far, some way from finding a convinced faith, was in tears because on that particular Sunday he hadn't come; she felt that it had been

---

[1] Mark 5.9

such a vivid demonstration of the reality of spiritual powers of good and evil, that it might have been a turning point for his cautious explorations into faith. A young man, who had with his wife been coming to church for a few months after making enquiries about the baptism of their baby, had been there that morning; I was having lunch when he rang me up and asked, "Chris, what did I witness this morning?"

This was a very good question. What had we all witnessed? What had been happening that day, and a few evenings earlier in my home? Were we right to take it at face value as a satanic or demonic manifestation? Or was this young woman merely mentally disturbed, with a good deal of exhibitionism and attention-seeking thrown in? Had I, and subsequently John, merely been deluded, and were we colluding with her fantasies? I have no doubt that the latter interpretation would be firmly asserted by many people – both unbelievers and many Christians; for there is a school of theological thought which regards any belief in miracles, of healing, deliverance, or anything else, with the deepest suspicion. Biblical accounts are dismissed as arising from the primitive and ignorant superstitions of the 1st Century culture.

The opposite point of view is that which at the time I was happy to accept; that the New Testament descriptions of demonic possession, or of miraculous healing, were to be taken wholly literally, and that we should expect to see such things continuing to happen today.

Now I suppose my position is somewhere between the two. I still have no problems with taking the New Testament accounts at face value. If I believe that Jesus was the Son of God, then I believe that he spoke with divine authority; when speaking of spiritual matters, he knew what he was talking about, and I regard it as an arrogant impertinence for modern theologians, while claiming to be his disciples, to say that they know better than him about spiritual realities.

But I am much more cautious now about seeing the work of Satan or his demons behind every situation of spiritual disturbance. I do not dismiss such a possibility out of hand; but I keep in mind that the human psyche is exceedingly complex, and simple, black-and-white answers are likely to be misleading. In those years when I was very ready to speak about demons, all too often I encountered suggestible souls who saw this as a nice, simple answer to all their problems. "That is why I so often feel depressed! That is why my teenage son is so intolerable and hostile to church! That is why I suffer from such strong temptations! It's all because I / he / we are demon-possessed! All we need is deliverance ministry, and our problems will be over." One particular lady at one church became totally convinced that this was her condition; and when I expressed some doubt about it, she was highly indignant. Some of us privately chuckled about her case; but for many people such delusions were very far from laughable, and had tragic consequences.

In later years I encountered the strongly demon-oriented approach to human problems a number of times. Ellel Grange, a centre for healing and deliverance in the North of England with which I had some contact, developed a system of teaching and belief, which seemed to see a demonic cause for a vast range of human problems, including such things as homosexuality and anorexia. They seemed to me to be erecting a huge edifice of demonology often on the slenderest of biblical foundations, which resulted in confident assertions about the likelihood of demonic involvement in all sorts of surprising situations. Some of these I found deeply offensive and potentially enormously damaging, such as their teaching that after a miscarriage the next child conceived is likely to be demonised.

And yet I could not dismiss their entire theology as superstitious rubbish. At a three-day teaching event there, I found one episode very thought-provoking. Two members of the party were men from a Sikh background; one had been a Christian believer for some years, but the younger man was recently converted. On one of the evenings we had divided into groups in different rooms to minister to one another in various ways, and so I did not see how this particular episode started; but when I entered the lounge I found a group, including the leader of the Centre, Peter Horrobin, gathered round the younger Sikh man who was lying on the floor. It seemed that they were trying to deliver him from demonic powers associated with his former Sikh faith.

For many people – Christians as well as Sikhs – this would be a profoundly offensive idea. The Sikh faith is monotheistic, and has many fine and noble elements. The school of thought which holds that all faiths are of equal validity and to be held in equal respect would particularly resent fiercely any suggestion that a faith such as Sikhism was in any way demonic. Ellel Grange would have had no truck with such liberal universalism; the assumption would have been that every non-Christian faith, with the possible exception of Judaism from which Jesus sprang, had a substantial demonic component.

However it seemed that the deliverance ministry being attempted was encountering problems, and the repeated commands in the name of Jesus for the spirit of Sikhism to depart was being met by a defiant refusal. The young man was being held down on the ground by several people, and the voice with which he was answering questions was quite unlike his usual light tenor voice; it was deeper with a snarling timbre. It brought vividly to my mind the descriptions of the unclean spirits answering Jesus from the mouth of a suffering man.

They paused to consider what to do next; and the older ex-Sikh said that his young friend still possessed some of the symbolic religious objects associated with the Sikh religion; the only one I can recall was the comb, used to control the long, uncut hair under the turban. This was not just a cosmetic object but an item of deep religious significance. So it was suggested that these five religious objects should be brought downstairs from his bedroom. The older ex-Sikh, and Peter Horrobin, believed that each of these objects might be linked with a specific spirit, each of which must be expelled individually. The central Sikh spirit was, so to speak, surrounded and protected by the other five subsidiary spirits.

The comb was held in front of the young man's eyes; and the spirit of the comb was commanded, in the name of Jesus, to leave this child of God. The comb was then deliberately snapped in half in front of him. The result of this was startling: the young man screamed, coughed violently, writhed around, and was then still, panting. There was a similar response to dealing likewise with the other four symbolic things (the dagger, the bracelet, the shorts, and the uncut hair); in each case when it was broken or disposed of in some other way, there was a brief, violent reaction, screams and coughs, and then a moment of rest.

It seemed that this procedure had stripped all the defences from the central, controlling Sikh spirit. The strange voice suddenly cried out: "Leave me alone! I'll have nowhere to go but the Pit!" This caused a roar of triumphant laughter from those around, and the leader firmly ordered the spirit to go – to the Pit, the place reserved for the devil and his angels[1]. Another shriek, and it was all over. The young man sat up, smiling and laughing. He felt that he was free.

Many people might find this story disturbing, even horrifying, not least because of the explicit insult to such an honoured religion

---

[1] Revelation 12.9, 20.3

as that of Sikhs. I would respond first, that the result of the experience seemed – as far as I could see – a wholly positive one for the young man concerned; but I freely admit that I never saw him again after the few days were over, and have no idea what the longer-term consequences may have been. But secondly, I would totally repudiate the "all religions are equal" theory, as being firmly contradicted by both Old and New Testament.

This is a very large subject on its own, and cannot be dealt with in a few lines in this context. All I would say here is that I would maintain that every non-Christian faith (except Judaism) has three constituent elements. There is the divine element, arising from the fact that every human being is created by God, for a relationship with God; and God reveals himself in creation, and builds into us the capacity to respond to that revelation, and to seek for God. So every religion has within it the God-implanted element of the search for the eternal, the ultimate, the divine. Secondly, these religions have a purely human element; the human ideas and theories of what God is like, and how we can find and please him – ignorant and false theories, which are inevitable if we have not encountered God's revelation of himself through his written word, the Bible, and the Living Word, Jesus. All we can do is come up with our own ideas – which may be apparently reasonable, or may be (in Christian eyes) totally weird.

But the third element is indeed the demonic. If human beings grope into the spiritual realm, they are likely to find it – but not everything in that realm is of God. They will find what Paul calls *"deceiving spirits"*[1], who, like their leader, Satan, are very good as masquerading as angels of light[2]. They are a substitute for the reality: a deity to replace the one true God. Sometimes these demonic elements of non-Christian faith are more easily discerned,

---

[1] I Timothy 4.1
[2] II Corinthians 11.14

such as in various occult practices and phenomena; but other forms of religion seem eminently reasonable and very spiritual. The one thing which reveals their true nature is this: they turn their adherents away from Jesus. Jesus is the light of the world; whatever turns someone away from him is from the realm of darkness. As John wrote, *"Every spirit that does not acknowledge Jesus is not from God. It is the spirit of antichrist."*[1].

It is because the Christian Church has always since New Testament times seen non-Christian faiths in this light that there has usually been an element of exorcism or spiritual deliverance as part of the liturgy of baptism. In the modern Common Worship service, after the candidate has been marked with the sign of the cross, and challenged to confess the faith of Christ crucified and fight under his banner, the priest says:

"May Almighty God deliver you from the powers of darkness, restore in you the image of his glory, and lead you in the light and obedience of Christ."

So however "non politically correct" and offensive such an unfashionable view may seem, it has an honourable pedigree, and I would maintain is far more faithful to the witness of the Bible than the somewhat naïve view that all religions are basically the same, and even that all are equally valid ways to God. This is of course no reason to treat adherent of these faiths with contempt, or to speak or write of their religious beliefs in insulting or derisory ways. A Christian is to love all people, however mistaken we may regard their beliefs; if I love someone, I will treat what is precious and sacred to them with respect, even while I seek ways to lead such a person to the true light and love of Christ.

Healing

The healing ministry has never been limited to churches which would consider themselves part of the charismatic renewal. There

---

[1] I John 4.3

have been various healing societies within the church which have encouraged the development of such ministry, though with different emphases.

But healing has also been central to those churches and para-church bodies involved in the charismatic movement. The basic premise was that healing is seen throughout the earthly ministry of Jesus, and in the Acts of the Apostles, and is referred to and commended in several of the New Testament epistles, and *"gifts of healing"* are among those listed by Paul in his "Gifts of the Spirit"[1]. So - argues the charismatic Christian – we should expect to see the same gifts exercised today wherever the Holy Spirit is at work, bringing new life to the church.

It must be admitted that this doctrine was promulgated in different ways, and some ways are definitely less balanced, wise and biblical than others. At one extreme end of the spectrum were those who held that to use medical means at all in time of illness reveals a lack of faith. Perhaps the opposite extreme would be the attitude that the only proper way to pray for healing is to ask God to give wisdom and skill to the doctors.

However between these two extremes are many Christian leaders, clergy and teachers, who grapple with the very real problems, and without in any way claiming that they had all the answers, they encouraged believers and churches to expect God to work in healing power today. I found various books on the subject helpful and encouraging; those of the Roman Catholic priest, Francis MacNutt, are among the most balanced and wise.

There are many methods and approaches which can be used. One of the most frequent actions associated with the healing miracles of Jesus was the laying-on-of-hands, and this is often used in conjunction with healing ministry today, whether in public services, or privately in the home or even a hospital ward. At the

---

[1] I Corinthians 12. 9,30

simplest level, a loving touch can convey a sense of caring to the troubled soul or pain-wracked body. But when I have been using this approach I have often prayed that God will be touching the patient, as I touch him.

Obviously there can be dangers especially when a man is ministering to a woman; many prefer only to minister in such circumstances if there are two people involved, preferably including a woman. This is particularly important when ministering in private. Sometimes it may be appropriate to lay a hand on the area of pain or sickness – such as on an arthritic shoulder. But obviously it would be totally unsuitable for a man to lay a hand on a woman's breast in a case of breast cancer!

A curious variation of the practice of laying-on-of-hands has come to be associated with the ministry of the late John Wimber, a very gifted preacher and writer with a valued healing ministry. His fellowship, and those influenced by them, used to stretch a hand in the direction of the person being prayed for, without actually touching them. Often several people around the patient would thus reach out their hands as one person prayed. I heard that the practice arose for a very prosaic and practical reason – in the summer in California when the weather was very hot, a lot of sweaty hands touching people was not felt to be a blessing, and so the "do not touch" suggestion was made!

Another method mentioned in scripture is anointing with oil[1], and in many Anglican dioceses provision is made for flasks of oil (ordinary olive oil, though some people like to use various herbal recipes to add a fragrance to the oil) to be blessed by the Bishop for this ministry, often called Holy Unction; it may also be used in the liturgy of baptism and confirmation. (In the Roman Catholic Church, the ministry of what is called Extreme Unction is well known, for those on the point of death; I would not disagree with

---

[1] E.g. James 5.14

that, so long as it is not the only kind of anointing ever offered which would suggest that any faith or expectation that a person might actually be healed has been completely lost.)

But it must be remembered that Jesus did not limit himself to one method or approach. Yes, frequently he laid hands on people, but on other occasions he simply spoke a word of authority. Sometimes he spoke to the sick and disabled person, commanding them to stand, or to stretch out an injured or crippled limb[1]. At other times he spoke a word of rebuke *to the illness itself*.[2] Sometime the sick person was not even there but was healed at a distance[3]. Sometimes he indicated that their primary need was not their obvious physical problem, but something spiritual, such as when he said to the paralysed man, *"Your sins are forgiven"* – and only after that healed the paralysis[4]. Francis MacNutt, in one of his books on healing, gives an interesting example of this, which concerned himself. He had found that God seems to use different people in different ways for healing – one was successful in one area and one in another. He himself seemed to be particularly effective in praying for people with back problems. And yet he himself seemed to suffer from chronic back pain, which was resistant to all prayer, by himself and others who tried to minister to him. And then somehow (I forget how) it was brought home to him that his primary problem was low self-esteem, which caused bad posture – he tended to stand with a stoop, as if to express a subconscious conviction that he was not a person who was worth very much. It was as he learned to deal with this, to remind himself that he was a child of Almighty God, made in his image, redeemed by Christ, of infinite value and precious to God, that he

---

[1] Mark 3.5
[2] Luke 4.39
[3] Matthew 15. 21-28
[4] Mark 2. 4-12

started to "walk tall" and straighten up – and his back pains were healed.

Most frequently people were healed instantly as Jesus spoke or touched them; but sometimes the healing occurred a little later, such as in the case of the ten lepers who were healed as they went to the priests[1], or the blind man who was healed when he washed his eyes in the pool of Siloam[2]. On one occasion, Jesus even had a second go, when the healing was not complete first time – the blind man who saw people like trees walking, but then saw clearly after a second time of prayer[3]. (I have often been very glad that the Bible records that particular incident – so often I find that people need more than one prayer for healing!)

Sometimes people speak of "faith healing", but I do not like the phrase as it does not specify what the faith is in – it may be faith in positive thinking, or in spirits, or in the person ministering, or in some technique. I prefer the term "Christian healing", as this emphasises that it is Jesus that heals.

But there is often misunderstanding about the place of faith even in Christian healing. I have even heard people say things like: "If you believe, you will be healed!" It may even be implied, "If you are not healed, it shows that you do not have enough faith!" This is a wicked, cruel and totally unbiblical thing to say. Of course on one or two occasions Jesus did say, *"Your faith has healed you"*[4]; but those incidents need to be examined carefully to see what the words meant. But in fact in all the many healings of Jesus, in only three or perhaps four cases was the faith of the sick person even mentioned.

A lot of people are surprised by that; but it is true. In several instances, it is not the faith of the sick person but that of someone

---

[1] Luke 17. 12-14
[2] John 9.7
[3] Mark 8. 22-25
[4] Matthew 9.22

else which was critical. When Jesus healed the centurion's servant, it was the faith of the centurion, not that of the servant, which thrilled Jesus[1]. When the four men lowered their friend through the roof, it says that *"Jesus saw their faith"*[2]. This may have included the faith of the paralysed man, but at least as important was the faith of the four friends. So no one praying for a sick person should ever say, "You're still sick because you haven't enough faith". It is just as likely that he is still sick because the people praying for him have not enough faith!

Mark tells us that in Nazareth Jesus *"could not do any miracles there... and he was amazed at their lack of faith"*[3]. Matthew's account of the same episode actually says *"He did not do many mighty works because of their unbelief."*[4] This suggests that our failure to see many miracles of healing today is because of the poverty of our faith and of that of the western churches. In some Third World countries, it seems that healing miracles are far more commonly witnessed because there is not in their culture the suffocating blanket of scepticism and unbelief that permeates ours.

It was not only Jesus who healed people; he gave this power and authority to his disciples[5]. This was so both during the earthly ministry of Jesus, and also throughout the book of Acts. As far as the early Christians were concerned, Jesus was still busy healing people through his followers. Several of the Epistles mention that miraculous healing was the experience of the early church. Paul writes to the Corinthian Christians, *"My message and my preaching were not with wise and persuasive words, but with a demonstration of the Spirit's power."*[6] He does not specify there what this

---

[1] Luke 7.9
[2] Mark 2.5
[3] Mark 6.6.
[4] Matthew 13.58
[5] Matthew 10.8
[6] I Corinthians 2.4

"demonstration" consisted of, but it is at least probable that it included healing.

The Letter of James has a famous passage (alluded to above) in which he urges his readers, if they are sick, to call for the elders of the church, who will come and anoint them with oil and pray for them, and *"the prayer of faith will make the sick person well."*[1] I firmly believe that this kind of practice should be as regular and familiar a part of our faith and of the life of the church as prayers, hymns and Holy Communion.

It may be argued that it is not always God's will that a person be healed. This is of course a huge subject about which many books have been written; I would just say here that there is no single instance in the Gospels of Jesus refusing to heal anyone, or of him saying, "God wants you to remain sick". On the contrary he often said things that implied that an illness was the devil's work, or that healing revealed the power and glory of God and was a sign of his kingdom. It is true that his healing seems sometimes to be *selective* – he apparently only healed one of the many sick people at the Pool of Bethesda[2], and it has been pointed out that Jesus must often have passed the cripple at the Beautiful Gate, who was not healed until the day when Peter and John stopped beside him; I would take it that while it is always, I am convinced, his will to heal, it is not always his will to heal *now*.

I have heard about, read of and witnessed many experiences of healing ministry, and been involved in quite a number myself; but I will frankly admit that in my own ministry some prayers for healing have been more obviously successful than others. Indeed, there has been little or no apparent result when I have prayed for someone, in far more instances than the occasions when God has wonderfully answered a prayer! One example of "success"

---

[1] James 5.14,15
[2] John 5

occurred when I was doing what I frequently do when giving people the bread and wine at Holy Communion: if I happen to know that someone has some need for healing, I lay a hand on their head or shoulder, and say a short and simple prayer for healing. On this occasion, the man kneeling at the rail was a regular member of the congregation, and I had heard that he was off work with a bad back, so I followed my usual practice and laid a hand on him and prayed for deliverance from the pain. I then passed on down the row, and thought no more about it. I certainly did not "feel" anything special at that moment.

It was eighteen months later that the man, very shyly and diffidently, confess to me that when I touched him, it felt as if electricity had passed through his body. By the time he had returned to his pew, he was completely free of pain, and he whispered to his wife, "I think I've been healed!" He had a doctor's note to be off work for two weeks; but on the Tuesday he thought, "This is ridiculous!" and returned to work. And I knew absolutely nothing about it!

Another remarkable case involved what might have seemed a trivial problem, an injured finger. My friend Jenny had been out with the family for a picnic on a Sunday afternoon, and on their return when she slammed the boot of the VW Camper down it caught her finger, which was thus split down both sides of the top joint. It was exceedingly painful, and she arrived in church that evening with a fat bandage around it. When chatting after the service, I did what I have hardly ever done before or since: I felt strongly moved to pray for that finger then and there, and grabbed her wrist, saying aloud "Lord, heal Jenny's finger, and take away the pain, in Jesus' name!" Jenny stood for a moment, and then swayed, and had to sit on a nearby chair: "It's stopped hurting!" she gasped. Yes, the pain did return later that evening, but much more mildly, and the finger healed up very quickly.

I wish I could report that that always, or even often, happened when I pray; but it doesn't. However I cannot see that frequent "failures" are a reason for giving up. How often, after all, are people converted through my preaching? Thankfully, it has sometimes happened; but more usually I just do not know what the results of my words have been, and I have to leave it in God's hands. But I still go on preaching God's word, sometimes including an appeal to turn to Christ in faith for salvation. The same, I believe, is true of the healing ministry.

I have also been on the receiving end of healing prayer. I had fallen off my bike and broken my arm – not a bad break, but enough to have to go to Casualty to have it X-rayed and bound up. Two days later I was due to speak to a group in a neighbouring church about "Physical Healing", and I arrived with my arm in a sling, which provoked a good deal of merriment! I have often enjoyed the Lord's sense of humour. At the end of that meeting there was a time of prayer and anointing, led by the host vicar, who asked if anyone would like this ministry – and of course I raised my hand. Before he prayed for me, he said he was going to pray for "accelerated healing" – that my arm should get better more quickly than expected.

At my follow-up appointment at the fracture clinic, the doctor carefully moved my arm this way and that, bending my wrist up and down, and even twisting it, and asking each time, "Does that hurt?" "No," I responded to each query. And in the end he said, "Well, that is remarkable! It has healed a good deal more quickly than I would have expected. There is no need for you to come back." I am still ashamed that I never told him why I believed it had happened!

As I say this is a huge subject, and this treatment of it will inevitably be very inadequate and perhaps raise more questions than it answers; but in telling of my gradual exploration of the charismatic dimension of spiritual life the healing ministry must be included.

Worship

Despite the elements of conflict and unhappiness sometimes associated with these early years of the charismatic renewal, and the mistakes and misjudgements that frequently occurred (and I am well aware of many of my own), I am still convinced that the balance of the legacy of the charismatic movement was overwhelmingly positive, for a variety of reasons.

The experience of worship in many churches has been transformed. When I am worshipping in a church which still seems untouched by the charismatic movement, to me (this is of course a purely subjective judgement, and others may strongly disagree) it seems overwhelmingly dull and dead. It is not that the liturgy is badly led; it is not that the worshippers have no faith. It is not even that the music is entirely traditional. Rather it seems that there is no life, no joy, no sense of the presence of God. It is entirely formal. "Take not thy Holy Spirit from us," they may chant; but I tend to suspect that He has already departed.

But when a substantial number of the worshippers, and of those who lead the worship, have entered into some experience of spiritual renewal, there is a marked change. There is a frisson, a buzz, an expectation that they are going to be meeting with God. There is joy and exuberance in the praise, there is a holy hush in the times of silence, there is a lively expectancy and responsiveness in the preaching of the Word and its reception.

There are several different elements in this transformation, the first and most fundamental of which is the transformation in the worshippers themselves and in their own personal relationship with God. Their relationship with one another is also of great significance. Such a church usually has a network of house groups where personal relationships, sharing of faith, and mutual support and encouragement, all grow; and this inter-relatedness of faith and spirituality – what may be called the fellowship of the Holy Spirit – profoundly affects the dynamic of the Sunday worship.

Other elements include the openness to the use of the many gifts that members of the congregation are discovering in one another. I am not referring primarily to speaking in tongues or prophecy – such gifts may hardly ever be experienced in ordinary Sunday worship, even in a church being touched by renewal. But the traditional "one man band" leadership has been replaced by a variety of contributions to the worship. The ordained president will still preside, of course; but many lay members may also be involved, not only in reading the scriptures, but in leading in prayer, in leading music in various ways (of which more anon), in giving a testimony or interviewing another person about God's working in their life, and in sharing in the ministry of prayer for healing.

The use of the newer worship songs will be found alongside the great hymns and anthems from the past; and these new songs cannot just be dismissed derisively as "happy-clappy". Yes, some are indeed bright, lively and joyful, and may indeed invite participation with clapping – for which there are several good Biblical precedents! Songs with children and young people in mind may particularly be of this style, and when you have experienced the noisy and enthusiastic worship – "hearts and minds and hands and voices in our choicest psalmody", as the hymn "Angel voices" has it – in such settings as a Pathfinder camp, which young people find exciting and uplifting, you can only sympathise with them when they return to their parish churches and find nothing but a dirge!

But many hundreds of the songs which have emerged from the renewal of the past forty years have been of much more weight and substance than the perhaps more light-hearted choruses for the children – not that I would ever suggest that the diet of children's worship should only be of lightweight material; that would very seriously short-change them and impoverish their explorations into faith. Some of the new songs are nearly as rich in Scripture as the great hymns of a Watts or a Wesley, even if the style of music and rhythm is that of a different era. Others may have very little "content", but in simple, perhaps repetitive words, they allow the worshipper to express the deep love and longings of their hearts; he would be rash who would dismiss such heartfelt worship as trivial, any more than are the words of intimate love between man and wife.

Inevitably there will be different tastes in the music of worship. Though my own background is of classical music and traditional Anglican forms of worship – I can happily sing chanted psalms and canticles, appreciate many of the great hymns of the eighteenth and nineteenth centuries, and revel in choral anthems – I have also found enormous blessing in many – not all! – of the worship songs of the last quarter century, and even tend to feel that worship without any of these newer contributions is lacking an essential ingredient.

The discovery and release of creative, artistic and musical gifts is one of the most positive aspects of the Renewal. Fundamental is the insight that every Christian has gifts, for the blessing of all; and many who have felt that they have nothing to offer but faithful attendance in the congregation (which I would in no way despise), and that it would be an impertinence to expect anything more, have found that God has given them some unexpected ability which has been welcomed joyfully by other members of the church family.

Instrumental music is one of these. Though the organ is a magnificent instrument, and for certain styles of music is incomparable and irreplaceable, it has its limitations, one of which is that only one person at a time can play! Yet there may be many in the Body of Christ who can contribute, and in recent years old and young have been able to play – strings, woodwind, brass, percussion. The first instrument which started to invade the organ's sole rule was the guitar, which while excellent for leading informal worship in home or clubroom, has considerable inadequacies in church. But as more gifts and abilities began to emerge unexpectedly in many congregations, worshippers began to thrill to the trumpet adding drama to a descant, violin and cello playing an obligato to some gentle song, a flute to soar above the melody. To have such instrumental music takes a lot of work and preparation, and if this is skimped the results may be disastrous, and not in the least glorifying to God. Neither is it usually wise to try to involve all the available instruments all the time, though when there are the resources worship led by a symphony orchestra is a thrilling and uplifting experience. But even a solitary recorder, played by a nervous child, can bring joy and variety to the worship, as well as letting the player understand that he or she has a gift to offer God.

Vocal music in a style different from the traditional church choir can also add richness to the worship. Singers can express their faith in very personal and individual ways, whether as a solo or in a group; whether singing alone while others listen, or leading the worship of the people. Leading musical worship is a very valuable gift, needing personal resources which are not only musical and artistic but spiritual; a music group of singers and players who are called to lead God's people in worship must not only rehearse the notes and words, but also prepare spiritually and with prayer both privately and corporately. (Sadly, I have known traditional church choirs where the opposite seems to be the case, and instead of loving, sharing fellowship among the members, informed by a deep personal faith, there is conflict, bitchiness and a contemptuous readiness to criticise and deride any form of worship or aspect of church life where spirituality is valued. The music led by such a choir, however technically polished, is unlikely to draw worshippers into a sense of the presence of God.)

Dance too has emerged as a form of worship. I have met earnest Christians who profoundly disapprove of this, and feel that it is entirely "of the flesh" and therefore unspiritual. I suspect that behind this attitude lies a theology which misunderstands what older translations of the Bible, particularly the words of Paul, mean by "the flesh". Paul indeed contrasts "flesh" with "spirit", and uses the word "flesh" (Greek: sarx, σαρξ) to mean the unredeemed, base human nature; but he is in no way implying that our physical being is evil or debased. How could it be, when it is created by God, and was the central aspect of the incarnation of Christ? (This view, that human nature in its physical elements is intrinsically corrupt and evil, is a very ancient Christian heresy called Manichaeism.) "The flesh" when contrasted with "the spirit" refers to our sinful nature; while it may include sins of the body, like drunkenness, greed and sexual immorality, it also includes such mental evils as jealousy, spite and lying.

Paul also told us to offer our bodies as a living sacrifice; and while that includes any of the multitudinous ways of serving God, why should it not also include moving our bodies in dance and physical worship? But this too, like any form of worship, requires the dancer him- or herself to be worshipping. I remember an occasion when a well-meaning leader had invited a local dance teacher, who was not a church member, and perhaps would not even have claimed to be a Christian, to perform a dance when a worship song was being sung, and it was painfully obvious that the dancer had not the slightest conception of what worship is about. In such a case the dance had become merely a performance, which seemed to be saying, "Look at me! Don't I dance superbly?"

But when the dancer is a person with a real faith, who is learning to express in movement such elements as joy, or humility, or thankfulness, or yearning, or adoration, all clearly focussed not on the dancer but on God, it can be inspiring and uplifting, and indeed deeply moving. Sometimes a dance of exultation can include streamers, flags or banners, which add powerfully to the sense of celebration.

This brings me to another gift which has been associated with the Renewal. The decorating of churches with banners is not of course a new phenomenon, and the church furnishing companies often have a fine selection of magnificent banners in the section of their catalogues that deals with vestments. But when banners or hangings have been created by members of the local fellowship of believers, so that in a very real sense they are their own personal offerings to God, a dimension is added which nothing bought from a catalogue can match, even if the latter is superbly and professionally executed. Many churches have started a banner group, in which the more skilled can encourage the ideas and contributions of the less experienced, and such colourful works of art, whether displayed permanently or only put up for a particular occasion or season, enrich the visual environment of worship.

The whole area of gifts of art and craftsmanship has started to emerge as a gift of the Spirit, in line with what is said in the Book of Exodus with reference to the leading craftsmen in the construction and decoration of the Tabernacle in the time of Moses:

"See, the Lord has chosen Bezalel the son of Uri, the son of Hur, of the tribe of Judah, and he has filled him with the Spirit of God, with skill, ability and knowledge in all kinds of crafts – to make artistic designs for work in gold, silver and bronze, to cut and set stones, to work in wood and to engage in all kinds of artistic craftsmanship. And he has given both him and Oholiab the son of Ahisamach, of the tribe of Dan, the ability to teach others. He has filled them with skill to do all kinds of work as craftsmen, designers, embroiders in blue, purple and scarlet yarn and fine

linen, and weavers – all of them master craftsmen and designers."

These were very gifted men and women! Not only were Bezalel and Oholiab multi-talented in terms of craftsmanship in many different media, but – even more useful when a major enterprise is in hand – they were able to lead and teach a team. But note this: their gifts are specifically attributed to the Spirit of God. When the Spirit of God, then and now, is being poured out on God's people, one result is a burgeoning of gifts of music, art and craftsmanship, which enormously enriches the life and worship of the whole community, as well as bringing joy and fulfilment to the individuals concerned.

So the gifts and enrichment brought by the Holy Spirit of God, to individuals, particular congregations, and indeed the whole church, are enormously varied, some of them more obviously supernatural than others. I have found some Christian people to be very cautious and even scared of spiritual gifts, or of any unfamiliar manifestations of the Spirit. This is entirely understandable; but perhaps we need to be reminded that in the passage which concludes, "How much more will the heavenly Father give the Holy Spirit to those who ask him?" he had earlier assured his disciples that fathers do not give their children snakes or scorpions when they ask for food. We can trust our heavenly Father totally that the gifts of his Spirit will not be dangerous or hurtful.

12

Theological College and Ordination

In the summer vacation before I went to Clifton to start my two years' theological training course, the college sent me a list of books which they recommended that I should read. As I mentioned earlier, I had already started a collection of religious books, mostly bought from the OICCU bookstall in the Northgate Hall. The great majority of these were paperbacks written specially for students, though a few were more substantial works.

I had also been given one or two second-hand books, like the devotional *Quiet Talks* book that David Fletcher had given me; and about that time I started to enjoy searching through second-hand bookshops, as became the fashion among OICCU members, especially those who were considering ordination or other "full time Christian service" – a phrase often used, but also disapproved of, as surely – it was rightly maintained – every committed Christian was in "full time Christian service", even if he or she was in secular paid employment.

In order to guide such treasure-hunting, Jim Packer (the author of *Fundamentalism and the Word of God*, and a tutor at Tyndale Hall, another evangelical Anglican theological college in Bristol) produced a type-written list of recommended books, especially Bible commentaries, with coded symbols to indicate how worthwhile he considered them. I recall that the top grade he awarded was "$$ - Sell your shirt to buy this!" This grade was attached to such classics as Spurgeon's great seven-volume commentary on the Psalms, *"The Treasury of David"* (which sits on my shelf as I write), or Matthew Henry's Commentary on the whole Bible.

The one thing that all these books had in common was that they were written from a firmly evangelical theological standpoint. They were "sound". But the books recommended for my reading that summer of 1961 had a much broader base. One was *"Oxford Apostles"*, Sir Geoffrey Faber's account of the founders of the High Church "Oxford Movement" of the nineteenth century: men like Newman, Keble and Pusey. I found this deeply stimulating and fascinating. Not only did it open up a whole area of Christian faith and Anglicanism of which I knew virtually nothing – and what I did know, I had always been taught to disapprove of and even despise. But now I was starting to understand the men who had been so enormously influential on the character of the Church of England in the last century, and what "made them tick". Newman, in particular, intrigued me, as he had been a fervent evangelical in his early years, but moved steadily away from that position; and after being so instrumental in introducing "catholic" (later known as "Anglo-Catholic") teaching and ceremonial into the Church of England, he gradually became utterly convinced that the only right and logical home for himself was within the Roman Catholic Church.

I was forced to examine my own position in the light of these developing convictions; and though it never led to my turning to Rome, or even to Anglo-Catholicism, it did at least broaden out my views and sympathies from what, it must be admitted, had been exceedingly narrow and intolerant.

But another way in which the College suggested that I should prepare for my first term was that I should study the First and Second Books of Kings in the Old Testament. I had no commentaries except the IVP's New Bible Commentary, which covered the whole Bible in one volume, and therefore was inevitably limited in how it dealt with a single chapter, let alone a single verse. So I approached the Vicar of my Gloucestershire parish, and asked if he had a commentary I could borrow. He lent me the Clarendon Bible commentary – a series which covered most if not all of the Bible; I expect he had used it when he had been at college himself.

I found this not so much stimulating as intensely irritating. The author was of the school of thought that took for granted that most of the Bible was merely mythical, and certainly any account with a miraculous element was, by definition, a pure fable. By the time I had read a few chapters of I Kings with comments from the Clarendon Bible, I remember expostulating to a friend, "If I believed about the Bible what this man believes, I cannot see why I would ever want to read it!" However this too exposed me to an unfamiliar way of theological thinking.

When we actually started term, I found that the tutors were all of a firmly conservative evangelical standpoint; but this was by no means because they had never considered any alternative point of view. We were not allowed to say of a particular doctrine or interpretation, "But the Bible says so!" We had to examine different ways of expounding the text, and adduce good reasons if we were to maintain that the conservative one was right. Other subjects which inevitably exposed us to different points of view were Church History and Doctrine. Liturgy (the study of worship, including all its historical permutations), the New Testament World, Pastoralia (caring for people in a parish), and so on – all these were part of the preparation for ordination.

Inevitably some lectures, and some lecturers, were better than others. Some subjects were rather boring, or presented in a boring way; other tutors had a gift of combining deep scholarship with a profound spirituality. But there was a lot more to college life than academic lectures; the two years spent there were designed to prepare us spiritually and practically, as well as academically, for perhaps forty years of ordained ministry. The regular diet of worship in the chapel, and our personal discipline of prayer and Bible study, were also fundamental.

Clifton had extensive gardens, and when it was discovered that I had a Forestry degree, I was put in charge of them. It was in vain that I protested that Horticulture was quite a different science, and I knew nothing about any plant that was less than sixty feet high! The routine was that every Friday afternoon, the whole student body was to work in the gardens, and I was in charge. I soon found that if my knowledge of gardens was limited, that of other students was virtually non-existent. At least I came from a home where there was a garden, and a keen gardener – my mother loved her garden, though her efforts to persuade me to help in the garden met with little success, apart from the male preserve of mowing the lawns. But I discovered the total ignorance of some of the other students when on one afternoon designated for weeding, I was just in time to rescue a clump of healthy Lupin plants from the bonfire. I fear that quite a number of other valuable perennials were incinerated. My one success in the garden was the planting of a long beech hedge beside the drive, using a large number of self-seeded beech seedlings from a wild area of the garden. Digging up seedlings or saplings from one place, and planting them in another, was not too taxing in horticultural skills, and as far as I know that hedge is still there.

We were also set to work in spiritual sowing and planting in various ways. We were attached to local parishes, and did door-to-door visiting. I was also seconded to a non-denominational youth movement called Crusaders, and not only did I enjoy it, but I developed my skills of dealing with youngsters and delivering talks and lessons with a wide variety of visual aids. On Sunday evenings students were sent out to preach, mostly in village churches around Bristol, but also in some of the city churches. We had to submit our sermons in advance to a tutor; and as well as the student who was to preach, a group of other students and usually a tutor went too, so that afterwards there could be a general discussion of the merits and faults of the sermon and its presentation. I'm sure some of the efforts presented before the long-suffering congregations were abysmal; I recall one (not mine, I hasten to add) which took as its text the parable of the Treasure in the Field.[1] To fill the allotted fifteen minutes, the student elaborated on this simple story, which occupies but one verse in Matthew's Gospel, describing in minute (imagined) detail the man wandering through the field and finding the treasure. As far as I recall the application of this simple story was sketchy and trivial. As an exercise in Biblical exegesis it was lamentable.

However I am sure that my own efforts were not much better. I recall with a hot flush of shame some of the sharp comments my sermon outlines sometimes elicited from the tutor in charge, the redoubtable Alec Motyer. "You are in danger of becoming a purveyor of devotional claptrap!" was one comment I recall written on the paper he returned to me. Nevertheless how can a person learn to preach, without doing it and inflicting his immature ramblings upon a patient congregation? So long as there are opportunities for review and frank comment afterwards, with a measure of encouragement to leaven the more critical verdicts, it can be a helpful and instructive process.

My first-ever effort to preach to a real, live congregation, and to lead a whole service, took place not through the college but

---

[1] Matthew 13.44

before I started there, by request of my own village vicar. He had approached me because a neighbouring vicar was unwell; could I take Evensong on Sunday in that village church? He suggested that there was no need to preach a sermon – a suggestion which I dismissed scornfully.

It happened that an OICCU friend was staying with us for that weekend, and so he accompanied me to the service and sat in the congregation. I was glad of his support and encouragement, and knew that he was praying for me. For my sermon I cribbed a passage from a book I had on my shelves by Maurice A. P. Wood, a regular speaker at OICCU meetings, who was later to become Bishop of Norwich. Afterwards, my friend Mark chatted to some of the congregation, and gleaned some reactions to my efforts. "He's got a lot to learn!" was the only comment (from an elderly villager) that I can recall. I could not deny the truth of that observation.

A village church near Bristol at which we students regularly ministered was singularly unresponsive; and the problem was exacerbated by the design of the building, which was L-shaped – the transept was almost the same size as the nave, and also had an exit door. So when the preacher went to one door after the service to shake hands with the worshippers, at least half of them left by the other. Within thirty seconds of the end of the service, the building was empty; the idea of staying to chat to the preacher or their fellow-worshippers was obviously quite alien to them. I recall that I preached there the Sunday after the Cuban missile crisis, when many people had been genuinely terrified that the Third World War was about to break out, until Khruschev backed down and removed his missiles. I alluded to this in my sermon; but it received as little response as any of our other efforts in that particular church.

The training for ordained ministry which I received in those two years at Clifton was, like the Curate's Egg, excellent in parts. It was very strong on Biblical content, and the syllabus required for the General Ordination Exam was supplemented by Clifton's own Bible Studies Certificate (I forget the precise name). Church History and Doctrine were both well taught – the Doctrine tutor was Peter Dawes, who had been a curate at St. Ebbe's in Oxford, and who ended up as Bishop of Derby. New Testament Greek was no problem to me, with my Classical Greek A-Levels, though men who had a different educational background struggled with it; and I also had the opportunity to learn a little Hebrew – not necessary for GOE, but optional lectures which I was willing to attend, and glad that I had, as it gave me a valuable insight into the writers of the Old Testament.

But one of the weakest areas in College training was in pastoral ministry. I was to discover in parish life that taking funerals was a major area of ministry, and offered great opportunities to come alongside people who usually had virtually no contact with church, but who wanted the church at this time of crisis. There must have been some teaching about funerals and ministry to the bereaved at Clifton, but I confess I have no recollection of it. I certainly know that after ordination, when within a few days of starting work in the parish I was involved in funerals, this was the first time in my life that I had ever been to one!

In retrospect it is appalling how ignorant I was about that enormously important area of ministry. It was made worse by the fact that I received virtually no help on the matter from the vicar of my first parish, Canon Druitt. It was of course recognised that a man left college with a lot of facts in his head, but that it was in his first curacy that he had to learn the practical realities. The parish was as vital a part of his training as was the college. It was therefore a pity that Canon Druitt's sole instruction to me about taking funerals was this: "You are not there to talk about the dead person; you are there to talk about Jesus!"

One feature of the parish in Walthamstow was that our parish clergy were responsible for a large cemetery used for funerals of people from a wide area, far beyond the parish boundaries. So at the great majority of the funerals I had to take, I had never met the family before they arrived for the service, and knew nothing whatever about the deceased person beyond name, age and sex. It would be hard for even the most experienced and sensitive pastor to make a service personal and helpful in such anonymous circumstances; for as brash and ignorant a curate as I was, with as little helpful support as I received from my vicar, it was a disaster, and I shudder as I think of the numbers of grieving families who must have left the cemetery deeply hurt and frustrated after such a totally inadequate and unhelpful ceremony.

It took many years for me to learn better ways in this sphere. It was some ten years later, after taking the funeral of a dear old Christian lady whom I knew well and of whom I was very fond, as she was a regular worshipper at my church of Emmanuel, Tolworth, that someone said to me, "You never even mentioned her name!" And I realised that it was true; it had never been suggested to me that mentioning the name of the deceased person was a good thing to do! My funeral addresses and prayers had always been wholly general – theologically sound, no doubt, but with no personal element whatever.

One trouble in this area of ministry, as in many others, is that few clergy ever have the chance to learn from one another. We don't go to funerals, or any other services, taken by other clergy, unless we happen to be there in a private capacity. So it is all too easy if we have got bad habits or serious deficiencies, for these to continue uncorrected for many years. But I still blame Clifton for the almost total failure to give me a proper grounding in the whole area of dealing with death and bereavement.

Preparation for leading Sunday services was also inadequate, but for different reasons. This was still the era before any revised or updated forms of service; it was the Book of Common Prayer, and nothing else. There had been, of course, the attempt at revision in 1928, and some clergy regularly used sections of the 1928 book; but we were taught to regard that with great suspicion, not only because the 1928 book was never made legal (it had been passed by the Church Assemblies, but was rejected by the House of Commons), but also because it had started to let in certain dubious doctrines from the more "catholic" wing of the church.

There were attempts at college to use some more modern elements. The Bible was read in a modern version, the Revised Standard Version (though the New English Bible had come out in the late 1950s, it was never regarded as acceptable in evangelical circles, largely because its freer approach gave it something of the character of a paraphrase; we felt that the RSV, sticking more closely to the original Greek or Hebrew, was more reliable.). There was the gradual appearance of modern hymns; Hymns Ancient and Modern, which was the basic diet in most Anglican Churches, was not used at Clifton, being replaced by a modern compilation, Christian Praise.

We still, of course, used chanted psalms and canticles, but these were supplemented by modern canticles derived mostly from New Testament passages. There were two such canticles in use when I arrived at Clifton, but I was instrumental in adding about ten more, and bound them into booklets which were used regularly in Chapel services. (I added the pointing, the little ticks and asterisks that indicate to the experienced chanter where the note changes; and I even selected appropriate chants for each one. My years of experience in the chapel choir at Shrewsbury had equipped me with such skills!) I don't know how long these booklets remained in use at Clifton.

But these were days before the revolution in worship styles broke upon the church. Modern services – "Series 2" and "Series 3", leading eventually to the Alternative Service Book of 1980, and then to Common Worship twenty years later – were still no more than a twinkle in the eye of certain liturgists. The explosion of new songs and hymns was still in the future – the only "modern" ones were those of Geoffrey Beaumont and the Twentieth Century Church Music Group. Books like Youth Praise 1 and 2 were still a few years in the future, and then were used almost exclusively for youth groups and youth services. The totally new styles of worship songs spawned by the Charismatic Movement had not yet been dreamed of.

Prayers used in church were also entirely formal and read from books. The diet was limited; books of prayers had been published, but Canon Frank Colquhoun's great book, "Parish Prayers", containing almost 1,800 prayers, did not appear till 1967. When I was responsible for leading prayers in chapel I mostly used prayers from a little *Anthology of Prayers* published in 1934, which I had been given at my Confirmation. Though we used extempore praying at prayer meetings, it was not generally felt that this was an appropriate form for use in formal church services.

We were unmistakeably and deliberately being trained for ministry in evangelical Church of England parishes. Evangelicals were still at that time a rather despised minority in the Church of England; but we had little contact with the theological colleges of different traditions. There were occasional sports fixtures with Wells and Warminster colleges; but I think we regarded the students there with some caution, as definitely unsound, and perhaps not even real Christians at all. On one occasion a student from Mirfield, the strongly Anglo-Catholic college in Yorkshire, came to visit Clifton and stayed for a few days – I think he was a friend of one of our own students. I remember him being pressed hard in discussions about the nature of salvation: "What would you say to someone, obviously not a believer, who was dying?" I can't recall quite how he answered, but it was not "Turn to Jesus and be saved!" which was what we were looking for.

At length the time came when we started to look for parishes in which to serve our first curacy. There was a network whereby vicars looking for evangelical curates could approach the evangelical colleges, and the Principal would try to suggest an appropriate candidate. This would lead to a visit to the parish and an interview with the Vicar. I am not sure who was interviewing whom; I fear that we students were judging and assessing these godly men very carefully, to decide whether we wanted to entrust them with the next stage of our training!

I visited two parishes, one in Bournemouth and one in Clapham, South London, but rejected them both – I can't remember why I felt them unsuitable. But then I was sent to St. Mary's, Walthamstow, and met Canon K. H. Druitt, and decided that that was where I wanted to serve. This was to prove a momentous, indeed life-changing decision – it was where I met the girl who was to be my wife.

Before I went to Walthamstow, however, three things happened – two of them a necessary part of the process, and the third my own choice. First there was "GOE" – the General Ordination Exam, the basic academic requirement which all candidates for ordination needed under their belt. This was no serious problem for me; the academic standard was less rigorous than the Oxford Degree exams I had already taken two years earlier.

The second requirement was, of course, ordination itself; as my chosen parish of St. Mary's, Walthamstow, was in the Diocese of Chelmsford, it would be the Bishop of Chelmsford who would ordain me as a deacon. But I decided to delay this by a few months, and to use my last few months of freedom for travel. This is commonplace nowadays, but was less so in the early 1960s. Two factors influenced my decision: first, that I was still nominally a student, and there were various "students' rates" available which considerably saved the cost of travel. Secondly, I was aware that once I started my parish ministry, holidays would be limited, and there would not be opportunities for taking several months off for exploring the world for nearly forty years. This was my last chance!

I decided to head for the USA. There were two main reasons for my choice. One was that there were several other students at Clifton who had been or were planning to go to the States, and they pointed me in the direction of BUNAC, the British Universities North America Club, who had several schemes to aid and encourage student trips to North America. The other was, of course, that I had been born in the USA, and my family had lived there for about eight years before my birth; and my mother was still in touch with quite a number of people from New York to California. In addition there were various other friends and relations in both Canada and the States. All this meant that when I set off on my travels I had a notebook with a long list of addresses of possible contacts.

This is not the place to tell the full story of my adventures. Suffice it to say that I was able to use the deal on Greyhound buses which offered "$99 for 99 days", and this enabled me to travel, during those 99 days, through thirty-six states and six Canadian provinces. I ended up in Illinois where I stayed for some weeks with the lady who had been my proxy godmother at my baptism, Jean Deansley and her husband Dick (Jean had stood in for my real godmother, May Nugent, who was in England); and I was able to get a job in the toy department of a Sears Roebuck store, to recoup some of my expenses.

There were a number of experiences which have a bearing on my Christian faith. My first visit to church in the USA was in a very up-market suburb of New York where I was staying with some quite wealthy friends of my mother. They attended the

Episcopal Church (a sister church of the Church of England), and the one thing that struck me straight away was that every single female, down to the littlest baby, was wearing a hat – it was obviously still a fundamental rule that women wore hats in church, as it had been in England a generation or two earlier.

One of the Clifton students who was going to be in the States at the same time as me had spoken of a little Christian community in New York City, who did social and evangelistic work there; and so I decided to spend a few days with the folk at St. Paul's House. It was a strange experience in a number of ways. The leader was an ex-episcopal clergyman, but the other members were a very mixed bag, denominationally, racially, and socially. There was a lovely spirit of warmth and love among them which quickly made me feel at home, and I joined in several of their evangelistic forays. We would go to various street locations, set up the Stars and Stripes (a legal requirement for any street preachers or performers) and start preaching and singing. One place we went was Wall Street, and there, in the streets which were like deep canyons surrounded by the soaring skyscrapers of down-town New York, we preached to the financiers and clerks in their lunch hour. I was astonished how the crowds quickly gathered to listen. Another spot was a long way up-town, outside Columbia University, again in the lunch hour; and again I was amazed that the students came out in throngs to listen to us. I was utterly certain that if we had been in Oxford, the reaction would have been totally different, ranging from complete indifference, to abuse and ridicule. But not in New York; the students listened respectfully and, rather than heckling, asked serious questions.

For these outings the St. Paul's House community were joined by a number of other people, with whom I felt less at ease. There was an older couple, of which the man had a truly patriarchal beard, and the woman had a face like flint. She was the preacher of the two, and strode up and down threatening doom and disaster to all who rejected her severe message. Another was a young man who looked vaguely odd; I did not find out who he was, but he had a little bundle of cloth banners, about A4 size, with slogans crudely printed on them saying things like "SALOONS – A DOOR TO HELL!" As we walked along the street on the way to our venue, he would thrust these into the faces of passers-by, often yelling out scripture texts at the same time. I walked as far from him as I could, trying to dissociate myself from his behaviour which to me was both weird and offensive; but to a New Yorker perhaps it was more commonplace. Certainly when I mentioned it to our leader, he was very relaxed about it, and just smiled tolerantly.

I was asked to speak at some of these venues, and though I had nothing prepared, I gave it a go; I probably used old sermons as the basis in this very different setting. My British accent, after the various kinds of American speech which had preceded me, aroused some interest, and once again people were prepared to listen courteously.

But the incident which really caused me to writhe with embarrassment and distaste was when, one evening, we were helping with a youth club among Hispanic people, in a very poor part of the city. Two or three of us were invited to go to visit the homes and parents of the youngsters after the club finished, and the club leader – not a member of the St. Paul's House group – saw this as a wonderful opportunity to evangelise. His method of doing so horrified me.

"All you have to do is to say to Jesus, 'Come into my heart!'" he insisted. "Come on, say it!" he urged our shy and nervous host. The man demurred, saying that he was not certain of what such a commitment entailed. This was brushed aside rudely. "Go on, say this after me! Say it! Say it!" he kept repeating aggressively. Eventually the man reluctantly agreed, and repeated the words after the evangelist. "There now!" the speaker said triumphantly. "You are now saved! Praise the Lord!"

I was utterly appalled by this; it seemed to me not only a gross assault on the dignity of the victim, but it was a travesty of the Christian gospel itself. I do not remember if I tried to express my horror to the perpetrator of the outrage; I am certain he would have been quite impervious to any such protest, and would have dismissed me as lacking in true evangelistic fervour.

However that was the only totally negative Christian experience I had during my time in the States. I attended many services in many churches; some were no more lively or inspiring than some of the typical Anglican churches I knew in the UK, but others were helpful and enjoyable. Some of the church buildings I worshipped in were themselves uplifting. I recall two whose east windows were clear rather than stained glass; one, in a convent church, looked out upon an enormous tree whose mighty limbs formed a marvellous sculpture on which we could gaze and meditate; the other looked out over Lake Tahoe in Nevada, with the great mountains in the distance.

At one stage on my travels I was staying for a few days with a cousin who had a ranch in British Columbia. Pam had been part of my childhood, but I had not seen her for many years; but she and her husband Hugh welcomed me to their home, where they farmed with their two young children. On the Sunday of my stay they were going to go to their local church some five miles away, which was celebrating Harvest Festival. "What are we going to church for?" asked their young son innocently. "Morning Prayer!" responded his mother repressively. I gathered that Sunday worship was not a regular feature of their family life! But it was a good service, with the Bishop as preacher. (During the service when he was being bothered by a wasp, he grabbed a nearby banana, part of the Harvest decorations, and slew the wasp – a memorable little episode!)

I recall one thing the bishop said in his sermon. He was speaking about Christian giving, and said that how much – or how little – we gave to God was an accurate reflection of how much our faith really meant to us. "I would like to introduce a new versicle and response when the offerings are brought up!" he suggested. "It would go like this:

Priest: 'Whatever we may say or do:'
People: 'Here's what we really think of You!'"

On my travels around the States and Canada I worshipped at a variety of churches, and also saw many others in passing. One tiny little urban chapel, little bigger than a shed, which I saw in Los Angeles, had a grandiose sign outside: "The Church of the Lord Jesus Christ of the Apostolic Faith, inc." I particularly liked the "inc."

I had made no specific plans about quite when I was going to return to England. I thought I had arranged with the Diocese of Chelmsford that I was going to be ordained at Advent, in mid December; but in November I started getting anxious messages from my mother. Somehow the system had broken down or information had been mislaid; she was being approached by the church authorities with enquiries about me and what I was doing. Normally if a candidate for ordination is ordained straight from college, the college provides all necessary references and documentation, but in other circumstances three ordained clergymen are required to give some kind of reference as to the worthiness of the candidate. My mother was frantically seeking three clergy to sign the necessary documents; only one local priest, our own village vicar, knew me personally, but she found two others who were acquainted with her and were prepared to take me on trust, and sign the papers. I am not sure why she could not have approached the college for the necessary signatures. But it all indicated that I should bestir myself and make plans for my return.

As soon as I returned to Britain (though I had flown out, I got a berth on the Queen Mary for my return) I started making plans for my ordination and my move to Walthamstow. I learned that Canon Druitt, my vicar-to-be, had arranged for me to have digs with an old lady in the congregation; and the date of the ordination in Chelmsford Cathedral was to be on the Sunday before Christmas.

The three days before the ordination were taken up with a Retreat at the Diocesan Retreat House. I recall little of what was said at the various addresses we listened to. Only one, very mundane and practical, suggestion remained in my mind, and was indeed useful throughout my parish ministry. This was the warning that often in the years ahead we would find ourselves being given money which was not our personal property but for the church. It was suggested that we should always keep such cash in a pocket different from where we kept our personal money. I have always done this ever since; my own small change goes in my trouser pocket, but other money I am entrusted with goes in the pocket of my jacket. Then I know for certain that any money in my jacket is not mine. This idea was perhaps hardly the most inspiring word of wisdom with which to set out on a lifetime's parish ministry; but perhaps I should be thankful for any memorable advice at all!

Finally came the morning of the ordination service. The little group of candidates gathered for breakfast, looking sheepish and uncomfortable in our brand new clerical collars. Of the service itself, attended by my mother and my eldest brother, I remember almost nothing, except that I had refused, on conscientious grounds, to wear the sacramental stole that the other candidates were to be draped with during the service. (A deacon wears it diagonally; when he is ordained priest, usually the following year, it hangs around his neck and down the front of his surplice.) I believed that the stole implied a sacerdotal doctrine of ordination (see page 57-8), which I could not accept. The bishop, John Tiarks, himself had evangelical leanings, but told me firmly that he had no sympathy whatever with these scruples about dress! Nevertheless he did not try to force me to wear this garment. (Twenty-five years later, my wife Mary made me a white stole to mark the 25th anniversary of my ordination; and by that time my rigid scruples had softened sufficiently for me to be able to wear it in the appropriate seasons – I felt that that particular theological argument was no longer of any relevance to almost anyone, and my love for and gratitude to Mary for her gift far outweighed such considerations.)

The only other thing I recall about my ordination service was that afterwards, when we went to a hotel for lunch, my brother remarked that as he looked at the back view of all the candidates, I was the only one whose ears didn't stick out. I am sure that holier thoughts should have been in his mind!

13

❧

The Start of Parish Ministry

I was 27 years old when I started my ministry. I had a tremendous feeling of "At last! For all these years I have been preparing for this ministry; now, at long last, I am actually doing it!"

This excitement and enthusiasm did not have entirely positive results. The parish staff consisted of the Vicar, Canon K. H. Druitt, who was a bachelor in his 60s; a "lady worker", Sister Miller, who had served with him for many years, and was only a little younger than he; and four curates. Peter had been serving in the parish for two years; two other men had been ordained only that September; and I was the "new boy". Unfortunately I very soon began to give everyone the impression that I felt that now I had arrived on the scene, everything was really going to come alive.

This sprang from my feeling of bubbling enthusiasm to get stuck in to the job; I felt that I was bursting with ideas, and could not wait to start putting them into practice. In particular I was impatient with what I considered old-fashioned, stuffy ways of doing things.

Within a very few days of starting I had mortally offended poor Sister Miller. I was put in charge of a group of young adults called the YCF (Young Churchmen's Fellowship), which met each week in one of the rooms of the Church House. I felt that the room was drab and institutional, and set about brightening it up with a few travel posters – one of them portrayed the Taj Mahal. That evening Sister Miller looked in to have a word with someone, and I said brightly, "Do you like our new decorations, Sister Miller?"

"No, I don't!" she said grumpily. "I don't see why we need pictures of heathen temples!"

I was a little hurt and taken aback. "Well, it at least brightens up the room, and stops it looking quite so dull and institutional!" I protested.

"It's been perfectly good enough for everyone till you came along!" she snapped, and swept out, slamming the door behind her.

I was startled at her attitude, and raised my eyebrows to some of the young people around me. One of them said something like, "Oh, don't worry about her – she's like that!" But next day I learned that she had been in deep distress all night, wondering whether to resign – somehow my brash arrogance had made her feel inferior and despised.

I did it again shortly afterwards. I had also been put in charge of the junior section of the Sunday School, with about 60 children in the 7 to 11 age range. After my two years helping with Crusaders in Bristol, I was pleased with this responsibility, and set about planning an exciting programme for them. This was to include the occasional use of filmstrips – not cine films, but more like colour slides. On reporting this to the Vicar at the Monday morning staff meeting, to check that the hire fees were acceptable, I mentioned that I thought such filmstrips would "brighten up the programme".

I had put my foot in it again. Sister Miller had been running the Sunday School for years before I arrived, and of course took my remark as implying that *her* programme had been dull – and once again she was deeply hurt and affronted, and needed a lot of apologies and smoothing of ruffled feathers. She was a very faithful soul, but with what nowadays would be called a desperately low self-esteem; it was this that made her terribly touchy, and ready to take offence at the most innocent remark that somehow she managed to interpret as a criticism of herself.

Canon Druitt, too, was not the easiest of men. I had felt that he was the man I wanted to train with, as he had been in Walthamstow for eleven years, and in Deptford in the true East End for some twenty years before that, including all the war years and the blitz; such a man, I felt, would "know his onions", and would be someone I could learn a lot from. To some extent that was true; but I also found that he was a man with a gift for upsetting and offending people. This, too, arose from a sense of inferiority, and I found that my public school accent and breezy approach did not help. He was a man from more humble origins; and while a more confident man would have been proud of that, and indeed used it to identify with his parishioners, Canon Druitt felt that it put him at a disadvantage, and was therefore prickly.

I found the senior curate, Peter, very supportive; he knew both Sister Miller and Canon Druitt well by now, and helped me to deal with their foibles. He was a married man, but the other two curates were also bachelors like me, and we got on well together. Peter once described Canon Druitt to me as like a crab – hard and spiky on the outside, but desperately soft and vulnerable under the hard exterior. On one occasion before I understood this I responded to some brusque remark of his by "giving as good as I got" – not meaning to be rude, but good-naturedly chaffing him. I was startled that he was deeply hurt by my ill-judged comment.

I knew I had a lot to learn, and a major part of it was learning to get alongside people with a very different background from my own. I started a programme of door-to-door visiting, which was still in those days regarded as an essential part of the work of a clergyman. "A house-going priest makes a church-going people" was a slogan taken to be revealed truth. In a rural parish a vicar might gradually get to know, and be known by, his parishioners in this way; but in an urban parish of some twenty thousand souls, going down the street knocking on doors proved a discouraging and fruitless occupation. Most residents were puzzled to find a "vicar" on their doorstep, never having experienced this before, and not being likely to see him again for some years. Maybe a man with an outstanding gift for building relationships quickly in one brief visit (I was not such a man) could have achieved something worthwhile; but after a few months I abandoned the exercise as a waste of time.

(In common parlance, every clergyman, of whatever denomination, was (and still is) known as a "vicar". I have always had a streak of pedantry in me, and would try to explain laboriously that no, I was *not* a vicar; I was just a curate. A vicar was the man in charge of the parish church; his assistants, who were rather like apprentices, were just curates. I would further baffle people with references to rectors, and to priests and deacons. Eventually I learned just to accept whatever title people chose to pin on me, and to swallow my urge to correct their inaccurate usage.)

On one occasion the resident I found myself calling on was a young Irishman, and unsurprisingly a Roman Catholic. "Come in, Father!" he greeted me warmly. I was still liable to be rather suspicious of Catholics (and shuddered at being called "Father"!), but I had to admit that his warm and friendly welcome was in marked contrast to the suspicion that I usually met from people who would perhaps have claimed to be "C of E". This young man and his wife had only been in Walthamstow a few weeks, and had come straight from deepest rural Ireland. I found to my surprise that they hated the new English Mass that had comparatively recently been introduced into the Roman Catholic Church – the Latin one with which they had grown up was far to be preferred.

But their simple and genuine faith shone out from them, and was a great encouragement to me on a cold winter evening after experiencing several doors firmly shut in my face.

What I found hardest to deal with was the combination of total indifference to matters of religion, and blank incomprehension if I tried to explain some aspect of faith. This was particularly the case when I was speaking to people who had asked for their baby to be baptised. In those days, this was still the practice of the majority of people, who took it for granted that they were Christians, and that their baby should therefore be "done". Yet any suggestion that being a Christian had any connection at all with being a member of the church or a regular worshipper was dismissed out of hand. They weren't the type. They didn't have time. You can be a Christian without going to church. Churchgoers were all hypocrites anyway.

In vain would I point to what the baptism service said, or what the Bible said. I was perceived as simply trying to put pressure on them to go to church, probably in order to boost the collections. They never actually said that, but I strongly suspected that this was their assumption – and that the collections were given straight to the vicar – me – so it was my own income I was trying to boost. Not unnaturally they resisted any such pressure, especially as they couldn't see the point of churchgoing anyway.

And yet in those days there was still a large measure of residual Christianity in the culture. It was often dismissed as "folk religion", and indeed was mixed with a good deal of superstition and other attitudes that were scarcely compatible with real faith in Christ. But most people assumed that (a) they were Christians (what else would they be? Heathens?); (b) they believed in God; (c) the Church was a good thing (the Church being the building, and the traditions, and the vicar). Compared with the much more secularised culture today, coupled with the mix-and-match, do-it-yourself spirituality of the New Age that we find at the start of the new millennium, it was a very different age.

I encountered an interesting manifestation of the vague feeling of approval of the church (so long as no one expects you actually to go there) two or three years after I started work in Walthamstow. I was sent to be curate in charge of what became our daughter-church, St. Stephen's. The actual church building had been condemned as unsafe; it had been damaged during the War, but though substantial repairs had been carried out, in the early 1960s it had been discovered that the walls were gently leaning outwards. It was a Victorian building which could seat some 600 worshippers, and the congregation was now no more than thirty people. It was felt totally unrealistic to seek to raise the hundreds of thousands of pounds needed to effect the necessary repairs, and indeed a wrong use of money for such a huge building of little architectural merit; and so the congregation moved next door to the very pleasant little church hall. But for some two or three more years the old church building still stood there on the corner, with signs warning people to keep out, as it was unsafe. Eventually the necessary, laborious legal processes were complete, and the building could be demolished.

Inevitably crowds gathered to watch; several hundred people stood around for most of the weekend as the operation proceeded. I was surprised to find not only some sadness that the old place was coming down – many of the residents had been christened or married there – but a real sense of anger. It was *their* church; how dare the authorities just knock it down? It was a part of their background, their neighbourhood, their heritage (though this was not necessarily how they expressed it). Never mind that they themselves hadn't given any money or attended a service for years to help to make the church viable. They still resented it being demolished.

However the church hall that we had been using for two or three years before the actual demolition of the church made for a far more homely and friendly place to meet for worship. Initially it had been converted into a church simply by lowering the stage to be the "chancel" with a bright orange, velvet curtain as a back-cloth, and having rows of chairs for the congregation; but when it became clear that it was to be a permanent move, we were able to get funds from the diocese to make more worthy arrangements. In particular we installed a new beech strip floor, and pitch-pine pews from the old church, stripped of their old, dark varnish, and polished to a beautiful honey-colour. Later in my ministry I would never have agreed to use pews – I came to regard the flexibility of chairs as highly preferable to the rigidity of pews; but in fact the old pews were singularly comfortable ones, and made people feel that it was now a "proper church".

I spent nearly five years in Walthamstow; for half of this I was the junior curate at the Parish Church, St. Mary's, but when I was promoted to act as curate in charge of St. Stephen's, this gave me a measure of independence and the opportunity to use my initiative and to be responsible for developing the life of that church; but I still had the other clergy to give support, and we all met together for a staff meeting in Canon Druitt's study every Monday morning.

What did I learn from my years in Walthamstow?

(a) Practicalities of parish ministry.

In all sorts of ways a new curate, fresh from college, is an ignorant and raw creature, who has to be knocked into shape by his vicar. Such things as preparing for services and being in church in good time, dressing properly – with clean shoes! – dealing with all types of services including the "occasional offices" of baptisms, weddings and funerals, preaching clearly, audibly and not for too long, and so on – all needed to be learnt. Mistakes were often made, sometimes to the amusement of the other curates or the parishioners. One of my colleagues often seemed to get in a muddle. He had to be taken off doing weddings for a time, as he so often made mistakes – at one service, the Vicar, who was supervising him, had to interrupt, as he was in danger of ending up married to the bride himself. At a burial, he stepped back, and fell off the raised heap of soil around the grave, covered with imitation turf matting, ending up on his back on the muddy ground.

Leading the prayers in a service is important, and in those days, and that parish, was a matter of selecting some from a book. I have always believed in including a short time of silence for people to make their own, silent, intercessions; but on one occasion when doing this I dropped off and awoke with a start – I think it was only for a few moments, but I was horrified at the vision of the silence stretching out for several minutes, until someone came to shake my shoulder – or alternatively leaving me there asleep, finishing the service and going home, so that I would eventually awake in an empty church….

One curate came from a wholly urban background, and sometimes it was evident that the rural or agricultural setting of many Bible stories was unfamiliar to him. One time, when he was telling the story of Gideon in the Old Testament, he said that "the angel of the Lord had spoken to Gideon while he was threshing sheep…" There was not a flicker from any of the congregation. They were as ignorant of farming practices as he was. (Perhaps they thought the angel was rebuking Gideon for cruelty to animals.)

Although in the years ahead I was to develop my own style and approaches to parish work, inside and outside the church building, the basic foundations of learning how the job is done were well laid by Canon Druitt, and I am grateful to him – despite the many occasions when I disagreed with him.

(b) The Cultural Divide

The steepest learning curve concerned social and cultural issues. I very rapidly discovered that there was a wide gulf between my own background and that of most of our parishioners, especially those who didn't come to church. I was from a middle class home, and had attended Prep School and Public School – that is, fee-paying schools in the private sector; and then I had been to Oxford for four years and had post-graduate training for a further two years. This was totally different from the vast majority of people in Walthamstow who had left school and started work at 15 or 16.

The difference between them and me was not primarily a matter of money. I had not come from a wealthy background, though if my father had not died when I was 2 we would no doubt have been in a higher income bracket. The only reason that my mother had been able to send my brothers and me to fee-paying schools was because she had a great deal of financial help from various grandparents and uncles. Mind you, I have frequently met the assumption that I was rich, simply because I was a clergyman. People from a professional walk of life were well aware that clergy were paid a pittance, but among the working classes it is commonly believed that they are well off. This conviction may be because the vicar lives in a large, detached house – sometimes virtually the only such house in the parish; but it may also be derived from more intangible assumptions, including "speaking in a posh voice" and even the folk memories of "the squire and the parson". The first time I encountered this attitude was when, as a curate earning £16 a week, I had a picture framed – it was a cheap Constable reproduction. When I went to collect it, the framer said that another customer had brought in an identical picture for framing. The framer had mentioned that he was framing one for "the vicar", and said that I had chosen a slightly more expensive frame than the other customer was considering. "Yes, but I don't get a vicar's wages, do I?" retorted the man. I obviously have no idea what wage he did get, but I doubt if it was as low as mine.

About thirty years later, when I was in Barrow-in-Furness, it was reported in the local press that when the Poll Tax was replaced by Council Tax, the diocese was going to pay the clergy's Council Tax for the first year of the change-over. The Evening Mail published a letter about the Mayoral Service which had recently taken place in my church, when the Bible Reading had been Romans chapter 13, including Paul's words "Pay taxes to whom taxes are due". The letter made some sarcastic comment about it being easy for me to talk, as I didn't have to pay Council Tax, so that I could continue to live in the style to which I was accustomed… I was able to reply (and my contribution was published) that while it was true that my Council Tax was being paid for me that year, it was also the case that my stipend, and that of other clergy, would remain at the same level as the previous year - £12,900. I am sure that many readers would have been startled at the slim wage packet drawn by clergy.

I never resented my modest income. When I was at Oxford, a booklet called simply "SACRIFICE" (in 1½ inch white capitals on a red cover) was being widely read in the OICCU. It was a challenge to young Christian men and women to accept a sacrificial lifestyle for the Lord's sake. I wholly accepted this message, and knew that if I went forward for ordination I would never have the level of income expected by most other Oxbridge graduates. But this didn't matter; if it was what God was calling me to, he would supply all my needs.

So the gulf between me and the residents of Walthamstow was not financial, but both educational and cultural. I was very aware that I had a much more extensive vocabulary than people around me; but I was also uncomfortably aware that it would be very easy for me to appear patronising if I tried to use simpler words. When trying to explain the Christian faith in the context of a baptism visit, I would find it very hard to make things clear. It was not that I was using complicated theological terms like "epistemological" or "exegesis"! I had, I hope, more common sense than that. But I still became used to a glazed look coming over their faces, and realised that I had lost them – they had no idea what I was talking about.

It was not a matter of intelligence, but of culture. My thought patterns were just totally different from theirs. Sometimes I felt I was making contact, and we could have a good discussion; but there were other people with whom I was simply not communicating - the cultural gulf was too wide. I know that other people from an identical background to me were happy and successful in inner city parishes; David Sheppard, who later became Bishop of Liverpool, started parish life in Canning Town in the inner East End of London, and loved the people there and was loved by them. But I never felt that I was as capable as he was of crossing the cultural divide.

Over the years I have learned a little better how to communicate spiritual truths in simple language. I have become very aware of how much alien jargon we clergy inflict on people who come to our churches, and how incomprehensible – and usually unnecessary – it is. Some words and phrases which are in common use in church circles are odd and puzzling to those without a religious background. Even a phrase like "reading the lesson" is not immediately understood. A "lesson" in common parlance is something that happens in school, or in contexts like a driving lesson; but we mean a reading from the Bible. Then why don't we just call it "a Bible reading"? There are enough barriers facing a person who is starting to try to find out what the Christian faith is about; why do we need to put extra hurdles in their way by using words like "the Gradual", when we mean the hymn before the Gospel reading, or "The Collect" when we mean the special prayer for today? I don't think many regular worshippers realise how alien church life is to those who are unused to it, and how intimidating.

(c) **Marriage**

I have mentioned my problems with baptism, and my incompetence in taking funerals; the third "occasional office" which afforded an opportunity to minister to non-worshippers is of course a wedding. St. Mary's, Walthamstow, is a beautiful, old church, and was much in demand for weddings; from April to September there were commonly four or five weddings every Saturday. In those days you had to get married between noon and 6 p.m., so each wedding was allocated 45 minutes, including coming in and going out, and the signing of the registers. Luckily the church had a side door; so it was not uncommon for one wedding party to be leaving by the side door while the next was coming in by the main West door.

The Vicar did not expect anyone to take all five weddings on the trot; after two or three it was someone else's turn. On one occasion when I was to take three services, I started feeling rather unwell. By the time I was starting the third service, I was beginning seriously to doubt whether I would be able to finish it. I gulped, and took deep breaths, but I was coming out in a cold sweat. As I was concluding the vows, I realised I had no more than two or three minutes before I was sick. So I stopped, assured the couple that they were actually married, but that I was too unwell to complete the service; and then almost ran into the Vestry, where there was a lavatory. I was just able to reach this and slam the door before I vomited violently.

When I was able to return to the Vestry, I found that the party had found their way there, and I was able to supervise the signing of the registers. But after the wedding party had departed, I felt I should write to the couple to apologise for spoiling their day. I addressed the envelope to the address in the parish which one of them had recorded as their home address – a couple could only get married in a church of the parish where one of them lived. However, the letter was returned to me a week or so later, marked "not known at this address"! Obviously they had given a false address; I felt that a service spoiled by a vomiting vicar served them right!

Apart from the actual wedding ceremony, there was of course the so-called "preparation meeting". I sat in on one of these, taken by Canon Druitt, and then had to do the job myself. Canon Druitt's "marriage preparation" (he was a bachelor) consisted of a 20-minute meeting in church with all the couples due to be married next day; he took them rapidly through the service, making single-sentence comments on the significance of some of the phrases in the book. That was it! When I started to do it, although I too was a bachelor, and 35 years younger than him, I felt that his brief comments were somewhat inadequate, and while keeping to the same pattern, I started to enlarge upon the explanations of the meaning. But when Canon Druitt found that my marriage preparation meetings had expanded to take 45 minutes, I was firmly rebuked. "They don't want to hang around all that time!" he grumbled.

When I had my own church, I tried to arrange more substantial wedding preparation, with at least one meeting in my home which might take a couple of hours, as well as the actual rehearsal in church. Over the years I tried various approaches, including using published courses, but I never felt satisfied with what I was doing. I told one fellow-cleric that I might think I was getting it right if people started cancelling their weddings afterwards! This would indicate that the seriousness of the commitment had got through to them, and some would feel they were not ready for it.

I recall one couple I was preparing when I was in the Isle of Wight. The bride, whom I knew slightly, was an unmarried mother with a little girl. I asked the young man what he felt about taking on not just a wife but also a child. His response was along the lines of "Well, I love Sarah, so I don't mind taking on her kid." I should have picked up on the inadequacy of this response from a future stepfather, but I missed it, and let it go. It was only a few months after the wedding that I heard that the couple had split up; the problem had been entirely his attitude to her little girl. I always blamed myself for not helping them to think through that issue beforehand.

Two other aspects of marriage also became increasingly problematical over the years, and these were first, couples who were already living together before marriage, and secondly the matter of remarriage after divorce.

Living together before marriage started being much more common in the '80s, and by the '90s it was virtually the norm. The vicar of a neighbouring parish to mine in the Isle of Wight took a hard line on the issue: if a couple were already cohabiting when they came to arrange the wedding, he would refuse to fix a date until they were living apart and promising to remain apart until they were married. I was never able to take such a firm stand, although I entirely sympathised with his position that the Christian moral standpoint is "chastity before marriage and faithfulness within it". I still believe that. The gulf between traditional Christian morality and secular standards is nowhere as wide as in the matter of sexual behaviour, and it seems that now the church has virtually stopped even trying to uphold the traditional line.

However I could not agree with my neighbour's stance on the matter. (I wonder how long he maintained it! I suspect that by the turn of the Millennium he would have virtually stopped officiating at any weddings at all if sticking to that rigorous policy.) Indeed, if the couple already had a child or more than one, he would have been breaking up the family by insisting on a separation.

In the mid '90s, after being approached by a couple who had just moved in together, and now wanted to book a wedding in a year's time, I wrote a somewhat intemperate letter in my parish magazine, denouncing the hypocrisy of couples who wanted to use the Christian church, while casually ignoring Christian teaching. I later regretted this ungracious and judgemental attitude, realising that I had to start where people were, not where I thought they ought to be; and I wrote another magazine letter (many months after the first, I fear) expressing my regret.

I still, however, found it hard to know what approach to adopt when such a couple was before me in my study, for an evening of "marriage preparation". My own experience was so totally different from theirs. Before I was married, I longed to be married. I hankered after sexual intercourse with a woman I loved. I wanted very much to have children. And I was often lonely, and much desired the warmth of companionship that I hoped marriage would give me. When I eventually found the right girl to marry, after various unfortunate, occasionally embarrassing, and sometimes hurtful attempts to fall in love with the wrong ones, my wedding day marked a whole new start in my life. And all the things I had wanted so much came to pass. We were blessed with a satisfying sexual relationship; we were given, eventually, four healthy children; and we enjoyed – with the inevitable ups and downs of married life – a warm and loving companionship. All this started on my wedding day, and that was what made that day so enormously special and significant.

But if you already had it all, then what on earth did getting married mean? I was then, and I confess I remain still, puzzled how to answer this question. I felt it right, quite often, to discuss it with these young couples; I hope I did so without any sanctimonious or moralistic attitude, but just in a genuine spirit of enquiry, trying to understand what the occasion we were planning together was actually to *mean*. We had some interesting and

255

amicable discussions; I felt I was being honest about my own convictions, without being condemnatory towards their different position. And I still set out to make their day as special as I knew how, without being unrealistic about what they and their guests believed. The comments I often received afterwards indicated to me that I had not gone too far wrong.

(d) **Christian Fellowship**

I had never actually experienced Christian fellowship in the context of an ordinary parish church before I was ordained and started my ministry at St. Mary's. All my experience of fellowship at Oxford and at Clifton had been almost exclusively in the student world. Though I had attended St. Ebbe's Church in Oxford regularly, I never got to know any of the congregation apart from fellow students. I only visited our village church in Painswick occasionally, when home for the vacation; I knew the other worshippers solely as my mother's friends. But when I started working in Walthamstow, my Christian fellowship was with the other members there – not only with my fellow-clergy, valuable though their support was, but with lay believers. I started to get to know fellow Christians of all ages, and from a wide variety of backgrounds.

One task I had been given was to visit the Alms Houses – there were three groups of these in the parish, with about six homes in each, and I had to visit each resident each month. I confess that sometimes this was more of a chore than a pleasure – with some of these dear old ladies, the conversation went round in the same, very limited circles, month after month. I hope my visits broke their monotony by giving them someone to talk to; but I suspect that in some cases they were politely humouring this ignorant young man! However there was one old lady who was still a Sunday School teacher at the Baptist church; and she was a lovely, gentle, Christian lady who was always a pleasure and a refreshment to meet. I was often able to share things with her, and we would pray together.

The other end of the age range was also a source of great enjoyment – not only the Sunday School, but the teens and early 20s. We did all the usual things that such church groups did, and had a good laugh together, as well as getting involved with Christian service of various kinds. Two examples of this are worth mentioning; one was the hospital ward services, and another was our monthly "Gospel Pub Crawl". In the wards of the little hospital across the road from the church hall we took short services on Sunday afternoons, taking in a tape recorder with the accompaniment for the hymns, and taking it in turn to lead, or to pray, or to "do the Talk", before going round the beds to chat to the patients. (I always remember one man who was telling me how hard he found it to reconcile the doctrine of a loving God with the suffering in the world. "It's not just people getting sick and that; it's all the dreadful carnation…" He kept on speaking of the "carnation" of war and revolution, while I did my best not to giggle.)

The Pub Crawl was a matter of going into various pubs (with the agreement of the landlords), sing a song or two accompanied by a guitar, and then chat with the customers. I have never been a particularly "pubby" person – not for any reasons of disapproval, but just because "it's not my scene". But it was good experience to meet a very different sort of clientele from our usual church contacts, and to meet them on their own ground. Occasionally we encountered anger at our invasion of their space with our gospel songs, or deliberately offensive, blasphemous and lewd comments; but usually people listened politely, and then were willing to chat. I don't know of any positive results from the exercise as far as the patrons were concerned; but it was a challenge to us to get out of our comfortable environment to share our faith.

I entitled this section "Christian Fellowship", and perhaps this term needs some unwrapping. The word "fellowship" is used with a wide variety of shades of meaning, denoting all sorts of friendship, matiness, comradeship and so on. All of these are valuable aspects of human experience, but "Christian fellowship" is something rather more specific. It refers to the shared experience of faith in Christ and a relationship with God. When a group of Christian believers have a close enough relationship that they are able to be open with each other, and pray together, about what they believe, what God means to them, and the problems and struggles they may face in their faith, this is fellowship. The word translates a Greek word (again!), the word Koinonia (κοινωνια), which means "sharing" or "having in common". It is sometimes used of sharing material things – homes, food, money; but going beyond and behind this practical sharing is the sharing of a living faith.

Sadly many Christians have never experienced this! In many churches, there is a degree of friendliness, but it virtually never includes talking together, let alone praying together, about what our faith means to us. If you asked people the meaning of the phrase, used in "the Grace" at the end of many services, "the fellowship of the Holy Spirit", you would probably be met with blankness, or inarticulate fumblings for some kind of definition. Yet the picture of the relationships that existed among the Christians of the churches of the New Testament reveals a deep and powerful degree of sharing together of spiritual experience.

I recall, during my time in Walthamstow, taking part in a Diocesan Clergy Conference which took place over a few days at the Butlin's Holiday Camp at Clacton. (The invasion of the camp by over one hundred collared clergy was not to everyone's taste; we heard that one family of holidaymakers demanded their money back, as it had ruined their holiday!) For several sessions we were divided into discussion groups of about ten, meeting with the same group every day, so that we were getting to know each other by the end of the conference. One elderly priest, of a more "catholic" persuasion than myself, confessed to a great feeling of loneliness in his parish ministry. "I so very seldom have the opportunity of fellowship," he lamented. In my brash way, I ventured to disagree with him, and spoke of the wonderful fellowship I had enjoyed with the lay Christians in the parish, thinking both of the young adults group, and my elderly Baptist lady in the almshouse. "No," he explained patiently, "I was referring to spiritual fellowship." It appeared that he was unable to conceive of enjoying spiritual fellowship with anyone but a fellow-priest. How very sad and limited a view that seemed to me.

(e) **Romance**

Before moving on from my years in Walthamstow, I must mention one other result of my time there which eventually became a life-long joy; it was at St. Mary's that I first met Mary, who was ultimately to become my wife. Ever since my conversion, one constant item in my prayers was that I would one day meet the right girl to marry. When, as an Oxford student, I attended the group at St. Ebbe's for men who were considering ordination as a vocation, I remember Basil Gough, the vicar, telling us how enormously important it was to marry the right woman. "The right wife will double the effectiveness of your ministry," he asserted, "and the wrong one will halve it!"

I had never had a real "girlfriend" since that time, though I had had casual friendships with a number of Christian girls; but I was not good at relationships with the opposite sex, perhaps as a result of coming from a family with three brothers, and attending all-male schools, a preponderantly male university, and a wholly male theological college. Mary was only 16 when I first met her, more than ten years younger than me; and it never occurred to me at first to think of her as a potential girlfriend. She was just one of the teachers in the Sunday School. She came from a typical

Walthamstow family; her father was a self-employed plumber, and they lived in a council house. Mary had left school at 15, with no "O" levels (though subsequently she took and passed one in English, and years later became a qualified nurse), and worked as a filing clerk for an Insurance Company in the City. Thus her background was not at all what I would have been looking for in a potential wife!

However we very gradually became more friendly, and enjoyed doing things together. When I moved from St. Mary's and started work at St. Stephen's, she sometimes came to help with the activities and events there, like the Sunday School outing or the church ramble. At one stage, our Church Army Sister, Sister Neate, who was a simple soul and a very faithful worker in the parish, took me aside and asked me earnestly, "Christopher, are you courting Mary?" I didn't know how to answer – it was not a phrase I would ever have used. Peter, the senior curate, also was uneasy about what he saw in our growing closeness; although I am sure that our behaviour was morally faultless – I don't think I had even kissed her at this stage – he obviously felt that we were just indulging in irresponsible flirting, and that because of the gulf between our social backgrounds nothing could possibly ever come of it. Mary had been one of the regular baby-sitters for their two little children, but the invitations to do this abruptly ceased. Mary was very hurt by this.

However when my time came to move on from Walthamstow, nothing had come of our friendship; I still needed to be shown by God that Mary was the answer to all those prayers! The next stage of our relationship was to come some years later.

14

❧❧❧

Further Parish Experiences

The time came when it seemed right to move on, and I was invited to become Curate-in-Charge of Emmanuel Church, Tolworth, the daughter church of Christ Church, Surbiton. I might perhaps have expected to have a church of my own after being ordained nearly five years, including the period as curate in charge at St. Stephen's; but I felt that, as Emmanuel was a much larger and more thriving church than St. Stephen's, with a firmly evangelical tradition and a good team of lay workers, it would give me valuable experience.

Emmanuel had been built in the 1930s when a large housing estate (of owner-occupied semis and bungalows) was being built within the parish of Christ Church; the population of the Emmanuel "sub-parish" would eventually be some 7,000 people, and the PCC of the parish church had the vision to have a centre of worship and ministry in the middle of the new estate. Unfortunately their vision only extended to building a small, dual-purpose building, which was a hall during the week and a church on Sundays. The developers offered the church a quite extensive plot of land, but the PCC turned it down, feeling that a more modest plot would be quite sufficient. Some years later, after the

261

war, Emmanuel was thriving and growing, and it was felt they needed to expand the buildings; the old dual-purpose building was enlarged with a chancel, and a new external profile, while a modern hall was built alongside. The buildings were now strikingly modern and wholly occupied the limited site.

Later still there were further developments, and it would have been enormously valuable to have had access to more ground, for further rooms, or for car parking space; but by now the site originally offered had been fully developed with houses. How we regretted the limited vision of the PCC in the mid-'30s! What an opportunity was lost.

Since the church had started, there had been a succession of mostly youngish curates, not usually staying for more than four or five years. The church had been started by a group of lay members from the parish church, who had from the beginning seen it as their task to build up the congregation by witnessing to their faith among their neighbours, and taking the lead in various church activities among adults and young people. This resulted in a very lively, out-going tradition, far from the very conservative and somewhat stuffy character of many parish churches – including, I felt, our own parish church, Christ Church. Being used to fairly rapid changes with a succession of enthusiastic younger clergy, the members were willing to go along with any new ideas that the next man came up with.

I found this enormously refreshing and invigorating, and looked forward very much to working in this parish. Moreover the clergy house, 181 Elgar Avenue, was merely one semi-detached house just like all the others in that end of the parish; there was no apparent barrier between clergy and parishioners caused by being saddled with a large, detached, old-fashioned house. However I found that I had arrived there at a time of transition; all the young couples who had moved into that parish in the pre-war years were now, in 1968, reaching retirement age together, and many of them were moving out to smaller houses, perhaps on the south coast. This included quite a number of the older church people, the founder members who had started the church and built it up over the years, and had taken various leadership roles and responsibilities. Several important posts were falling vacant, and we would need to find younger people to fill them. However the other side of the coin was that many new families were moving into the area, a number of whom were keen Christians, so there was an infusion of "new blood" into the church.

In the end I stayed in that church for nine years, and very happy, rewarding years they were. The church grew numerically; we started a monthly Family Service, attended by all the Sunday School children and uniformed groups, and this resulted in a packed church of over 300 people, which always gives a good buzz. I had always been keen on using visual aids in Family Service talks, and this gave me the chance of developing my style in this respect. Perhaps one of the most dramatic ones was when I borrowed a real stuffed lion – I had seen it in the window of a travel agent, advertising safari holidays in Kenya, and immediately said to myself, "I must have that in church!" It was quite a complicated operation to obtain and insure it, but that Sunday my sermon on Daniel went with a roar!

House groups became an important part of church life, with about half the adult members taking part in small groups in peoples' homes, particularly in Lent and Advent. This had a marked effect not only on people's growth in faith, by being able to discuss the Bible and our own experience with one another, but led also to a stronger sense of fellowship.

All sorts of church activities were arranged with the particular purpose of strengthening the sense of fellowship within the church community. Some were for particular parts of the church membership like the YCF or the Women's Fellowship, but others were for everyone, like the Sports Day when we challenged Christ Church, our mother church (one time Mary and I won the three-legged race!), and the Peaslake Picnics.

Peaslake is a little village in the Surrey countryside, and after summer picnics in one or two other locations, we settled on Peaslake for our annual outing. After a picnic lunch – every family or individual bringing their own – there was an afternoon with various activities for all ages, or a lazy snooze or chat for those who preferred. Then we went to the village hall, where the valiant ladies of the village had kindly prepared for us a simple cooked evening meal, with the sweet course contributed by the picnickers. Finally we all trooped across to the parish church for a short family service. The local parishioners were also invited to join us for this – they seldom had an evening service; and I recall two or three elderly ladies sitting at the back with Evening Prayer open in their Book of Common Prayer. I think they may have been a little taken aback when I took the service without robes, indeed with my shorts on; and everyone joined enthusiastically in a variety of worship songs including some action choruses for the children! We usually got fifty to sixty takers of all ages from infants to the very elderly for these popular occasions.

Evangelism

I have mentioned in an earlier chapter the charismatic dimension, with its joys and its problems that were a major part of my time at Emmanuel. But another key development in my own ministry was in the sphere of evangelism.

From my earliest days as a newly-committed Christian at Oxford, I had been wholly convinced that one of the main purposes of the Christian Church was evangelistic mission. Every Christian was to be ready to speak of his or her faith whenever the opportunity offered. All means should be used to lead people to faith in Christ. That was why God had saved us; that was why Jesus had founded the Church. "Go into all the world to preach the Gospel," he had said.

That was the theory; but increasingly I was feeling that it wasn't happening very much. In particular, I personally was not very good at it. I was often in situations where I was talking to people about the Christian faith – particularly at times like baptism visits, or when I was calling on people who had newly moved into the parish (I always made a note of "SOLD" signs outside houses, and tried to call within a few weeks with some of our church leaflets). But people weren't getting converted! They were not unwilling to talk about religion; but I didn't know how to take it on to the point of helping them to a personal faith. We sometimes were able to use major evangelistic events like the visits to London by Billy Graham, and we had seen people converted that way, both in Walthamstow and at Emmanuel; but when the "crusades" (as they were called then – it was before anyone was aware of the wholly negative connotations of the term, particularly for Muslims) ended, so did the conversions.

I then started to hear about a scheme of personal and parish evangelism called "Evangelism Explosion". It was a system which had originated – like Billy Graham – in the USA, being devised by James Kennedy, a young Presbyterian minister in Fort Lauderdale, Florida. My first enquiries about it did not attract me – it seemed too much like high-pressure salesmanship. But after much discussion, we decided to make it the main theme of one of our annual Parish Weekend Houseparties, at which the speaker would be a Vicar from North London, David Bubbers, who was one of the first British church leaders to introduce this method of evangelism into his church.

David's explanation and description of "EE", together with his accounts of how it had worked in an English parish, allayed our fears and misgivings; and shortly after that weekend the church paid for me to attend one of the "Evangelism Explosion Clinics" arranged by the British arm of the movement. This was a six-day event particularly for church leaders, clerical or lay, attended by members of several different denominations. The first three days were concentrated instruction classes; the next three included going out around the town in threes, calling on people's homes (by appointment), to put into practice what we had been learning in theory. During those three evenings, we witnessed several people responding to the Gospel and giving their lives to Christ in a prayer of commitment in their homes. I found this enormously encouraging.

The "EE" system has two main strands. First, there is a carefully-worked-out way of leading a conversation round to talking about a personal faith, leading up to two so-called "Diagnostic Questions". These lead on to an explanation of the Christian message in five stages. At each point there were Bible verses to quote, and helpful illustrations to use. It culminates in the question, "Does this make sense to you?" If there is a positive response, the evangelist – an ordinary person like me, not a high-powered Billy Graham type – will say, "In that case, would you like to receive this free gift of eternal life, right now?" This is the critical point. It is so easy to leave that direct challenge out – and result in an interesting conversation, but no conversion. But we found that if we had the faith and courage to ask the question, people would often respond. This method has to be learnt virtually by heart, including the scripture verses that can be used, and the illustrations that are often helpful.

The second strand of "EE" was the scheme for gearing up the entire church to learn and use this method of personal outreach; people converted would be recruited to join the classes learning the method, so that right from the start of their Christian life they would be learning to pass on their faith. Special emphasis was put on actually doing the work – not just learning about it - under the guidance and instruction of more experienced workers. As new recruits started to go out to call on people, always with an older guide, at first the "apprentice evangelist" would only watch and listen to how it was done. Gradually they would learn to make a contribution, the first being to give their own personal testimony – taking no more than three minutes! Ultimately the pupil would take over the entire conversation and the presentation of the message, the tutor only chipping in if particular assistance was needed.

Returning from this Clinic, I felt that at last I knew how to do it! This simple, point-by-point presentation of the Gospel could be dismissed as merely technique, a "spiel" learned by rote, and grossly over-simplifying the message. However it had been strongly emphasised throughout that while a "method" could not convert anyone, and this depended wholly and entirely upon the Holy Spirit, a learned method enabled otherwise inarticulate and stumbling Christians to explain their faith clearly. As far as the accusation of it being over-simplified or even simplistic, I would respond that all too often Christian preachers leave their hearers lost and confused; a straightforward outline of the message is a great advantage. Of course having once responded to the appeal the hearer will never stop learning and exploring greater depths of religious truth and experience.

The day after I got home from the Clinic, I had an appointment to visit a young couple about the baptism of their baby. The mother was a fairly new worshipper at our church, as the family had only recently moved into the parish; the father, however, described himself as an agnostic. This was the first opportunity for me to use my newly-acquired skills on my home ground, and it all went smoothly. When I reached the final question, "Does this make sense to you?" my hearer paused and then said thoughtfully, "Yes, it makes a lot of sense. I can see I need to do some more thinking about this!"

I responded, "Well, maybe you need to do some more thinking; but I must ask you this: do you feel you would like to receive this gift of eternal life that I have been describing, right now?" Again a pause; then the firm reply, "Yes, I would!" And so, after a few brief clarifying points to ensure there were no misunderstandings, I had the joy of leading him in a prayer of commitment to Jesus Christ – and the young wife had the joy of seeing her husband at last joining her in her faith.

That man became a very regular worshipper at Emmanuel, and took on various responsibilities within the church, and was still highly involved until the family moved away, more than thirty years later.

Although I started to use the "EE" method of running an on-going evangelistic programme in that church, it never wholly fulfilled my expectations in that respect. Nevertheless the actual method of personal evangelism – the framework of five stages of presenting the Gospel, with the illustrations and Bible texts used – I continued to find of great value throughout my personal ministry. Sometimes, it must be confessed, even after a person had apparently responded to the message and prayed a prayer of commitment to Christ, nothing seemed to come of it, and unlike that first man, they never actually became worshippers, or showed other signs that their commitment was genuine. I had perhaps been too pressing, and urged them into a "decision" which was not in fact real for them, and this is highly regrettable – not only because it indicated on my part an insensitive over-pressurising of the person which insufficiently respected their integrity, and perhaps did not sufficiently listen to their hesitations or uncertainties; but also because such an experience might sadly inoculate them against a more genuine response on some later occasion. However there were other people – particularly, perhaps, those who had already had some contact with the Christian faith, and even were nominal Christians – for whom the "EE" approach was enlightening and marked a real turning point in their finding a personal faith.

A conclusion I came to was that, in the British context, a method which had the expectation of a person moving from "Square One", with no faith and only the haziest understanding of the Gospel, to a full Christian commitment, in one single evening, was for most people unrealistic. In the American, much more religious, context, where the fundamental truths of the Gospel are familiar to most people, it can be highly effective; but in the UK, where ninety percent of people nowadays are almost wholly ignorant of what the Christian faith is about, a much more gradual approach is required. Something more along the lines of the Alpha Course, which has proved so enormously effective in recent years, allows for this more gradual, step by step, opening up of the message, with ample opportunities for people to voice their doubts, their questions, and even their objections and hostility to religion.

Marriage

I mentioned the start of my hesitant friendship with Mary before I left Walthamstow. It seemed that when I moved to the opposite side of London this tentative relationship had fizzled out. However this was not to be the case. When I left, Mary felt that a major change of direction in her own life was necessary, and she decided to seek new employment. As she had always enjoyed working with children – as well as being a Sunday School teacher she had also been heavily involved in Guides and the other uniformed groups – she felt that she should seek some job involving children. At first she explored the possibilities of being a nanny, but having none of the necessary qualifications, she found a job as an "assistant matron" at a boys' preparatory school in Winchester. While there she observed the work of the school "Sister", who was a trained nurse; and she found herself thinking, "I could do that much better than her!" This led to her applying for nursing training, and she started work at the Lord Mayor Treloar Hospital, in Alton, Hampshire. Apart from anything else, both these jobs brought her to the same side of London as me.

I would phone her for a chat sometimes, and on a couple of occasions she joined a holiday party I was leading on our family Island in Scotland. We had holidayed together before – while still in Walthamstow, she and another couple of friends had joined me for a fortnight on the Isle of Wight, which was where I first started to teach her to sail – and we found we enjoyed all the same sort of things.

That first experience of sailing was memorable. The other friends we were holidaying with had no thought of doing anything on a holiday but sitting on a beach in the sun – a fragile and uncertain hope in an average British summer. I had found there were sailing dinghies available for hire in Yarmouth, and booked one for the following day. The day dawned wet and windy; I asked Mary if she still wanted to go sailing, and she replied cheerfully, "Of course!" We collected our dinghy, dressed in whatever waterproof gear we had, and went zipping across the estuary with the boat heeling vigorously and the rain slashing our faces. Was Mary scared or miserable? No – she loved it! Wind and rain did not bother her in the slightest. This was perhaps when I began to feel, "This is my sort of girl!" But our relationship was an on-off kind of affair; months would go by with no contact, and then one of us – usually me – would phone the other, and it would start off again.

It was nearly ten years after we first met – nearly five years since I had moved to Surbiton – that once again, when I was making up a party for an Island holiday, that I felt that an experienced female would be a useful asset. "Just for a holiday!" I assured her; "No ulterior motives!" So once again she joined me in Scotland, with a group of other friends.

I should mention that our family links with this Island went right back to the early years of the twentieth century, when my grandfather and great-uncle had built a little Hut there as a base for sailing, and the family had been having holidays there ever since. The Island – it has a name, of course, but for our family it was always just The Island – is a place with its own magic. Scenically it is spectacularly beautiful; the panoramic views seen from the Hut, over the Sound of Jura, with the three symmetrical peaks of the Paps of Jura in the far distance; the ever-changing light over the swirling tides, the rocky islands, the rugged hills; the amazing sunsets over the Gulf of Corrievreckan and the mountains of Mull – all these we find haunting and enchanting. The wildlife too charms us – the seals, and sometimes otters, dolphins or porpoises; the gulls, cormorants, gannets and guillemots; the red deer seen on Jura or Scarba, and the shy roe deer or fox very occasionally glimpsed on the Island.

Each type of weather we experience there has its own attraction: the days with sun and a north-west wind, which brings an improbable brilliance of the blues of sea and sky, and purple of the far hills; the south-westerly gales, with huge curtains of rain sweeping up the loch over the marching, steel-grey waves and blowing spindrift; the glassy calm evenings, with wisps of mist drifting between the islands and points, and a silvery light over it all… staying in a simple little hut on the exposed tip of the Island, you are far more aware of every permutation of wind and weather than you ever are in normal urban life.

Furthermore it is a place redolent of a century of memories, of family stories passed down through the generations, as well as the recollections, both happy and painful, of my own holidays there since childhood. Perhaps the guests we invite to share a holiday – and guests have to be carefully selected: such a retreat is not to everyone's tastes and there have been some disastrous and embarrassing misjudgements, not least my own invitations to girls in my bachelor years – have become bored by the recounting of these tales; but they are a part of the place's character, together with the quirky names bestowed upon different objects and rooms around the Hut.

It was always a very special place for us all, with its own magic. My parents got engaged there, as did my mother's brother and his wife; and in my own youth two of my brothers had got engaged on the Island. So perhaps it should not be too surprising that the magic worked again, and I returned from that holiday in 1973, engaged to Mary.

In fact there was more to it than that. In our ten-year friendship, we had from time to time discussed whether we were "suited", and should get married; but there was always uncertainty – mostly on my part, perhaps because I was just not very good at male-female relationships – and so nothing ever came of it. But one evening on the Island, when everyone else had gone to bed, Mary and I were talking, and again I said, "I wonder if I'm just being stupid about this!"

I have mentioned my settled conviction that God had a plan for my life, including such major matters as matrimony, and the most important thing was for me to find and follow his plan; and I had often found that the Bible had spoken to me powerfully, and helped me to discern his guidance. I had by my bedside a little book of Scripture readings called "Daily Light", with a set of themed Bible verses for every morning and every evening of the year. Though I did not read it without fail every day, I often would look at it, particularly before going to sleep, so I said on this occasion, almost flippantly, "Let's see if God has anything to say!"

I opened it at that evening's readings, and found among the verses there were the following: *"The Lord God said, It is not good that a man should be alone"*. (Genesis 2.18) *"Two are better than one."* (*Ecclesiastes 4.9*) This was a startling shock; I had looked for guidance, and the guidance could hardly have been clearer. Some of the other verses on the same page reinforced the message. By the time we went to our (separate!) beds that evening, we were not only engaged; we had fixed the date of our wedding. We had decided that, as we (I should say, "I") had wasted so much time already, that it would be sensible to get married as soon as possible, and we settled on October 8th, which happened to be my birthday. This would give us just under three months to arrange it all.

We did not in fact tell anyone else at that point; there were particular people we wanted to tell first, before it got around the parish. The way I announced it to the parish was by reading my Banns, the legal requirement before any marriage in church. I stood up at the usual point in the service, and opened the Banns Book; and, as usual, most people switched off, glanced through their notice sheet, or looked up the next hymn, as I started, "I publish the Banns of Marriage between Christopher Cameron Jenkin, bachelor of this parish...." Some heads jerked up in a wild surmise; but others were totally unaware, until the buzz started going round after the service.

The wedding took place in St. Mary's, Walthamstow, Mary's home church, and it was Canon Druitt who conducted the ceremony. We were getting married at 5.30 p.m. on a Monday evening. The reason for this was that I had already had my full quota of holiday, and though my vicar in Surbiton agreed to give me an extra Sunday off, I did not feel I could ask for two. But getting married on a Monday would allow us a honeymoon of twelve days. The late hour was to enable as many people as possible to come, without missing a whole day's work. Two coachloads were coming across London from Surbiton. Unfortunately one driver got lost, and it was 5.45 before they arrived. We couldn't start the service until they had come, as 52 people coming in late would have created a considerable disturbance! Mary was actually standing on her doorstep waiting for the signal to come to church, when the lost coach passed along her street (completely off the proper route) and all the Emmanuel people waved madly at the bride! Meanwhile Canon Druitt was getting more and more agitated as the time passed, knowing that the legal deadline was 6pm. I still don't know if we got our vows in before that point; we certainly hadn't signed the registers, so we have probably been living in sin all our lives, as our wedding was not legal...

After a wonderful honeymoon in a boat on the Canal du Midi in the south of France, we returned to set up our married home together. I had of course been living in that house for five years, and had all my set, bachelor ways of doing things and the places where things were kept; and in my selfish and thoughtless way sometimes caused Mary considerable hurt, as I made her feel like a visitor rather than someone with an equal stake in the home. However we worked our way through such problems, and Mary was warmly welcomed by the whole church.

We had a further four years in Surbiton, and two of our children were born there. There were a considerable number of young families in the church, and the friendships between the couples and their respective children were a great joy and full of laughter. Emmanuel was very much a "family" church; the year our eldest was born, there were four other children born to church couples in the first few months of the year, and as they all grew and became toddlers together they made their mark on the atmosphere in services! Our eldest was a highly mobile youngster, and squealed vigorously if held; but if Mary put him down and let him wander round the church, he hardly made a sound. However while one toddler was no problem, when two or three of them started having races down the aisle during the prayers, it was a bit too much! So a crèche became an essential feature.

Moving on

The time came when we started to feel that we should move on and find a new sphere of service. For some reason, the usual practice in the Church of England is to keep such a matter a total secret from the parishioners, until one can triumphantly announce one's departure. I have never been able to see the reason for this secrecy; I made a point of telling Emmanuel folk that we were looking for a move, and asked them for their prayers, both that we should find the right parish, and that the right man should be found to follow me at Emmanuel. In fact it took two years before we found the place to which we felt that God was calling us.

We had looked at various parishes, both in the London area and further afield. We visited one parish in Derbyshire, and were surprised to meet there a young couple who were originally from Emmanuel, and whose wedding I had conducted some three or four years earlier. They had both been active members of the YCF, and I was delighted to see them again, now with two young children. I was even more pleased at what their Rector told me. He had only been in that parish a matter of months (the post which I was being invited to consider was being a Team Vicar at an associate church), and under his rather elderly predecessor the church had become very moribund. This young couple had arrived in the parish, as the husband was starting a new job in Derby; and though they were the youngest members of the church by some thirty years, they felt that God had led them to their new home in the town, and so to this particular parish church. It was not easy for a solitary young family to fit in; but after a while, another young couple joined the church, and then one or two more. This group of young couples became a centre for new life in the parish, and when the old Rector retired and the new one came, he felt that it was this young group from whom new life and growth began to spread throughout church life. It would have been so easy for the first couple to seek a more congenial church with other younger people; but it was their faithfulness to their sense of God's calling that enabled them to be a valuable catalyst in the church. I was very gratified to hear that story, and to feel that my ministry at Emmanuel, as the "exporting church", had played a part in it.

Guidance

I have mentioned several times my belief in seeking God's guidance, both in terms of a sphere of ministry and more personal matters like finding a life partner. For some people this is a concept hard to understand. I remember discussing it with one of my brothers. "All you have to do is to ring up for orders!" he said – he was an officer in the Royal Navy. "I don't do that; I have to make my own decisions, and take responsibility for them."

Well, no; seeking God's guidance is not quite "ringing up for orders", as if I don't have to think matters through, or use my judgement, and am thereby absolved from all responsibility for the result, in a kind of "God has spoken!" sort of way. It is certainly a matter of wanting to do what God wants; and behind this is the conviction that God *has* a plan and purpose for my life, and is concerned about all the major – and sometimes minor – decisions I have to take. Fundamentally I try to conduct my entire life in trust and obedience to him, and in a living, day-by-day relationship with him. Of course I don't always do it! I am as liable as anyone else to drift away from him and make decisions on a more self-centred basis than that. But that is the aim, and I have constantly to remind myself of it. If I am living close to God in this way, with prayer being something not relegated to Sundays or a particular point in the day, but in the background of all my living, then I believe I am in the best position to be living all my life in accordance with God's will.

If there is a particular problem facing me, or a decision to be made, then I will make that a specific matter of prayer, sometimes over a considerable period; and if it is something that concerns us as a couple or as a family, we will try to pray about it together (though I confess shared prayer was a much more regular feature of our married life in the early years). But the fact that I am praying for guidance does not absolve me from all the normal means of thinking through the issues, and weighing up the various factors and considerations. God has given me a brain, and commonsense, and he expects me to use them. He has given me a measure of wisdom and experience, and Christian friends whose judgement I respect, and various sources of information; all of these are to be employed, not as alternatives to God's guidance, but as the means of it. But I am also very aware of my fallibility. I do not always see things clearly. I sometimes give different factors affecting a decision either too much weight or not enough. I am selfish, and lazy, and greedy, and my motivation is not always precisely what it should be – in other words like everyone else I am a sinner, and my sin can easily distort my judgement. The same is true of even the wisest friend or mentor whose advice I might seek. So I continually have to ask God to keep me on track and overrule my faulty judgements.

How do I expect God's will to be made known to me? I know people who feel they have heard God speak to them in an audible voice – sometimes so vividly that they have looked round to see who it is. The Bible speaks of such experiences; but it has never happened to me like that. I have heard of others who feel they have seen a word written up in front of them as a visible message from God; again this has never – yet – been my experience.

There have been quite a number of occasions when it is the Bible through which a sense of guidance has come; sometimes gradually, as my regular reading and even my study in preparation for preaching has gently influenced my thinking, but sometimes much more directly when a verse or phrase has leapt from the page and hit me between the eyes. I have mentioned one or two such instances. There was another which occurred during my years at Emmanuel, and this concerned my relationship with my bishop.

The Bishop of Southwark at that time was Mervyn Stockwood, who was a powerful figure with various idiosyncrasies. I had a good deal of respect for him; more than that, I liked him. But in one matter I disagreed with him profoundly. Perhaps because he quite enjoyed being a controversial figure himself, he sometimes appointed other controversial clergy around him. One of these was Canon Pierce Higgins, who was more of a Spiritualist than an orthodox Anglican Christian. Bishop Mervyn was obviously intrigued with some of the phenomena associated with Spiritualism. One time on two successive Saturdays he wrote major articles in The Times, whose theme was aiming to challenge complacent secularists, by taking the line, "There are more things in heaven and earth than are dreamt of in your philosophy". But instead of adducing Christian arguments or experience in support of his argument, he described various spiritualistic séances he had attended, and some of the startling phenomena he had witnessed.

I was dismayed and horrified by this. I have always regarded such aspects of the occult as totally opposed to true Christian faith, and utterly condemned in and forbidden by Scripture, and it was appalling to find a Bishop of the national church giving credence to them. I wondered if I should myself write to The Times to make this point; but felt that I should wait a day or two in case someone more qualified than I did so. But two issues of the paper came out, and there was nothing. I drafted a letter, quoting various verses of the Bible. But I was still unsure whether it was right to post it. So in prayer I picked up my Bible, and flicked over a few pages in the New Testament. My eye fell on these words:

The Lord's servant must not be quarrelsome but kindly to everyone, an apt teacher, forbearing, correcting his opponents with gentleness. God may perhaps grant that they will repent and come to know the truth, and they may escape from the snare of the devil, after being captured by him to do his will. (II Timothy 2. 24-26)

This struck me as a fairly direct and clear answer to my prayer for guidance! I reviewed my letter, in case it was "quarrelsome", but felt it was adequately "gentle"; and I was certainly wanting not to attack my bishop, but to influence him to "escape from" this particular "snare of the devil". So I put a stamp on the letter, and posted it. On the Thursday it appeared in the leading position on the Letters page.

I have no idea if my letter did indeed alter Bishop Mervyn's views in the slightest. I did not hear it but that weekend he was on the panel of the BBC "Any Questions" programme, and a question was asked about this topic. I gather he referred in his answer to a "fatuous letter" from a member of his diocese! But he never mentioned the matter to me; whenever we met, he remained perfectly friendly and courteous, so he seemed not to hold my perhaps impertinent rebuke against me.

This example of my feeling that I had received God's guidance from words of Scripture might horrify some people, who would dismiss it as mere superstition. It would certainly be possible to quote many cases where well-meaning but naïve Christians had claimed guidance from God by using some verse totally out of context, and this might indeed lead people to disastrous actions. I have often quoted the story (probably fictional) of the man who sought guidance by opening the Book at random and stabbing the page with a pin. To his dismay it had landed on the words, *"Judas went and hanged himself."* So he tried again; this time, it was *"Go and do thou likewise."* In horror he had one more go, but the pin fell on the words, *"That thou doest, do quickly!"*

Though one can rightly deride such methods, I do not believe that this rules out seeking God's guidance from Scripture in more careful ways. Lying behind the reverent approach that I favour is the conviction that the Bible is the Word of God. This assertion of course raises huge questions, and theological, cultural, historical, and literary arguments have raged about them for at least the last one hundred and fifty years. Without going into all these issues, and I wholly accept that one must use all the methods of sound scholarship in order to interpret the words of the Biblical writers wisely, I do not believe that historical and textual criticism in any way rules out God's direct involvement in the writing of Scripture and his inspiration of the forty or more writers over some fifteen centuries. And if, as St. Paul wrote, "All Scripture is inspired by God" – literally, "God-breathed – *theopneustos* - θεοπνευστος"[1] (and he was of course referring to the Old Testament scriptures, as the New Testament was still largely unwritten) – then it seems perfectly logical to believe that God can use these words, inspired by the Holy Spirit, to speak to his people in every age by the same Spirit. Certainly this has been my experience, and that of many others.

---

[1] II Timothy 3. 16

As one reads the Bible, it is written of many men and women of God from Genesis to Revelation that God guided them. *"The word of the Lord came to..."* or *"they were led by the Spirit..."* are frequent phrases; though it seldom spells out exactly what happened, and how they discerned the word of the Lord or the leading of the Spirit, they had no doubt that this was what was happening. *"My sheep hear my voice"*, said Jesus[2], and he also implied that these same sheep had to learn to distinguish his voice from that of other, more malign, guides: *"They know his voice... they do not know the voice of strangers."*[3]

Paul was well aware that people who did not share his and his readers' faith in Jesus and experience of the Holy Spirit, would find such things absurd or incomprehensible. *"The unspiritual man does not receive the gifts of the Spirit of God, for they are folly to him, and he is not able to understand them because they are spiritually discerned."*[4] I have often found, for instance, that when a secular, non-Christian journalist is trying, even genuinely, to report some matter of faith and religion, where not just financial or practical issues but spiritual ones are involved, he or she invariably gets it wrong, and shows a fundamental misunderstanding of what is at stake. When this spiritual obtuseness is coupled with a mischievous hostility to the person involved, such as a political leader, the scope for distortion and caricature is boundless. In the week in which I wrote these words, the Prime Minister, Tony Blair, had mentioned in a TV chat show that he had prayed for wisdom when facing the huge decision of whether to send British troops into Iraq. Even those who share his religious faith may argue about whether he rightly discerned God's answer to that prayer! But various secular commentators poured scorn and ridicule upon

---

[2] John 10.27
[3] John 10. 4,5
[4] I Corinthians 2.14

281

the very idea, and implied (a) that he was using wholly irrational criteria to make the decision, rather than using his and other people's intelligence; (b) that he was claiming "This was the will of God", in an attempt to be above all criticism; and (c) that he was giving the Iraq war the character of a religious crusade against Islam, because "God is on *our* side, not theirs." Of course he said none of these things. He merely said that he prayed about it. As a man of faith, how could he not?

To the Isle of Wight

I wrote above that God expects us to use our brain, and weigh up all the criteria as best we can when making decisions. When the time came that Mary and I felt that we had found the right parish to move to from Emmanuel, I do not recall that there was any direct "word from God". We were invited to consider a parish in the Isle of Wight – which was unexpected, as we were always being told that the North of England was where the greatest needs were. Initially the Revd. Teddy Saunders of the Church Patronage Trust told us that he thought that it was likely to be a mixture of elderly people and holidaymakers. Parts of the Isle of Wight could be described like that, and we said that it didn't sound like us at all! However a day or two later he phoned again, having made some enquiries, and assured us that St. John's, Newport, was in an all-age area, with few holidaymakers. So we felt it right to explore this opening and pay the parish a visit.

We set off to Portsmouth to catch the ferry. We had left the two children with friends. It was a beautiful autumn day and we sat on a seat on deck as we crossed the Solent; it felt like being on holiday! We were met by the churchwardens, and they drove us into Newport and showed us around. We saw the vicarage, the church and the hall; we had a glimpse of the streets of the parish, including the rural, agricultural end of it, and met various parishioners; we were told about the life of the church with its strengths and weaknesses. Finally we returned home to Tolworth that evening.

Somehow from the start we both just felt that this was right. We had felt at home there. It was the type of parish we were looking for – not already a thriving, strongly evangelical fellowship like Emmanuel, but a simple parish church of a "low church" tradition. We heard that a number of young families had started coming to church while their children were in Sunday School, as the elderly vicar, at the end of his twenty-seven years of ministry there, had managed to get a new church hall built, right beside the church, to replace the old one nearly half a mile away. This hall, and the youth activities that went on there, were already beginning to change the age profile of the church.

We decided to give ourselves a few days to reflect and pray. But our conviction that this was right remained firm. The door to this new ministry had been opened, after two years of searching; all the aspects of the church and parish fitted with the kind of thing we had been looking for. Our inner conviction was untroubled by any contrary feelings of unease, as if God might be saying "No!" or even "Wait a moment!" Rather we felt that he was smiling upon us, and saying, "Go ahead!"

So the decision was made. The churchwardens were happy to ratify the invitation of the Church Patronage Trust (churchwardens cannot choose a new vicar; they can however refuse one who is being presented to them), and the Bishop of Portsmouth was in agreement. So a date was fixed, and early in the New Year we moved to our new home.

I Believe – I Think…

15

Caulkheads and Overners

Going overseas requires learning a new language! Before I even arrived in Newport, I got it wrong. I thought it would be a good idea to write a letter to be published in the Parish Magazine, to introduce myself and my family to them, and so I started it, "Dear Islanders..." However one of the churchwardens edited this; he explained to me that the local residents would understand the word "Islanders" as referring solely to people who had been born on the Isle of Wight, and there were quite a number of members of the congregation of whom that was not true – they were people who had moved over to the Island from the mainland, and were therefore known as "overners". So my letter appeared in the Magazine, starting "Dear parishioners..." which I felt was rather limp and boring!

I later learned that the traditional term for born-and-bred Islanders was "caulkheads", derived from the old boatbuilding industry. The other category of people, apart from the overners, who featured in Island life was the tourists or holidaymakers; these were known as "grockles", though we didn't have many of them in Newport. There were various other characteristic features of Island speech which intrigued me; words like "anywhen" and "somewhen", which are a perfectly logical parallel to "anywhere" and "somewhere", nevertheless struck me, when a newcomer, as charming and quaint.

My predecessor as Vicar had been there for twenty-seven years, and finally retired through ill-health at the age of seventy-seven. I was some 35 years younger when I arrived; there may have been some apprehension among some church members that I would be a "new broom" who would instantly set out to change everything, but in the main there was a recognition that changes were necessary if the church was to move forward. One of the first things I had to do was to start a crèche, even if just for the sake of our own family. Our two children were eighteen months and two-and-a-half, and were both extremely lively and restless toddlers; when I was at the front taking the service, Mary was having to cope with them on her own. One feature of the church building was that the pews had doors, and at first we thought that this would make it easier to control the youngsters; but they very quickly learned how to twist the snib or latch, and then it was great fun to bang the doors vigorously – and sometimes catch small fingers in them!

A young mother struggling with noisy children in a largely elderly congregation (though as I have mentioned there were other young families who were starting to come to church) is far more aware of, and on edge about, the disturbance her children are making, than any of the people around her. But although Mary was the object of turning heads and "looks", the looks were mostly smiling and sympathetic, rather than scowling and disapproving as if saying "Why can't you keep those brats quiet?" Nevertheless a crèche was a necessity; the questions to be explored were, "Where is it to be?" and "Who will man it?" The Hall next door was used by the Sunday School, so we decided to use the Choir Vestry; but on Family Service Sundays, when there was no Sunday

School, and there might anyway be more little children, we would use the Hall. As for crèche minders, in those early months it was mostly the older ladies who volunteered, until some of the younger ones, mostly newcomers to church, were ready to take over. We really appreciated the kindness of those older women.

The crèche started at our first Family Service which was the Mothering Sunday Service. The church was packed, and when I announced after the first hymn that pre-school children could be taken out to the Hall where they would be looked after, a sigh of relief went up all over the church, and about a dozen young mums got up to take their little ones out. I was quite surprised, however, when both on that Sunday, and when the crèche was mentioned in the local paper, the Isle of Wight County Press, the reaction was generally, "What a good idea! However did you think of it?" – as if no one had ever thought of such a thing before!

Although there were one or two younger families who were established church members, the great majority of younger people were newcomers to church. They had started to bring their children to the Sunday School, which started off in the morning service in church, and then after some ten minutes the children and teachers went next door to the hall, and the rest of the adults – including these young mums and dads – stayed in church for the rest of the service. When I looked around at these younger members, I could see that most of them were not confirmed; probably few of them were committed, converted Christians; most of them had a pretty hazy idea of what the Christian faith was about. But – for whatever reason – they were there! And I felt that this was where the future of the church lay. I was delighted that the older, long-established church members welcomed these newcomers, and helped them to feel at home; and I found that many of these "oldies" would say to me, "It's lovely to see them there! We've had our day; of course the church has got to change, so that these new, younger ones can be happy there." This attitude made it much easier than it might have been to introduce some changes of style.

I say "for whatever reason" they were there. I came to understand that another reason, apart from any searching for a faith (come on, get real!), and apart from wanting their children to go to Sunday School to learn about Jesus – or, more likely, "to learn right from wrong" – another powerful incentive concerned the Church of England Middle School.

The Island school system divided the children into Primary (4-9), Middle (9-13), and High (13-18). In Newport there were three Middle Schools; Archbishop King, the Roman Catholic one, known as ABK; Node Hill, which was just across the road from the church, and the Church of England Middle School in Wellington Road, usually known as "Welly Road". "Welly Road" was where many parents wanted their children to go; it had a very good reputation for both academic standards and behaviour, and it had been set up specifically to cater for the children of church members – first Anglicans, and then Free Church – from all over the Island. But to get your child in there, you had to get a form signed the previous autumn by your Vicar or Minister, who would confirm that you, the parents, were regular worshippers. It was surprising how many young parents – particularly mothers, as fathers tend to feel that such matters are women's business – turned up in church after the summer holidays, perhaps a year before the dreaded form must be signed! It was sad, though perhaps less surprising, that all too many of them abruptly stopped attending church once the coveted place in the school had been obtained.

Every year the Archdeacon wrote a letter to all clergy, urging them to be absolutely honest about what they said on the form; to interpret "regular churchgoer" to mean "normally weekly", and, if that were not the case, to spell out as precisely as possible how regular the parents' attendance at church was, and any other family involvement with church. Inevitably some clergy were more rigorous with this than others; I certainly got the impression that some of my brother-clerics were happy to sign the form with no qualification if a parent had turned up a couple of times. But I tried always to be scrupulously truthful.

As the years went by, the pressure for places at Welly Road became greater and greater; in my final year on the Island, there were 150 or more applicants for 90 places. This led to a very painful episode for one church family, and for me. This particular family had had strong links with the church for some years, although the father only worshipped occasionally. But the mother was not one of those who I saw in church every Sunday without fail. When she came with her form, I wrote "Mrs X is in church most Sundays, and Mr. X comes occasionally." Perhaps the fact that – as I learned later – the family had been on holiday for two weeks, and on the third Sunday they had attended the Chapel of the private school where their eldest child was a pupil – all meaning that I felt I hadn't seen them for a few weeks – may have influenced my precise wording, although the parents both later acknowledged that what I wrote was strictly accurate.

However that year, because of the pressure for places, the Selection Panel had decided only to offer places at the school to children whose forms in no way qualified the "regular worshipper" statement. Anyone else, even with such a qualification as I had added, had regretfully to be turned down; and that meant that this particular family found that their beloved child was refused a place. What made it worse was that the mother was actually a teacher at the school (she was my daughter's excellent class teacher), and she was able (quite wrongly) to go into the school office, and examine all the forms to see what I had written about other parents. Then she hit the roof, and was

289

incandescent with fury, and I received in one morning three increasingly abusive and distraught phone calls, accusing me of "ruining a little girl's life".

There was of course an appeal process, and I willingly appeared on their behalf, explaining the long-standing links that the family had had with our church, and happily the child was in the end offered a place at the school. But I don't know if that mother ever forgave me.

Although the practice of attending church purely in order to get your child into the school of your choice raises all sorts of moral questions, not least about the system that encourages such behaviour, nevertheless I saw it as an opportunity and a challenge. Could we, in the year or so that these parents were coming to church, convey to them the essence of the Christian message, not only by sermons and services but by the Christian love they experienced, enough to persuade them to continue their attendance when it was no longer necessary for their ulterior motive? Thankfully in quite a number of cases this was so; I can recall one couple who became very committed believers, but who confessed that their initial motive for coming to church was entirely selfish. But as they say, "You can't win them all", and others disappeared rapidly once their child had been given a place in the school.

For the first time I was now genuinely a Vicar, and Mary was a Vicar's wife. I never really got used to being called "Vicar", rather than Christopher, or more formally Mr. Jenkin, but I recognised that for older people it was hard to change the habit of a lifetime. (A man of my own age, who was our part-time organist, was prone to call me "Vicar", and so I would respond by addressing him as "Organist"!) There was a recently-formed Young Wives group, and in our first month we learned that there was a problem with the usual venue, the church hall, as it had been double booked; so we invited them to meet in our very large drawing room, even though at that point the house was far from organised, and there were still stacks of boxes of books in various places. At one point, one of the young women said to Mary, "How are you settling in, Mrs. Jenkin?" "Oh, please call me Mary!" said my wife. This request was met by a shocked silence. Even though they were the same age group as her, many of them obviously felt it was dreadful to call the Vicar's wife by her Christian name. It took quite a long time for many people to recognise and understand that Mary was just another young mum – and often, in this new place, a very lonely one. It never occurred to any of them just to drop by for a chat; unlike our home in Tolworth which was indistinguishable from anyone else's, the Vicarage was a large, detached, six-bedroom house, with a number of similar houses on either side. It was daunting for someone who lived in a terrace house or even a semi to brave the drive and the large garden and approach the imposing front door.

But we did soon settle in and make friends, and the ten years we spent on the Island were perhaps the happiest of our entire ministry together. Our two younger children were born there (and so were true Islanders!), and our three older children were happy in local schools (the youngest didn't start school till we had left). Church life, while not of course without its problems (is it ever?), was rewarding and encouraging. The church grew both numerically and in terms of spiritual life and maturity; many of those young couples who were new and uncertain when we first arrived, went on to be confirmed, and indeed converted. Though many of the real Islanders had never in their lives been to any church but St. John's – and therefore were apt to assume that the patterns of church life they were accustomed to were the right and indeed the only way of doing things – we had a steady inflow of overners who had had a variety of experiences of other churches;

and these people were very ready to suggest (or to respond positively to my suggestions of) changes and new developments. I was aware that there might be some resentment on the part of traditional Islanders about these newcomers who were changing "their" church. This danger was the greater because very often it was the newcomers who were willing to take leadership roles, while many of the Islanders were reluctant to recognise their own gifts, and were diffident about "putting themselves forward". But in fact there was very little real friction over this issue, and there was usually a very happy and positive atmosphere in the church.

Music

We were very blessed with our choirmistress, who was also the deputy head and music teacher at the local church Primary School. This enabled her to recruit a number of children, both boys and girls, into the choir, and a further feature was that there were several families with both parents and children in the choir. It was a traditional robed choir, but not an imitation cathedral choir with the attendant formality associated with that. We were affiliated to the Royal School of Church Music, but were also very ready to tackle more contemporary, informal styles of music from various sources, as well as traditional anthems and hymns and psalms.

One particular development which we started to explore was the Gospel Musicals of Roger Jones. The first one we tackled was "A Grain of Mustard Seed", which this Birmingham music teacher had composed in 1986 to mark the 250th anniversary of the birth of Robert Raikes, the founder of the Sunday School movement. This music was of a rather different style from anything we had sung before, being slightly syncopated, very tuneful, and sometimes slightly comic and light-hearted. Roger Jones also has a habit of using words of some traditional hymn, and composing a totally new tune to it. One used in this work was "Tell me the stories of Jesus", which was performed to a lively melody by all the children (representing the children in Raikes' eighteenth century Sunday School) marching round the church, playing kazoos!

We performed this work in semi-dramatized style, with the three main soloists (I was Raikes) in costume; it was enormous fun, and was greatly appreciated by the whole congregation. The next year we decided to do another work by the same composer, "Saints Alive!", which told the story of the Day of Pentecost and the growth of the early church, as described in the early chapters of Acts. As we started to learn this, it became apparent to me that this was a rather different work; it was not just a religious entertainment, but was potentially both worship and evangelism – we were not just singing about the Holy Spirit but experiencing him and ministering him to our hearers. So we determined to learn the work by heart so that we could present it without books, so that we could make more direct contact with our audience; moreover I felt that it would be wholly appropriate to have an evangelistic appeal at the close, to invite anyone who felt that God had touched them to come forward for counselling and prayer.

I also decided that we needed to use part of our weekly rehearsal time for Bible Study and prayer, so that we could better understand and enter into the story we were presenting. Once again the work contained some familiar hymns set to new tunes. One such was "Breathe on me, Breath of God"; another was "When I survey". The first one was used in the part of the story when the disciples were praying that the Holy Spirit would come upon them, as described in Acts chapters 1 and 2. It led straight into a free time of interweaving melodies, where although there were three suggested musical lines, the singers were invited to extemporise and sing their own spontaneous tunes. In other words it was a portrayal of, and indeed an opportunity for, "singing in the Spirit" or singing in tongues. This was a totally new experience for most of the choir members, and it took some getting used to, but many of them started to find a freedom to express their own yearnings and worship even if they didn't actually have the gift of tongues. The other song, "When I survey", was set to a haunting, beautiful melody, sung first by a soloist (in the context, a new believer responding to the Gospel message), and gradually supported and accompanied by other singers, till in the last verse the whole choir joined in a triumphant chorus. It was intensely moving.

At the end one or two members of the congregation did respond to my low key appeal; the young husband of a regular churchgoer, who himself was a fairly infrequent attender, was in tears as he acknowledged how God had spoken to him through the performance, and as I led him in a prayer of commitment to Christ.

In subsequent years we presented several others of the Roger Jones musicals; our most ambitious production, using a 60-strong ecumenical choir and orchestra in the local theatre, was "From Pharaoh to Freedom", a work which – as the title suggests – presents the Passover story. It starts and finishes with a modern Jewish family celebrating Passover; it then tells the story of the Exodus, and then moves to the Gospel account of the Last Supper as Jesus and his disciples celebrate Passover. Light-hearted moments include the plagues of Egypt, portrayed by children dressed as frogs, gnats, and locusts – though it becomes much more serious for the final plague, the Angel of Death. This was acted and danced by a fourteen-year-old girl from one of the local village Methodist chapels, who had worked out all her own choreography by listening to the tape and studying the Bible story. And I always found myself close to tears as I watched her. The new hymn setting which was most powerfully moving was "Man of Sorrows", sung as Jesus hung on the cross; it rises to a great climax, with a change of key and the entry of the brass in the orchestra, in the final verse, "When he comes, our glorious King, All his ransomed home to bring"; Jesus descends from the cross, and the cast gather at his feet. The trouble was that I could never sing that bit – my throat would seize up with emotion!

As well as the robed choir, and its activities both in formal services and more ambitious drama, we also started to develop a Music Group with guitars and other instruments, with some quite accomplished musicians – some of them members of the choir, but others who were not. This group would quite often accompany some of the more modern worship songs in Sunday services, but also on other occasions and elsewhere, as I will describe shortly. Instruments such as a flute and a trumpet, played by talented young people in the choir, would also be used to enhance hymns.

As a choir affiliated to the Royal School of Church Music, we were heavily involved in RSCM events both on the Island and over in Portsmouth. This gave us an opportunity to meet members of other choirs; and it was very evident that the great majority of church choirs, on the Island at least, were composed of members who were very much more elderly that we were. One village church choir had just three children in it, all boys from one family; at one RSCM event these boys were chatting to our large bunch of youngsters, who were telling them about all the things our choir got up to. The boys went home to their Mum, and said, "Why can't we join that church, instead of our boring one?" This led to a lot of heart-searching in that family; eventually, fearing that there was a real risk of the boys becoming so disenchanted with church that they rebelled and stopped going altogether, the parents transferred their family allegiance to our church. We were of course glad to welcome them; but at the same time I felt very guilty, and sorry for their vicar who was losing the one and only young family from his church and choir.

Youth

There was a good Sunday School at St. John's, and a Pathfinder Group for the 11-14 year olds. The latter, however, only really took off and came to life when we were able to encourage eight of the youngsters and one of the assistant leaders, a young man of about 20, to go away to a Summer Camp in South Devon. My successor-but-one at Emmanuel was the leader of this Pathfinder Camp, which was why I chose that particular one to suggest to our group; but at first it proved very difficult to persuade the parents to agree to let their youngsters go away for ten days without them – and to the Mainland! The big, bad, remote and dangerous Mainland! I exaggerate a little, but that anxiety about crossing the Solent was real for some. So Mary and I decided that we would have to go too, and Stuart, the commandant, agreed to take me on as Padre, and Mary as Medical Officer. We also took our three children – the third had his 2nd birthday while at camp. One memorable episode with this toddler occurred when he was sitting on one of the chemical toilets; unfortunately the ground was uneven, and child and loo together toppled over. Fortunately it had only just been recharged so there was nothing in it but the chemical solution, but Ross still suffered from a blue backside, as well as the indignity of having to be rescued from his predicament!

That Camp was a life-changing experience for most of those young people. They had never experienced a large and lively group of young Christians before. The young assistant leader, too, was thrilled, after years of being almost the only one in his age group in church, to find a large team of energetic, crazy, fun and deeply committed young Christian men and women. One by one, our Pathfinders gave their lives to the Lord; it was like picking fruit, with one after another ripening and dropping into our hands! The weather that summer was atrocious, far from ideal camping conditions, with frequent torrential showers, though with spells of sunshine between, when all the wet clothes and bedding were dragged out of the tents and strung up to dry on the guy ropes – until the next downpour approached. But none of it mattered. The fellowship, the worship which was of a liveliness and authenticity which was inspiring, the imaginative teaching, and of course all the fun things of camp, with outings, games, and swimming – all conspired together to make it an unforgettable ten days. The group came back to their homes, their schools, and their church and Pathfinder group, fizzing with their newfound faith, and the positive fall-out from that first camp continued to influence church life for several years, both in the young people's work, and also – as four or five of the girls were in the choir – in the life of the choir too.

Most of them went to the same camp the following year; that summer was glorious, with almost unbroken sunshine. A memorable episode was the baptism in the sea of a fourteen-year-old boy from Emmanuel Church, which I described in Chapter 10. The Camp was the usual mixture of fun and games, worship and teaching, laughter and noisy singing; and as I drove our minibus away at the end, laden with happy, tired and deeply tanned young people, I asked them, "Well, have you enjoyed it?" "Oh, yes!" they enthused. "But..." there was a pause; "Last year was better!" It seemed that there were more important factors than the weather!

Inter-Church Events

The Newport Clergy Fraternal was not a large group – there were usually about six or seven of us – but it was a very warm and friendly fellowship, with several Anglicans, a Methodist, a Baptist, a Pentecostal, and a Roman Catholic as very regular attenders. We had a varied programme, of discussion and study, but just chatting and sharing our joys and troubles was always a major part. The Baptist minister was part-owner of a yacht kept in Cowes

Harbour, and on one occasion he took us all for a sail in the Solent; on another occasion the Roman Catholic priest cooked us a curry.

It was from that little group that a number of major initiatives sprang, involving church life not just in Newport but sometimes the whole Island . There were the usual things like the Week of Prayer for Christian Unity, in which we not only had a united weeknight service, but on the Sunday we exchanged preachers, and sometimes lay people to lead prayers too. (I always remember the visit to St. John's of an enthusiastic and fervent Pentecostal lady to lead our intercessions. Her vigorous and eloquent appeals to the Almighty were not quite in the style we were used to – but that was partly the point of the exercise. I particularly recall her prayer for the inmates of the three local prisons; "Lord, let them study the Scriptures – they've got plenty of time….")

But there were also other events which were organised by Newport clergy, being in the centre of the Island, including the annual Whit Monday devotional service. This had been for some years a worthy but – dare I say? – perhaps rather dull event, with an appeal limited to the more devout church members. One year, however, we decided to "push the boat out", and not only invited an extremely well-known speaker, but moved both the night and the venue to allow for the expected larger attendance. This was encouragingly successful, and there was standing-room only. The following year, we went a step further, and as Portsmouth was hosting a week-long mission by the Canadian evangelist, Leighton Ford, who was incidentally the son-in-law of Billy Graham, we invited him to come to the Island on the Sunday afternoon, for an open-air service in Carisbrooke Castle. The so-called Bowling Green within the Castle walls made a superb venue, and we were thrilled that about one thousand people, from all over the Island, came to the event.

This was the start of a number of Pentecost Celebrations, as we called them. In several subsequent years we used the grounds of a Stately Home, Gatcombe Park, about three miles outside Newport. The first year we went there it was empty; but when the new residents moved in, they graciously allowed us to meet on their lawn on two or three occasions. As we were well aware that not everyone would know where it was, I produced a quantity of fluorescent signs, saying PENTECOST CELEBRATION, with an arrow, which I placed a few days before the event on signposts at strategic road junctions for miles around the venue. This not only directed people to find the place, but also had an even more valuable function, in advertising the event to a wide audience. Each year we had from 800 to 1000 people. The music at all these events was provided by the St. John's Music Group.

At least two major Christian events took place at the largest indoor venue on the Island, Sandown Pavilion. The first of these was the visit of the noted evangelist, writer and teacher, Canon David Watson. This was in fact only a couple of months before his death. It had been planned over a year earlier, as the first stage of a five-day Island-wide Mission and Festival led by David Watson and his team. His usual practice for these events was to have a one-evening visit about six months before the main Mission, as an appetite-whetter – to give the local Christians a taste of the kind of style and content of his team events – the music, the drama, the dance, the banners, as well as David's address. The main five-day event was to be right in the centre of our parish, in the playing fields of a local school, using a large marquee.

However his diagnosis with liver cancer put a stop to all the plans, to our deep disappointment, and everything was put on hold. But in the summer, as his cancer did not seem to have progressed (he had received healing ministry from his great friend, the Californian John Wimber) it was decided to reinstate the Sandown meeting in November – the five-day event was to have been the following May. On the Saturday morning, there was a seminar for Christian leaders of all kinds, and David shared with us his faith and his uncertainty about his future. He mentioned that he was booked to lead a three-week mission in Seattle the following autumn. The organisers had asked him, "But will you be here next autumn?" "I don't know!" he answered frankly. "Will you?!"

Sandown Pavilion was packed to the doors with 1,100 people on the Saturday evening – it was said that it was probably the biggest Christian gathering on the Isle of Wight in history! It was an uplifting and inspiring occasion. A coachload (or was it two?) went from St. John's; I recall that one lady who was a little on the fringe of our church life, a close neighbour of ours, told me afterwards that half way through the first hymn, "Praise my soul", she started crying, and hardly stopped all evening. I have often found that tears are a sign of the movement of the Spirit in someone's life.

Tragically, though David told that great audience, "I still have cancer, but I *think* I am being healed..." it was not so, and the following January he became very ill, and died in a couple of weeks. I was personally particularly disappointed, as I had had great hopes of the May event in the centre of my parish. But despite the prayers of thousands, David – that great believer in, and practiser of, healing ministry – was not healed.

Of course I was far from alone in my disappointment; and many were not just disappointed but had their faith severely shaken. David Watson had had such a remarkable ministry, with the gift of reaching so many different kinds of people. He was deeply respected by the highest in the land – he was a frequent guest of parliamentary groups; and he was able to reach across all denominational boundaries to people who were inclined to be very suspicious of and uncomfortable with most evangelists. Many felt that he might be the one who would spearhead a real spiritual revival in our country. So why did God not heal him? It seemed so terribly wrong.

In his final illness, he had to be protected by his friends from all kinds of cranks (one of them a lady in the Isle of Wight whom I knew well) who were convinced they had a Word from the Lord for him, and rang constantly to tell him so. Some wanted to assure him he would be healed if he underwent believer's baptism by immersion; others, that he had to renounce the Church of England as an apostate and heretical body. Maybe some of these still feel that his refusal to heed their revelations was the cause of his death. I don't have any answers to why he was not healed, but I do not believe that reasons such as these are the explanation. I too believe in healing ministry; but it is my experience, and that of everyone who is honest about such ministry, that sometimes it "works", and sometimes it doesn't. And there is no simple answer as to why. I believe that we just have to obey God, do our best to pray and minister as guided by the Spirit, and leave the results with him. At the end of the day we can only pray with Job, "The Lord gives, and the Lord takes away; blessed be the name of the Lord." We may weep before him, and rage at him – and that's all right! His shoulders are broad. But in the end we can but acknowledge that we see only a tiny bit of the whole picture; God is the only one who sees it all.

I was also instrumental in organising another great evangelistic event in Sandown Pavilion. I had read that the converted New York gang leader, Nicky Cruz, whose name had first become known in the '60s through David Wilkerson's best-selling book, *The Cross And The Switchblade*, and who had developed an international evangelistic ministry, was to tour England; so I approached the organisers of this tour to explore the possibility of his including the Isle of Wight in his itinerary. This led to my booking Sandown Pavilion, and undertaking most of the local arrangements, including recruiting and training of counsellors, and all the publicity. ("Counsellors" in the evangelistic context has nothing to do with psychology or therapy; a Counsellor is a person who, when an evangelistic appeal is given at a meeting, goes forward with the people who respond, and then talks to them, one to one, to help them to make their own personal commitment to Christ in prayer, and also makes sure their name is fed into the system for linking the person with a local church so that their new faith can be properly nurtured. This system was first developed by the Billy Graham Evangelistic Organization, and the pattern, training programme, and literature of their system became a model followed in many subsequent evangelistic events.)

Because Sandown Pavilion seated over one thousand people and needed to be filled, and because all reports indicated that Nicky Cruz's ministry was singularly effective, particularly with younger people, publicity was absolutely crucial. I had already developed an all-Island publicity vehicle, which I called CHAIN (Churches All Island News) – a duplicated single-sheet newsletter which I sent two or three times a year, free and unsolicited, to every church of every kind for which I could acquire a contact address; my mailing list had nearly 180 addresses. I had started this newsletter because I was so aware of many valuable Christian events which took place at various Island venues, which might be of much wider interest than to the immediate locality, but which were never heard about by most ordinary church members. So I used this mailing list to send out publicity about the Nicky Cruz meeting. The first letter, asking church leaders to put the date in their diary and to recruit potential counsellors, went out some three or four months before the event; and there were two subsequent mailings, the final one being a couple of weeks before the visit of Nicky Cruz, including posters and handbills, all of which I had produced myself.

However, on this occasion and many others, I discovered that the hardest problem is the "clergy block": in all too many cases the information never gets further than the Minister's desk (and perhaps his waste paper basket). This became clear a few days before the Nicky Cruz meeting, when I was at a Committee Meeting of, I think, the local auxiliary of the Bible Society. One member of this committee was the wife of the vicar of a village church not far from Sandown. I mentioned the Nicky Cruz meeting, and my hopes and excitement about it, and the vicar's wife pricked up her ears. "Oh, is Nicky Cruz coming to the Island? I'm a great admirer of his!" This, after her own husband had received three different mailings about it!

Because of this problem in publicising any event – such a mission, the Pentecost Celebration, the Roger Jones Musicals, the annual Sponsored Walk for the Bible Society known as the Wight Wander – I knew I had to use every possible means of reaching past the clergy to lay members of churches. If there was a Deanery Synod (the Isle of Wight was divided into two Anglican deaneries, East Wight and West Wight), a Methodist Circuit meeting, a concert, or any other occasion when Church people might be gathered together, I made sure there was a handbill for "my" event on every chair. There were also posters everywhere, of course – but I believe that posters are an over-rated means of publicity, whether put in a public place or on a church's internal notice board; for while some people (I am one) cannot pass a piece of writing without wanting to read it, many others, perhaps most, can pass the most eye-catching poster a dozen times, and remain totally unaware of it.

However, for the visit of Nicky Cruz, the venue was packed, the organization went smoothly, the counsellors had been recruited and trained, and the response to the appeal was encouraging. As always, of course, it is hard to gauge the long-term effectiveness of any evangelism; even Jesus obviously experienced the disappointment not only of the seed falling on stony soil, but of apparently enthusiastic responses fading away and coming to nothing. But I hope that for some, at least, of those dozens of people who flooded forward at the close of the meeting, it marked the start of a new relationship with God which was to prove life-long.

I mentioned above that one of the events which I publicised was the Wight Wander, a sponsored walk which I initiated as a result of my involvement with the local Auxiliary of the British and Foreign Bible Society. (For some reason it is only the Bible Society which calls its local support groups "auxiliaries".) We decided that some kind of fund-raising effort was required, and it was before sponsored walks had become quite such a cliché as was the case in later times. So I agreed to take it on. In fact the hardest task was done by a faithful member of St. John's, David Copp, a schoolmaster who was a keen walker. It was he who, that year and every year, devised the route, and then walked it all to check that there were no problems and to write precise directions. My task was to publicise it, to recruit teams of checkpoint marshals, and to produce sponsor-sheets and route guides.

The first year the total distance was 28 miles; there were quite a number of people who completed this impressive total, but we reduced it to 20 miles in subsequent years. Every five miles or so there would be a check-point, where check-cards were signed, and those who had reached their energy limits could drop out; a soft drink was offered to those continuing, and then on they plodded. We had walkers of all ages; I remember that my elder daughter, when aged about eight, had almost completed the entire 20 miles when she collapsed, sobbing, on to the pavement. "I just can't go any further!" she wept. But I was able to say, "Look! Just along there, beyond the trees! Can you see the church tower? That's the finish! You are nearly, nearly there!" And so she struggled to her feet and limped on the final few hundred yards. Five minutes after finishing and having her check-card signed off, she was playing tag around the churchyard with her friends...

The Wight Wander not only raised a good sum of money for the Society every year, but it was an ecumenical event which involved considerable numbers of people from several different denominations and churches, not only in Newport but from all around the Island.

Freemasonry

It was at St. John's that I encountered Freemasonry for the first time. It was strong on the Isle of Wight, and there were half a dozen mostly older men who were members of the Lodge. All but one came only to the evening service on Sundays. At that time I knew very little about Freemasonry, but had a vague feeling that I was against it; but the presence of such men in my church prompted me to start reading up on the subject. In addition, at a meeting of the Portsmouth Diocesan Evangelical Fellowship the speaker was a vicar from Aldermaston, and his topic was Freemasonry; it seemed that Aldermaston parish had a tradition of very strong links with the Craft, and his experiences there of conflict over the matter had led to him almost having a breakdown. (His battle had started when, nearly a year after he moved to that church, he received a letter from the secretary of the local Lodge asking for permission for the annual Masonic Service to be held in his church. His reply was to give consent, so long as all prayers were offered in the name of Jesus. At this modest request the skies fell in!)

I was concerned that as most of our Masons were elderly men, the chances were that one of them would die before long, and his widow would request a church funeral with full Masonic rituals. There was no way in which I could accede to such a request, and yet I had no desire to find myself in conflict with a grieving widow. But I was reluctant to attack Freemasonry openly. From time to time, however, I alluded to it in passing in sermons or parish magazine articles, normally not mentioning its name, but referring perhaps to "religious societies which exclude the name of Jesus". But the time came when, one Sunday evening, I was preaching about the Old Testament reading from Exodus chapter 4, where Moses learned the Name of God, "I AM". I mentioned the name for God used in one Masonic ritual, JAHBULON, and explained that this was an amalgamation of JAH, for Jehovah; BUL, for Baal; and ON, for the Egyptian God, Osiris. I said that such an identification between the Lord God and pagan deities would have been utterly abhorrent to Moses and other writers of Old and New Testaments.

This was the first time I had ever mentioned Freemasonry by name in any public sphere, and a few days later the wife of one of the Masons spoke to me.

"The Masons in this church are very hurt that you keep attacking them," she said. "Did you know that it was the Masons who donated the oak choir stalls to the church?"

I protested, "I have never mentioned Freemasonry till last Sunday evening!"

"No, but you keep attacking it indirectly," she insisted.

I was interested, and quite pleased, that my various oblique allusions to the Craft had been understood by those involved. But I felt that now it was out in the open, I must confront the Masons honestly and directly. I had in my files a copy of a talk by Rev. Dick Lucas at St. Helen's, Bishopsgate, in the City of London, spelling out in detail what the Christian objections to Freemasonry are; so I made copies of this, and sent them, with a covering letter, to each of the freemasons in the church. In my letter I expressed my appreciation for their loyalty in worship, and the various ways in which they had supported St. John's over many years, but said that my conviction was that no Christian should also be a Freemason as the two systems of belief were incompatible; the enclosed paper would explain my reasons. I assured them that I was not in any way suggesting they should leave the Church; I would far prefer that they left the Lodge.

I had one reply to this letter, in which the Mason accused me sharply of ignorance and bigotry. The following Sunday all the Masons were in church as usual; the service was Holy Communion in the modern liturgy, which included The Peace. At that point in the service I felt it important to go over to the letter-writer to greet him and shake his hand. He looked startled as I approached him, but then grinned at me and shook my hand. I hope that I conveyed the fact that although we disagreed on that one matter, I still regarded him as my brother in Christ. I would have been uncomfortable giving him Communion if I had not expressed that reconciliation after the sharp words that had been expressed between us. It is on that sort of occasion that I really value The Peace as an element of worship.

Sesquicentenary

1987 was the 150th anniversary of the founding of St. John's (and I found that the formal title for such an anniversary is "sesquicentenary", but we didn't in fact use the word in any of our parish publicity – the church does enough baffling people with abstruse words without adding any more!), and we decided to make it a whole year of celebration, with special events arranged virtually every month. The actual weekend of the founding date was marked by a visit of our Bishop, with a great hotel dinner on the Saturday night (we felt it merited more than a church hall buffet!), and a special service on the Sunday. For that service, as people came into church they were given a block of wood (offcuts, 12″ x 3″ x 1″, from a local timber firm whose owner was a church member), and a pen; and they were asked to write their name on one edge. Then later in the service, each person came forward, and the Bishop built a great erection of timber blocks on the font. This vividly expressed the fact that the church is not bricks and mortar, but people – old and young.

We had several other bishops preaching during the year – men with whom I had some kind of contact. Bishop Pat Harris, whom I had known at Oxford, and who had visited my home to assure my mother that Clifton men were all right; Bishop Ban It Chu, late of Singapore, and the Rt. Revd. Dehqani Tafti, the previous Bishop of Iran; and I had even invited George Carey, later to be Archbishop of Canterbury, who was at that time Principal of Clifton, but subsequently he had to withdraw his acceptance as he was appointed Bishop of Bath and Wells.

Other major events during the year were a weekend led by Graham Kendrick (which was the first time I met the hymn, "Shine, Jesus, shine" which he taught us at the Saturday evening celebration in Node Hill School); a weekend led by John Stott, including a high-powered seminar on "Issues facing Christians Today" in the local Theatre; a visit by the London Emmanuel Choir; and another by the Prom Praise orchestra from All Souls', Langham Place, under the baton of Noel Tredinnick. This latter I expected to be enormously popular and quite a money spinner. They were to give two performances in the Theatre, an afternoon one for younger families, and the full Prom Praise works in the evening. I knew that Prom Praise events in the Royal Albert Hall were always sell-outs very quickly; but I discovered that no one in the Isle of Wight had ever heard of Prom Praise or of the orchestra, and tended to be suspicious of Classical music anyway. Tickets went very, very slowly, and I began to panic that the orchestra would be playing to an almost empty Theatre. Among our efforts to drum up some support was a handbill distribution on the Saturday morning to the crowds in Cowes! In the event, although for the afternoon performance the Theatre was less than half full, for the evening it was three-quarters filled, and all who went found it – perhaps to their surprise – an enormously enjoyable and inspiring occasion. On the Sunday morning, the orchestra divided in two, half of it playing in our church, and half at the Baptist Church. Each ensemble invited local musicians to join them after a brief rehearsal before the service, and this was a splendid opportunity for a number of our young instrumentalists. (Though I got into trouble with one protective mother – "Why was my daughter not invited to take part?")

Perhaps the most memorable event of the year, however, was our Marriage Reunion. We planned to send a personal invitation to every couple who were still alive and still together, who had been married in St. John's. My wife Mary took on the task of doing the vast amount of research to try to trace all these couples. This involved going through six marriage registers which covered a period of over sixty years. There were several elderly people in the parish who had lived there all their lives and were valuable sources of information: "Oh, yes, I remember them – but he died… That couple moved to Southampton, but they still have relatives in Shanklin…" And so on. In the end we sent out about 350 hand-written invitations (one of our teenagers did superb calligraphy), and at one point we thought we were going to have exactly 150 couples coming – which would have been splendid for the 150th Anniversary! However one or two dropped out, and there were about 145 couples. One couple had been married 62 years; another for six weeks! Both those couples were church members.

We had a service in Church, at which all couples were invited to stand and renew their vows. One couple in the choir sang a duet (from Roger Jones' *Saints Alive!* "I am yours and you are mine.") Then everyone went up to the Carisbrooke High School Hall, where there was a Reception complete with three-tier wedding cake. Another couple – our choirmistress and her husband – sang a duet there: the Alan Jay Lerner and Frederick Loewe song, "I remember it well!" It was a tremendously happy occasion. An additional and exciting bonus was that the BBC had heard about the event and sent a TV crew, who filmed during the service and the reception, and interviewed me and several couples. It appeared on that evening's 6 o'clock news, with a longer item on the Monday evening regional news. My brother was sailing his yacht in the Mediterranean and listening to the BBC World Service – and was astonished to hear my voice speaking about the event there!

Moving On Again

The time came when we began to feel it was time to move on. I had made it clear when I first went to St. John's that I did not envisage staying for twenty-seven years like my predecessor! I thought seven to ten years was more likely, as I felt that if vicars stay too long in one place, they can get stale and run out of steam. (I don't now feel that that is necessarily true.) In 1986 I had answered an advertisement in the Church of England Newspaper, for the Director of Evangelism in Carlisle Diocese, coupled with the incumbency of a small village church, and Mary and I had been invited to go for an interview in Penrith. How to get there was a problem – it is a long way from the Isle of Wight. We looked into driving, or going by train, but it all seemed laborious and expensive. An acquaintance on the Island, to whom we had been able to give some help in a family crisis, was part owner of a Cessna plane, and he had told me once that he had flown to Perth

(Scotland, not Australia) and back in a day, for a wedding. I said to Mary, in jest, "Perhaps we ought to ask John to fly us up to Penrith!" The very next day I found myself sitting beside him at a committee meeting of Marriage Guidance, and at a dull moment in the Agenda, I leant across to him and whispered, "You wouldn't like to fly me and Mary to Penrith next week, would you?" "Yes!" He exclaimed. "Which day?"

It emerged that he loved doing this sort of trip. He had to check with his co-owner that the plane was available, but then phoned me to say it was OK. I asked about the cost; he said that it cost £32 an hour to keep the plane in the air (Sandown to Carlisle would be about 2½ hours), so the round trip would normally cost about £160. However he said he would be happy to charge us no more than the train would cost – which I knew was almost exactly £100. So we agreed on that price – it was a very generous offer - and made the arrangements.

It was quite an adventure for us to do the trip in a small plane. He let me wear the spare headphones so that I could hear all the dialogue with the various Air Traffic Control areas; and although on the trip north there was a heavy overcast, on the journey south it was clear and we enjoyed a wonderful view. In fact when we were due to come home, it was blowing a gale, and he didn't think we would get off the ground safely, so we begged beds for the night, and flew back next day.

As far as the interview was concerned, there were two other candidates. We were all interviewed for both the parochial and the diocesan parts of the job, the latter being the more substantial. I understood (later and unofficially) that I was the choice of the parish representatives, but nevertheless the diocesan team selected another man for the appointment. In fact by the end of the day, Mary and I were coming to the conclusion that it was not quite right for us anyway, so we were not too disappointed. In particular, we felt we should not leave just as the church was going to celebrate this major anniversary with all the year of festivities and special events planned. (Later I got to know the successful candidate, and felt that he did the job superbly, much better than I could have done.)

However a year later, a purely parochial post in Carlisle diocese was advertised, and I wrote to the Bishop to ask for particulars of the parish concerned, St. Paul's, Barrow-in-Furness. I waited and waited, but no letter came. After some two weeks, I phoned the Bishop of Carlisle; his secretary answered, but the Bishop then came on the phone, and said that he was very sorry, but they had never had my letter – and interviews had now been arranged for the following week. However he said, "In case we don't make an appointment then, would you like me to send you the particulars, so that you can still ask for your name to be considered?" I replied that I would be grateful if he could do so.

When the description of the parish arrived, they seemed to both Mary and me to be just the sort of thing I was looking for, and so I filled in the application form. This form also, however, asked for three references; and as a year previously the Bishop of Penrith, the suffragan bishop, had received three references from me, I phoned him up to see if he still had them on file. Bishop George Hacker greeted me warmly, remembering me well from the previous interview (my arrival by plane may have helped to render me more memorable!) but regretted that when that appointment had been made, the references of the other candidates had been destroyed. This was very efficient, but inconvenient. "However," he added, "knowing the parish of St. Paul's, Barrow, well, I think you might well be a suitable candidate. I am seeing the Bishop of Carlisle tomorrow, and I will mention you to him."

An hour or two later, I had a phone call from the Bishop of Carlisle. It seemed that Bishop George had decided on reflection not to wait until the meeting next day, but had phoned Bishop David Halsey that afternoon – and now Bishop David said, "Could you come up for the interview next week?"

This time Mary could not make arrangements for the children to be looked after, and I decided to go by train, and on my own. I felt excited about the possibilities, feeling that the previous visit to Cumbria, though seeming to come to nothing, had in fact done two things: it had made Mary and me feel that we would quite like to work in that lovely county, and it had also prepared the way for me, by making me known to the Bishop of Penrith. There was only one other candidate, and the interviewing panel of six (three parish representatives, the Bishop of Penrith, the Archdeacon, and a clergyman from the Simeon Trust, who were the patrons of the parish) offered me the job. I asked if I could have forty-eight hours to discuss it with my wife and family, and they readily agreed. I took photographs of the Rectory and its garden, the church, the hall, and some views of the parish, and when I got home next day the whole family gathered round to see them and talk about the possible move to a new home. There seemed to be complete happiness and agreement that this was right, and after further prayer I phoned the Bishop to tell him of my acceptance.

This experience seemed at the time another instance of being comfortable that we were following the guidance of God. Later, when we were finding our life in Barrow far from happy, we wondered if we had got it terribly wrong. In particular, we could not recall quite why we had felt it right to move on from Newport at all at that stage. Because I had always said to people that I expected to stay there seven to ten years, and in fact we stayed almost exactly ten years, had I simply got that time span stuck in my mind? And yet, with our prayers for guidance, the various circumstances that seemed to point in that direction once we started considering the move to Barrow, the definite invitation of the selection panel, and the sense, when we were discussing it as a family – even including the children, as it was their lives that were going to change too – that we were all happy about it, with no sense of unease or contrary indicators – it all seemed to confirm that this was right.

So, for good or ill, with a sense of excitement and facing a new challenge, we headed for Cumbria. I particularly remember our final service at St. John's. At the end of a moving and inspiring time of worship, during which not only I but Mary and each of the children were given farewell gifts by the parishioners, the service concluded with the congregation singing, accompanied by our lively music group, "You shall go out with joy, and be led forth with peace, and the mountains and the hills shall break forth before you..." Our family moved to the door to greet people as they left; but no one else moved, as they were all singing so enthusiastically! I was thinking about the mountains and the hills to which we were moving; but also, despite feeling a little foolish as we stood waiting in the porch, I felt glad that the worshippers' attention was more on worshipping God than on saying goodbye to us!

16

Hills of the North

A s we left the M6 and headed west along the A590, the rugged hills and scars on our right provoked cries of joy and excitement from the children, reminding them of happy holidays in the West Highlands of Scotland. When we arrived at our new home, which Mary and I had seen (we had spent a couple of days measuring up for curtains and carpets) but the children had not, they quickly recovered from the long and weary drive as they rushed around to explore. One of the first things I did was to climb a tree and fix a rope with a tyre on the end, as a swing – it remained there, much used and enjoyed by our own and many other children, until we left more than thirteen years later.

One serious misjudgement was that, though moving from a large, Victorian house to a considerably smaller, 1960s residence, we had decided not to select which items of furniture we would keep and which discard until we arrived and saw what fitted where. This is a course of action I would not recommend! It meant that virtually every room was packed with furniture, and there was scarcely room to move. In addition we had no less than forty-two cartons of books. I was reminded of *The Hunting of the Snark*, and the character of whom Lewis Carroll wrote:

"He had forty-two boxes, all carefully packed,
With his name written clearly on each;
But since he omitted to mention the fact,
They were all left behind on the beach!"

But ours were not left behind; they all came, and were stacked high in every room, including the garage. The movers from the Island were dismayed at the state in which they were leaving us; they liked to take a pride in settling people comfortably into their new homes. However we assured them that we would be all right, and set about trying to sort things out.

It had already been arranged which schools the three elder children would go to; the fourth was only three. The eight-year-old had been intended to go to the Church Junior School, of which I would be Chairman of Governors; but we were told there was no room, and were advised that although I could "pull rank" and insist that he be accepted, this would not be appreciated within the parish, especially by parents who had been denied a place at that school for their child. So we accepted the situation, and on his first day I walked to a more distant school with him, skinny and freezing on that January day in his shorts. We soon learned that long trousers were a necessity in the north!

When I started going to services in my new church, I decided for the first two or three weeks to let the existing clergy (a curate and the hospital chaplain who was on the strength of the parish) lead the services so that I could pick up the flavour of what the people were used to. The first thing that struck me was how very old-fashioned and formal it all was. It took me back twenty-five years to my curacy in Walthamstow. At both Emmanuel and St. John's I had become used to modern, forward-looking churches, with a good deal of informality and relaxation, using contemporary hymns and songs as well as the traditional repertoire. Instead of the large, youthful choir of St. John's, I found a small, mostly elderly choir, with about three children. When I asked if anyone played any instruments other than the organ, I was met with blank looks.

I had been given to understand that the church had had evangelical leadership for at least the past thirty years. My immediate predecessor, Frank Dean, had died very suddenly in office a few months before he was due to retire, after seventeen years in the parish. As a result all his papers were still in the filing cabinet in the Rectory study, and as I sorted them out it was clear that he had been a faithful, biblical teacher. But I also gathered that he had been a very gentle man who had shrunk from any confrontation; and perhaps there had been therefore less change, development or modernization than there might have been with more forthright leadership. Certainly I would not have described the church as an evangelical church; not only would most members not have been at all clear what the term meant (which is unimportant) but concepts like conversion were not part of their thinking. I did however meet some members who were definitely of an evangelical persuasion, and I had great hopes that they would form the foundation of the developments which I hoped to lead.

This was not how it turned out. Some of our most committed members left the area within a short time of my arrival. One family moved their membership to another church in the town because they did not find my ministry charismatic enough; another little clique left the church because I was too charismatic. Those who were left were "middle-of-the-road Anglicans"; faithful, loyal and godly indeed, but with no particular understanding of my theological style, which was coming to be described in church circles as "open evangelical".

It was not that I met with opposition to my ideas, or hostility of any kind within the church fellowship. On the contrary the church members as a whole, and those in positions of leadership and responsibility in the church, were invariably friendly and kind. But I felt that there was no appetite for change. Every initiative of any spiritual kind had to come from me; I don't think I can recall any lay member suggesting a new idea, saying, "Why don't we...?" I remember talking to a minister of another denomination in the town, who said of his own church, "As long as I don't try to change anything, they are all perfectly happy!" I knew what he meant.

But the feature which I found hardest to deal with for quite a long time was the reserve. I had had a naïve expectation that northern people were blunt-spoken, heart-on-the-sleeve type of folk, who would call a spade a spade. I suppose I had picked this image up from books like *All Creatures Great and Small*, which was of course about Yorkshire. But I found Barrovians to be very reserved, certainly about matters of faith. My very first Sunday, as I stood at the door and shook hands with people as they left the service, I was expecting welcoming greetings like "I do hope you and your family settle in quickly and feel at home!" But hardly anyone said a word but "Good morning, Rector!"

At my previous churches I had been accustomed to getting some response or reaction to services I led or sermons I preached. I am not just talking about a casual "Nice service, Vicar", but specific comments about things I had said – sometimes a query, sometimes a disagreement, sometimes a "that was helpful." If the choir sang an anthem, or even a descant, usually someone would express appreciation. But at St. Paul's in those early days, that virtually never happened. I would preach my heart out, perhaps sharing something that was deeply important to me and about which I felt strongly, and which I felt God had led me to speak about. And at the end, nothing but a polite "Good morning, Rector." I felt like saying, "Hullo? Is anyone there?" Did they agree or disagree? Was anything I had said remotely helpful to anyone? Had it sparked off any thoughts or ideas, or been challenging, or encouraging? I never knew. I never even knew if people listened, or just switched off when the sermon began.

I eventually concluded that one possible reason for this reserve, this reluctance to react or comment in any way, was a kind of deferential hangover from old-fashioned attitudes - as if people felt, "Who am I, to comment on what the Rector says or does?" It didn't mean in the slightest that they found what I said to be unhelpful or irrelevant. On one occasion, an older lady did phone me after the service to take me up on something I had said. I had mentioned my conviction that Jesus was for everyone, including people of other faiths like Jews or Muslims (of whom there were and are very few in Barrow). This lady's husband came from Holland, where he had witnessed Nazi persecution of the Jews, and she felt strongly that the gracious thing for Christians to do was to leave Jews in peace and not try to evangelise them. I disagreed, but appreciated very much her willingness to say what she felt. However she was very apologetic about daring to mention it at all; it was only the strength of her feelings that gave her the courage to do so. I did my best to assure her that in no way did I take offence, but indeed that I far preferred that someone should take issue with what I said than show no apparent response or reaction at all.

One occasion when this lack of response particularly upset me was after our first Carol Service. I had been used in my previous parishes to the Carol Service being the biggest service of the year, with a packed church. But when I looked through the Service

Register at St. Paul's, I found to my astonishment that the numbers attending previous Carol Services had been very modest, with not many more than one hundred people present, though the church would seat over four hundred. So as my first Christmas approached, I started to make ambitious plans and preparations. For a start, it was going to be "Carols by Candlelight" – so we constructed plywood hoops to hang from all the light fittings, each with about eighteen candles on them, and also little boards to hold rows of candles on each window sill. On the reredos behind the Holy Table was a further row of thirty-six tall candles. We had a total of some four hundred candles in church. Then we invited men, women and children to join an augmented Christmas choir, and this led to a choir of thirty-six people, who started practising five special carols. Scripture readers were recruited and rehearsed; colourful Order of Service leaflets were prepared. And then there had to be publicity; so we produced dozens of coloured posters which were displayed all over the area, and thousands of handbills which teams of church members loyally posted through every front door in the parish.

In the event, the church was packed to the doors, and everything went splendidly. But as I stood shaking hands at the door at the end, just five people out of four hundred made any comment. Two complained that candle wax had dripped on them; two said they found it hard to hear the readers. One said it had been a lovely service. And as I went home in a state of exhaustion, I asked myself, "Why did I bother?" In the following few days, I kept hearing second-hand reports of what a splendid and inspiring service it had been, which was more encouraging; but why had no one said so at the time?

When I had been in Barrow for a year or two I mentioned in a Parish Magazine letter how puzzling and indeed discouraging I found this apparent unresponsiveness. I was not angling for fulsome but insincere praise, neither did I expect everyone to agree with everything I said. I just wanted some indication that someone was listening, and that I was not wasting my time. Perhaps partly as a result of this, gradually people did pluck up the courage to respond. There was one couple, fairly new churchgoers, whom I found particularly heartening. One time when I was visiting them, the man said, "A few months ago you said…." And he quoted a point I had made in a sermon, and asked if I could explain it further as it had puzzled him. I was amazed that not only had he listened, but he had also pondered what I had said. I could ask for no more!

Within weeks of arriving in the parish I found myself embroiled in a fierce controversy. I was told that in March – we had arrived in early January - the Church Primary School would perform a musical show generally called "The Spectacular". This was an annual event which had been a major feature of the school's life for some years, and was an important money-raiser for school funds. The producer had had children in the school when the show first started, but they had left some years before my time there. I was looking forward to seeing this show; but I also picked up certain "vibes" that raised question marks in my mind. "I'll be interested to hear what you think of The Spectacular!" people would say – but would not elucidate.

I was a bit surprised when I learned that there were always five evening performances, each lasting two hours; this seemed a heavy burden to lay on children aged between 7 and 11. But when Mary and I went to a performance, we were very impressed. The school hall was packed out. The musical accompaniment was provided by a competent adult ensemble of six players. It seemed that about half the school were taking part in the succession of "songs from the shows". The performances were lively, sparkling, meticulously rehearsed and polished. The stagecraft was superb.

At the end I warmly congratulated the Head Teacher – a member of the church, and ex-churchwarden - for his school's achievement.

And yet there had been certain elements of the show which had left me uncomfortable and uneasy. I felt that the children, especially the little girls, had been rehearsed to behave not as children, but as sophisticated adult women, with actions and gestures which had suggestions of a mature sexuality which troubled me. In addition, when they were performing "Nothing like a Dame" from *South Pacific*, the only adult performer in the show appeared – a man wearing a grass skirt, and an imitation bra made of coconut shells. In an adult show this would have been harmless; in a children's show at a church school I felt it was in bad taste and unsuitable, even though it evoked shrieks of mirth from many in the audience.

Every Monday I had a meeting with the Head Teacher to discuss school affairs, and a week or two after the Show I mentioned to him, "When you start to plan next year's show, would it be possible to allow the children to *be* children, rather than imitation Tiller Girls?" And I briefly mentioned my misgivings about certain elements of the show which had made both Mary and me uncomfortable. I had no idea at all what I was starting. Neither did I realise till much later that Frank Dean, the previous Rector, had so hated the Spectacular for precisely the elements that troubled me that he just stayed away. His gentle nature would not allow him to make any comment, especially when to criticise would have been publicly to set his opinions against the judgement of his church school's Head Teacher. It might have been wiser had I emulated his example, but to quote the proverb, "Fools rush in..."

A few days later, the Head Teacher said that some of the parents whose children had been performers, and who had themselves been involved in various ways in the production, had heard of my reservations, and would like me to explain to them what I felt; would I be willing to meet them? "Of course," I replied; and a date and place were set.

Now I recognise that I didn't handle that meeting at all well. One background factor was that on television, the evening before I met these parents, I had seen a programme about the sexual abuse of children. It was at that period that such issues were beginning to emerge from the shadows, and this programme gave some horrific details of little children being abused, and being encouraged to develop sexual habits and appetites at an appallingly young age. I particularly recall one case reported, of a little boy of about three or four who had been frequently seduced by his teenage baby-sitter; he had developed strongly sexualised behaviour which horrified his mother. I had been very disturbed by this programme, and I am sure it was in the background of my mind when I went to talk to these decent, well-meaning parents about my unease about aspects of the show in which their beloved children had taken part.

I had not prepared a statement, and it had not occurred to me in any way carefully to formulate my concerns; I was ready just to try to explain frankly how I felt. But to start with I was taken aback when I entered the room and found twelve men and women awaiting me – I had thought it was going to be perhaps three or four. When I tried to explain my misgivings about certain parts of the show – perhaps a small percentage of it – I probably did not express myself well, and I soon found that I was provoking a considerable measure of hostility. I mentioned my sense of disapproval about the man in the coconut bra, and said that I regarded it as coarse and vulgar; I later learned that I had been sitting beside the man's wife, who had designed his costume. Unsurprisingly she was mortified and deeply hurt, though she said nothing at the time. I recall one man who kept on saying – in the famous words of the tennis player John McEnroe - "You cannot be serious!" I realised that they were reacting as if I was accusing them of sexually abusing their children; I never said this, of course, but I did feel that teaching little girls to dance seductively was the thin end of the same wedge. But the parents found this utterly incomprehensible: how could young children like theirs be anything but wholly innocent? And what sort of mind did I have, that I could suspect anything else?

I had found that meeting difficult, but much worse was to come. The convenors of the meeting sent a long letter to all the parents whose children had taken part in the Show, saying that the Rector was wanting to stop future shows. (This was not true.) There were statements in quotes purporting to have been made by me at that meeting, which I felt seriously misrepresented my views – though after that hour of heated discussion I could not guarantee that I had never said precisely those words. But it gave the impression that I thought the whole show had been disgusting.

And the next thing was that someone sent that letter to the local press, and there was a half-page article about the controversy, with a large photograph of six scantily dressed little girls, captioned in huge print, "WAS THIS THE WIGGLE THAT WORRIED THE RECTOR?" From then on there was a steady stream of letters to the paper, all anonymous, attacking me savagely. "What disgusting minds some people have!" they accused. I never mind people disagreeing with my views; but I had stood by my convictions openly – why did these writers not have the courtesy or the guts to do the same? Not only that, but we started receiving anonymous letters and abusive phone calls at home. Mary took to answering the phone herself and not allowing me to take calls until she had vetted them; anonymous ones she just fielded and quickly rang off.

A special school meeting was called (according to the rules, the governors were compelled to call an extraordinary meeting if sufficient parents requested it). I found myself under fierce attack once more. In the front row were four ladies who were church members, who I knew sympathised with my views; but not one of them said a word. Afterwards I asked one of them, "Why didn't you speak up?" "Oh, I don't like to put myself forward!" she replied, shaking her head. I had some sympathy with this diffidence – but the lack of any overt support whatever left me feeling desperately isolated. Interestingly enough, one speaker at this meeting said that over the years five different clergymen had criticised the show. He said it to demonstrate, I think, how stupid and narrow-minded the clergy tend to be. I responded that if the show had often evoked such criticisms from clergy, it just might perhaps indicate that there were indeed elements of the show which were contrary to Christian standards. But this suggestion was derided.

The issue was discussed at length at the next Governors' Meeting, and the conclusion was that the producer of the show should be invited to produce another show the following year, "but to bear in mind the concerns felt by some governors and parents about some elements of this year's show". I felt this was a very restrained and courteous request on the Governors' part. However the response of the lady concerned was flatly to refuse ever to produce the St Paul's School Spectacular again unless and until she received a public apology and full retraction from the Rector.

So that was the end of it. I was not going to retract my views, and I did not think I had anything for which to apologise. Shortly after that the Head Teacher took early retirement – he assured me that his resignation had nothing to do with this controversy (despite mischievous allegations to that effect in the press) but was for reasons of ill-health and his responsibilities towards elderly relatives. When a new Head was appointed, he knew nothing, of course, about the details of the issue, but said firmly that he disagreed with anything which so totally monopolised the spare time of the pupils and staff for so many months each year, and he was relieved that the show had been discontinued.

The controversy, however, rumbled on. On the one hand, I started to hear from more and more people who had been as unhappy about these aspects of the show as I was, and who congratulated me on the stand I had made; I appreciated their comments, but would have valued their open support when the battle was at its height. On the other hand, my own children were frequently accused, for years to come, that "Your Dad was the one who stopped the show!" And in the local paper, the North West Evening Mail, whenever my name was mentioned for any reason, I became known as "Barrow's controversial rector".

This could have been amusing, if it hadn't become rather irritating. I have mentioned my interest in the whole subject of publicity, and one aspect of this has always been that I have felt it important to keep the press informed of anything the church is doing which is newsworthy. At one stage I asked a church member who was a retired journalist if he would be our Parish Press Officer; but I obviously failed to explain the purpose of this role. He seemed to assume that he was just there to field any questions from the press - if there ever were any; but he couldn't see the value of anyone but the Rector doing this, as (a) the press would contact the Rector if there were any questions, and (b) the Rector is far more likely to know the answers than a lay "Press Officer". I tried to make clear that his role was to be proactive rather than reactive; instead of waiting for questions from the Press, he should be regularly feeding them stories and press releases. He should be on the lookout for anything remotely newsworthy in church life; not only sales and fayres, but interesting stories about people, about the children and teenagers, about any unusual activities that the church was arranging. But in the end, I had to do it myself; either you have an eye for such things or you do not, and he just didn't. I tired of phoning him to ask, "Have you sent anything to the Mail about…?" He never had as it hadn't occurred to him, and it became embarrassing. So I just did it myself. This was one of many tasks which I should have been able to delegate, to share the church's ministry and work among the laity, but in the end I did everything myself.

However the monthly church magazine was always sent to the Mail, and from time to time they published items from it. These were mostly snippets from my own "Rector's Letter", and it was usually something which could be portrayed as in some way controversial. Now I have to confess that not only have I not generally shrunk from controversy, but I have sometimes courted it. Too often the church in general, and clergy in particular, are seen by the public at large as desperately dull – worthy, but bland and utterly predictable. So from time to time I have deliberately "trailed my coat" and made comments which I hope will grab someone's attention. There is partly, no doubt, an element of exhibitionism in this; but I also have the conviction that the one thing Jesus never was, is dull and predictable, so if that is what the church is being, then it is not faithfully reflecting its Lord. The Gospel is good news – not just exhortations to be good. And news is worth listening to and reading about.

On two occasions in my magazine letters, over a year apart, I mentioned sex. I have no recollection what I said either time – but of course the word "sex" is gold dust to a newspaper which has sensationalist tendencies (as the Mail undoubtedly did), so whatever I wrote about sex was worth printing. In between those two letters, I no doubt wrote a dozen others on many other subjects, unnoticed by the Mail. But when sex was once more mentioned, there was my name again! This time it provoked a reader's letter in the Mail: "Why does this Vicar never write about anything but sex?" she complained. Oh, I do, I do; but for some unaccountable reason, when I write about prayer, or the Resurrection, or overseas mission, or showing practical love to our neighbour, not a word on those topics was deemed to be worthy of printing in the Mail. I can't think why!

My patience snapped, however, when a report in the Evening Mail distorted my words in a way which was seriously damaging, not just to me but to other vulnerable people. I had been writing an article about "Respect", deploring the decline of this quality in an age when it seemed to be equated with forelock-tugging deference. At an "Any Questions" event a few days earlier where a local Head Teacher and I had been on the panel, a question had been asked about respect, and the Head Teacher had said that a schoolteacher has to earn his pupils' respect. I knew what he meant, but I challenged him: "Supposing a class has a new teacher; do you expect the pupils to afford the teacher no respect, until he has earned it? Surely not! He is entitled to their respect, simply because he is their teacher, before he has said a word. He can *forfeit* their respect if he shows by his behaviour that he is unworthy of it; but the 'default position' is that a class should respect their teacher!" The Head conceded that he had to agree with this view.

It was that exchange which prompted me to write further about the subject, and almost as an aside I mentioned that I had been brought up to believe that a man should show respect to a lady in such ways as opening the door for her or offering her his seat. But the extreme feminists deride this as patronising, and I suggested that they have thus contributed to the loss of respect for women which is perhaps one element in the shocking growth of sexual assaults on women.

The Mail's headline was "Rector Slams Feminism", and the article went on to assert that I had written that if a woman is sexually assaulted it is her own fault. I was outraged by this caricature of my paragraph, especially because if any woman who had been sexually assaulted read it, and so gathered that I was blaming her for the trauma, she would be deeply hurt and furiously angry – and she would have every right to be.

I wrote to the Editor, demanding an interview, and threatening him with the Press Complaints Commission. After several days, when I had had no response, I turned up at his office, insisting on seeing him. By chance this happened to be the morning after a General Election, and he had been up all night. He was sitting in his office, looking weary and unshaven. Taking advantage of the fact that perhaps his resistance was low, I thumped the desk and demanded an apology and retraction.

"What would any assaulted woman think if she read your garbage?" I fulminated.

He looked a bit sheepish. "We have had a few letters," he admitted.

"I'm not surprised!" I raged. "Time after time you twist and distort anything I say or do, and I've had enough of it!"

"We're not out to get you," he assured me.

"It certainly feels like it!" I said.

"No, you should take it as a compliment that you are considered worth reporting!" he insisted.

"Well, what are you going to do about this sexual assault story? Or do I have to take you to the Press Complaints Commission?"

"I'll give you right of reply," he conceded. "Let me have an article in a day or two and I will publish it."

I went home and wrote my article. I think the paper steamed as I thumped it out. And, to his credit, under the headline, "Sexual

Assault: What the Rector Thinks" he published it, virtually in full – the only sentence he cut was where I had said, "The Evening Mail totally distorted what I had originally written"! On the same page, but below my article (which filled half a page – I hadn't asked how many words I could have, and he didn't think of limiting it when promising to publish what I wrote), he published some of the letters the original item had provoked. As expected, they were savage attacks on my reported views – but my article above the letters more than answered them.

But the painful controversy over the Spectacular in my first few weeks in the parish, and the continuing attacks, mockery and misrepresentations in the Mail, year after year, contributed to my feeling increasingly that I was in an alien, hostile land. I fear that I sometimes reacted badly, and met perceived hostility with aggressive attitudes. I think I hurt my congregation very much by my critical stance on various topics, though of course none of the attacks I had suffered had come from them. Because I was feeling, rightly or wrongly, that the church was unresponsive to my ministry, I began to imagine that they were actively resisting it. This of course was a gross distortion of the facts, and these good people will be terribly hurt that I could have thought this.

Some years later I was reminded by my daughter of the ways my ministry had influenced many people in Barrow and sowed seeds for the future, though at the time I was unable to see it. Two church members have been ordained since I left, and two others explored ordination. A study group which started as a "Saints Alive!" Bible Study course which I led, but which continued to meet for a year or two more, was influential in the life and faith of one of these. Other people have become leaders in the ministry of St. Paul's Church or other churches – one is a leader of Alpha Courses, another a worship leader and elder in her church; one is a regular lay preacher; one became a Christian youth worker for a while.

She reminded me of the several assistant curates whose ministry I supported and helped to develop. Many other people, she assured me, had found their faith nurtured and deepened, including those involved in the various inter-church musical events I led.

One lady was encouraged to start fostering and Mary and I supported her application, and many children's lives have been changed through her and her husband. Another only joined the church because her children attended, but has now become such a stalwart that the church could scarcely function without her.

She insisted that my incumbency had a huge and positive impact on the St. Paul's Church family and that I was and still am much loved there. Indeed Mary and I are very aware of this; and in the years since we left, quite a number of St. Paul's folk have continued to show us much love and support, in coming to such events as my 70th birthday party, inviting us to accompany the Barrow Ramblers when their programme leads them to the vicinity of our new home, and particularly in very generously supporting our fund-raising which is described in Chapter 18.

And a week or two after Lucy reminded me of all this, I received a letter from a lady who left Barrow about the same time as us. She wrote, "I am eternally grateful to you both, and to Mary Day" (the curate), "for the spiritual guidance you gave me whilst I was living in Barrow. It certainly resurrected my Christian faith and helped me enormously through life… I am sure that you will be pleased to hear that David and I have recently completed a Worship Leaders' course."

How precious are words of encouragement!

The fact remains that my years in Barrow were the least happy of my whole ministry, even though we stayed there nearly fourteen years, until my retirement. I felt increasingly stressed, year by year, until I was put on anti-depressants by my doctor. He asked me during that consultation whether I ever felt suicidal; my response was that I would never put my wife and children through the anguish that killing myself would cause – but I did not deny that the idea had entered my head, especially when lying awake in the small hours. I totally lost my confidence. I found that at meetings of the Clergy Chapter and other such gatherings I now seldom contributed to the discussion. This was in marked contrast to previous years when I would have been one of the more vocal members; but now I felt I had nothing to say. I wondered about looking for another parish; but when I read advertisements for parish posts in the church press, I found myself thinking, "Who would want to appoint me? I have absolutely nothing to offer!"

One of the problems with an organisation like the Church of England is that there is no straightforward means of support for struggling clergy. The Bishop is of course meant to be, in the traditional phrase, "Pastor pastorum", or "shepherd of the shepherds"; in other words, looking after his clergy is precisely what he is meant to do. But he was also my boss! If I went to him with moans about failure I felt that this would go down on my file as a black mark. In other such spheres, like Social Workers, there is a clear demarcation between the person who is the worker's support and counsellor, and the one who is his or her "line manager". But when I was in my slough of despond, I felt there was no such distinction. The Diocese did, in my later years in Barrow, send round details of an inter-diocesan counselling service, which for some reason I perceived as being largely for clergy couples with marital problems; but at the time of my deepest despair, I was aware of no such avenue in which to seek help.

But I did, in the end, discuss my unhappiness with the Bishop of Penrith. I was reluctant to do so, as I felt I had failed him: it was he who had thought that I had the gifts that made me the right man to lead St. Paul's, and now I was whingeing that I was a failure and miserable. When I asked him whether I should look for a move, he suggested that I should "test the waters".

I did answer one advertisement, from a parish in Plymouth. When the application form arrived from Plymouth, one question asked, "What makes you think that God is calling you to serve in Plymouth?" I answered it as honestly as I could, that I was by no means certain that he was! But because I was not happy in my present post, I had felt it right to explore other possibilities.

Although the train journey from Barrow to Plymouth was something of a nightmare, involving four changes (and at the first change I missed the intended train because of line repairs, which resulted in missed connections all the rest of the way) I enjoyed the visit. I was staying with a church member, and met several others including of course the wardens. I found that these were people who "spoke my language": they understood concepts like conversion, and evangelism, and guidance, and the work of the Spirit, and had the same kinds of priorities and vision for church life that I did. It was a forceful reminder of how seldom I had been able to share such thoughts with my Barrow parishioners, and how I had missed doing so. And yet at the interview after a morning of being shown around the parish (there were several other candidates there at the same time), when the Bishop asked me if I was any clearer as to whether I would be happy to go to Plymouth if they offered me the post, I had to acknowledge that I was still far from sure.

I suspected that the panel wanted to offer me the post, but delayed saying so because I had been quite frank about my doubts whether it was right to leave Barrow. However I remained uncertain, not in the least because I had doubts specifically about the Plymouth parish, but particularly because I had a continuing, strong and nagging feeling that I would be running away from the task God had called me to if I moved south now. Over the next few days as I awaited the phone call from the Bishop, either with an invitation or with the news that one of the other candidates was to be appointed, I came to recognise that I was hoping they would say "No", as that would settle the matter; if they invited me to go, that would still leave me in a turmoil. When I discerned this, it was obvious that I really felt in my heart that this was not God's call; so I phoned the Bishop of Plymouth and said so.

In the matter of seeking divine guidance I can only conclude – without the blithe certainty of my younger years – that (a) we can very easily get it wrong; (b) when God calls to a task, it doesn't necessarily mean that it will be easy or even happy; but also (c) we still have to stick at it, and trust him with all the consequences, for ourselves and our families.

Apart from my personal difficulties and unhappiness in Barrow our move there had profound implications for both Mary and our children, and their lives might have been very different if we had stayed in the Isle of Wight. I am tempted to say, "would have been much better" in all sorts of ways – though who can tell what "might have been"? The thriving young people's groups at St. John's would perhaps have offered a more positive influence upon their developing faith than happened at St. Paul's. They would have had very different friendships. More than one of them was to go through deep traumas and miseries of their own in Barrow, which they might have avoided had we stayed in Newport. But for all those things, too, I have to trust God. The new influences that came to bear upon them, the new kinds of friends they made, in many instances are things Mary and I regret. But God uses the uncomfortable, the painful, the failures as well as the successes; and I repeat that I cling on to the conviction – if that is not too strong a word for my often faltering faith - that it is all, good and bad, in his hands and under his loving control.

This account of my 13½ years in Barrow may seem a very negative one, which will undoubtedly paint a very misleading picture; for I certainly did not pass that entire period in gloom and depression. There were of course happy times in church life, like the annual church picnics.

I remember our very first weekend houseparty with particular pleasure. About sixty church members went to a conference centre in an old farmhouse; we were self-catering, and decided that children should be free of charge, and so there were about a dozen young children in the party. On the final Sunday morning our Communion Service was held in the lounge – the first experience of such informal worship for many. (For part of the service all the children had their own activity in an adjoining room, and then were summoned back to join the adults at The Peace. We waited quietly for them to appear; and the first one to rush into the room was my 3-year-old daughter, who shouted enthusiastically, "Hello, everybody!" This splendid "peace" greeting caused much merriment.) In the closing hymn of our worship, I became aware that the singing was a bit feeble. When I looked up at the congregation I realised the reason: many of them were in tears, often a sign of the Holy Spirit working.

Although Mary, too, never felt at home in Barrow and regretted our decision to go there (for which she accepts an equal responsibility with me), especially because of the damage she feels it did to our children's lives, she found a measure of contentment when she was able to go back to work once our youngest child started school. She had expected to go back to nursing, but at that time this was very hard to do as she had been out of the profession for seventeen years, and to undergo the necessary retraining would have required her to work full time. This she was not prepared to do, with four children to care for. But she found her nursing qualifications opened the way for her to work with Special Needs children in schools – irrespective of whether their Special Needs included anything of a medical nature; and so for some eleven years she found great satisfaction in working about 12 hours a week in a local school. One of the reasons she enjoyed it was that in parish life she was always "the Rector's wife"; in school it was irrelevant who her husband was or what he did, and she could just be respected and valued for herself and the contribution she could make.

She had always played an active part in parish life. Though she was never a public speaker, and had no desire to do such traditional "clergy wife" things as leading the Mothers' Union, she not only fully supported my ministry, but found various roles in parish life where her gifts could be used. For some years she led the Sunday School, and for most of our time in Barrow she also edited the Parish Magazine. But she too, like me, lamented the lack of responsiveness of the church members. She had always felt strongly that the Sunday School children were an important part of the family of the church, but got the impression that many church members took little interest in what they did, though she knew that some elderly folk faithfully supported the work in prayer. And she remained convinced to the end (quite wrongly, I am sure) that hardly anyone ever read the parish magazine! This was simply because, though several hundred copies were printed and distributed each month, almost never did anyone comment on anything published in it. She felt just as I did about Sunday services. Is anyone there? Is anyone reading it? Is anyone remotely interested in any of the articles and stories which had involved a good deal of effort to produce? One lady did often congratulate her on an excellent magazine; but this was almost a unique reaction. Mostly all her efforts were met with silence.

There were many aspects of parish life that I found quite positive. One of these was taking funerals, surprising as this might be; but the reason is that I felt I was learning to exercise this ministry much better than I ever had before. I mentioned in a previous chapter my early inadequacies in bereavement ministry; but I felt that at last I was doing this important work more helpfully and effectively. Not infrequently people would say, as they left the church or Crematorium chapel, "That was one of the nicest funerals I have ever been to." Contrary to what I was taught by Canon Druitt as a curate, that the minister is there to speak about Jesus, not about the deceased, I had at last come to grasp that the deceased person was the person the mourners had come to think about and whom they wanted to hear about, and to neglect this was seriously to short-change them. As the great majority of people whose funeral I had to take were people I had never met, I might find it hard to say much about them, and I offered the bereaved families a choice. The ideal thing, I suggested, was for some old friend who had known the person well to stand up and speak about them. This would be genuine and from the heart, so that their words would be met by a sense of recognition from the hearers. Another possibility, if there was no one who felt able to take on this task (and I was well aware that for people unaccustomed to speaking in public this was a daunting and even terrifying prospect), was for the family to write something out for me to read. But the third way was for them to tell me all about the one who had died, and I would do my best to use the insights they had given me to speak about the person. It was important, anyway, whoever was going to pay this tribute (I dislike the word "eulogy", as to me it implies an insincere talk which only mentions the good things, and makes every dead person out to have been some kind of unreal plaster saint), for me to allow the bereaved family to talk to me about what their loved one had meant to them.

I did also speak about Jesus! I would try to do so in ways which recognised that most of my hearers probably had pretty hazy and indeed distorted ideas about what Christians believe about death, and would admit that they themselves were uncertain about what they believed. After some deaths, there would be a good deal of anger as well as grief.

People hear what they expect to hear. A fellow-clergyman in Barrow hit the front-page headlines of the Evening Mail when an aggrieved, as well as grieving, family complained to the paper that all the Vicar had done at the funeral was tell them they ought to go to church on Sundays. When I read this account, it struck me as most unlikely. I phoned the minister concerned, knowing what it was like to be vilified in the press; and he told me that of course he had said no such thing. He had never mentioned the words "church" or "Sunday". What he *had* done was to talk about faith in Christ, which can be an enormous support when facing the pain of death. But for some, at least, of his hearers, "faith in Christ" was a nebulous phrase which meant little; what the vicar must be talking about is going to church.... I had found similar misunderstandings from time to time, not only at funerals but at weddings. One of my often-used wedding talks mentioned, in the context of John's account of the Wedding at Cana[1], how good it is to invite Jesus to your wedding – but that he wants to be invited not just to a Wedding, but into a marriage, and into our life.... It was once reported back to me, by a church member who knew one of the guests, that I had told them all off for not going to church more.

---

[1] John 2. 1-11

I had the usual series of requests for baptisms, and initially tried to follow my accustomed procedure – of spending an evening with the family, explaining the implications of baptism and the meaning of the promises and statements of faith, and then suggesting that if they felt that they could not honestly make such promises, another option is the Service of Thanksgiving, which involves no such promises. Then I would leave a copy of each service with them, say we would leave it for a few days for them to discuss it, and make a date for a further visit at which I would learn their conclusions. This, as I say, had been my practice for some years in both Surbiton and the Isle of Wight.

But in Barrow I very soon discovered that parents instantly dismissed out of hand any suggestion of an alternative to baptism. "We know what we want, Vicar – it's a proper christening!" There was no point at all, I found, in giving them time to think about it, and come back later; I might as well accept the request for baptism without wasting any more time.

It was one way in which I found that people in Barrow who were not churchgoers were in a sense *closer* to church than I had found them to be in the south. It was still, when I went there in 1989, the custom of many non-worshippers to send their children to Sunday School, very much as I had found was the practice of the people of Walthamstow in the early '60s. In the Isle of Wight, almost all our Sunday School children had parents who were at least occasional worshippers; not so in Barrow.

Another way this desire to maintain church links, without actually going to church, showed itself concerned Confirmation. I was astonished in my first year in Barrow, when I announced the start of Confirmation Classes, to find about 25 children appearing at the first class, most of whom were not members of Sunday School or of a group like Pathfinders. Some of them were Guides or Scouts; but quite a number had no apparent link with the church at all, except that they had been baptised there twelve years earlier. My first reaction was to be delighted at this opportunity to spend some weeks explaining faith in Christ to this large bunch of youngsters. But it soon became evident that they were there not out of any interest in faith, but because Mum had sent them. The sooner they could get it over with and stop coming, the better. In other words the parents regarded Confirmation as a rite of passage, with no necessary connection with an on-going membership of or attendance at church. The other side of this same coin, I discovered, was that the normal worshippers tended – at least in the more rural parishes of Cumbria – to regard the actual confirmation service as nothing to do with them, especially if it was on a weekday evening. It would not occur to such church members to turn up at a confirmation unless they had some connection with the families of the young people being confirmed, any more than they would go to a wedding uninvited. I learned of this attitude from a slightly pained letter from the Bishop to his clergy, urging them to encourage their regular worshippers to attend a confirmation in their parish to support the candidates.

This whole culture of assumptions was something very puzzling to me. In my previous churches not only had the Confirmation Service always been on a Sunday, but it was recognised that it was one of the major occasions of the year, and was a valuable opportunity for the church to welcome new members and their families. The northern attitude of it being largely detached from normal church life struck me as needing to be grappled with. (This, I fear, was yet one more case where I found myself working not with but against the grain of local people's culture.)

After two years of Confirmations after which, despite my best efforts, almost all the newly-confirmed instantly disappeared and were never seen at church again, I decided to do it differently the next year. The classes usually started in September; so that year I wrote an article in the magazine asking for names of potential candidates at Easter. I also sent letters to all the Guides and Scouts of confirmation age, making the same request, that although actual confirmation classes would not start till September, I would like those considering Confirmation to attend church or Pathfinders from Easter onwards, as part of their preparation for the great event. My thinking was that their rapid disappearance in previous years was at least partly due to the fact that they just did not experience what it was like to be regular members of the church or the fellowship of Christians of their own age group. If they had longer to become accustomed to this, it might reduce the dropout rate.

It did; but it did so by drastically reducing the take-up rate too. That year, instead of the two dozen candidates of previous years, we had five candidates, all of whom were already Pathfinders. Obviously the response to my well-meaning change of policy was to say, "What? Go to Church for eight months? This is blackmail! Count me out…."

On the positive side, the classes were easier to handle, and much more responsive spiritually, because these were youngsters with a good background of Christian teaching, who had some degree of familiarity with the concepts of faith in Jesus and the value of worship. The negative side of the coin was that I had now lost the chance – however unfruitful it had generally been in the past – of drawing in young people from right outside normal church contacts. The Confirmation Services in subsequent years seemed much more real, with some indication that the candidates were genuine and sincere in the vows they were making, rather than just going through an empty ritual; but I still felt sad, and a little guilty, that this was at the cost of scaring away other potential candidates.

I did eventually emerge from that deep pit of despair which led to my seeking medical help and getting anti-depressants prescribed, and my later years in Barrow were rather happier. I never felt that my ministry at St. Paul's had the rewards and encouragements that my ministry in Surbiton and the Isle of Wight had afforded, even though many people may have seen it as a "successful" church. The annual carol services remained high points, attended by hundreds from all over Barrow for whom they were a central part of Christmas. This included the Children's Candle Service, a shorter version of the Carol Service held at 4 p.m. on Christmas Eve, which was always packed out. It concluded with the entire congregation singing "Shine, Jesus, shine" and spilling out into the dark streets with their candles still lit, to symbolise taking the light of Christ out into a dark world. After one such service, the young father of a family whom I had met during the year for a baptism said to me as he left, close to tears, "Thank you for making our Christmas!" Such words of encouragement mean a very great deal.

Another annual service which, though not as hugely popular as the Christmas services, meant a lot to many people, was the Service of Remembrance and Hope, which took place in the weeks after Easter, and to which we invited all who had been bereaved throughout the year. An additional feature of it, introduced by Ian Hook, the curate who joined me a few years before I retired, also involved the lighting of candles. Members of the congregation who had been bereaved, whether recently or long ago, were invited to come forward during a particular hymn, and light a small candle to place in a tray of sand on the Holy Table. "Sometimes we don't know how to pray," I would suggest. "We are perhaps not sure what we believe, or what words to use. But a candle with its silent flame can be an unspoken prayer, a sign and symbol of our love and our hopes." This point in the service was deeply moving, and there were often many tears. I hope it was also a stage in healing and moving on along the path of grief. I particularly recall a young man whose mother had died during the year; he lived hundreds of miles away on the south coast, but had travelled north to attend the service, and as he waited in the line to light his candle he sobbed inconsolably, while a hymn was sung and the violins played.

Two things gave Mary and me some relief and refreshment when we were feeling low and despondent. One was the proximity of the beautiful scenery of the Lake District, which was where we frequently went on our Day Off, walking for miles over the fells and valleys. But it was music which was perhaps the largest element in my own healing and encouragement. After the first year or two, I took over the leadership of the church choir myself, as the new organist who had joined us did not want that responsibility. We made a good team, the organist and I, and although the choir never grew to the numbers that we had known in Newport, and we were always especially short of basses, the choir became a more and more important part of our worship.

This was not in any way as a substitute for congregational singing – I have never had any desire for the type of worship experienced in some cathedrals and other large churches which seems largely a "spectator sport", with superb music provided by an almost professional choir, to which the congregation just listen respectfully. I have met organists, highly skilled and perhaps with rows of initials after their name indicating their academic and musical qualifications; and yet in some cases (not all, of course) they seem to have no spiritual sensitivities, no understanding of worship being for the glory of God – perhaps no real faith, though I cannot of course pass such judgement.

I remember one such man I met when I was doing a two-week chaplaincy in Zermatt during the winter sports season. We had a rather creaky old harmonium in the English Church there, and on my first Sunday there was a lady to play it to accompany the hymns; but her holiday came to an end after that, and I did not know who would play for the service on our second Sunday. During the week, at an *après-ski* party for English-speaking people, I found myself speaking to a man who was the Director of Music of one of the big West London churches. He was telling me about the European tours of his church choir, and the records they had made. "I'm so glad I have met you!" I exclaimed, and told him of my chaplaincy duties in Zermatt. "I wonder if you could accompany our service on Sunday? I am afraid we don't have much of an instrument, just a harmonium, but I am sure you could make a good sound on it!" "Hah!" he responded, "I wouldn't prostitute my art on an instrument like that!" I was so taken aback by his attitude that I was speechless. It was sadly obvious that contributing to God's people worshipping their Lord was exceedingly low on his scale of priorities.

I have heard of choirs, too, with a similar attitude. One church was planning a week's Mission, with services and addresses every night. The choir insisted on being there to lead the singing, but at the end of the hymn before the Missioner's address, they all processed out and went home. When I was told that story by the priest concerned, my reaction was to say that I would have dismissed the entire choir – and if that led to the organist resigning too, so be it. Such an attitude of contempt for worship and mission could do nothing but harm to the life and work of the church and they would be better without such "musicians". Thankfully I have never been faced with such organists or choirs in any church where I have ministered.

Our choir did sing anthems – of a wide variety of styles, but seldom of the plainsong styles of Tallis and Byrd, beautiful though these are; I felt, rightly or wrongly, that for the great majority of our church members such music would be above their heads, and I tended to opt for a slightly more "accessible" genre, though it included Bach, Brahms and Schubert, as well as Rutter or Negro spirituals. But mostly the choir were there, in my view, to help the congregation to lift up their voices and lift up their hearts; and when taking choir practices I usually included some comments to help both children and adults to understand and feel what they were singing about.

We were also able to gather a group of quite talented musicians who played at services from time to time. We had two very good violinists, several brass players, and some flutes; and as we were a bit weak in the lower registers, I bought and played a bass guitar. I was able to find some excellent instrumental settings of quite a number of the contemporary worship songs, and for others I would sometimes write arrangements myself. Sometimes the whole ensemble would be used, together with the piano, for the livelier songs; for the quieter and more reflective numbers, perhaps a flute, or two violins in harmony, could gloriously and movingly enhance the music. My one regret was that I was never able to find anyone to take responsibility for leading the group; every time we played it always had to be initiated and rehearsed by me. I enjoyed doing it, but it was time consuming, and I felt it was yet one more aspect of church life which was wholly dependent on me, which it should have been delegated to someone else. Despite my convictions about using all the gifts of all the church members, all of whom have a valuable contribution to make and gifts given them by God, in practice I was just not very good at such delegation and gift-recognition and encouragement.

Occasionally I rehearsed and conducted a combined choir of our own and neighbouring churches for a united service or festival event. One Palm Sunday we sang "Worthy Is The Lamb" from *The*

Messiah (with one of those near-disasters in the fugue in the middle, when I felt that the various parts were not together either with each other or with the organ, and the whole thing was in imminent danger of falling apart – but a strong entry by the tenors pulled it all together again and saved the day). On Good Friday another year we sang Stainer's *The Crucifixion*.

But I also initiated an inter-church choir which started to perform some of the Roger Jones musicals which had been such a joy in the Isle of Wight. We usually had a choir of about sixty voices for these events, which took place in one of the local public theatres in Barrow or Ulverston. Sometimes they were part of Roger Jones' own national tours with his teams of actors and soloists, but sometimes we performed the whole work ourselves. When we put on "*From Pharaoh To Freedom*" Mary was much involved in making costumes, especially for all the children who played the parts of the plagues of Egypt – dressed as gnats or frogs or locusts. The youngest child, a tubby little girl of four, was a gnat, and though she took her task with extreme seriousness, she kept getting left behind by the others and trotted anxiously after them; the audience were rocking with laughter at this charming little mite!

Perhaps the climax of such presentations was in the Millennium year when we put on a musical written specially for the Millennium, *Hopes and Dreams*. This was not by Roger Jones but by Graham Kendrick and other writers, and was performed by groups, large and small, all over the country. It needed dancers, actors and puppeteers as well as the choir and soloists. For this reason I invited two other co-producers to share the leadership: I did the music, and the other two did the drama and the dance. We had a total of about 130 people on stage.

The whole work was based on the different clauses of the Lord's Prayer, and the final item was the whole Lord's Prayer sung to the tune of Auld Lang Syne. This seems at first glance cringingly awful, and when I heard that item on its own on Top of the Pops, sung by Cliff Richard, it was indeed wince-making. But in the context, and as the climax of the whole show, it was stunning.

The song starts with the melody played on the bagpipes. I found quite a good young piper, a teenage girl from the Methodist Church who played in Barrow's St. Andrew's Pipe Band – but we then found that her pipes did not play in the same key as the rest of the song on the backing track, and you cannot tune bagpipes into a different key! Obviously the sound-track had digitally retuned it. What were we to do? The piper mimed it, as the soundtrack played! There she was, in full Highland fig, apparently playing away – but in fact she had reversed her reeds, so was playing silently. No one saw through the deception.

Then we needed a team of drummers, and I recruited six Sea Cadets whom I had encountered at a summer carnival. They were desperately nervous, but did very well. The production book had suggested getting members of the cast to come on stage with brightly coloured flags, perhaps silver and gold. We modified this, and Mary made about forty flags of the nations. The whole cast of actors and dancers marched down through the audience with these flags, and gradually filled the stage, as the choir and audience sang:

> *Let all the people say Amen*
> *In every tribe and tongue;*
> *Let every heart's desire be joined*
> *To see the kingdom come!*
> *Let every hope and every dream*
> *Be born in love again;*

Let all the world sing with one voice,
Let the people say, Amen!

And the song ended with the stage lights gradually dimming, with a spotlight first on the lone piper on her platform high up to one side, and then on the drummers, narrowing to one solo drummer who finally played all alone, dum tara tara tara dum... I tell you, it was a stunning and moving experience!

Always in the rehearsals of these musicals, I had a break in the middle for a brief Bible Study and prayer. I feel very strongly that such works are not just entertainment; the choir is not singing them for fun, as if we were a secular choral society, though we did indeed derive a great deal of enjoyment from both the rehearsals and the performances. We are presenting them as an act of worship and an act of witness. There is a tangible difference between singers, whether soloists or chorus, simply performing for their own enjoyment or for self-glorification, and their doing it as an expression of their own heart-felt faith and conviction, and for the glory of God. More than one person has found taking part in such an event to be a faith-enhancing and even a life-changing experience.

I have subsequently been a member of choral societies, singing exclusively sacred works, and have often found it disappointing and indeed frustrating that the gifted musicians who train the choir almost never make any mention whatever of the words we are singing or their significance. Yes, the music is magnificent; but what is it *about?* Of course these choral societies are not specifically Christian bodies, and many members probably claim no personal faith. But that wouldn't stop me, were I leading (though far less talented musically than the actual conductors), from trying to explain the profound significance of the great Christian and often biblical words which the composers have expressed in music. When I am singing "Sanctus, sanctus, sanctus!" ("Holy, holy,

348

holy!") from some work of Bach or Mozart, I am not just singing; I am worshipping!

Another Millennium event took place in our own church. A national recommendation that was sent down from on high (I mean from the bench of bishops, not the Almighty!) was that at noon on 1st January 2000 all the church bells around the country should ring. There was only one church in Barrow with a full peal of bells, and at the time that building was closed for substantial restoration and repair, and so the bells could not be rung. St. Paul's had but one bell! But I determined that we would still ring it.

So we devised a "Celebration of Bells". Every member of the church received a personal invitation to the event, and on the "RSVP" slip they were asked to circle the decade in which they were born. We borrowed a set of hand bells from another church, and recruited a team of ringers, children and adults, who learned how to play them. We planned a short service of worship, including such songs as "Ding dong merrily on high", and the hymn including the verse "Whene'er the sweet church bell Peals over hill and dell, May Jesus Christ be praised!" And then we had drawn out of a hat the name of one representative of every decade of the twentieth century, who was invited to heave on the bell-rope and toll our solitary bell, ranging from a lady of 92 to a child of six. The event closed with sherry and soft drinks being served. It was a splendid occasion, and well attended; the fact that the bell rope snapped as one enthusiastic ringer tugged too heartily at it, and had to have a knot tied in it to conclude the campanology, all added to the fun.

When the time came for me to retire in 2001, planning the music for my farewell service was of course something that exercised my mind; and yet in the event in one respect I was taken by surprise. I wanted to involve the whole instrumental group, and also the choir and organ, but also to have uplifting and inspiring congregational hymns. So the service started with Vaughan Williams' splendid arrangement of *All people that on earth do dwell*, with organ and a six-piece brass ensemble. The choir sang Stanford's *Te Deum* in B♭, a rousing piece which we had sung only once before. The instrumentalists and piano accompanied some children's songs. At the end, I had been warned that something was to follow, and I was to go and sit in the congregation beside Mary. I was expecting some kind of speech or presentation; but what actually happened was that the whole choir moved out from the stalls into the centre of the Chancel, and then sang, completely without sheet music, Rutter's *Clare Benediction*. I had been totally unaware of any clandestine rehearsals going on, and I was completely broken up by this performance. At the conclusion I was asked to come forward, and I tried to compose myself as one of the children handed me a copy of the music, signed by all the choir members. This is a precious gift that I will always treasure.

17

❧

Gender, Sex and Sexuality

Two issues which have been sources of controversy within the church for many years seem to have risen to such powerful prominence in the twenty-first century that they threaten to tear the church apart. These issues are whether women can or should be consecrated as bishops, and what the Church's attitude to homosexuality should be. I have, I confess, been thankful that it has largely been since my retirement from parish ministry that these bitter wranglings have seemed to eclipse all other matters, certainly as far as the way the Church is featured in the secular media is concerned. I no longer have to face up to them, and am tempted to keep my head down and hope they will go away!

But of course they will not, because they concern not theories or theologies, but people; men and women loved by God, who must also be loved by the Church of Jesus Christ, whatever the rights and wrongs of the disputes.

In such a book as this, in which I have undertaken to be honest about my own struggles of faith, I want to be honest about matters which exercise the church to which I belong, even if I have no confident answers.

Female Bishops

When I was converted, and when I was trained for the ministry, it never occurred to me or most of my contemporaries that ordained clergy could be anything but men. Certain other denominations promoted women to positions of pastoral ministry – the Congregational Church, for example, had had female pastors for many years, and I remember the Revd. Elsie Chamberlain coming to speak at a meeting in Bristol (which I did not attend) when I was at college there. However I well recall, when the issue of whether the Church of England could, at some point in the future, ordain women began to surface, and my church newspaper illustrated an article on the subject with a line-drawing of a woman in a clerical collar, my spontaneous reaction was to laugh aloud; the idea seemed to me droll, rather than offensive.

My attitude might have been not wholly dissimilar to that of Dr. Samuel Johnson, as recorded in Boswell's *Life of Johnson:* 'I told him I had been that morning at a meeting of the people called Quakers, where I had heard a woman preach. *Johnson:* "Sir, a woman's preaching is like a dog's walking on his hind legs. It is not done well; but you are surprised to find it done at all."'

And yet I had heard some excellent women preachers. I recall, when on holiday in Scotland, visiting the local Baptist Church one Sunday, and hearing a woman missionary preaching. At the time I felt it was one of the best missionary sermons I had ever heard. No "hind-leg walking" there!

It was not until my final few years before I retired that the definitive decision to allow women to be ordained priest was taken by the General Synod of the Church of England. One of the early batch of women ordained under that legislation became my curate at St. Paul's, Barrow. By that time, after many years of discussions at all levels, and much reading of articles in church newspapers and theological journals, I had reached the point of seeing no valid objection to the change, and indeed I welcomed it.

The opposition in the pews was largely a matter of finding such a change difficult to get used to; disciplined and intellectual theology played little part in it, and in inviting a young lady to become my curate, after discussion with the PCC, I was sure that the warmth and gentle sweetness of the girl concerned would very soon smooth away most opposition. This indeed proved to be the case, though three or four people did leave our church and move to another. (It was interesting to see the differences of attitude among those who left. One lady, the daughter of a high church priest, did have serious theological objections, and told me that she and her husband would slip away before the lady curate arrived, as they did not in any way want her to see it in personal terms; and subsequently, when the curate met her at some deanery function, the lady was courteous and friendly towards her. Another objector, however, on meeting the lady curate, pointedly ignored her existence, and looked through her...)

There were, however, serious theological objections to ordaining women, one held by the "high" or catholic wing of the church, and the other by the more extreme evangelicals. The "high" view was two-fold: one, that the priest at the altar was representing Christ, and as Christ had been a man and not a woman, only a man could represent him; and secondly, that Jesus, while very ready to challenge wrong religious or social attitudes in his contemporaries, and indeed treating women with deep respect, nevertheless chose twelve men as his apostles, and following that precedent this had been the universal practice of the church for twenty centuries. Coupled with this conviction was the belief that the Church of England, as only a small part of the world-wide Universal Church, had no right to make such a radical change unilaterally, and if it did so, all the tentative moves towards attaining unity with other churches, such as the Church of Rome and the Orthodox Church, would come to an abrupt stop.

Those on the evangelical wing with firm objections to women's ordination based their opposition on various Scriptural passages, particularly in the writings of Paul. These concerned what they saw as the Biblical view of authority, which, within the church, is a male preserve. (This was bluntly expressed in the title of a book by the Baptist minister, David Pawson, called *"Leadership Is Male"*.) Such evangelicals had no problems with women presiding at the Eucharist; what they did object to was women having authority over men, which a woman vicar would certainly exercise. Whether that precluded women preaching was a matter on which evangelicals had different opinions, some ruling it inadmissible, and others allowing it so long as she did not enter the pulpit but spoke from the chancel step!

At one stage I would have had a good deal of sympathy for this view of authority, and would have taken very seriously Paul's strictures against women having authority over men. But gradually my views softened and were modified. I think there were various elements in my change of position. One was that I increasingly came to recognise a purely cultural attitude lying behind Paul's views; I felt that in certain matters he spoke as a 1st century Jew in a Graeco-Roman society, and that this coloured his views. I therefore felt able to disagree with him, without feeling that I was disobeying the authoritative Word of God.

This cultural factor was vividly illustrated when we had a Nigerian clergyman staying with us for some weeks when we were in the Isle of Wight. He was a man of great faith, warmth and godliness, but when the subject of women priests came up in discussion (this was in the 1980s, and even then it was already a very live issue in the church) he expressed strong disapproval.

"Suppose a woman, celebrating communion, was actually pregnant? Or menstruating? This would be deeply offensive!" he insisted.

I was astonished at this argument, which I had never heard expressed in all the discussions I had encountered in Britain. But I recognised that he was speaking and reacting out of his own cultural background. I did not argue with him, as I felt it would be pointless and discourteous, and I did not want to offend him as a guest in our country, our church and our home.

Another element in my own gradual change of view on women's ministry has been the practical experience of the gifts of women in many spheres of life, both Christian and secular. This was, of course, the period of Margaret Thatcher's premiership, and she was just one of a number of extremely powerful and talented women on the world stage. It was also, I felt, illogical for any Anglican to maintain conscientious objection to a woman exercising authority in the church, while belonging to a national church whose Supreme Governor is a woman – Her Majesty the Queen. (And of course many of her female ancestors, right back to Queen Elizabeth the First, had held the same position of authority.)

Within society and the church many women exercised leadership, often extremely effectively and positively. The whole Missionary movement of the church in the past two hundred years had been very largely dependent upon godly women, often working not only as pioneer evangelists but as leaders of emerging churches where there were simply no men to do the work. God had blessed their ministry abundantly in many lands. No, they had not been ordained; but they were leaders in the church of Christ. I found myself unable to deny the gifts that God had given the church in the dedicated lives of women.

I must admit that part of my change of view was influenced by secular feminism – not the strident and militant feminism which I found (and find) either distasteful or comic, and sometimes both, but rather the steady and growing demand for justice and equality of opportunity in society as a whole. Was I being "conformed to this world" in the sense that Paul criticised in Romans 12. 2? Some Christians may well make this accusation. But increasingly I felt unable to hold to what looked and felt like an outdated and prejudiced position.

But throughout those years, the issue was whether a woman could be a priest; the further question, of whether she could also be a bishop, was still hovering in the background. At an evangelical conference I attended sometime in the 1980s a straw vote was taken by a show of hands, whether the people there would approve of women priests (about 60-40 in favour) or women bishops (about 30-70 against). I think I probably voted against the second motion at that time.

But there were many who insisted that there was no logical way of separating the two issues; if the church decides – rightly or wrongly – that a woman may be ordained priest, then it can only be a matter of time, not of any modification of theological principle, before the decision to allow her to be consecrated as a bishop. My own position now is that I would be happy to accept this. And though I am sad for other Christians who feel conscientiously unable to accept the ministry of a woman bishop, even to the extent that they must leave the church which has been their home all their lives, I do not believe that this consideration can indefinitely hold up the progression towards what I see as the inevitability of accepting women to the episcopate.

Homosexuality

Homosexuality is an issue which causes me much more uncertainty and heartache. There are many aspects which

356

influence my attitude, which must be true of everybody; for it is impossible to consider moral or theological issues in a hermetically sealed vacuum, totally insulated from one's own emotions, one's own sexuality.

For some people their emotional response to homosexuality is simply disgust. They cannot begin to have any sympathy for such desires or behaviour. It seems utterly abhorrent to them, and they can only see it in terms of perversion and even corruption. This may be because they themselves are wholly heterosexual in inclination; but it may be because they do have homosexual desires, which they are violently denying and suppressing, so that they perceive the whole issue as a threat to themselves.

When it is Christians who have this "gut reaction" they will roundly condemn homosexual desires or behaviour in terms of sin, designating it "an abomination unto the Lord". Some pronouncements from Christian leaders have been in such immoderate and harsh terms, and seem to me totally lacking in the Christian qualities of compassion and mercy.

I grew up in single-parent family, with three brothers and no sisters; apart from my mother and other female relations I had little social contact with the opposite sex. I attended largely single-sex boarding schools, especially during my adolescent years, and like many boys in such establishments I had some homosexual fumblings with other boys, as well as solitary sexual activity. I also knew what it was to have a powerful "crush" on younger boys, an emotion by no means dissimilar to being in love. So I can indeed sympathise with homoerotic emotions and desires, even though I have been blessed by a happy marriage for many years, and am the father of four children. This therefore is the emotional standpoint from which I approach the moral and theological questions posed by the issue of homosexuality.

Sex and sin

Morally I was brought up to believe that genital sexual experience should be reserved solely for marriage. All other sexual desires outside of marriage, whether heterosexual, homosexual or solitary, were therefore seen in terms of temptation and sin. The only actual sexual experience I had had at the time of my conversion to a personal Christian faith at the age of 21 was the homosexual variety at school, mentioned above, and masturbation. I had while serving in the Army encountered pornography in the form of crudely written little booklets, passed around among the soldiers. (I think that the soldier who passed them to me, as his platoon commander, was mischievously amused to give such things to someone from a very sheltered background such as myself; I imagine virtually all the "other ranks" I encountered as a National Service officer would have had considerable sexual experience, and regarded a "virgin" like me with pitying amusement.) But I certainly found the (hetero)sexual encounters described in this pornography as very arousing; I was perhaps reassured that in this respect my reactions were "normal".

The Christian teaching I received on sexual matters in my newfound evangelical fellowship was no different from that acquired in my younger years: namely that sexual expression, while a gift of God of great significance and beauty, was to be enjoyed in no setting other than that of the marriage between a man and a women. Heterosexual intercourse before marriage was fornication. Heterosexual intercourse, for a married man or woman, with a partner to whom they were not married, was adultery. Both of these, I was taught, were totally sinful, and should be resolutely shunned by the disciple of Christ.

Homosexual behaviour, likewise, was to be rejected as contrary to the will of God. I do not think that I was taught that it was *more* sinful than heterosexual fornication; it was however

358

sinful, and that was that. The difference, of course, was that the person with heterosexual temptations and desires could look forward to a legitimate outlet for their expression, in the event of their finding a person to marry; the person experiencing homosexual desires had no such possibility, so that the only legitimate course was a life of celibacy, and the renunciation of sex altogether.

To write in these terms in the twenty-first century may seem to many quaint in the extreme. Leaving aside for a moment the homosexual issue, for the vast majority of people in our modern secular society – and not just young people either – sexual expression, with any willing adult partner, is considered healthy and normal. Most people would still frown on being unfaithful to one's partner – whether married to them or not; but if you are not "attached" in any way, to refuse to express your liking for someone of the opposite sex on some moral grounds would be regarded as at the very least odd, and almost certainly unhealthy.

And yet I have to admit that I still believe that those moral convictions which I was taught both before and after I became a committed Christian are sound. I am still convinced that chastity outside of marriage, as well as faithfulness within it, are God's will for mankind, and his prescription for a healthy, happy life, and a wholesome society and a stable civilization. I am glad – thankful, rather than self-righteously boastful – that my wedding night, at the age of 37, was my very first experience of sexual intercourse. I am thankful, too, that in the nearly forty years of happy marriage I have never been unfaithful to my wife. Sins of the mind and imagination there have been (and Jesus was severe about these); but I thank my God that I have never been put into a position of such temptation to unfaithfulness that I was unable to resist.

I mentioned earlier that before I was married I very much wanted to be married. As the years passed and I saw no wedding on the horizon one of the aspects of marriage I particularly longed for was to be a father. When eventually at the age of 37 I did get married to Mary, and children came along quite rapidly, this was an enormous joy to me. I am aware that I have hardly mentioned my four children in this book, largely because I did not want to embarrass them or invade their privacy; clergy children often suffer too much from the high profile of their parent. But I would hate anyone to get the impression, from their near-invisibility in these pages, that my children were on the periphery of my life, crowded out by the more important parish ministry. Many children who have parents with very full and busy lives, whether clergy, politicians, or many other professions, grow up with feelings of resentment or anger that they were marginalised and unloved.

I don't think that any of my children accuse me of that, though they were sometimes given a hard time at school because of press publicity given to something I had said or done; and they certainly suffered embarrassment when for example I came and led an assembly at their school. (My youngest especially squirmed if I said something that revealed my age, as I was of a similar age to the grandparents of some of her friends. If I said "I remember when I was a child in the war…" *"Dad! Don't say things like that!"* she agonised afterwards. However all parents embarrass their children, especially in their teens!)

I was privileged to be present at the birth at each one of our children, which I always found a profoundly moving experience. Although I worked a six-day week, and not infrequently a ten- or twelve-hour day, one advantage of my lifestyle was that I was almost always there at mealtimes and at bedtime when they were young. We always had breakfast together – Mary and I don't approve of help-yourself, running breakfasts! I usually took them to school (on foot). It was almost always I who read to them at bedtime. Indeed when they were little or even babies, I would say a prayer with them and usually sing a little song. "Jesus, tender shepherd, hear me," was one (to thc tune "Stuttgart") which had been sung to me in my infancy. "Jesus, Jesus loves Toby" (or Lucy, or Ross, or Zoë) was another, which I had found in the book, "Fresh Sounds". And of course, at Christmas, "Away in a manger".

Stories and games (not football but board games and "silly" games) were very much a part of our family life. On one occasion when they were in their teens the children wanted a party for their friends, and at first they suggested that Mary and I should go out and leave them to it. We weren't having that (and having read more recently of some of the disastrous parties of teenagers when the house has been trashed by gatecrashers who have learned of the party online, I am glad we never went down that route!). Instead we said that we would also invite their friends' parents, in the cases where we knew them, and have a party in the garden with games. They were initially appalled by that idea; in the event it was an enormous success, and it was their teenage friends who told us they hadn't enjoyed a party so much for ages!

Like all Christian parents, and all clergy families, we had to allow our children to make their own decisions and to find their own way; and like many such couples, we had to watch our children making decisions other than what we would have preferred. All our children had been brought up to go to church, until they were old enough to choose not to go – and to be left alone in the house when we went. They were all given Christian teaching; and each one in turn turned, or drifted, away from it. Sometimes the course they chose made us literally weep for them; thankfully none of them went down the dangerous roads that all too many young people found, of drugs or other addictions, and they all are now young people of whom we are proud and whom we still love deeply. One has rediscovered the Christian faith; the others, as yet, have not, while wholly respecting ours.

At one stage one of my children had apparently totally abandoned the faith to which she had once seemed so committed, and was living with a partner who was deeply hostile to all religion. Then, gradually and occasionally, she started appearing in church at parade services, as she was helping with one of the uniformed organizations for young boys. Normally these were not eucharistic services, but just occasionally, if for example it fell on Easter Day, it did include communion. On one such occasion, my daughter came up and knelt at the rail to receive communion.

Earlier in my ministry I had taken the line that someone living in a sinful relationship should not receive communion until they had repented and amended their life; I found justification for this strict approach in the rubric at the start of the Prayer Book service of Holy Communion, which referred to someone being an "open and notorious evil liver… so that the Congregation be thereby offended." Perhaps in the sixteenth century when Cranmer wrote those words, living in an unmarried sexual relationship would have fitted this description; in the late twentieth century it is considerably more doubtful whether it was appropriate to apply such a rule. But certainly when it was my own daughter, taking the first tentative step back towards the faith she seemed to have abandoned, there was no way I could have rejected her, and I do not believe for an instant that my Lord Jesus Christ would have required me to. I was very moved as I put the consecrated bread into her outstretched hand. I am sure that had I taken any other approach, it would have made her subsequent return to faith in Christ much more difficult, and might have stopped it altogether.

My encounters with homosexuals

When I was curate-in-charge of Emmanuel Church, Tolworth, we had a large and lively young people's group. This was not a "Youth Club" for unchurched youngsters, but a Christian fellowship for teens and twenties, with a regular diet of Bible studies, worship and prayer, as well as outings and social events of various riotous forms. One young man, a little older than most of them, was a quiet and earnest person, very regular in attendance. He had a girlfriend in the group, and I was aware that their relationship was sometimes stormy, though I did not know why.

He worked for the BBC in some technical capacity, and on one occasion he was sent to Glasgow for a week, where he shared accommodation with an older man. On his return, he asked if he could come and see me. It emerged that the older man was a homosexual; not only that, but Neil (as I will call the young man) by the end of the week was in love with him, and was convinced that he, too, was a homosexual. (The word "gay" was not in such universal use in the 1970s as it is today.)

However Neil knew well what the Christian teaching he had received said about homosexual behaviour, and as a devout and committed Christian he was now in a state of considerable confusion and distress. Was he a Christian, or was he a homosexual? It seemed to him that he could not be both – and yet he was.

This was the very first time that I was brought face to face with this issue in the life of someone I knew, respected, and cared about. I don't remember what I said to him, but almost certainly it would have been along the lines that the only right way forward was celibacy. I don't suppose it helped him much. I think he moved from the area soon after that, and I lost touch with him.

A few years later, when I was a vicar in the Isle of Wight, I felt it right to write an article on the subject of homosexuality in the parish magazine. (I never shrank from tackling controversial issues; I far preferred that, than to be bland and predictable.) I tried to be balanced, and compassionate. I condemned harsh and prejudiced attitudes, which nowadays are called homophobia – the word was not used then. I insisted that Jesus loves all people, whatever their sexual desires and temptations, and even if and when they give in to them. Especially I insisted that there is a profound difference between "being homosexual" in tendency and inclination, and indulging in homosexual genital behaviour. A person's nature and temptations cannot be condemned, and are not sinful. But – I said – homosexual genital intercourse is sinful, in just the same way as fornication.

Shortly after this issue of the magazine was published, I received a long letter – two handwritten sides of foolscap - from a homosexual man, who apologised that he felt he must write anonymously. He gave me, perhaps, six marks out of ten for trying, but still felt that I had no idea at all what it felt like to be a homosexual who still tried to maintain a Christian faith. I kept that letter for a long time, but sadly in one of our moves it has been lost. But I recall some of the things he said. One was that most homosexuals hate the church with a virulent hatred, because of what they have suffered as a result of its attitude. In another passage he described how he himself had tried very hard to have heterosexual relationships, and the attempts had been humiliating and disgusting, not just for him but for the women concerned. He ended by asking for my prayers.

I was very moved by that letter; and it perhaps helped me to be a little humbler, and a little more compassionate, in my attitudes and words. But the places where my ministry has taken me have not been large metropolitan centres where no doubt I would have frequently met homosexual men and lesbian women. No doubt there were such people in the Isle of Wight and in Barrow, but like my anonymous correspondent they kept their heads down. Would it have been better if they had "come out" and even had Gay Pride marches on the streets? The fact that they did not allowed me to continue my ministry without confronting the issue. I did know a clergyman who was undoubtedly homosexual, but not in any open way. When the clergy chapter congratulated me on my Silver Wedding, in a subsequent discussion he invited the clergy to consider with sympathy the fact that a gay couple could not, generally, celebrate openly and joyfully such anniversaries of their relationship.

While I was in Barrow, PCCs in evangelical parishes were invited by a para-church organization to pass a resolution that they would not accept practising homosexuals in any leadership role, clerical or lay, in their church. This led to a lively and interesting discussion at the PCC meeting. I was appalled by the naked homophobia of one older man, who was convinced that every homosexual was inevitably also a paedophile. Another older man, who had served in the Royal Navy as a petty officer, and whom I might have expected to have a hostile attitude to same-sex relationships, turned out to be surprisingly gentle and understanding. I discovered some time later that his son was homosexual, and the young man died in London of an AIDS-related illness not long after that. The love and kindness with which the gay community treated the bereaved parents as they mourned their son was deeply moving to them both. As I had discovered in the very different case of my daughter, when it is someone you love who is involved in some "moral issue", your attitude cannot but change.

What do I believe now about the rights and wrongs of homosexual or lesbian relationships? Do I now accept the almost universal secular standpoint that such relationships are every bit as "valid" as heterosexual ones? Would I be content for the Church to bless such relationships or even conduct homosexual marriages? Would I be unconcerned if an openly gay or lesbian priest were living in the vicarage with his or her same-sex partner? Is it acceptable for a practising homosexual to be a bishop? Is the moral distinction which I clung to for many years, between homosexual feelings and homosexual behaviour, totally unreal, since it involves demanding that homosexual people renounce sex, which means denying a central part of who and what they are?

I might use several pages here to examine the various passages in Scripture which are adduced to indicate God's hostility to homosexuality, but will be brief. The story of Lot in Sodom and Gomorrah[1] features a threat of homosexual gang rape, and I am not convinced it has much to tell us about the homosexual condition *per se*. A verse in Leviticus[2] prescribes the death penalty for male homosexual intercourse, but certain verses in the previous chapter also denounce such sins as wearing clothing woven of two kinds of material, or eating bloody steak; it makes one cautious about taking one verse as still declaring an immutable law three thousand years later, while others in the same passage are set aside as irrelevant to us. Paul has strong words about women pursuing *"unnatural relations"* (the only passage where lesbianism is mentioned) and says that men *"committed indecent acts with other men and received in themselves the due penalty for their perversion"*[3]. Certainly the most obvious understanding of these words is that any male or female same-sex sexual acts are forbidden.

---

[1] Genesis 19
[2] Leviticus 20.13
[3] Romans 1.26-27

Why am I reluctant – as I admit I am – to accept this as a binding ordinance, in the way that I once did? One way to soften this severe teaching is to suggest that Paul is writing about deliberate same-sex experimentation by heterosexuals, as a perverse distortion of one's natural desires, rather than about homosexual desires which are experienced as wholly "natural" by those who – for whatever reason – find their orientation that way inclined. I find that interpretation unconvincing. Another approach is simply to say that this was Paul's view, as a 1st century Jewish Christian trying to maintain sexual purity in a Graeco-Roman culture where every conceivable sexual perversion was exulted in; and we are at liberty, and indeed obliged, to find our own convictions of moral and ethical behaviour according to the Christian law of love, without necessarily feeling ourselves bound by Paul's strictures.

Jesus himself never mentioned the issue at all, though he did not hesitate to denounce the behaviour of his contemporaries, including in matters of sex and marriage. What he did do was insist that the primary obligation is love; he had no time for the judgmental and legalistic attitudes which he so frequently encountered in the scribes and Pharisees. It troubles me that so often the attitudes of Christians who maintain a traditional "hard-line" approach to homosexuality tend to resemble the stance of the Pharisees rather than that of Jesus himself. I have been like that in the past, and deeply regret it.

In the last few years the legal position has changed through the introduction of "civil partnerships". Civil partnerships in the United Kingdom, granted under the Civil Partnership Act 2004, give same-sex couples rights and responsibilities identical to civil marriage. Civil partners are entitled to the same property rights as married opposite-sex couples, the same exemption as married couples on inheritance tax, social security and pension benefits, and also the ability to get parental responsibility for a partner's children, as well as responsibility for reasonable maintenance of one's partner and their children, tenancy rights, full life insurance recognition, next of kin rights in hospitals, and others. There is a formal process for dissolving partnerships akin to divorce. More than 100,000 people have entered into civil partnerships since they became legal – several times more than were expected at the time of the legislation.

However in 2012 a further controversial issue has come to the fore, namely "Gay Marriage". The Prime Minister and Deputy Prime Minister have made it clear that they favour the introduction of homosexual marriage, as has the leadership of the Scottish Assembly. But many Christian leaders of various different churches and denominations have condemned the proposals, as have leaders of the Jewish and Muslim faiths, despite the assurances that no religious body would be forced to conduct or solemnise such marriages. (Serious doubts have been expressed about the validity of such assurances, some people envisaging legal action being taken by militants under the terms of Human Rights legislation.)

When this controversy began to attract more and more media coverage, I was very puzzled. What was it that homosexual couples actually wanted that they could not already have under the Civil Partnership legislation? I had an email correspondence with a younger Anglican priest – whom I knew to be sympathetic to the demands – to seek clarification. And I concluded that what it all centered on was the word "Marriage". Not rights or rites, not legal or financial issues; they just wanted to be able, like their heterosexual friends and neighbours, to describe their relationship as a marriage, and to say they were married.

I confess that I found it hard to feel a lot of sympathy for this desire. If a homosexual couple in a Civil Partnership wanted to call it marriage, or to tell people they were married, what was stopping them? Did they fear they might be prosecuted for some kind of Trades Description infringement? Indeed some such couples do speak of their union, or the ceremony to solemnise it, in precisely these terms. Why does it require a change in the legal definition of marriage, from what has been universally been recognized as such for thousands of years?

All right, the term "Civil Partnership" perhaps lacks a sense of romance; it is clumsy and infelicitous. "I love you – will you enter into a Civil Partnership with me?" has not quite the ring of "Will you marry me?" ("Will you partner me?" sounds a little like an invitation to dance.) Perhaps gifted writers and poets should be invited to set their minds to find a better terminology. But must marriage itself be redefined in law?

However when I went online with the term "Gay Marriage", one thing I discovered was that in many "first world" countries, homosexual marriage was already enshrined in law. Since 2001, eleven countries (Argentina, Belgium, Canada, Denmark, Iceland, Netherlands, Norway, Portugal, Spain, South Africa, Sweden) and some sub-national jurisdictions (parts of Mexico and the United States) have begun to allow same-sex couples to marry. In Canada, for example, the High Court had held that it was unconstitutional to make any legal distinction between men and women, and the 2005 Civil Marriage Act defined marriage throughout Canada as "the lawful union of two persons to the exclusion of all others."

All this has made me feel that it is pointless and impractical to go on fighting a rearguard action to prevent it happening in UK. The majority of the population is probably in favour; the overwhelming majority of those under 35 are quite unable to see what the problem is.

What about the church? Irrespective of whether clergy might somehow be forced by law to conduct same-sex marriages, which we are assured will never happen (never say never!), what is the Christian – by which I mean the Christ-like – attitude to the issue, or, more importantly, to the individual people, or the loving couples, whom we are seeking to love in the name of Jesus?

To some extent it is a similar issue to the remarriage of divorcees. Some clergy feel bound by their conscience to take a firm line, and refuse to conduct the wedding of any person who has a former spouse still living. Others are much more liberal and relaxed, and will marry anyone who asks them. And in between there are those who try to apply conditions, such as the question of whether the new relationship started when one of the partners was still married to their former spouse, and indeed whether it was instrumental in causing the breakdown of the previous marriage. I seem to recall guidelines of this sort (the infamous "Option G") being circulated to clergy when I was still in parish ministry; but increasingly clergy who tried to apply them found themselves in a totally unwelcome position of imposing judgmental criteria upon couples – which felt far from Christ-like.

Already there are many ministers in many churches who will happily "bless" a Civil Partnership, and conduct a ceremony which is virtually indistinguishable from a wedding. Their attitude will be along the lines of: "If a couple love each other, who am I to judge whether that love is right or wrong? Surely to enter into a lifelong, committed, mutually caring and supportive relationship, must be wholly good, and certainly far better than the sordid, promiscuous lifestyle so often associated with the homosexual community. I cannot believe God will condemn them for a love which to them is as wholly 'natural' and instinctive as any heterosexual 'falling in love' may be. If God approves, then let us happily, joyfully and publicly seek his blessing upon them." Any minister of any church who already conducts such services of blessing would be totally happy to go the further step and conduct a full marriage for a same-sex couple – only held back by any strictures which their church or supervisors might impose.

A major factor which the Anglican Church must keep in mind is the totally different attitude which many branches of the Anglican Communion in Africa and other Third World countries hold. They regard all homosexual relationships as intrinsically, deeply sinful; in several such countries they are illegal, and even liable to the death penalty. Bishops and clergy in such countries would find it horrifyingly offensive to be associated with a church which is blessing blatant sin. The accusations of the Muslim community that Christianity is totally corrupt would reinforce the unhappiness of Christian leaders at any proposal to recognize, let alone to celebrate, same-sex relationships.

Any Archbishop of Canterbury, who by virtue of his office is bound not only to seek to lead his church in Christian witness to this nation, but also to be the leader of the world-wide Anglican Communion, will certainly find this an increasingly impossible task, and the newly-appointed Archbishop is felt by many to be likely to preside over the break-up of the Anglican Communion, largely over this one issue.

Where do I stand, personally? I am glad I am no longer in the front line of having to make such decisions! I do not know what my convictions are on the matter. Some will be dismayed at this pusillanimity, particularly in one who used to be firm and unafraid to make controversial decisions and statements. I do not think I am yet ready publicly to bless a same-sex relationship; but I would be ready to say private prayers with such a couple, if requested – and those prayers would not be that the couple would repent of their sinful desires (!), but rather that God would bind them ever more deeply together in love. If I would do that, why not go the further step and do it publicly? A fair question, and one I hope I will not be asked any time soon. After all, the title of the

371

book is "I believe – I think!" This is one subject about which I no longer have certainties. Like much of our discipleship, it is "work in progress".

18

❧❧❧

What Next?

From the start we found retirement almost intoxicating. A major part of this feeling was that, for the first time in either of our lives, we were living in our own house. Clergy nearly always have to live in a "tied house"; the vicarage or rectory is provided, and that is where the parish priest lives. There are advantages, of course, not least financial; a free house of four or five bedrooms represents a substantial addition to what is otherwise a fairly meagre salary. (Some purists will correct me; a clergy stipend is not a salary, or a financial reward for the job; rather it is a subsistence allowance, so that the priest can do the job.) There is an allowance towards redecoration, and major repairs are paid for by the Diocesan Parsonages Board, which is a very considerable financial saving, and affords relief from anxieties. Costs for heating and lighting are not paid by the church, but an element of them is tax-deductible.

The disadvantages are, first, that the clergyman or his family have very little freedom to make any alterations to make the house more to their liking. The house is as it is, take it or leave it – and if your preference is to leave it, that means leaving the job as well!

Secondly, upon retirement, you have nothing; you have to move almost at once, and find a new house to live in. If a clergyman dies in office, his widow is given a very limited period in which to vacate the property, even though the authorities will try to be compassionate.

We were very fortunate, in that I had inherited from various relations a sum of money sufficient to buy a house for my retirement, and we had done so some five years before I actually retired. In the intervening years we let it, and when our final tenants left we had nearly a year in which to get a new room added and various other improvements carried out. It was about one hour's drive from Barrow, and we often drove out to do jobs like mowing the lawns; and seldom did such a trip end without Mary saying on the way home, "I wish we could live there *now*!"

But now at last we could move in, into a house which was our own to do what we liked with! The house itself, the garden (beautiful, even though a great deal of work was needed to get it under control), and the village and surrounding area all brought both of us enormous pleasure. Not infrequently, as I walked across the lawn, and gazed up at the old grey stone walls and slate roof, with the Virginia creeper and the rambling roses, I laughed aloud from sheer joy. We found our neighbours in the village warm and welcoming, and the peace and quiet of village life – after thirteen years of living on the main road into Barrow, with the roar of traffic day and night – totally delightful.

It was not only a new home; it was a new life, in all sorts of respects. Many of the domestic details of our home were new. For the first time in our lives we had an *en suite* toilet, shower and washbasin attached to our bedroom. We bought our first-ever new sitting room suite – we had lived with a succession of second-hand ones all our married life. Even such trivialities as the new breakfast set and cutlery gave us pleasure, and helped to mark the start of a totally new chapter of our lives.

A retired priest is still a priest, for life (unless he is unfrocked for disgraceful conduct!). But I told the vicar of our new parish that I wanted to do no work in the church, and take no services, for the first six months. I needed time to learn to be retired. Working as a parish priest is far more than a job – it is a total way of life, and to a far greater degree than most other jobs it impinges on all aspects of the life not only of the priest but also of his wife and children. It is a 6-days-a-week job, with not infrequently twelve-hour days or more. It takes time to wind down from that, and to find a new pattern for living.

The church does arrange various events – day and residential conferences – for those who are approaching retirement, to think through some of these issues. At one of these which I attended, a retired priest said, "When I retired, I decided to take no services at all for three months. It was a great mistake." He paused. "It should have been at least six!" So I took my lead from that man's experience.

But I still was certain that God had work for me to do, even though I did not know what it would be. In the spring before I retired, I had had an interesting experience, which I felt had been a word from God. It happened while I was having my morning Quiet Time, as I usually did.

Many clergy were taught at their Theological Colleges that it was the duty of a priest to "Say the Office"- to read and pray through the service of Morning Prayer, including the two Bible passages set by the Lectionary – every day of his or her life, and many do this as a life-long discipline. They would no more drop it than they would give up brushing their teeth. At the evangelical college that I attended, no such instructions were given. We were urged very strongly to have a daily time of prayer, Bible reading, and meditation; but it was never even suggested to us that the only way, or even the best way, to do this was to use the liturgy of Morning Prayer. At one point when we were on the Isle of Wight, the subject came up at the clergy fraternal meeting, and I was chided by a priest of a more catholic tradition, who said that my "quiet time" style was entirely individualistic; to Say the Office was to share in the prayer of the whole church. So for nearly a year I tried it. I really did; sometimes at home, and sometimes in church, I read through the canticles and psalms and prayers, and read the lessons for the day as prescribed in the daily lectionary. But I confess that I found it more of a chore than a blessing, and eventually I returned with relief to my Quiet Time pattern – reading a daily passage of Scripture, for which I usually used a scheme published by the Scripture Union, pondering it, and spending some time in prayer.

So that was what I was doing that spring morning in 2001. It was a Friday, which was my Day Off; that is significant, because it meant I was about half an hour later than I would have been on a working day. The passage set by my Scripture Union booklet was Exodus chapter 3, which tells the story of Moses and the Burning Bush[1]. The notes suggested that sometimes God uses some material object, maybe something very mundane and ordinary, to speak to us; and the writer suggested that I should look around and see if anything round me spoke to me of God.

I lifted up my eyes and looked out of the window. In our garden was a large Magnolia bush, and as I looked at this, the morning sun, coming over the roof of the house, was just touching the top three or four feet of it; and the creamy buds were glowing brilliantly in the sunlight. If I had been there half an hour earlier, it would have been in shadow; but as it was, it looked to me like a

---

[1] Exodus 3.2-4

burning bush! Moses was 80 years old, I pondered, when he began his life's work of leading the people of Israel out of Egypt. I felt as if God was saying to me: "So you are looking forward to retirement, are you, because you are nearly 65? Just going to put your feet up, are you? Forget it! I still have work for you to do – and it may be as much more significant than anything you have done yet, as Moses' work was for him! You ain't seen nutt'n yet!"

Well, something like that, anyway! But from that point on, my attitude towards retirement began to be different. God did still have work for me to do, even though I did not yet know what it would be. It was likely to include helping out in the parish of my retirement and others nearby; very often the ministry of retired clergy is enormously helpful to country priests with four or five churches to look after. But though I would (after my six months' rest) be happy to help in such ways, I felt that there was more. But I might have to wait some time – perhaps, like Moses, till I was 80! – to find out what God had in mind.

In fact I was very seldom asked by my vicar – a man from a very different tradition of churchmanship from mine – to take services or preach, even after the first six months of idleness; occasionally I would stand in if he were away, but this was rare. The village Methodist Chapel asked me to take a service and preach every few months, which I enjoyed; occasionally I was approached by other churches a bit further afield to take services in the absence of their vicars. This included the occasional funeral, baptism or wedding, which also entailed visiting the homes of the people concerned. I even had to take the funeral of my elder brother, an occasion which gave me a good deal of anxiety in advance, but satisfaction on the day, especially as there were several warm expressions of appreciation from both family members and other people. Perhaps the most moving tribute was from the crematorium organist, who shook my hand very warmly, but could hardly speak for the depth of his emotion; something in the service had touched this man's heart, despite the hundreds of funeral services for which he must have played.

All these opportunities to minister in God's name were rewarding in various ways; but I still felt that this was not what God had had in mind in my "burning bush" revelation (if that is not too dramatic a word for it). I mentioned my conviction about some future but as yet unrevealed ministry to various people. But I was still a good many years short of Moses' age of 80, so I waited patiently.

But then a new and very different opportunity for Christian ministry offered itself after some seven years of retirement. My old friend David Bendell, whom I had first met when he had been my churchwarden in Surbiton in the '60s, had in the intervening years left his career in Barclays Bank, been ordained to non-stipendiary ministry, and after working for a while for Tearfund (The Evangelical Alliance Relief Fund), became the UK Chairman of an Anglo-Canadian Mission society, Emmanuel International. This society specialises in sending small teams to Third World countries to work in both evangelism and humanitarian projects like health, nutrition and water, always in full cooperation with the local indigenous church. Often these teams contain young people working on one-year contracts after receiving three months' training in Canada. David had first encountered the society when his daughter Sarah, at the age of 18, worked in Jamaica for a year, and when David and his wife Jenny went to visit her there, it was their first face-to-face encounter with real, abject poverty. This was for both of them a life-changing experience.

As UK Chairman, it was his responsibility to pay regular visits to areas where teams of British people were working, and sometimes he was able to take other people such as members of his home church in Surbiton with him; he liked to do this to expose them to direct contact with Third World churches, particularly in Africa. Thus it was that he invited me in 2007 to join a party going to Tanzania for two weeks. A particular role he had in mind for me was to share in leading a Day Seminar for local village clergy and evangelists.

I found this visit both fascinating and challenging. We were shown various projects around the district of Iringa, including rural health clinics and water projects. We were invited into the homes of some of the local clergy, and shared meals with them, which was a great privilege. On Palm Sunday we attended a small Anglican church in the town, taking part in their worship (which included marching all round the outside of the church singing, dancing and waving real palm branches), and I was asked to preach the sermon, which was translated into Swahili by our host, Andrew. But undoubtedly the high spot of the visit for me was the day seminar.

This took place in a large, newly-built church some miles from Iringa, up in the hills, in a village called Kilolo. Kilolo had been designated a few years before by the Diocese of Ruaha as a Mission Area. The Seminar was to be on the theme of "The Evangelist", and I was to give the first and third talks ("The Call of an Evangelist" and "The Work of an Evangelist"), and David's son-in-law, Stewart, a vicar working in Cambridge, was to give the second talk, on "The Personal Life of the Evangelist".

We met in the large but simple, modern church. About forty-five of the evangelists and pastors who were working in the region had come to the seminar, many with their wives – brilliantly dressed, many with babies; one man, we were told, had walked for 5 hours with his wife and baby, just to be there! And five hours home again. I was amazed and humbled; no one had ever walked for five hours to hear me speak before! They were all gathering in the church, and while waiting for the seminar to begin (time is relaxed in Africa) they were spontaneously singing and dancing. One would go out to the front and start a solo line, and then all would join in quite naturally in 5- or 6-part harmony. Sometimes the women would ululate at moments of special exaltation. Mostly women sat on one side, and men on the other.

When the meeting started, first there were introductions all round, and then the Pastor in charge, Canon Ernest Lejeto, told us something of the recent history of the local churches. We were told that in the last ten years, this church, St. Michael's, had planted forty new churches in the surrounding area – seven of them in 2007. Many do not yet have any kind of church building, or just temporary ones; they will build more as the churches grow.

I had prepared very carefully, writing it all out in full (not my normal custom), in short sentences to aid the translation into Swahili. I was rather apprehensive, very aware that I had little understanding of their culture, their level of education, and their theological knowledge, and fearing that I could be completely on the wrong wavelength. Hearing about all these new churches - started by the men and women sitting before me - I felt all the more, "I am *talking about* evangelism – they are *doing* it!" I almost felt it was something of an impertinence for me to pontificate to these front-line workers. It became evident, especially in the question time after the talks, that these were no ignorant peasants, but intelligent, thoughtful people with a strong and deep faith. Later reports came back how valuable they had found the day; I felt enormously privileged to have been a part of it all. Altogether the whole day was a memorable experience. My heart was very full as we drove back on the uneven dirt roads to Iringa.

The following year there was another invitation to go to Africa, this time to Uganda. Mary had not accompanied me to Tanzania, feeling that she would just be a passenger, an onlooker; but for the

Uganda trip it was particularly her skills in needlework that were required, as she and Jenny were to lead a week-long seminar for a Women's Learning Centre which was one of the projects run by the Mothers' Union of the Diocese of South Rwenzori, in the town of Kasese in the south west of the country. The African women were to learn to make church banners and clergy vestments, and other craft work including knitting and rag rugs as an additional source of income for their families.

The invitation for me to come too was almost an afterthought, but it had occurred to David that another clergy seminar might be arranged. There were several differences from the previous year's seminar at Kilolo. First, I would be the sole speaker for all three sessions. Secondly it would be an ecumenical event, with not only Anglicans but Roman Catholics, Baptists and Pentecostals. And thirdly I could not simply re-use the talks prepared for my previous year's seminar, as the theme was to be different.

We were expecting about 80 clergy at the Seminar. All the planning had been done by Alan Parrett, our host in Kasese, who had been working there for several years. He had consulted with Rev. Nelson Isebagheen, our main Ugandan contact, and other diocesan clergy, especially a Church Army captain, Reverend Captain James Tumwesigye, whom we had met at the Diocesan Centre, and whom I had very much taken to. Emmanuel International were financing the event, including not only the hire of the premises and provision of two meals, but also 3,000/- (Ugandan shillings) travelling expenses (about £1.00 sterling) for each delegate – possibly a critical factor which would influence whether they could afford to attend the Seminar.

When discussing the theme (by emails between me and Alan) in the previous weeks, I had originally suggested that, like the seminar I helped at last year in Tanzania, the theme could be evangelism. However Captain James, in particular, felt that many

Ugandan church leaders are quite good at preaching the Gospel evangelistically; what they tend to be much less good at is the subsequent teaching and pastoral care of those who have been led to a personal faith in Christ. So it was agreed that the overall theme would be "Discipleship", with three sessions: Making Disciples, Training Disciples, and Discipleship and the Holy Spirit.

The timetable planned was that the Seminar should start at 10 o'clock, with people arriving for registration from 9.30 a.m. Worship was to be led by a man and a lady, Musa and Alice, accompanied by a keyboard. When we arrived shortly before half past nine there was hardly anyone there. Alice arrived shortly, and I was able to discuss with her how the worship in the final session could be run. She listened carefully, saying, "Yes, please" to all my suggestions – I had discovered that this form of words is often used in ways which strike a British person as odd. But I had confidence that she would lead the worship sensitively, and pass on to Musa my suggestions.

We already knew that African ideas of time tend to be very relaxed, but we were still a little anxious as 10 o'clock approached and the hall was still nearly empty. It was raining too; would this keep people away, or make travel difficult? However there was a steady trickle of delegates, and by about 10.15 it seemed right for the singing to begin. Musa had arrived, as had the keyboard player, a young lad called Chris, so they started off in lively, upbeat fashion. There were no books, of course – but the assembled (and still assembling) Reverends, Pastors and Fathers seemed to have no difficulty in joining in with enthusiasm.

As Bishop Jackson Nzerebende Tembo, Anglican bishop of South Rwenzori, had arrived, Alan thought it appropriate to invite him to say a few words before the first session – which he did, for 25 minutes! So by the time I stood up to speak, it was after 11 o'clock, and there was a pretty full house, a total of some eighty-six men and two or three nuns.

I had three different translators for my three talks, the first one being Alfonse, a Baptist. Joseph, a Roman Catholic, would do the second talk, and Nelson the third. After the first talk, there were refreshments (called "breakfast tea") served on the veranda, consisting of a plate of chicken, two vegetable samosas, a banana and a cup of tea or coffee.

Before the second session, there was another time of lively worship led by our three musicians, and all the delegates joined in with vigour. I noticed through the window that the three or four hotel waitresses, who were clearing up on the veranda, were also joining in the worship with singing and dancing, and I slipped out to greet them.

Alan then invited the Pentecostal bishop to speak; he was a grizzled older man called Silas, wearing a bright yellow and red figured cotton suit, and he too spoke (or perhaps roared) at considerable length. After Session 2 we all repaired to a dining room across the courtyard for a late lunch. I noticed that the delegates all piled their plates really high – rice, maize, two kinds of stew, potatoes (boiled potatoes are known in Uganda as "Irish potatoes"), and various vegetables, followed by fruit salad, with various fizzy drinks available. Knowing how limited is the income of these men, I was not surprised at their heaped plates; if a free meal is being provided, make the most of it! They probably would eat nothing more that day.

I was planning that at the end of the third session, on the Holy Spirit, there would be an opportunity for people to come forward to receive prayer with laying-on-of-hands, and so about ten men, representing all the four denominations, had been approached to share in this. After lunch I had a briefing session with them to explain how I planned to introduce the time of prayer ministry. I could only trust that they were spiritual men who would minister with sensitivity.

Before the third session Alan invited the Baptist leader to "say a few words" (apparently the Roman Catholic Vicar-General had been invited, but was not available), and I was relieved that he spoke quite briefly, majoring on how good it was that we could all come together from our different denominations – he could remember a time when Baptists and Catholics threw stones at each other!

I had to shorten my third talk a bit as time was getting on, but when we came to the point where people were invited to come forward for prayer, quite a considerable number did so. Some of the prayer needs that were mentioned to me were heart-breaking - desperate financial hardship and children to educate, a man's wife's chronic illness, and such like; how does one pray for people who are burdened with such needs, and yet who have such deep faith?

Finally the Seminar came to a close. David, Alan and I chatted to a number of the men as people were leaving, and there were many warm handshakes and expressions of gratitude and blessings received. I was particularly interested when I spoke to Musa, the man who had led the worship with Alice: he told me his main sphere of ministry was evangelism among Muslims. I asked whether this was a controversial or even dangerous work, but he said, "At present it is possible; it may not be possible for very long, and so we have to use the opportunity while the door is open!"

After this demanding but – to me at least – inspiring day, I was totally exhausted; we all came home and I collapsed upon my bed.

Another opportunity for ministry came on our second Sunday in Uganda. I was to preach at All Saints' Church, Kasese three times, to three different congregations; the first service was to be in English, the second in Runyoro/Runyankole (known as R/R), and the third in Lhukonzo, the main local language. The first service was meant to start at 7.15 a.m. – though, as usual in Africa, that was not a precise starting time!

I had gathered that the All Saints' congregations now worshipped in a new church, and had moved from the garage where they had started in November 2003; but when we came round a corner and saw this "new church" I was quite taken aback, as it was nothing but a large, timber shed, with considerable gaps between the planks, roughly whitewashed on the inside; the floor was earth, and there were simple forms with no backs for the congregation. There was no electric light, and when we arrived it was still fairly dark; I hoped I would be able to read my sermon notes. But as the morning brightened the light inside was adequate, and by mid-morning the sun had come out, and it became not only bright but very hot. I started the morning wearing a jacket, but I ended in shirtsleeves.

Nelson, the parish priest of this and twenty-six other churches, explained that this was a temporary building, and they planned to build a new, brick church outside the wooden one, and then remove the shed when the brick building was complete. There was already a pile of bricks nearby, though many more would be needed. The present building seated some 150 people.

Before long the church was fairly well filled. The English service (Morning Prayer according to the Alternative Service Book) was fairly staid, though the singing was quite lively. It was mostly accompanied only on two hand-drums.

My sermon was not translated. I asked Nelson later why they have an English service, as Cheryl (our hostess), Mary and I were the only white faces in church (David and Alan were worshipping in the Cathedral). He explained that, because of the large number of different languages in the country, and since people from many tribes and communities have moved to Kasese to find work, for many of them the majority languages like Lhukonzo are not well known. But if they know no other "foreign" languages, they will know some English, having learnt it from infant school, so for such people the English service meets a real need. All Saints', as a town centre church, was determined to meet the needs of all sections of the community.

The second service followed on almost immediately after the first. The changeover of congregations seemed to happen quickly. Nelson himself seemed much freer and livelier in the African languages than he had been in English – he had been almost "British" in style as he led the first service. I suggested before we began that perhaps I should shorten my sermon a little as it had to be translated, and would therefore take twice as long, and so I omitted a section in the middle (I had been somewhat uncertain how appropriate that part was, anyway.)

Because of the freer style of worship, I felt more relaxed myself. At each service, before preaching I called Mary to me and introduced her, and she was always warmly greeted, especially by the ladies. We also pointed out Nelson's chasuble which she had made, and he did a little twirl! Mary also spoke a few words, particularly bringing greetings from our own church, All Saints', Orton.

Between the second and third services, there was a pause during which we went round the corner to the Lay Reader's home, where a breakfast of fruit, chapatti and coffee was served.

For the Lhukonzo service the church was packed to overflowing, with dozens of children. We were met at the side of the church by the (unrobed) youth choir, who started singing and dancing as they led us into church. As they reached the front they parted, and we passed between them to our places. There were so many children in church that a lot of the little ones (aged perhaps 3 to 6) were beckoned forward to sit at the communion rail and behind it on the floor. There they were quite close to me and to Mary, and some of them moved closer to us so that they could reach out and touch us, perhaps to see if we were real, or if the white came off! There are very few white people to be seen in Kasese.

The Sunday School children – all in green uniforms of skirts or shorts and tabard tops (which they change into when they get to church) - enthusiastically sang a lively song about the healing of King Hezekiah (see II Kings chapter 20). The congregational singing was really inspiring and joyful, accompanied by an electric guitar (battery operated) as well as the two drummers. I felt really uplifted and moved as I came forward to preach, and Mary too was close to tears as I introduced her. I told the youth choir and all the Sunday School children that I had enjoyed their singing so much that I wished I could have taken them *all* home to my church! This evoked a great cheer.

At the end of each service there were lengthy notices from the Lay Reader, which included a warm welcome to anyone who was worshipping there for the first time. Such people were invited to stand and introduce themselves; and at each service, and especially the final one, there were several people who did so. It was a vivid demonstration of how the church is growing week by week; we had learned that since they had started in November 2003 in the garage with a very few worshippers, they had grown to over 450 members, which represents growth at a rate of 100 people a year, or two new people every week.

Then the Lay Reader and two other people said they had gifts for us, and came forward with shiny wrapped parcels. We were told that when we unwrapped them we would see which one was for which person, and indeed it turned out that Mary's was intended for me! The swap caused much merriment. I had a superb shirt, and Mary was given a beautiful length of material.

Their Mothers' Union ladies also presented some beads which they had made; one string was for Mary herself, one for the leader of our Mothers' Union at home, and one for the first person who would greet us at our home church. We found all this very touching, and were rendered almost speechless by the generosity of these very poor folk.

Then they said that they wanted to create a long-term link between All Saints', Kasese and All Saints', Orton, our home parish. When we introduced ourselves, we had shown them photographs of the congregation from Orton waving in greeting. I responded that I personally would love to see such a link established, but that I was not in charge of All Saints', Orton. I could promise nothing, but I would certainly try. Once again there was a burst of applause.

Though such a link would start with mutual prayer and news-sharing, they were obviously hoping that before too long there might be a considerable financial element. We kept on meeting this attitude. Several of the schools we had visited also hoped for a link with a British school. The *Mzungus,* or whites, are inevitably perceived as rich, and therefore as a valuable source of funds. We could totally understand this! We are of course vastly better off than them in material terms, but at the same time we were unhappy about fostering this kind of dependency culture. It is a very complex and sensitive area.

They had ambitions to replace their temporary worship building – which they referred to as a shed – with a more worthy, permanent structure; they indicated that the Kasese Town Council authorities would not tolerate this kind of shed for long. The third congregation was already outgrowing it; and they had a vision for this town centre church to reach out into the surrounding area, with all its bars and clubs. Nelson told us that their first need was for a Public Address system – not for audibility within the church, but to broadcast their worship to the neighbourhood. I was not sure how welcome this would be to the neighbours!

Though taking part in three services, and preaching three times, was tiring, we both felt that it had been a moving and inspiring morning, and our hearts were full as we pondered what we had shared with our African brothers and sisters in Christ.

There was one more experience during that visit to Uganda which was to have a powerful effect upon us both when we returned home. Nelson had planned a day visiting all sorts of schools and colleges, all of which were fascinating, and at all of which we received an enthusiastic welcome. At all of them, too, it was made clear to the visiting party of *Mzungus* that they very much hoped that our visit would lead to their receiving financial support, perhaps by our arranging a twinning agreement with some British school. Though their needs, compared with any British school, were huge and pressing, it became embarrassing to hear these appeals, time after time. We felt that they saw us as an unending source of wealth; we feared that the warm and smiling welcome we received from them all was tainted with this expectation.

By the end of the day, when we still had one more school to visit, we were getting weary, and were not best pleased when yet another stop was inserted into the programme. "Now what have we got to see?" we wondered. This, it emerged, was not a school, but a project working among a group of street children, led by a young man named Enos Kyibibi. Enos introduced us to his bunch of some thirty boys, ranging in age from about 6 to 16. Unlike our experience at all the schools we had been visiting, we were not greeted with cheerful, smiling faces here. Their expressions were etched with suffering and poverty. One of the older boys came forward and read a statement, describing their way of life. Many were orphans through HIV-Aids or Malaria. Others were children of prostitutes. Many had been dreadfully abused. They were reduced to sleeping in the trees, and getting what food they could from the town rubbish dump. Sometimes, said the boy, a lady would give one of them work for a day, perhaps sweeping a shop, and would pay them with food. When that happens, "she is our mother for the day." Enos was trying to provide both food and shelter, and to arrange vocational training of various kinds so that they could support themselves, rather than slip into petty crime which was all too easy.

We felt rebuked and guilty for our resentment at having to stop off to visit them; and when David was asked to say a prayer for them, he was nearly speechless, confessing that he felt shame for our wealth and their poverty.

When we flew back to UK and returned home to Cumbria, our minds were buzzing with all that we had seen. In particular, we did want to respond to some at least of the appeals for help that we had heard, even though we could not possibly respond to them all. I hoped to make good my promise to All Saints' Church, Kasese, to try to arrange a link with All Saints', Orton, but nothing could be done for some months until a new Priest-in-Charge was appointed. Likewise we wondered if our village school would like to link up with a Ugandan primary school, but this too would have to wait until a new head teacher was in post.

But we also felt strongly that we ourselves as a couple should support something; and Mary had no doubt that it should be the street children. We learned that Enos had a scheme to buy land and build a Hostel, to get the little children back into school, and give vocational skills training to the older ones. (We had the impression at first that this was a project already under way, which we could support; but it soon emerged that it was nothing but a vision, a "twinkle in his eye", and he had no source of income at all for it but us!)

So that was the start of what was to become over four years of fund-raising. At first there were such things as selling Ugandan beads, and copies of my Uganda Journal, copiously illustrated with photographs (mostly taken by David). We opened our garden to the public for one weekend, with refreshments and crafts for sale, and music from the Appleby Town Band in which I play. People gave generously to the cause, and over £800 was raised; when sponsorship by Barclays Bank through their charities foundation was added, we were able to send £1,500 out to Uganda, which would be enough for Enos to buy a 2-acre plot of land, both for building a hostel and for agricultural projects. Alan Parrett, our Missionary host in Kasese, had agreed to oversee the receipt and spending of the money we were able to send out.

A personal effort which I undertook was prompted by the fact that very shortly after our return from Uganda we found ourselves watching the London Marathon on TV. There were runners as old as me (I was 71) or even considerably older; and I started to wonder, would it be a mad and absurd idea for me to apply to run in the 2009 London Marathon? I prayed about it, and felt that I was given positive promptings by the Holy Spirit to pursue this idea. When I was at school, over fifty years earlier, cross-country running had been almost the only sport at which I had excelled - I was useless at anything with a ball. But I hadn't run for fifty years, and my initial rash attempt to start training runs led almost at once to a strained Achilles tendon! I would not know for six months whether I would be allotted a place in the Marathon, and so as an intermediate step I applied for a place in the Great North Run, a Half-Marathon from Newcastle to South Shields which took place in October. When my tendon was better I started more cautiously on a training regime once more.

I was amazed at the generosity of family members, friends and neighbours whom I had invited to sponsor me. Within weeks the pledges had topped a thousand pounds. The training runs, even after my Achilles tendon had healed, were causing me a good deal of pain, especially in the buttocks, but I pressed on. My target time for the half-marathon was 2½ hours, but with all my aches and pains I felt this was more and more unlikely to be achieved, and I just hoped I could finish the run, however long I took. On the day of the Run I had no pain at all; as my physiotherapist had told me, adrenalin is a wonderful drug. There was an amazing atmosphere with 52,000 runners and many thousands of cheering supporters; to my great satisfaction I achieved a time of 2 hours, 29 minutes and 46 seconds! Even better, the sponsor money topped £3,000.

We continued raising funds throughout 2009 with various events and talks, and were supported by some exceedingly generous donors. In March 2010 we planned to revisit Kasese. By then we had been able to send out £12,000; the land had been bought, a hostel had been designed, planning permission (or the Ugandan equivalent) had been obtained, and, we were told, foundations had been laid and building had begun. We could not wait to see it.

This time we were not travelling with our experienced friend, David, but on our own, but we would still be staying with Alan and Cheryl Parrett as we had on the previous visit. A day or two after arriving in Kasese we were driven the two or three miles out of town to the site where the new Hostel was to be built, and there we met Enos Kyibibi whose vision this had been and who had been carrying the work forward; and while we were there, Rev. Captain James also arrived on his motorbike.

We were astonished at the size of the building whose foundations and footings we saw, with a team of about a dozen men and some women hard at work. We marched all round the 2-acre site, singing songs of praise, and claiming the land for God; and then we gathered together for a time of prayer. By the end

Mary was in tears – it was a profoundly emotional experience for us both that after two years of fund-raising we could actually see the building growing around us. By the time we left Kasese some ten days later, the walls had grown to waist height.

During this visit too a clergy seminar had been arranged, and I had been preparing my talks for some weeks. But this time Alan had entrusted some of the planning arrangements to the Diocesan Secretary. African clergy have many spiritual gifts, but it seemed that administration was not one that had been given to this person, and it turned out that few of the invitations to clergy of the Church of Uganda and the Baptist Church had actually been sent out, and unlike the nearly ninety men who had attended the seminar two years earlier, there were only about thirty this time, most of them Roman Catholics and Pentecostals. Captain James, who was there, told me afterwards that he was particularly upset about this, as he felt that the teaching given would have been very valuable to his colleagues.

Once again I preached at All Saints' Church, with which a parish Link had now been set up with our home parish in Orton, Cumbria, and enjoyed the uplifting and inspiring worship. The collections at the two previous Christmas Carol Services in Orton had been designated for our Link church, and so after the service, when we were invited to a meeting with the church council, we were able to pass on this gift to the church leaders. We were shown a plot of land immediately behind the wooden church, which we were told they were buying as a site for their proposed new church building, but they were still paying off the bank loan for this purchase. At each service there was not one but two collections, the second one being for the paying off of the loan, and raising funds for the new building; and for each collection, instead of passing round bags or plates in the way familiar to British churchgoers, the people came up to the front and put their gifts into the box or basket. But when the contribution from Orton was counted, to the joy of all the council it was found that it exactly paid off the bank loan. Both Alan and I were given new African-style shirts (which of course we had to try on then and there: "See, I am white all the way down!" joked Alan), and Mary was given a costume in local material (which she didn't put on there!).

Though Nelson still had links with All Saints' and had translated for me, he had in fact been moved by his Bishop to a new sphere of ministry, as Missioner to an area of some forty villages in the hills about thirty miles north of Kasese; and there he had another task lined up for me. He was arranging a two-day Prayer Conference in Rwensande, the central village, to which Christians from many of the villages all round the area were expected to come. He asked me to give three substantial addresses on the theme of prayer.

We were disturbed to learn that when the Bishop sent him to be Missioner in this very extended area in the hills, covering some forty parishes, "to care for the welfare of these people", he would not actually get a stipend or salary of any kind, because he does not have his own church where he is vicar. Apparently he asked the Bishop, "But what about my own welfare?" And the Bishop simply replied, "I don't know what to do about your welfare!" We are aware that the Diocese is desperately short of funds; but to send a man to a very responsible job which entails him living fifty kilometres from his wife, Yoleda, and his children, some of whom are in school in Kasese, but to make no provision whatever for his financial support, seems dreadful. I really do not know how he and his family survived.

As we were to stay in the village overnight, we would be sleeping in the "Guest Bungalow". We had been warned that there was no electricity in the village so we had brought a torch; but we had not realised quite how basic the accommodation was. I had been vaguely assuming that the bungalow would be similar to, though perhaps smaller than, the Parretts' bungalow in Kilembi, which is of almost European standards.

But no. "Basic" was the word. A corrugated iron roof, and no ceilings; no glass in the windows, just wooden shutters; simple wooden beds, with a foam mattress (thank goodness!), and we had brought our own bedding. The toilet was a pit latrine, with the typical foot-stands either side of the hole, in a little brick shed some 20 yards from the house, with a tiny window to let in some light and air (bring your own paper!). The "washroom" was a cement-rendered enclosure outside the back door with a drain hole in one corner, and no door, and not much roof. There was a sitting-cum-dining room with a long table, and some chairs and wooden settees with foam cushions. But we were in no way horrified or dismayed by these simple conditions, rather regarding them as a challenge and an adventure, and a way of living in Ugandan style.

We were summoned across the green under the trees to the church, from which lively singing had been emanating for quite a while. There were perhaps thirty people there in the large, bare, cement-floored building. There was no glass in the windows, but they had wrought-iron grilles. The congregation sat on wooden forms. The singing was in rich spontaneous harmony, accompanied by bongo drums, played by hand or by a stick. There was the usual solo and harmonic chorus style, and one song merged seamlessly into the next. No books were used.

When I gave my talks, there were different translators, some definitely more satisfactory than others, though of course I had no way of assessing the accuracy of the translation. But one young man, while translating fluently, had his mind elsewhere – looking out of the window, or fiddling with his mobile phone. I was very relieved when Nelson took over, and presented the message to the people with directness and expression. We were becoming very fond of him and had a growing respect for him; when we went back to Kasese, we met his wife, Yoleda, and their family again (as we had in 2008), and gave them little presents that we had brought from England. When we got back home we decided we must try to give him and his family some personal financial support.

On our return to UK we set out once more on the round of fund-raising for the Street Children's Hostel. With the photographs we had taken in Uganda I produced a PowerPoint presentation, and over the next two years we showed it and spoke at many groups – Mothers' Union, Women's Institute, Rotary Clubs, schools and churches. There were ceilidhs, a concert, a barbecue, an African Evening in the village Market Hall, and – a major fund-raiser – Mary's Multi-Vehicle Charity Challenge, in which over the course of six weeks she drove as many different kinds of vehicle as she could. The 63 means of transport she achieved included a tractor, a pink stretch limo, an Ullswater steamer, a narrow gauge steam train (the last two complete with passengers), a Model T Ford, a Harvest Forager, a donkey cart, three different fire vehicles, an armoured personnel carrier, and a penny-farthing bicycle (from which she fell, cracking a rib!). The sponsorship for these efforts raised a further £3,000, which enabled the roof of the Hostel to be completed. Alan emailed us regular photographs of progress with the building.

By March 2012 the Hostel was virtually complete, and an Opening Ceremony was planned. Some £40,000 had been raised by then, and so of course we had to fly out to be present at the Opening. By this time Alan and Cheryl, our hosts on the two previous visits, had been moved from Kasese and were stationed in Kampala, so we were expecting to have to find a hotel to stay in – on our previous visit, anticipating that this might be the case, we had inspected a number of hotels, ranging from the cheap and extremely basic to the luxurious and rather expensive. We had taken particular care to look at the toilets! However we were emailed by Enos who was arranging not only our whole busy itinerary in Kasese, but also our accommodation: we were to stay with Emmanuel Maate, the chairman of the Hostel Board.

I confess that we were slightly apprehensive about this, as well as excited. We had never met Emmanuel; but we gathered that he was a deputy Head of a Teacher Training College at Bwera, some fifty miles from Kasese, and not only had a rather larger house than most homes we had seen, but had himself been in UK when doing a course in Educational Special Needs in Sussex University. In the event we found the hospitality we were offered was quite delightful, and Emmanuel, his wife and 12-year-old son were warm and welcoming hosts. (They even had a flush toilet close to our bedroom, though the home was simple!)

Each evening the family joined us for family prayers; on the first evening, it was apparently the turn of Ephraim, the 12-year-old, to lead the prayers. He confidently started by leading an extempore prayer – in English, of course; and then started singing a hymn, in which we all joined; I think it was, "Jesus loves me, this I know." He read a scripture passage, and his mother, Gertrude, read a comment from a booklet, and we all shared in prayers at the end. It was a moving and heart-warming start to our stay. Emmanuel himself was only able to be there for one evening, as he was obviously a very busy man with many responsibilities, but we took to him at once, and found him to be a highly intelligent man with a profound faith and a wide knowledge of the scriptures. We felt that to have a man like that as the Chairman of the Board of the Hostel project was very encouraging, and gave us confidence that there would be a wise hand on the helm.

The Opening of the Hostel, the main purpose of our long journey from UK, was much as we expected - exciting, disorganised, lengthy, and very late in starting! When I had been preparing my address for the occasion, I remembered the boy who, four years earlier, had read the statement which had so touched our hearts, and wondered if he was still around. I emailed Enos to ask him, and he replied promptly, with the boy's name and an up-to-date photograph, and had promised me that he would be at the Opening. As soon as we arrived at the site, Enos greeted us, and said "Here is your boy!" This handsome young man – now perhaps 18 or 19 – came forward; his name was Ashiraf. He had no recollection of reading the statement, but I had with me a photocopy of his original scruffy bit of paper, in his handwriting, and showed it to him. He studied it, and then slowly smiled, and said, "Oh, yes!" He asked me if he could keep it, and I gladly gave it to him.

During my speech I called him forward (Nelson was translating for me; probably most of the adults there could have spoken English, but many of the street children could not and I wanted them to understand). I told Ashiraf before them all that he had played a crucial role in what I believed to be God's long-promised plan; it was because of what he, Ashiraf, had said that day in 2008 that this great building was there before us. I was told that Ashiraf was now working as a boda-boda man (a bicycle taxi), and was hoping to start a course in welding.

After many speeches, and songs by several choirs, at last lunch was served (about 5 p.m., instead of the midday scheduled – but after all, this was Africa!). The Hostel building was, in fact, not quite finished – there was still plastering to do, as well as fitting some of the internal doors, as things had been delayed in recent months because of a problem with the budget which took a while to sort out. So the boys would not be moving in just yet. Anyway even when the building was finished, further finance would be needed for furniture and other equipment.

We had always said that we would try to finish and equip the building, but could not take on the responsibility of day-to-day running costs; that would be up to the local community. In my speech I illustrated this with the Olympic torch – I had actually acquired an inflatable torch, which Alan held as he trotted round the compound; but, I insisted, we were now handing the torch on to the community of Kasese – and Alan passed the inflatable torch to a Ugandan guest in the front row.

Enos, we knew, had hopes that by using the land for crops and also selling wooden items made by the boys, it would be to some extent self-financing, but we also hoped that the local authority might give financial support, and so he had arranged an appointment with the Mayor of Kasese. I had a nasty tummy upset that day so Mary had to go on her own; but I think she handled it well, not least when she found that the Mayor was a Rotarian, and he suggested that we explore the possibility of funding from Rotary International.

On the Sunday I was to preach at All Saints' Church once again, this time just for the early service, as we were then to be driven forty miles south to the new parish where Nelson was serving, among the nomadic cattle herders of the Queen Elizabeth National Park. We were also to stay there for one night, so that on the Monday morning we could visit one of the Primary Schools in his parish, as Orton Primary School had now decided that they would like to form a Link with a Ugandan school. Having heard about his parishioners' way of life, I wondered if we would be staying in a tent! However Nelson had an attractive little house, quite recently built, and indeed he explained that most of the cattle herders were now settled in houses; this had been encouraged by the church, to enable to people to have easier access to health care and education for the children.

We were welcomed into Nelson's home by his wife Yoleda, now very pregnant, together with his two youngest children, Brompton, aged 6, and Atwanzire, aged 3. There was of course food, preceded by the usual washing of hands; and then we moved across to the church for a service of Holy Communion. In view of their traditional nomadic lifestyle, I had decided to base my sermon on the story of Abraham's encounter with God when three mysterious men visited his tent. I helped to administer the Communion, dipping the wafers into a chalice held by Nelson, as the worshippers came forward while there was quiet, worshipful singing. As always we found the African worship moving and uplifting, and felt it a privilege to be able to share it.

After the service the men moved outside for a discussion with Alan and me, while the women stayed in the church; Nelson had emailed before we left UK, "Mary will speak to the women", which alarmed her considerably, as she does not see herself as a public speaker. However she had prepared a little talk about some biblical women – she has a particular soft spot for Mrs Noah, who just supported her husband even while not understanding what was going on! The women gave her (and Cheryl, and Sue from the Emmanuel International head office in UK, who was also visiting Uganda) a little demonstration of certain marriage customs from their culture; and then they all stood in a circle, each woman laid her right hand on the shoulder of the woman to her right, and each prayed out loud together for that person.. Obviously when African was praying for British woman or vice versa, the one prayed for might not understand what was being said, but it was still a heart-warming experience as the murmur of all the prayers filled the little church, and the breeze gently moved the long skirts and shawls of the African women.

That evening Nelson took us parish visiting. The houses were widely scattered over the flat, parched landscape, perhaps half a mile apart; normally Nelson would have walked around his parish, but we were able to use the car which had brought us from Kasese. (Next day, when this car was still being used to take us to various appointments which Enos had arranged for us in Kasese, Mary asked, "Who has provided this car?" Nelson answered firmly, "God!" We gathered that some well-wisher, whether a friend or member of his extended family, was happy for his vehicle to be used in God's service.)

The first home we visited was that of a desperately unfortunate little family: "the husband is blind, the wife is paralysed, and their daughter is mad," explained Nelson. The tiny house was dilapidated with an earth floor and holes in the thatched roof. We did not meet the blind husband, who had apparently been taken by a neighbour to find someone who might mend his roof; but when the old lady heard that the vicar was outside, she begged him to come in and pray for her. Nelson took me and Cheryl into the dark little room at the back of the house, where the poor old soul was huddled on the floor, partly covered with a ragged cloth. When she spoke, Nelson told us she was not complaining of her lot, but was upset that she could not look after her husband. He asked us to pray for her, and we knelt beside her, held her hand and prayed; though she spoke no English, I am sure she derived comfort from these prayers. When we left the house, we found some young women standing outside, and we gathered that these were neighbours whom Nelson had arranged to take turns to bring food, milk and water to this sad little household. It suddenly struck me that in the dark bedroom, there had been no unpleasant smell of urine; these good neighbours must have been attending to even her most intimate needs, a wonderful example of Christian love.

We were taken to some other homes, poor and simple but in good order, and were welcomed to each; in one we met Yowesi

Yombo, an elderly man who was the first Christian in this community, converted in his teens through an American missionary; he had returned to the tribe, and with two others had set about preaching the Gospel to them. This was a "first generation" church, whose existence was largely due to the faithful labours of this evangelist. (I describe him as elderly, and Nelson had referred to him as an old man; but I found he was two years younger than me!)

We returned to Nelson's home in the pitch dark, and he started his generator to give us a little light – there is no electricity there. After the evening meal, as we sat in the semi-dark, he told us of his ministry, not only in this parish, but in the early years since he was ordained. Our respect for him grew as we heard of his persistence with a charismatic ministry, against the disapproval of some senior clergy in the diocese, until the Bishop supported him. We asked him about walking around his widely-extended parish; could he not use a bicycle, because we remembered he used to have one? However he told us that since he had a bad motor-cycle accident the previous year (an antelope had knocked him off a borrowed motorbike on his way to visit his teenage son in hospital, and he suffered a serious knee injury; he had had to climb back on the bike and take himself to hospital, where he stayed for some weeks), he simply could not pedal a push-bike. So walking was the only option. "How much would a motor-bike cost?" we asked; he gave us the sum in Ugandan shillings, which we worked out at about £800, including insurance. We felt we would love to try to get him such a vehicle, which would be an enormous asset to his parochial work, as well as enabling easy trips into town. (Since we shared this desire with some supporters on our return to UK, a friend who used to be a biker as a young man told us he would like to give us the money for it.)

The accommodation for us in Nelson's home was much more basic than Emmanuel's, with a very narrow bed and an outside pit latrine; but we still really enjoyed his hospitality, and felt it a privilege.

Next morning we went to visit Busunga Primary School, which was to be linked with Orton Primary School in Cumbria. Orton School had lent us a camcorder, which we had already used extensively on our various activities, and we were pleased to be able to record the lively song of welcome by the pupils as we drove into the school grounds. Mary had also prepared a scrap book with a lot of photographs of Orton School, the children and some of their homes, and including some sheets of writing by the children; we felt as we handed that to our hosts that as they saw these pictures of the facilities in a UK school – facilities that they could only dream of – they would inevitably hope that the Link would lead to some of this wealth coming in their direction. When the speeches of welcome made frequent reference to such a hope, I whispered to Nelson that he must make clear to them that the purpose of this Link was educational and cultural, not financial, and it would cause great embarrassment if they started asking for money; when I got home I spelt this out more clearly, while also saying that perhaps small sums might be donated, perhaps from the takings at a school show. Nelson completely understood this point.

We had just two more days in Kasese, taken up with various visits and appointments which Enos had arranged for us – with the Bishop, the Mayor, another minister, another school, the Hostel Management Board, and Enos' own family. Finally we had to be up early on the Wednesday morning to catch the bus for the eight-hour journey back to Kampala. Nelson came to see us off, and as we waited for the bus, he laid a hand on my arm. "Chris," he said earnestly, "you cannot imagine how much it meant to Yoleda and me to have you and Mary staying in our home!" We were very touched, and assured him that we too had felt it a joy and privilege to be there.

When we finally arrived back home in Cumbria, after ten hours' flying and the final two-hour drive from the airport, unsurprisingly we were totally shattered and took several days to recover. But we still felt that the whole adventure had been enormously rewarding and worthwhile; and we started to report on our trip to all our many supporters, by an update email, reports on the Kasese Street Kids blog, and a sixty-page journal for those who are real gluttons for information.

What next? Will we go back? Various people asked us. We don't know. Despite the "passing on the torch" image, we have continued to do some fund-raising, but at a reduced level. We have sent out more money for bunks for the Hostel, and will try to help them with further furnishings, tools and equipment. As I write, we have just heard that the first eight children have moved into the Hostel. Our prayer is that this will represent not just a change of address, but a change of life.

19

But is there a "What next"?

I am well past the Biblical "three score years and ten". I am very thankful that I have good health and remain active. A few years ago on some website which claimed to measure your life expectancy I filled in the personal details of my height, weight and lifestyle, and it told me I could expect to live to the age of 89. Well, maybe; but I might be knocked down by a car tomorrow. Sooner or later like everyone else I will die.

Then "what next?" The atheist of course will maintain there is nothing next. Where is the candle flame when it has been blown out? Some people find this idea of "nothing" very comforting and reassuring. It is likely that the person who for whatever reasons chooses to end his own life is hoping that there will then be nothing.

Different religions suggest a variety of answers. Some of the oriental faiths believe in reincarnation. Born again? Yes, and again, and again and again. Perhaps eventually after a myriad of lives there will be Nirvana, which may be defined as "absorption into the infinite", or by imagery such as a drop of water falling into the ocean.

The Christian faith will have none of it. *"To die once, and after that comes judgement*[1]*."* Once, not many times. *"And after that…"* Yes, there *is* an "after that." The spiritualist movement which became very popular at the end of the nineteenth century and in the early twentieth century (and still of course has many adherents today) uses phrases like "passing over to the other side", which is apparently very much like this side, but nicer. But it does not seem that a judgement by a holy God features at all.

In popular thinking in our culture today there is a great deal of confusion about death and what happens after it. It has of course been strongly influenced by centuries of Christianity, but this has been much modified and distorted. Too often the versions of Christianity that people think they know about are a travesty of Biblical faith. "Heaven" is thought of in vague, cartoon-like terms of sitting on a cloud playing a harp, for ever and ever, which is about as inviting a prospect as an interminable wet weekend in Wigan…. And "Hell", if thought of at all, is seen in mediaeval terms involving demons with pitchforks (not a biblical image!). But few people take that seriously.

I have had to take many funerals, of course, the great majority involving people who have no Christian commitment and very limited Christian understanding. Occasionally bizarre assumptions emerge in the pre-funeral pastoral visit. I recall a young couple who had suffered the tragic loss of a little child, about two years old. As they discussed with me where he would be buried, the choice lay between two different cemeteries; the trouble with the one nearer to their current home where they had not lived for very long was that "He wouldn't know anyone there." There seemed to be some vague idea of the ghosts sitting on their graves, chatting, and the poor little boy being lonely. I do

---

[1] Hebrews 9.27

not mean to mock; in such matters of deep grief for most of us our heart rules our head.

A few years ago at the time of the scandal at Alder Hey Hospital, when it emerged that children's body parts had been stored without seeking parental consent, one sequel was that many of these horrified parents, whose children's funerals were long past, wanted further funerals for proper disposal of the stored remains. Sometimes funerals were even demanded for tissue slides, or families had three or four funerals as yet more organs were discovered. Leaving aside all matters of medical ethics in this case, it seemed to me that this obsession with the minutest fragment of a loved one's body indicated a very sad lack of any real faith about eternal life and resurrection.

From my youth the concept of heaven has been important to me. I recall my grandmother reading to me the same Victorian children's books she had read to her own children, and in one of them there was a kind of fantasy of the child who thought she was in heaven, and harsh and cruel people had become sweet and kind – and then she woke up, "and behold, it was a dream". As a little child I was gripped by that account, and I am sure it has coloured my thinking and imagining ever since. (How gratified the Victorian author would be!) Almost certainly too the death of my father when I was two was influential, so that the assurance that "Daddy is in heaven" was very much part of my thinking.

Other books have moulded my understanding since then, especially perhaps those by C. S. Lewis. Lewis himself thought a lot about heaven; his friend, the author and Bible translator J. B. Phillips, told of his last meeting with Lewis, who, as they parted, bellowed across the traffic-infested High Street, Oxford, "See you in heaven!"

In a sermon Lewis preached at the Church of St. Mary The Virgin, Oxford, came this passage:

407

"If we are made for heaven, the desire for our proper place will already be in us... In speaking of this desire for our own far-off country, which we find in ourselves even now, I feel a certain shyness.... I am trying to rip open the inconsolable secret in each one of you – the secret which hurts so much that you take your revenge on it by calling it names like Nostalgia and Romanticism and Adolescence; the secret also which pierces with such sweetness that when, in very intimate conversation, the mention of it becomes imminent, we grow awkward and affect to laugh at ourselves; the secret we cannot hide and cannot tell, though we desire to do both. We cannot tell it because it is a desire for something that has never actually appeared in our experience. We cannot hide it because our experience is constantly suggesting it, and we betray ourselves like lovers at the mention of a name.... The scent of a flower we have not found, the echo of a tune we have not heard, news from a country we have never yet visited... We remain conscious of a desire which no natural happiness will satisfy."[1]

But perhaps as well as books, sermons and Scripture it is a wide variety of hymns which have touched me, and clothed my thinking and believing about life, death and heaven. Not infrequently such hymns have moved me to tears, so that I choke and have to stop singing – tears not of sadness but of inexpressible yearning and joy.

"Imagine there's no heaven" sang John Lennon, with the obvious implication that the world would be a better and more peaceful place without religion. Yes, "it's easy if you try"; but no, thanks! I prefer to imagine – or maintain a firm conviction (I think...!) that heaven is a reality.

---

[1] The Weight of Glory, from *They Asked For a Paper* – Geoffrey Bles, 1962

There is so much about heaven in the Bible. Some people are troubled by the imagery and language used, which admittedly may be remote from our life many centuries after those words were written. White robes, palm branches, angelic choirs, and much besides: do these pictures inspire us or touch our hearts? But objecting to imagery when eternal things are being spoken of is a mistake; for how else other than by images and pictures can we speak of matters beyond our comprehension? I recall reading of a child whose parents were so determined that she should not have an image of God as an old man with a beard in the sky, that she ended up with a vague picture of him like a sago pudding – and the trouble was that she did not like sago pudding! Surely "Father" is an infinitely preferable picture, however anthropomorphic or metaphorical it may be (let alone the problems about gender that it may provoke for some).

We have been made aware in recent decades by leading scientists, both in the realm of astrophysics and at the other extreme, in sub-atomic particles, that very soon language and logic break down. I can imagine an atom – a very, very tiny *thing*. But when I read of ever tinier *things*, the sub-atomic particles, I learn that they may be waves rather than particles, or sometimes one and sometimes the other; and even – or is this crazy? – they can be in two places at once! At the other end of the scale we learn of black holes and quasars, and space being curved, dark matter making up three quarters of the universe, and string theory.... Some of these scientific truths, it seems, can only be explained in terms of mathematical formulae – that no ordinary illustration can do them justice. I don't begin to understand these things. And didn't Niels Bohr say anyone who says he understands Quantum Theory doesn't know the first thing about it?

So if this is true of scientific truth, how much more must it be true when talking about God, who *"alone has immortality and dwells* in unapproachable light, whom no man has ever seen or can see;"[1] "the high and lofty one, who inhabits eternity, whose name is holy"[2]? It must also be true when talking about heaven or life after death. Jesus gave a hint of this mystery when he was asked the test question about the woman who had been married to seven brothers, one after the other: which shall she be married to in heaven? His answer was *"In the resurrection, they neither marry nor are given in marriage, but are like angels in heaven."*[3] In other words, heaven is not just like earth: it is of a different order, a different dimension.

There is the story told of someone who tried to explain the colour scarlet to a man who had been blind from birth. "I think I understand," said the blind man at last; "Scarlet is like the sound of a trumpet!" Well, yes, that's not bad as an approximate comparison; but it can never be more than that. So if the images in which heavenly things are expressed in the Bible are earthly ones – jewels, and white robes; music like the sound of many waters or like thunder; brilliant light, and a river as clear as crystal – we have to recognise that we have no images other than earthly ones to use. Sometimes when we wake up from a dream, we can remember very clearly the details of the dream, absurd or bizarre as they may have been; but sometimes we can recall an atmosphere, a mood – of horror, or of ecstasy, or of anxiety - but cannot pin down the specifics of what we saw or heard which gave rise to those feelings.

Paul writes of an out-of-this-world experience which had once been given to him – though it had been so other-worldly that he was not even sure if it had happened to him or to someone else!

"I know a man in Christ who fourteen years ago was caught up to the third heaven. Whether it was in the body or out of the body I do

---

[1] I Timothy 6.16
[2] Isaiah 57.15
[3] Matthew 22.30

not know – God knows. And I know that this man – whether in the body or apart from the body I do not know, but God knows – was caught up to paradise. He heard inexpressible things, things that man is not permitted to tell."[1]

This experience had been one which he was not only incapable of expressing in words, but he had even been forbidden to try!

So before we mock the imagery – "sitting on a cloud in a white nightie, playing a harp" and suchlike – we can start by recognising that people in Bible days, and sometimes since then, have indeed had visions or experiences which have left them dazed, or exalted, or appalled, and often they have been totally aware that the terms in which they have attempted to convey this have been utterly inadequate. It is often worth seeking to analyse the phrases and pictures used, in the context of their time and culture - perhaps in the same way as a psychologist would seek to comprehend the recollections of someone's dreams – to see what they convey; perhaps a sense of worship and awe, of love and peace and beauty, of wonder and exaltation, of promise and hope, of celebration and triumphant joy.

I have spoken of how simple tales spoke to my heart and imagination when I was very young. It is often music which has enriched those longings and hopes. Some of the great oratorios with magnificent and uplifting choruses have moved me deeply, whether hearing them or singing them – Bach's Mass in B Minor, or Handel's Messiah, or Brahms' German Requiem, or in the twentieth century, Vaughan Williams' Sancta Civitas (Holy City). But it may be the repertoire of hymns which have given words in which to clothe the yearnings for heaven which are deep in my soul.

"Jerusalem the golden" is one such.

---

[1] II Corinthians 12. 2-4

"I know not, O I know not
What joys await us there,
What radiancy of glory,
What bliss beyond compare."

Does it not touch your heart? No, of course we do not know what heaven is like. But I remember reading of an elderly father going for a country walk with his son, and as they topped a brow they stopped to drink in the beauty of a spectacular sunset. They gazed for a while in silence; and then the old man said, "You know I've never been a particularly religious man, or much of a churchgoer. But when I see something like that it makes me feel that perhaps I have touched the hem of His garment."

Glory – a word often used in descriptions of heavenly things. Few sights on earth are as worthy of that word as a magnificent sunset. I totally identify with the man who perhaps broke the habit of a lifetime of reticence to speak of such an emotion to his son.

What is heaven like? Yes, beauty, and glory, and light; but it is more than just *looking* at it: the true wonder of heaven is that we will be a *part* of the glory. As C. S. Lewis said, "Something else which can hardly be put into words – to be united with the beauty we see, to pass into it, to receive it into ourselves, to bathe in it, to become part of it."[1]

Another hymn seeking to describe heaven is "Ten thousand times ten thousand":

"O then what raptured greetings
On Canaan's happy shore,
What knitting severed friendships up,
Where partings are no more!
Then eyes with joy shall sparkle
That brimmed with tears of late;

---

[1] Op. cit.

Orphans no longer fatherless,
Nor widows desolate."

The idea of heaven as a place of reunions with lost loved ones is common in popular devotion. Some gravestones have the inscription "Reunited", when both husband and wife have died. Not all of those who order such words to be inscribed necessarily have the sentiments of the above hymn in mind, but some other, vaguer reunion – even if only, at its lowest, that they are now in the same grave. But in fact almost nothing is said in scripture about such reunions with those we have loved. The only verse I can think of is in I Thessalonians chapter 4, in the passage starting *"We do not want you to be ignorant about those who fall asleep."* I think Paul would be horrified by the degree of ignorance among even committed Christian people today! But in spelling out what he expects to happen at the return of Jesus, he writes, *"The dead in Christ will rise first; after that, we who are still alive and are left will be caught up together with them in the clouds."* There is this hint of a reunion: *"together with them."* But the main emphasis is in the following words: *"to meet the Lord in the air."* The focus is not on meeting my deceased parents or wife, but on meeting Jesus! *"And so we will be with the Lord for ever."*[1]

To quote another hymn:

"My knowledge of that life is small;
The eye of faith is dim.
But 'tis enough that Christ knows all,
And I shall be with him."

"With Jesus": is that indeed "enough", to satisfy all our longings? Perhaps; but our understanding of being "with Jesus" is bound to be limited, with thoughts of being physically near to someone and enjoying loving conversation. In other words, as if

---

[1] I Thessalonians 4.13-17

the Jesus we are with is the Jesus of the Galilean road, rather than the glorified King of kings whose face shines like the sun and whose eyes are like blazing fire[1]. So we need, perhaps, some of the other images, like singing, feasting, glory, even if we have to work hard to grasp their significance.

A hymn I have requested for my funeral (though I confidently expect to be singing even better hymns, with a *much* better choir, at the time!) is based on Paul's words quoted above:

"'For ever with the Lord!'
Amen, so let it be!
Life from the dead is in that word,
'Tis immortality.
Here in the body pent,
Absent from him I roam,
Yet nightly pitch my moving tent
A day's march nearer home.

My Father's house on high,
Home of my soul, how near
At times to faith's foreseeing eye
Thy golden gates appear!
Ah! Then my spirit faints
To reach the land I love,
The bright inheritance of saints,
Jerusalem above."

One aspect of "glory", as well as the shining beauty mentioned above, is that of praise and fame. A few weeks before I wrote these words the Olympic and Paralympic Games took place in London, and huge television audiences witnessed the massive stadium crowds roaring out their support of an athlete striding to victory; more than one such athlete spoke of the "wall of sound"

---

[1] Revelation 1.14,16

which almost carried them forward on the plaudits of the multitude. If we carry the idea of the "glory" of Olympic victory into the realm of heavenly glory, we come close to the words of Bunyan: "And all the trumpets sounded for him on the other side."

A hymn which has echoes of this is "For all the saints".

> But lo, there breaks a yet more glorious day;
> The saints triumphant rise in bright array;
> The King of Glory passes on his way:
> > Alleluia!

> From earth's wide bounds, from ocean's farthest coast,
> Through gates of pearl streams in the countless host,
> Singing to Father, Son and Holy Ghost,
> > Alleluia!

Those are verses which I can seldom sing without a lump in the throat. The final chapters of Tolkien's "Lord of the Rings" catch a similar tone – the triumph of the returning King, and the "Praise them with great praise" which greeted the wounded hobbits being welcomed back after their journey of terrible suffering.

"Making everything right" is a concept which is certainly part of my personal hope for heaven. Putting right injustices; answering all questions; solving all mysteries; recognising and acclaiming faithful service – "*Well done, good and faithful servant!*[1]" That will include healing for all those fears of not being worthy, of awareness of so many dismal failures, of so many wounds of so many kinds. "*God himself will be with them and be their God. He will wipe every tear from their eyes. There will be no more death or mourning or crying or pain, for the old order of things has passed away.*"[2]

---

[1] Matthew 25.23
[2] Revelation 21.3,4

Every joy which we experience in this life is but a thin reflection of the joys awaiting us in heaven. The most unutterably glorious sunset; the most inspiring music; the most delectable food; the most hilarious laughter; the most thrilling sporting victory; the most huge relief when bad news is replaced by good; the most exciting drama; the most enormous satisfaction when a massive effort is met with success and acclaim – all these are but a pale echo of what awaits the children of God when we are welcomed into his home.

Yes, home; it is where we belong, the destiny for which we were created.

"I looked over Jordan; what did I see,
Coming for to carry me home?
A host of angels, coming after me,
Coming for to carry me home!"

It is not surprising that in the slave culture of the West Indies and the southern states of the USA, far from the African home from which they had been ripped, and with no hope of any improvement of their wretched lot in this life, there grew a rich repertoire of songs expressing that hope of joy and glory for which they longed.

"I got a robe! You got a robe!
All God's children got a robe!
When I get to heaven gonna put on my robe,
Gonna shout all over God's heaven!"

A robe! For a slave toiling in the fields in rags, that represents more than a trivial aspiration. Think of the whole world of fashion; think of the care than people take, the money they spend, to look good, particularly for special occasions. Why? Yes, too often it is just "me-centred" – but then think of a bride, and the love and admiration of her bridegroom as he turns and sees her. This is another Biblical image – the Holy City, representing all God's people, *"coming down out of heaven from God, prepared as a bride beautifully dressed for her husband.¹"* In this image, the husband awaiting us with love in his eyes is our Lord Jesus himself.

Am I sure of all this? Will I remain confident up to the hour of death? Paul used an interesting metaphor when speaking of the transition from this world to the next. He spoke of our earthly body as like a tent (and he worked as a tentmaker, which was perhaps why this image suggested itself to him). But we have waiting for us not a perishable tent but a solid building, what he calls "a heavenly dwelling". *"We groan, longing to be clothed with our heavenly dwelling"²*, But at the same time, there is dread at losing the only covering we have, this mortal "tent", lest at that point we are left naked. I find it touching and reassuring that even Paul, a man with apparently unshakeable convictions, who could write those triumphant assertions that *"We shall all be changed, in a flash, in the twinkling of an eye... The perishable must be clothed with the imperishable, and the mortal with immortality... Then the saying that is written will come true: 'Death is swallowed up in victory!'"³* – even this giant of faith could admit that he too shrinks from the prospect of nakedness when this "tent" falls away. As the hymn puts it:

"When I tread the verge of Jordan,
Bid my anxious fears subside!"

I am sure that when it is my turn, I too will need to pray such a petition voiced in an otherwise confident hymn.

That unutterable longing of which C. S. Lewis wrote so eloquently is one with which I totally identify. I will end with more words by Lewis, this time from the final Narnia book for

---

¹ Revelation 21.2
² II Corinthians 5.2
³ I Corinthians 15.52-54

children. Whenever I used to read these words to my children when they were young, I found it hard to complete the story, because they moved me to tears.

> "Aslan said, 'The term is over. The holidays have begun. The dream is ended; this is the morning.'
>
> And as he spoke he no longer looked to them like a lion; but the things that began to happen after that were so great and beautiful that I cannot write them. And for us this is the end of all the stories, and we can most truly say that they all lived happily ever after. But for them it was only the beginning of the real story. All their life in this world and all their adventures in Narnia had only been the cover and the title page: now at last they were beginning Chapter One of the Great Story which no one on earth has read: which goes on forever: in which every chapter is better than the one before."[1]

---

[1] *The Last Battle:* Fontana-Lions.

INDEX

A-B-C-D, 29, 33

Acts, 59, 67, 69, 86, 99, 101, 108, 131, 153, 170, 172, 175, 218, 222, 305

Adam and Eve, 46, 49

Alpha Course, 157, 283

Anglo-Catholic, 94, 128, 236, 245

art, 232, 233

atheist, 7, 413

banners, 232, 248, 311, 388

baptism, 10, 11, 36, 94, 107, 169, 170, 171, 172, 173, 175, 177, 178, 179, 181, 182, 183, 184, 185, 186, 187, 189, 191, 198, 217, 219, 247, 258, 264, 265, 279, 309, 313, 348, 385
baptize, 107

baptist, 5, 170, 172, 181, 190, 192, 203, 270, 272, 310, 321, 362, 364, 390, 391, 400

baptize. *See* baptism

Basil Gough, 90, 94, 162, 273

believe, 1, 2, 6, 8, 11, 13, 18, 29, 36, 39, 40, 43, 55, 56, 64, 65, 67, 69, 73, 85, 93, 105, 135, 139, 144, 146, 149, 158, 159, 169, 172, 173, 174, 179, 205, 223, 225, 352, 380

Bible study, 71, 73, 160, 238

Billy Graham, 5, 83, 279, 280, 311, 314

bishop, 10, 17, 78, 107, 112, 116, 125, 126, 130, 133, 136, 163, 219, 240, 241, 246, 250, 264, 290, 291, 292, 296, 320, 324, 325, 342, 401

Book of Common Prayer, 13, 131, 243, 278

born again, 9, 18, 37, 39, 40, 41, 43, 47, 61, 86, 104, 109

buildings, 68, 102, 162, 163, 165, 249, 276

Bultmann, 3

C. S. Lewis, 41, 55, 416, 421, 428

Carol Service, 42, 331, 351

charismatic renewal, 15,
205, 217, 227

cheque, 177, 178, 179

child of God, 39, 40, 50, 61,
74, 178, 215

christen. *See* baptism

Christian service, 60, 109,
111, 235, 270

Christianity, 36, 64, 85, 90,
95, 99, 163, 167, 196, 379,
414

Christmas, 10, 11, 12, 42,
142, 331, 351, 352

circumcision, 173, 176, 177

cohabiting
cohabitation, 267

Common Worship, 131,
217, 244

confirmation, 15, 17, 18, 78,
170, 219, 349, 350

confirmation
confirmed, 10, 16, 183,
244, 349, 350, 351

converted
conversion, 9, 18, 36, 67,
76, 77, 86, 87, 93, 95,
96, 101, 102, 105, 107,
127, 152, 156, 161, 170,
174, 213, 225, 279, 281,
299, 303, 314, 362, 409

crèche, 188, 287, 298, 299

dance, 231

David, 5, 8, 13, 57, 58, 87,
170, 236

David Bendell, 386

David Watson, 5, 8, 112,
190, 311, 313

deliverance ministry, 159,
204, 206, 207, 213, 214

demonic. *See* spiritual
warfare

devil, 45, 215, 223, 292

diaconos
deacon, 132

disciple, 43, 67, 101, 103,
368

discipleship
disciples, 389, 390

ecclesia, 68, 102, 163

episcopos. See bishop

eternal life, 6, 39, 40, 44, 47,
53, 60, 61, 64, 106, 115,
178, 179, 180, 280, 282,
415

evangelical, 4, 5, 9, 20, 36,
40, 55, 61, 71, 75, 82, 83,
84, 90, 95, 97, 112, 125,
126, 127, 128, 170, 172,
175, 195, 196, 199, 203,
204, 236, 237, 243, 245,
252, 275, 295, 329, 364,
366, 368, 373, 383

evangelism, 82, 127, 145, 278, 279, 282, 305, 316, 343, 386, 388, 389, 392

evangelistic, 26, 42, 63, 75, 76, 78, 83, 96, 111, 113, 124, 143, 147, 247, 249, 278, 279, 282, 305, 314

evolution, 56

exorcism, 204, 206, 207

fellowship, 63, 67, 68, 69, 82, 135, 137, 153, 155, 156, 157, 160, 166, 200, 219, 227, 231, 232, 269, 271, 272, 277, 309, 310, 350, 368, 371

fellowship of the Holy Spirit, 228, 271

feminism
feminist, 366

Fountain Trust, 196

funeral, 165, 242, 347, 385, 423

funerals
funeral, 181, 241, 242, 243, 261, 265, 346, 348, 414, 415

Garden of Eden, 49, 59

Genesis, 38, 49, 50, 51, 52, 53, 54, 56, 57, 285, 293, 374

grace, 46

guidance, 71, 73, 79, 118, 121, 123, 127, 281, 285, 288, 289, 290, 292, 293, 325, 343, 344

guide
guidance, 12, 80, 117, 127, 135, 152, 235

healing, 3, 6, 87, 102, 159, 160, 165, 199, 212, 213, 217, 218, 219, 220, 221, 222, 223, 225, 226, 228, 312, 313, 352, 395, 425

Holman Hunt, 29

Holy Communion, 15, 130, 133, 135, 136, 152, 223, 224, 319, 370, 407

hymn, 12, 20, 21, 27, 110, 186, 228, 305, 307, 422, 424, 427

hymns
hymn, 4, 12, 15, 17, 20, 186, 197, 228, 229, 243, 244, 304, 305, 307, 359, 417, 420, 423

immersion, 170, 171, 189, 190, 191, 192, 313

inviting Jesus into your heart, 61, 62

Isaiah, 59, 119, 122, 129, 418

IVF, 82, 94

Iwerne, 81, 95, 113, 127

James, 49, 82, 143, 219, 223

John, 3, 6, 9, 10, 27, 28, 29, 30, 31, 32, 33, 37, 38, 39, 48, 62, 69, 70, 77, 79, 81, 92, 95, 104, 112, 165, 217, 221, 223, 293, 294, 348

John Stott, 27, 28, 29, 30, 31, 32, 33, 62, 70, 77, 79, 81, 95, 104, 112, 117, 196, 320

Judaism, 214, 216

judgement, 13, 32, 53, 54, 66, 134, 158, 162, 164, 199, 227, 414

leadership
leader, 80, 127, 130, 135, 138, 139, 142, 143, 144, 145, 146, 148, 203, 228, 277, 304, 329, 365, 373

Limbo, 180

make a commitment, 63

Mary, 61, 161

Matthew, 64, 66, 120, 158, 164, 174, 220, 221, 222, 239, 419, 425

metanoia, 65

Mission Praise, 21

missionary

missionaries, 79, 80, 91, 105, 121, 150, 151, 205, 362, 409

Moses, 57, 116, 131, 164, 232, 318, 384, 385, 386

music, 15, 141, 145, 147, 154, 168, 227, 228, 229, 230, 233, 304, 311, 326, 352, 355, 359, 420, 425

Muslims, 98, 279, 331, 392

Nicky Cruz, 314, 315, 316

Nicodemus, 37

OICCU, 4, 25, 27, 70, 71, 75, 76, 77, 79, 80, 82, 83, 84, 85, 88, 89, 94, 109, 121, 126, 169, 170, 194, 204, 235, 240, 263

opening the door, 31, 62, 78

ordination
ordain, 78, 124, 125, 129, 130, 147, 175, 235, 238, 241, 246, 251, 252, 263, 273, 364

Packer, 82, 95, 235

parish magazine, 297, 332, 346

Paul, 29, 44, 45, 46, 47, 48, 51, 59, 61, 73, 87, 89, 92, 93, 98, 101, 121, 133, 134, 135, 142, 143, 153, 155,

156, 171, 173, 175, 176,
177, 189, 198, 201, 204,
216, 218, 222, 231, 263,
293, 294, 364, 366, 375,
419, 422, 423, 427

Pentecost, 68, 86, 93, 170,
173, 305, 311, 315

Pentecostal, 85, 86, 87, 88,
89, 90, 91, 92, 94, 113,
194, 195, 196, 201, 202,
310, 391

Peter, 37, 68, 102, 103, 119,
132, 133, 140, 143, 162,
170, 173, 174, 223

Philippian gaoler, 59, 108,
172

Philippians, 73

pneuma, 38

pray
    prayer, 24, 31, 74, 77, 87,
        88, 92, 105, 127, 145,
        147, 154, 155, 182, 208,
        209, 218, 223, 224, 225,
        270, 271, 289, 296, 313,
        352, 383, 392, 409

Prayer Book. *See* Book of
    Common Prayer

prayer meeting, 71, 75, 87,
    88, 90

priest

priesthood, 10, 76, 105,
    128, 130, 131, 132, 135,
    136, 147, 148, 149, 150,
    155, 157, 160, 189, 251,
    252, 272, 362, 363, 366,
    382, 383

Quiet Time, 72, 383, 384

repent, 63, 64, 65, 66, 105,
    208, 291, 380

resurrection, 33, 37, 45, 47,
    106, 171, 189, 209, 415,
    419

Roger Jones, 304, 306, 315,
    322, 355, 356

Roman Catholic, 83, 133,
    139, 159, 196, 218, 219,
    236, 257, 300, 310, 390,
    391

Romans, 17, 49, 51, 93, 105,
    119, 171, 175, 176, 177,
    263, 366, 375

RSV, 71, 243

salvation
    saved
        Saviour, 47, 60

SCM, 82

Sikh
    Sikhism, 213, 214, 215

sin, 32, 45, 46, 48, 49, 51, 52,
    53, 54, 57, 58, 59, 60, 61,
    115, 178, 290, 367, 368,
    379

speaking in tongues, 85, 86, 91, 194, 195, 198, 201, 203, 228

spiritual life, 38, 39, 40, 64, 87, 92, 226, 303

spiritual warfare, 204

St. Ebbe's, 75, 78, 89, 90, 123, 162, 170, 241, 269, 272

street children, 397, 398, 406

Sunday School, 110, 111, 141, 145, 146, 188, 255, 270, 273, 277, 283, 295, 298, 299, 300, 304, 308, 346, 349, 394

tree of the knowledge of good and evil, 50

unbelief, 149, 150, 222

USA, 246, 247, 279, 426

wedding, 265, 266, 267, 268, 285, 286, 348, 349, 369, 378, 385

worship, 3, 15, 20, 27, 68, 76, 103, 105, 111, 125, 135, 140, 143, 147, 152, 154, 155, 160, 161, 163, 164, 165, 166, 168, 182, 192, 197, 198, 200, 202, 227, 228, 229, 230, 231, 232, 233, 237, 238, 244, 278, 305, 306, 307, 309, 326, 353, 354, 357, 390, 391, 394, 401, 407, 420